Their Number Become Thinned

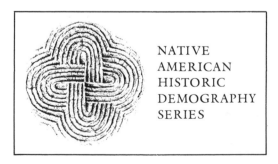

NATIVE
AMERICAN
HISTORIC
DEMOGRAPHY
SERIES

Published by
The University of Tennessee Press
in cooperation with The Newberry Library
Center for the History of the American Indian

Their Number Become Thinned

NATIVE AMERICAN

POPULATION DYNAMICS IN

EASTERN NORTH AMERICA

by Henry F. Dobyns

including an essay with
William R. Swagerty
as co-author

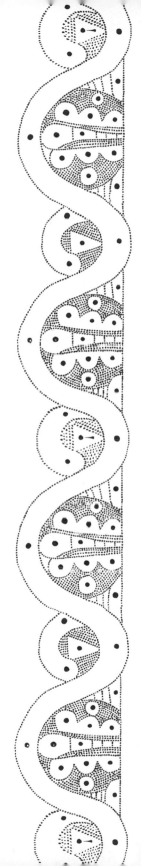

The border design used in this book was
adapted from *Authentic Indian Designs*
(New York: Dover, 1975), 23.

Clothbound editions of University of Tennessee Press
books are printed on paper designed for an effective life
of at least 300 years, and binding materials are chosen
for strength and durability.

Library of Congress Cataloging in Publication Data

Dobyns, Henry F.
Their number become thinned.

(Native American historic demography series)
Bibliography: p.
Includes Index.
1. Indians of North America—Population—Addresses, essays, lectures. 2. In-
dians of North America—Florida—Population—Addresses, essays, lectures.
I. Swagerty, William R. II. Newberry Library. Center for the History of
the American Indians. III. Title. IV. Series.
E98.P76D6   1983   304.6'2'08997   83-5952
ISBN 0-87049-400-7
ISBN 0-87049-401-5 (pbk.)

CONTENTS

ILLUSTRATIONS

ACKNOWLEDGMENTS

No author can complete a work such as this one without support and cooperation by other people. I deeply appreciate the crucial stimulation and assistance provided by key individuals and institutions.

This analysis became a reality only because of the dedication of my wife, Mary Faith, to the research goals it embodies. Her "public work" as a nurse enabled me to write it. The National Endowment for the Humanities supplemented Mary Faith's support in two ways. First, it gave the Newberry Library funding for fellowships in its Center for the History of the American Indian. A senior fellowship in the Center in 1979–1980 enabled me to work with William R. Swagerty, then associate director of the Center, on the fourth essay in this volume. More recently, the Endowment granted the Newberry Library funds to support my continued research on Native American historic demography. This support made possible Donald Rufkin's preparation of maps far better than those that would otherwise have been used.

I particularly thank Paul L. Doughty, then chairman of the Department of Anthropology at the University of Florida, who offered me a visiting professorship that led me to read about the aboriginal peoples of Florida. My thanks also go to members of the staffs of the Newberry Library and the University of Florida library, who without exception aided cheerfully in my quest for sources of information.

Their Number Become Thinned

INTRODUCTION

American Indians are often in the news. Journalists report that they are a "problem" in Seattle, San Francisco, Los Angeles, Phoenix, Tucson, Albuquerque, Santa Fé, St. Paul, Chicago, and other cities. What are Indians doing in cities, wearing jeans, drinking in bars, and scrambling for low-paid odd jobs? Are not Indians supposed to chase buffalo over the high plains and to wear feathers?

Reporters discover some Indians defying local sheriffs and other law enforcement officers as they pursue their own versions of the "Monaco solution" (gambling for nonresidents of a special area) to reservation poverty. In Broward County, Florida, the Seminole tribe has erected a multimillion-dollar bingo hall where games for high stakes are played every night. The county sheriff cannot stop the bingo games, although the state outlaws such gambling; Florida's jurisdiction stops at the edge of the Seminole Indian Reservation. In Pima County, Arizona, Papago entrepreneurs sell cigarettes on the San Xavier Indian Reservation without charging state taxes. The county sheriff cannot halt such sales because Arizona's jurisdiction stops at the edge of the reservation.

Such innovative use of reservation lands by Indians to earn relatively high profits after decades of poverty was not foreseen by the national policy makers who reserved lands for Native Americans in the late eighteenth and nineteenth centuries. Yet contemporary ethnic leaders claim that Indians have little choice except to branch out into new and lucrative fields of economic enterprise. The reason is that reservation populations have grown much too large to survive on a limited land base following traditional rural pursuits. This argument is quite legitimate. The number of Native Americans has been increasing rapidly since the Second World War. The population doubles with each generation. Consequently most reservations do have more inhabitants than their finite resources can sustain at a standard of living that would be considered decent in the United States.

The roots of the problem extend not only to early republican but even to Colonial times. When the government reserved lands for Native Americans, policy makers expected the Indians not to increase but to become extinct. From historic times until about 1890, the Indian population had steadily diminished. The U.S. policy of reserving lands for Native Americans rested upon the assumption that each group assigned some portion of its aboriginal territory would dwindle and disappear. What caused national decision makers to predict the wrong future for American Indians?

This book analyzes at least some of the reasons for the dramatic decrease of the Native American population during most of historic time in North America, which led Colonial and then national policy makers to believe that native groups would eventually vanish. I do not pretend to offer the definitive analysis of the population dynamics of American Indians throughout history. Several volumes of this type would be required to accomplish that goal. I do seek, however, to remedy somewhat what one analyst called the "paucity" of works on "basic demographic history of Native Americans"[1] by identifying the major dynamics of historic population trends and analyzing illustrative instances of them.

A book about demography is usually not viewed as controversial unless it delves into personally sensitive matters, such as abortion or the use of contraceptive devices, that affect contemporary population trends. This volume does not do so but will nevertheless be viewed as controversial by some readers, inasmuch as an increasingly lively scholarly discussion of Native American demography has been under way in scientific journals and monographs in recent years.[2] I have been a participant in that discussion,[3] and some scholars will no doubt view this book as presenting a thesis, or more than one thesis, with which they disagree. Still, historic facts are not always plain and certainly do not speak for themselves. Before a consensus of opinion can be reached, different analysts must seek to uncover and to evaluate the past, forming views that will sometimes conflict. In this book I have tried to set forth my own conclusions, and their basis, as clearly and persuasively as possible.

NOTES

1. Horsman, "Recent Trends," 1979, p. 140.
2. Major contributions to this discussion to 1976 are identified and evaluated in Dobyns, *Native American Historic Demography*, 1976, and in "Brief Perspec-

tive," (1976). Especially noteworthy works include Borah, "America," 1964; Cook and Borah, *Essays*, 1971, 1974, and 1979; Jacobs, "Tip of an Iceberg," 1974; and Crosby, *Columbian Exchange*, 1972.

3. My principal statements about Native American historic demography, in addition to those mentioned in the previous note, appear in "Indian Extinction," 1963; "Outline," 1963; "Estimating," 1966; and *From Fire to Flood*, 1981.

Widowing the Coveted Land

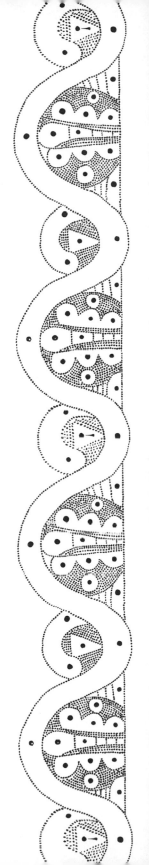

Policy makers in North America during the republican and earlier Colonial periods had good reason to suppose that Native Americans would disappear. From before the beginning of European colonization on the continent until the twentieth century, more Indians had died every year than were born, and for a simple reason. Colonists brought with them Old World pathogens that escaped from their original hosts to invade new territory. Because the native population lacked immunity to viruses and germs that evolved in the Old World, Indians succumbed in large numbers to ailments that scarcely afflicted the immune colonists. Epidemics of lethal pathogens began to spread widely through the Native American population no later than A.D. 1520 and did not end until 1918.

The North American continent was thus in one sense not the "virgin" land many historians and politicians have called it. It became "widowed" land by the time of widespread Euroamerican settlement.[1] The Indian population dwindled sharply during historic times to fewer than half a million survivors, simultaneously reducing Native American population density and, in the view of Europeans, opening up New World lands for European exploitation. It would be difficult to overestimate the extent to which diminishing Native American numbers reinforced the European belief that the human invaders could make better use of the widowed New World territory than its surviving aboriginal inhabitants had done. Native American depopulation during the sixteenth century far exceeded that of later times. Yet the number of Native Americans who did survive into the latter portion of that demographically disastrous century was great enough to prompt some Europeans to advocate measures for further thinning.

His years of captivity among the Calusa and Apalachee evidently left the Spaniard Diego de Escalante Fontaneda feeling resentment. Once

8

freed, he flatly predicted that the Calusa, Timucua, Ais, and Jeaga peoples of Florida would "never be at peace, and less will they become Christians." On that premise, Escalante recommended that Spaniards invite Native American couples aboard ship and then lock them below decks. Once betrayed, the North American natives could be sold for cash to colonists on the islands and mainland coast of the Caribbean Sea: "In this way, there could be management of them, and their number become thinned."[2] Once the number of Native Americans in Florida had been reduced, Spaniards might set up stock ranches there.[3]

The thinning of numbers by "natural" means was nevertheless extreme. The components of the Columbian Exchange of peoples, plants, animals, bacteria, and viruses between the Old and New Worlds that caused biological catastrophe among Native Americans are not at all mysterious.[4] They have, however, been masked by many myths and by much ethnocentric historical writing. Long isolated from face-to-face contact with residents of the Old World, Native Americans lacked any experience with or immunity to the bacteria and viruses that evolved there. Consequently, the Indians succumbed to what might be termed McNeill's Law of biological aggression.

Accusing other historians of neglecting the historical significance of diseases, William H. McNeill[5] synthesized the results of research aimed at reconstructing historic population trends. McNeill formulated a proposition that should long since have been obvious, namely, that as one society grows in population by conquering others, or through trade, its members acquire immunity to the viruses or bacteria that previously predated upon smaller polities. The conquerors fortify themselves at a cost in human lives, but eventually the new diseases that they have encountered are in a sense domesticated. That is, pathogens that have been lethal to adults become, in an enlarged society, childhood diseases. Thereafter the expanding group possesses a pronounced aggressive advantage when it encounters a previously independent, isolated people. Childhood illnesses in a cosmopolitan but disease-ridden population once killed adults as well as children but eventually conferred immunity on adults, thus significantly helping the society conquer previously isolated groups by keeping its troops alive, if sometimes sickly. The pathogens biologically invade the isolates, killing off their key leaders and fighters and demoralizing survivors. Precisely such a process occurred throughout the Americas during the Columbian Exchange.

In an epidemic the pathogen domesticated in one human population as a rule rapidly invades another susceptible population. One important task in the historic demography of Native Americans is, therefore, the identification of epidemic episodes of Old World diseases in the New World. The historic demographer of Native Americans needs to become an ecological historian, for epidemics were crucial biological happenings that produced significant changes in existing relationships between Native Americans and their habitat.[6] Transmitted to Native Americans, Old World pathogens became powerful biological influences new to the New World environment. The very novelty of Old World pathogens resulted in a high mortality among Native Americans during virgin soil epidemics[7] that was decisive for later cultural as well as ecological history.

Social anthropologists concerned with studying and predicting cultural and social change have improved their results by focusing on events for their data collection and analysis. Knowledge of how individuals interacted in varied situations reveals cultural dynamics instead of a static description of characteristics.[8] A similar method can improve the analytical power of historic demography. Consequently, this essay initiates my discourse by focusing on well-documented and widespread epidemics of Old World diseases among Native Americans.

The period of time to be analyzed spans four centuries. It is easier to differentiate between important and unimportant happenings during such a time period than it would be to do so in a synchronic study of contemporary society. The epidemic is not simply an event like any other in the biological and cultural history of a Native American ethnic group. In temporal perspective, epidemics have been "decisive demographic events." That is, epidemic mortality became decisive for future events and population trends in at least three major ways.

First, epidemic mortality affected later biological conditions among survivors by conferring immunity to a second invasion by the same pathogen—at least, exposure to many pathogens did so, although some do not provoke an enduring immune response. Second, mortality profoundly influenced Native American mental health, affecting the energy and effectiveness with which people engaged in subsistence activities. Third, mortality changed pre-Columbian Native American cultures in several ways. Epidemic mortality that diminished numbers thereby made inoperative many conventional understandings evolved by large populations. High mortality undermined the faith of many Native Americans in their respective versions of the fundamental postulate of ethnic superiority.[9] The loss of core confidence left them peculiarly vulnerable to the transculturation effected by invading Europeans.

SMALLPOX

The most lethal pathogen Europeans introduced to Native Americans, in terms of the total number of casualties, was smallpox. It was also the earliest Old World pathogen that we can be sure invaded the native peoples of North America. A Spanish ship carried one or more passengers or crew suffering from smallpox across the Atlantic Ocean about A.D. 1516. Apparently the initial transmission from Europeans to Native Americans occurred on the island of Hispaniola. From there the contagion soon spread to the Indians of Puerto Rico and then to Cuba. When the governor of Cuba dispatched Pánfilo de Narváez to the Mexican coast to attempt the arrest of Fernando Cortés, a member of Narváez's force transmitted the smallpox to natives of the continent. The disease spread like wildfire through a Native American population that was 100 percent susceptible. The virus found ideal conditions: millions of completely susceptible human hosts. One historical analyst has described these hosts as "virgin soil" in which the smallpox flourished.[10]

McNeill's Law operated in the theater of face-to-face contact between rapacious Spaniards and the principal Mesoamerican political empire. Capitalizing on Nahua beliefs that a bearded deity would one day come from the eastern sea and on other circumstances, Cortés marched into Tenochtitlán and seized its Aztec ruler, Moctezuma II. Other leaders of the Aztec conquest state mobilized resistance and forced the Spaniards to flee from Tenochtitlán on their Sad Night, with heavy casualties. As reinforcements Cortés needed the troops Narváez brought to arrest him. By his charismatic personality and the lure of riches, Cortés won the men over to his banner. Far more important to Native Americans and to future history, however, was the active case of smallpox among Narváez's forces. In a few weeks the smallpox pandemic swept through all of the native peoples allied with or against the Spaniards in central Mexico. It killed the royal heir whom the Aztecs had chosen to replace Moctezuma II, who had shown considerable ability in resisting the invaders. Large numbers of Aztec noble-generals perished with him. A less capable and more distant heir acceded to the throne.

Immunity to the disease among Spanish adults left Europeans hale and hearty while Native Americans died by millions. The apparent health of the invaders, in contrast to their own very high mortality rate, demoralized the Aztecs. Some felt simply betrayed by their gods; others concluded that the monotheistic deity about whom the pious

Spaniards preached must indeed possess greater power than the natives' own pantheon. How else could the invaders withstand a scourge that struck defenders in appalling numbers?

Even more important, once the smallpox had been unleashed among Native Americans, the virus spread rapidly through the native population of the Americas. We shall never know precisely how far this first smallpox pandemic spread. Its victims were not literate, so they could make no record of the arrival of the disease or of their own passing. Most of them lived far beyond the relatively small area of Mesoamerica reached by any Spaniard during the period of pandemic mortality. Consequently, contemporary Spanish descriptions refer to but a few tribal chiefdoms in Mesoamerica near the Aztec empire.

Later Spanish records do provide evidence of the widespread biological invasion that occurred in 1520–1524. When Spaniards led by Francisco Pizarro invaded the Inca empire in the Andean area of South America in 1532, they met with comparatively little resistance. Two half-brothers, contenders for the scarlet fringe of the Sapa Inca, were brawling so bitterly with each other that they could not unite to fight the Spaniards. The aspirants' father and the crown prince had both died from the smallpox when it reached the Tawantinsuyu in 1524, and half of the senior generals of the imperial army had also perished during the pandemic. Thus Pizarro's relatively small troop was able to capture one of the brothers and to execute him not long after he had executed his adversary.[11]

Although Pánfilo de Narváez failed in 1520 to arrest Cortés, Emperor Charles V later granted him the privilege of conquering and ruling the entire area then known as Florida. That area ran around the entire Gulf of Mexico coast of North America from the neighborhood of Pánuco, which Cortés had conquered, to and including the peninsula now known as Florida. Narváez botched this later Florida opportunity in 1528. He was last seen sailing a makeshift raft selfishly away from similar rafts carrying other members of his expedition after losing contact with his supply ships and deciding to raft from Apalachee Bay to New Spain.

The man who recorded the last sight of Narváez was Alvar Núñez Cabeza de Vaca, one of Colonial Spain's great survivors of expeditionary adversity. In 1535, Núñez and a few companions finally struck out westward toward the Pacific Coast in hopes of striking Spanish Colonial territory. When they came within sight of the mountains of west Texas, Núñez noted evidence of the earlier smallpox pandemic of 1520–1524: a high proportion of the inhabitants of one settlement were blind in one or both eyes.[12] There can be little doubt that the most lethal of all smallpox pandemics, the very first on the continent, swept through all of the most densely populated portions of the Americas.

The initial smallpox pandemic indelibly fixed in Spanish minds the image of Native Americans dying in droves. In the midst of a military campaign of conquest, Spaniards were not in any position to stop in 1520–1524 to take a census of any Native American group before and after the pandemic episode in order to obtain precise mortality figures. The "horseback" estimates that the Spaniards reported then and later therefore simply indicated that more than half of the natives perished during the pandemic.

Applying the principle of uniformitarianism, we are able to make a rather more accurate estimate of the scale of pandemic mortality. In 1898, smallpox spread from Euroamericans in New Mexico to residents of one or more Pueblos. Officials of the Office of Indian Affairs tried to quarantine each Pueblo to prevent further spread of the disease. Devout native believers in traditional religious doctrines flouted federal authorities and participated in communal dances or at least visited other Pueblos to watch communal dancing. Some of them transmitted the virus to additional Pueblos.[13] Among the afflicted settlements were Zuñi and some of the Hopi villages in Arizona. By the end of the nineteenth century, Christian missionaries had made some converts among the Hopis, and some non-Christians admitted the efficacy of Western medicine. Many Hopis continued to believe in their traditional religious system. Hopis of that persuasion who contracted smallpox refused any treatment by the Indian Service doctor assigned to the Hopi Indian Agency. That medical practitioner managed to compile reasonably accurate records of the outcome and reported to Washington the sad result. Of 220 traditionalist Hopis with smallpox who refused Western treatment, no fewer than 163 died[14]—74 percent of the known cases.

In 1898 not all Hopis were susceptible to smallpox. They had suffered repeated epidemic episodes of the disease, including a particularly serious one in 1853. Consequently, all or nearly all of the adults over about forty-five years of age in the population had acquired immunity by surviving an earlier onslaught of the virus. Thus mortality figures for the total population cannot be determined for that very first smallpox pandemic in 1520–1524. We can, however, estimate with some accuracy the case mortality among traditionalists. In 1520, no Native American had been exposed to the virus, so all individuals were susceptible. All or very nearly all Native Americans in 1520–1524 must have contracted the disease, so the death rate then was very close to the 1898 Hopi traditionalist case mortality. Spanish reports that half of the Native Americans died were almost certainly underestimates.

The relatively well documented Hopi mortality takes on great analytical importance, for it provides a chilling quantitative perspective on the magnitude of casualties caused by the biological invasion of American peoples by Old World viruses and germs. The discontinuity in Native American affairs that began on the continent in 1519 was catastrophic.[15] Depopulation constituted the major single component of a process that historians usually refer to as the European conquest of the Americas. In the northern Mesoamerican instance, Woodrow Borah and Sherburne F. Cook calculated that a population of perhaps 25,300,000 Central Mexicans on the eve of Spanish Conquest was reduced by 97 percent during somewhat more than a century.[16] The fate of conservative Hopis in 1898 when attacked by the smallpox virus tells us that the peoples of Central Mexico and all other areas of the Americas to which the virus spread in 1520–1524 lost nearly 75 percent of their numbers during the first pandemic of an Old World disease to afflict the peoples of the New World. Discontinuity and biological-cultural shock were immediate and massive.

After the first great smallpox pandemic had slaughtered millions of susceptible Native Americans, that virus could find significant numbers of new victims only after a period of years. The women who survived the 1520–1524 contagion with unimpaired genitourinary tracts had to bear children who would grow for at least several years before the smallpox virus could again encounter a susceptible population of any great size. Smallpox was retransmitted to Native Americans on an epidemic scale possibly more than three dozen times between the 1520–1524 continental pandemic and the 1898 Pueblo epidemic episode (see Table 1). It seems not to have become endemic among Native Americans, as it did in larger cities, at least in the Old World. Consequently, truly high mortality occurred during later years when the virus was transmitted to groups of Native Americans who had not been exposed for a long period—by which time survivors of the last epidemic had mostly died of other causes, leaving a largely susceptible population.

There is necessarily some doubt as to the exact number of smallpox epidemics between 1520–1524 and 1898. During Colonial times, some pathogens that produced red rashes, such as scarlet fever, had not yet been identified as separate diseases. Consequently some cases labeled as smallpox by contemporaries surely involved measles or chickenpox or scarlet fever or perhaps other diseases. As far as Native American mor-

TABLE 1

Probable Epidemic Episodes of Smallpox
Among Native Americans in North America, 1520 – 1898

Date	Peoples Affected
1520 – 1524	Total geographic extent unknown; at least from Chile across present United States, causing greater mortality than any later episode
1592 – 1593	Central Mexico to Sinaloa; southern New England; eastern Great Lakes
1602	Sinaloa and northward
1639	French and British Northeastern North America
1646 – 1648	New Spain north to Nuevo León tribes and western Sierra Madre to Florida
1649 – 1650	Northeastern tribes; Montagnais-Naskapi to Quebec, Huron, and Iroquois; Florida
1655	Florida chiefdoms
1662 – 1663	Iroquois, Delaware, Canadian tribes, and Central Mexico
1665 – 1667	Florida chiefdoms to Virginia tribes
1669 – 1670	French and British northeastern peoples
1674 – 1675	Coahuiltecan tribes of Texas, northeastern New Spain
1677 – 1679	Northeastern tribes in New France and British territory
1687 – 1691	Northeastern tribes on French and British frontiers; Texas tribes
1696 – 1699	Southeastern and Gulf Coast chiefdoms decimated
1701 – 1703	Northeastern tribes to Illinois
1706	Coahuiltecan tribes of Texas and northeastern New Spain
1715 – 1721	British northeastern tribes to Texas
1729 – 1733	New England; Creeks; California tribes
1738 – 1739	Southeastern tribes to Hudson Bay; Texas mission peoples
1746	New York and New England tribes; New Spain
1750 – 1752	Texas to Great Lakes tribes
1755 – 1760	From Canada and New England and Great Lakes to Virginia, Carolinas, and Texas
1762 – 1766	From Central Mexico through Texas and the Southeast to Iroquois, Potawatomi, Wea, Kickapoo, Miami, Shawnee, Arikara, and Northwest Coast
1779 – 1783	From Central Mexico across all of North America
1785 – 1787	Alaskan coastal tribes across northern Canada
1788	New Mexico Pueblos
1793 – 1797	New Spain
1799	Ottawa tribe
1801 – 1802	Columbia River peoples; Great Plains to Gulf of Mexico
1810 – 1811	Leech Lake Dakota to Lake Superior groups
1815 – 1816	Río Grande Pueblos and Plains tribes
1828	California tribes; Osage
1831 – 1834	Plains tribes; Great Lakes tribes; direct local transmissions from settlers
1836 – 1840	Alaskan, Columbia River, California, Plains, Plateau, and Mackenzie-Yukon tribes; Pueblos
1843 – 1846	Aleuts to Plains Crow
1848 – 1850	Plains Tribes; Coeur d'Alène; Kutchin

TABLE 1 Continued

Date	Peoples Affected
1852–1853	Columbia River tribes; western Pueblos
1854–1857	Among Plains tribes
1860–1867	Iroquois and Great Lakes groups in 1860–1862; northern Plains to Northwest Coast; 1863 to Southwestern and southern California groups; 1864 to southern Plains; 1865–1867 to northern Plains and Great Lakes
1876–1878	Lower St. Lawrence River peoples to Northwest Coast tribes and to Southwestern peoples
1896–1899	California to Río Grande Pueblos; Navajos; Jicarilla Apaches; Oklahoma tribes

Notes: Table sources follow the notes for essay I.

tality is concerned, however, chickenpox and measles and scarlet fever were only less virulent than the smallpox virus itself.

Several factors combined to increase mortality from all pathogens causing epidermal eruptions. First, the entire Native American population was entirely susceptible to each of these diseases the first time it was transmitted across the Atlantic.[17] That situation encouraged virulent strains of viruses to develop on Native American hosts. Second, the eruptive diseases cause significant complications among peoples with relatively heavy melanin deposits in the skin—especially among peoples who customarily purify themselves in sweat baths. Third, Native Americans typically lacked life-support services during illness. Consequently, when all members of a hunting-gathering family simultaneously fell ill, there was no one to obtain key animal protein food to strengthen resistance. There was no one to cook any food or even to obtain drinking water. Thus patients at times perished from dehydration in combination with a fever-generating pathogen. Fourth, groups which traded with each other helped spread such viral diseases,[18] as did the prevalent custom according to which Native American relatives and friends visited an ill person.[19]

MEASLES

Measles may have been the second largest killer of Native Americans among Old World pathogens, although other European ailments appear to have spread to the peoples of New Spain from Colonial Spaniards who arrived soon after the 1520–1524 smallpox pandemic.

Spaniards transmitted this second scourge to the natives of Meso-america in 1531, and the pandemic raged well into 1533. The contagion spread from New Spain through Nicaragua and the rest of Central America to Panamá and the crews and troops of Francisco Pizarro, who helped to spread it down the west coast of South America in 1531–1532. Measles caused very high mortality among the thousands of native auxiliaries whom Pizarro and his men pressed into service.

Once again, the virus swept through an entirely susceptible, or virgin soil, population. The Native Americans who had survived the de-moralizing mortality from smallpox had thereby gained no immunity to measles; they again perished by the millions. Because Spanish ships and slaving activities apparently facilitated the rapid diffusion of measles through Mesoamerica and South America, one cannot be sure that the virus spread along Native American trading routes as far north as it went south, although it probably did (see table 2).

TABLE 2

Probable Epidemic Episodes of Measles Among Native Americans North of Central Mexico, 1531–1892

Date	Peoples Affected
1531–1533	New Spain and probably far beyond the colony northward, including Pueblos and more
1592–1593	Sinaloa
1602	Sinaloa
1633–1634	New England, New France, and Great Lakes groups; Native Americans near Boston and Plymouth to Mohawks, Oneidas, Hurons, Montagnais, Nar-ragansetts, Delawares, etc.
1658–1659	Canadian tribes; Florida peoples to Mexico City—with diphtheria
1692–1693	Illinois peoples; Oneidas
1713–1715	New England tribes to Illinois
1727–1728	Mexico City to California tribes; Florida peoples; possibly New England groups
1748	Lower California peoples
1759–1760	Possibly among Southeastern peoples
1768–1770	Southwest; Mexico City to Lower California
1776–1778	Possibly in Plains, Hudson Bay, Texas tribes
1803	Caddoan tribes
1819	Lac Seul Ojibwa
1837	Florida Seminoles
1887	Walapai
1892	Indian Territory reservation populations

Notes: Table sources follow the notes for essay 1.

INFLUENZA

Influenza may have been the third most lethal disease for Native Americans. In recent decades, influenza has demonstrated that it can almost exterminate tribesmen in the Amazon River basin who have not been exposed to it in any of its various forms.[20] Consequently, the historic role of influenza is probably significantly underestimated in records of its extent because its symptoms do not include a readily perceived red rash or similar marker. Even so, at least ten influenza epidemics, or apparent combinations of influenza with another disease, sharply diminished historic Native American populations. Those influenza epidemics are dated in table 3.

Certainly influenza invaded the Americas no later than 1559. A combination of influenza with smallpox or with another rash-producing virus caused extremely high mortality. It was documented in Pamplona Province of Nueva Granada—present-day Colombia. Spanish officials sent an enumerator in June 1559 because of an earlier decline in numbers of Native American tribute payers. The epidemic subsequently caused rapid depopulation, and another enumerator counted survivors in April 1560. Within that brief interval, the province lost more than 58 percent of its population.[21]

BUBONIC PLAGUE

Bubonic plague vied with influenza as the third largest killer of Native Americans. Measles has the advantage of earlier transoceanic transmission, so that there were more susceptible Native Americans when it struck in 1531 than there were later. Influenza apparently had the advantage of invading Native American populations oftener than bubonic plague. Yet the Black Death that had terrified Europe reached the New World early enough to claim millions of victims during its first pandemic.

So great was the loss of life in Colonial New Spain between 1545 and 1548 that the decimation impressed even calloused Colonial Spaniards. Small as the overseas Spanish population then was, the new governing elite realized that the sharply diminished Native American population could no longer support Spaniards in the lavish style to which they had been accustomed. The prices of foodstuffs rose rapidly as Native American towns defaulted on their assigned payments of tribute. Spaniards in Colonial institutions competed against each other for the sharply diminished production of the postpandemic population.[22]

It is not clear whether plague became endemic among New World

TABLE 3

Probable Epidemic Episodes of Influenza Among
Native North American Peoples, 1559–1918

Date	Peoples Affected
1559	Southeastern tribes; Gulf Coast peoples to central New Spain
1647	New England tribes
1675	Iroquois and New England tribes
1696–1698	Possible component with smallpox epidemic among Gulf Coast and Southeastern peoples
1746	Possible component with smallpox among northeastern tribes
1761	All Native Americans in North America
1779–1783	Possible accompaniment to continental smallpox pandemic
1889–1890	Indian Territory reservation tribes
1892	Indian Territory reservation tribes
1918	All North American Native Americans

Note: Table sources follow the notes for essay 1.

rodents during the first pandemic or later. If it did, the plague organism may have been carried across the Atlantic only once. Known epidemic episodes are dated in table 4.

DIPHTHERIA

Diphtheria became epidemic on at least five occasions during the seventeenth and eighteenth centuries among Native Americans (see table 5). It caused frightening mortality among them as well as among European immigrants and their Creole offspring.

TYPHUS

Typhus was relatively difficult for people to diagnose prior to the mid-nineteenth century. Probably half a dozen typhus epidemics occurred among Native Americans during historic times. Certainly so-called ship's typhus was common among crews and passengers on European sailing ships carrying people and goods to the New World. It was therefore frequently available for transmission to Native Americans. Undoubtedly it was repeatedly communicated to them, but records of epidemic episodes do not exist or at any rate have not been located. Typhus so plagued historic sailing vessels that it was regarded

TABLE 4

Probable Epidemic Episodes of Bubonic Plague
Among Native American Peoples of North America, 1545–1707

Date	Peoples Affected
1545–1548	New Spain to Pueblos and perhaps beyond
1576	New Spain
1612–1619	New Spain to Florida and New England
1707	Louisiana groups

Note: Table sources follow the notes for essay 1.

TABLE 5

Probable Epidemic Episodes of Diphtheria Among
Native Americans of North America, 1601–1890

Date	Peoples Affected
1601–1602	Central New Spain to Sinaloa
1659	New England and Canadian tribes
1735–1736	New England tribes
1784–1787	New Spain
1880s	Kutchin of Arctic Canada

Note: Table sources follow the notes for essay 1.

more as an endemic, undifferentiated ailment than as a clearly distinguished epidemic disease. Consequently, its incidence is almost certainly grossly underreported in historic documents. Table 6 shows known incidence of typhus.

CHOLERA

During the nineteenth century, Native Americans suffered with immigrant Europeans and their descendants from worldwide cholera epidemics in 1832–1834, 1849, and 1867 (see table 7). This waterborne disease had not previously spread out of its South Asian and Middle Eastern habitat into Europe and the New World. By the time it reached North America, it roused considerable fear among Euroamericans, so that its spread was comparatively well documented in newspapers and other documents. Moreover, Euroamericans had by the 1830s colonized most of the continent that had been left sparsely populated by earlier mortality among Native Americans. Thus the demographic distribu-

TABLE 6

Probable Epidemic Episodes of Typhus Among
Native Americans of North America, 1586–1742

Date	Peoples Affected
1586	Tidewater Carolina tribes to Florida Timucua and Apalachee; probably Creek; extending to southern New England tribes
1611	Sinaloa peoples
1720	"Marseilles Fever" among Naskapi
1742	Lower California tribes; possibly Choctaw

Note: Table sources follow the notes for essay 1.

TABLE 7

Epidemic Episodes of Cholera Among
Native North Americans During the Nineteenth Century

Date	Peoples Affected
1832–1834	Potawatomi, Winnebago, Menomini, Ojibwa, Mexican groups, Panya
1849	Kiowa, Pawnee, Ojibwas, Menomini, Brulé Sioux, Maricopa, Pima, Papago
1867	Plains tribes; Wichita, Caddo, Pima

Note: Table sources follow the notes for essay 1.

tion of population approximated that of earlier centuries when Native American numbers had been far larger than they were by 1833. Consequently the pattern of cholera transmission serves as a model for many earlier and much less well documented epidemics, even though the disease is not inherently as lethal as the aerosol transmitted viruses.

Asian cholera reached North America in 1832, breaking out in Quebec on June 8 and in Montreal on June 10 among European immigrants.[23] The transatlantic mode of transmission and route were identical with those of a number of earlier pathogenic invaders. Case mortality ran to 43 percent in Montreal,[24] showing how lethal the disease could be among Native Americans, many of whom lived in conditions of household crowding and sanitation similar to those of newly arrived immigrants.

U.S. troops sent by Great Lakes steamers from Buffalo to Fort Dearborn carried cholera to the post near the southern end of Lake Michigan on July 10.[25] These troops carried the disease with them to the vicinity of modern Beloit and Fort Crawford/Prairie du Chien.[26] The soldiers were a precise analogue of earlier traders—European, of mixed blood, and Native American—who moved from the St. Lawrence or

Hudson river valleys almost as rapidly westward by water craft, then walking inland to Native American settlements, carrying germs and viruses with them.

Chicago's civilian population fled and possibly spread cholera among friendly Native Americans. At least some Potawatomis attending a council at Milwaukee contracted cholera, and a councilwoman died.[27] An influential Winnebago chief also died, having contracted cholera directly from the U.S. troops while meeting with Gen. Winfield Scott.[28] One Menominee attending the same council also caught the disease but reportedly survived.[29] General Scott's meeting with representatives of a number of Native American groups that contracted disease directly from the Euroamericans was, again, a precise analogue for many an earlier multiethnic frontier conference.

SCARLET FEVER

Members of the medical profession did not identify scarlet fever as a distinct affliction until the end of the eighteenth century. It was first specifically identified in epidemic form in North America in 1793.[30] Because earlier scarlet fever epidemics were variously labeled, identifying them is difficult. Table 8 gives the best list of probable scarlet fever epidemics that I have been able to compile.

The physician Percy M. Ashburn identified the 1708–1710 epidemic as scarlet fever on the basis of a mention of "purple" fever in *Jesuit Relations*.[31] This designation is the key to identifying the 1637 epidemic as well. Contemporary witnesses did not distinguish very well between the 1633–1634 measles epidemic, the 1637 scarlet fever, and the 1639 smallpox epidemic that decimated Native Americans around the Great Lakes and in the St. Lawrence River Valley.

TABLE 8

Probable Epidemics of Scarlet Fever Among
Native North Americans, 1637–1865

Date	Peoples Affected
1637	Tobacco, Neutral, Erie, Susquehannock, Huron Confederacy, Wenro
1708–1710	St. Lawrence River valley and Great Lakes area peoples; possibly Gulf Coast; Pueblos; Lower California peoples
1793	Miami, Potawatomis, Algonkians, and probably other peoples in the Great Lakes area
1862–1865	British Columbia and Mackenzie-Yukon tribes

Note: Table sources follow the notes for essay 1.

OTHER DISEASES

Several other pathogens introduced to Native Americans from the Old World appear to have become epidemic on at least one occasion. Some of these, and others, wrought most harm as endemic ailments that established themselves as perennial threats to human well-being throughout large areas of the continent. Several additional epidemics of these less lethal pathogens—less lethal at least in terms of major epidemic episodes—are listed in table 9.

Although seldom identified as causing epidemic mortality, whooping cough became a major ailment among Native American children.[32] Malaria is listed only once in table 9, but it was important as a debilitating endemic disease that made its hosts more likely to die when attacked by other pathogens. The disease arrived in North America no later than the seventeenth century and spread north into Canada.[33] One apparent disease index of previous viral infection bears mention. Researchers have reported incidences of diabetes among Native American populations ranging from half again to seven times the incidence in the general U.S. population.[34] Recent laboratory discoveries implicate prior mumps or coxsackie viral infections that destroy pancreatic beta cells.[35] Thus the diabetes incidences found among Native Americans suggest that they have suffered frequent viral infections. The frequency of smallpox and measles epidemic episodes in historic times implies that diabetes may have been a very serious health problem among Native Americans for most of the historic period.

Tables 1 through 9 list ninety-three epidemic episodes known to have

TABLE 9

Recorded Epidemic Episodes of Additional Pathogens
(Identified and Unidentified)
Among Native North Americans, 1528 – 1833

Date	Disease	Mortality	Peoples Affected
1528	Typhoid	50%	Gulf coast barrier islanders
1535	Unknown	low	St. Lawrence River valley, southern Plains, Southeast
1564 – 1570	Unknown	severe	Florida to Virginia and New England tribes
1711	Typhoid	7%	Native American slaves in Louisiana
1804	Tularemia	10%	Ojibwa
1830 – 1833	Malaria	75% and less	California and Oregon tribes

Note: Table sources follow the notes for essay 1.

taken a significant toll of Native American lives. This is no doubt an incomplete list of such pathogenic invasions of the aboriginal population of the New World. Enough of the viral or germ invasions of the Native American population have been identified in this chapter, however, to indicate rather clearly that Old World diseases were the primary cause of historic Native American depopulation. A serious contagious disease causing significant mortality invaded Native American peoples at intervals of four years and two and a half months, on the average, from 1520 to 1900. Many of the epidemics were continentwide. Yet the relatively long intervals between invasions by the same disease prevented Native Americans from acquiring much immunity for well over three centuries. Vaccination against smallpox materially slowed Native American depopulation during the nineteenth century. Until the decade that began in 1890, or even later, however, the Native American was in actual biological fact vanishing. During serious epidemic episodes, Native Americans perished very rapidly and in large numbers, as observers could not fail to note.

Every pathogen mentioned in this chapter evolved in the Old World and biologically invaded the peoples of the Americas. Viruses and germs constituted the true shock troops with which the Old World battered the New. Much has been written about Colonial mistreatment of Native Americans, and some exploitation did occur. Still, abuse killed comparatively few Native Americans compared with the destruction wrought by germs and viruses. There is today no great point in discussing the Black Legend of Spanish Colonial mistreatment of natives in terms of major Native American mortality, most of which stemmed from the Columbian Exchange process. Some colonials no doubt overworked Native American miners, oarsmen, and field hands so that they died. De las Casas did see Cuban natives put to the sword. Nevertheless, all Colonial mistreatment of natives killed fewer by far than did Old World diseases.

CONCLUSIONS

While this essay offers only an outline of the sequence of pathogenic invasions of the native peoples of the New World, it identifies enough epidemic episodes and pathogens that became endemic in various parts of the Americas to suggest a very important methodological consideration for historians and anthropologists. Simply stated, lethal pathogens, especially during virgin soil epidemics, spread to and decimated Native Americans far beyond the geographic limits of face-to-face contact between Europeans and aboriginal groups. This is an important matter for historians who usually depend upon written documents as sources of information. If historians are to analyze the significance of diseases in the human history of the New World, then they must identify and evaluate nondocumentary kinds of evidence of changes in the numbers and types of human settlements between 1520 and the beginning of a full written record of Native American life. In other words, historians must analyze events that occurred in what the eminent historian W.W. Borah has labeled "protohistoric" populations—those that changed because European influences reached them through other Native American groups or even through unrecorded European explorations or incursions. Europeans set loose diseases, technological changes, and territorial reshufflings that extended far beyond their own presence.[36]

Aboriginal lifeways for the native peoples of North America clearly terminated with the large-scale depopulation caused by the initial smallpox pandemic in 1520–1524. Those peoples cannot be considered to have continued their prepandemic ways of life unchanged and unaffected by a massive loss of manpower. Yet direct written documentation is lacking for all but a few marginal areas, so that historians cannot rely upon written records as sources of information about decisive demographic events.

Much the same methodological problem confronts anthropologists and archaeologists. It is made more difficult for them, however, by certain professional interests that they have pursued for some time and by specific definitions of intergroup relationships that anthropologists have formulated to further their research concerns. As the term was originally defined in the 1930s, "acculturation" means those kinds of cultural change that result from face-to-face contact between members of two societies.[37] Anthropologists have fallen into a careless habit of assuming that native peoples followed their aboriginal lifeways without change until they met Europeans. This misconception has resulted in the all-too-frequent use by anthropologists of the term "aboriginal" in place of "precontact." The tables in this chapter that show the impact of epidemic diseases on population clearly indicate the conceptual error in such a practice. Aboriginal ways of life influenced by entirely American causes changed for many Native American peoples long before they ever saw a European or an African. Aboriginal times ended in North America in 1520–1524, and Native American behavior was thereafter never again totally as it had been prior to the first great smallpox pandemic.

It is as important for anthropologists as for historians to think and to

analyze data bearing in mind that a "protohistoric" period existed between 1520 – 1524 and the creation of full, written records of face-to-face
intercultural contacts in any area. For anthropologists systematically to
rethink their approach to a protohistoric period that was very long for
many peoples will be a massive endeavor. The bulk of the early anthropological research conducted in the Americas was reported in the
form of an "ethnographic present." Ethnographers dated that "reconstructed" cultural pattern several decades prior to the date of field research, with little regard for historic reality, believing that they could
reconstruct aboriginal cultural patterns by interviewing informants to
elicit memories of precontact behaviors. Julian Steward pointed out in
an all-too-often ignored paper that intertribal trade and religious
movements changed aboriginal lifeways for many tribes in North
America long before their members encountered Europeans.[38] This
essay, brief though it is, marshals enough information about historically known epidemic disease to make clear that the pathogenic invasion of Native Americans by Old World diseases must be added to
Steward's incomplete list of precontact change agents. The human
mortality from protohistoric and historic epidemic disease needs to be
accorded even greater importance than the causes of change listed by
Steward.

In short, most of the anthropological literature that refers to an
ethnographic present may be termed "divorced from reality."[39] No
such cultural phase existed; ethnographies written in the ethnographic
present are like paintings of extinct birds based on hearsay and on the
artist's imagination. The methods and techniques traditionally employed by ethnographers are not capable of recovering from a very
small handful of survivors an accurate portrait of societies that have not
functioned for decades—and in many instances centuries—prior to the
arrival of an ethnographer. Field workers who thought that they were
describing stable cultural patterns to use as baselines for comparison
and analysis of acculturation actually inferred a stability of precontact
culture that had not existed. Demographic and consequent changes
began in 1520 – 1524, and continued depopulation generated cultural
changes that were often of a very fundamental order. These changes can
be accurately studied with the techniques of archaeohistory and ethnohistory but not with those of traditional ethnography.

NOTES

1. Jennings, *Invasion*, 1975, p. 15.
2. B. Smith, *Letter and Memoir*, 1854, p. 24. This translation has been reprinted several times: True, ed., *Memoir*, 1944, 1945; Quinn, ed., *New American World*, 1979, vol. 5 p. 12. French, comp., *Historical Collections*, 1875, offered a different translation.
3. B. Smith, *Letter and Memoir*, 1854, p. 24; Quinn, ed., *New American World*, 1979, vol. 5, p. 13.
4. Crosby, *Columbian Exchange*, 1972.
5. McNeill, *Plagues and Peoples*, 1976, p. 55.
6. Kimball and Pearsall, "Event Analysis," 1955, p. 61.
7. Crosby, "Virgin Soil Epidemics," 1976, pp. 289 – 99.
8. Kimball and Pearsall, "Event Analysis," 1955, p. 58.
9. Hoebel, *Law of Primitive Man*, 1954, pp. 13, 16, 260.
10. Crosby, "Virgin Soil Epidemics," 1976, pp. 289 – 99.
11. Dobyns and Doughty, *Peru*, 1976, pp. 58 – 65.
12. Bandelier, trans., *Journey*, 1904 (1922), 133.
13. Commissioner of Indian Affairs, *Annual Report, 1899*, p. 249.
14. Ibid., p. 159. Stearn and Stearn, *Effect of Smallpox*, 1945, p. 15, noted that this was 74 percent mortality, contrasting with only 10 percent mortality among 412 Hopis who accepted Western medical care, only 42 of whom died.
15. Borah, "Discontinuity and Continuity," 1979, p. 1, emphasized the importance of identifying significant discontinuities for accurately interpreting history.
16. Ibid., 11.
17. Crosby, "Virgin Soil Epidemics,", 1976, pp. 189 ff., ably discusses this topic.
18. Krech, "disease, starvation," 1978, p. 715.
19. See, for example, Kluckhohln and Leighton, *Navaho*, 1948, pp. 160 – 63.
20. Dobyns, "Estimating," 1966, p. 409.
21. Cook and Borah, *Essays*, 1971, vol. 1, p. 423.
22. Borah, "Population Decline," 1962, p. 175.
23. Glisan, *Journal*, 1874, p. 23.
24. Jenkins, *Montreal*, 1966, p. 287.
25. Andreas, *History of Chicago*, 1884, vol. I, p. 120.
26. Fonda, "Early Wisconsin," 1868, vol. 5 (1907), 259.
27. Le Baron, *History*, 1878, p. 235.
28. Whitney, comp. and ed., *Black Hawk War*, 1937, vol. 37, pp. 1232, 1403.
29. Ibid., 1128.
30. Toner, *Contributions*, 1874, pp. 94 – 95.
31. Ashburn, *Ranks of Death*, 1947, p. 92.
32. Krech, "disease, starvation," 1978, p. 714.
33. Duffy, *Epidemics*, 1953, p. 205, noted malaria in Canadian missions in 1684.
34. Dobyns, *Native American Historic Demography*, 1976, p. 27.
35. Onadera et al., "Virus-Induced Diabetes Mellitus," 1978, pp. 529 – 31.
36. Borah, "Historical Demography," 1970, pp. 179 – 80.
37. Redfield, Linton, and Herskovits, "Memorandum," 1935, pp. 149 – 52.
38. Steward, "Theory and Application," 1955, pp. 296 – 97.
39. Wheeler-Vogelin, "Northern Paiute," 1956, p. 1.

TABLE SOURCES

Table 1

1520 – 24. Crosby, *Columbian Exchange*, 1972, pp. 47 – 51; Dobyns, "Outline," 1963, pp. 494 – 97; Stearn and Stearn, *Effect of Smallpox*, 1945, pp. 18 – 19; Ashburn, *Ranks of Death*, 1947, pp. 83 – 86.

1592 – 93. Gibson, *Aztecs*, 1964, p. 449; Sauer, *Aboriginal Population*, 1935, p. 10.

1602. C.O. Sauer, *Aboriginal Population*, 1935, p. 11.

1639. Stearn and Stearn, *Effect of Smallpox*, 1945, pp. 22 – 28, 30 – 31, 128, 133; Thwaites, ed., *Jesuit Relations*, 1896, vol. 10, pp. 19, 27; vol. XVI, pp. 101, 221, 217.

1646 – 48. León, *Historia*, 1909, p. 148; Alegre, *Historia*, 1959, Tomo III, pp. 60 – 62; Bushnell, "Menéndez Cattle Barony," 1978, p. 419.

1649 – 50. Stearn and Stearn, *Effect of Smallpox*, 1945, pp. 28, 128, 133; Speck, *Naskapi*, 1935, p. 29; Schlesier, "Epidemics," 1976, p. 136 – 38.

1665 – 67. Chatelain, *Defenses of Spanish Florida*, 1941, p. 56; Duffy, "Smallpox," 1951, pp. 324 – 41; Gibson, *Aztecs*, 1964, p. 450.

1669 – 70. Stearn and Stearn, *Effect of Smallpox*, 1945, pp. 29, 31, 133; Duffy, *Epidemics*, 1953, p. 71; Speck, *Naskapi*, 1935, p. 29.

1674 – 75. Ewers, "Influence of Epidemics," 1973, p. 108.

1677 – 79. Stearn and Stearn, *Effect of Smallpox*, 1945, pp. 31 – 32, 128; Thwaites, ed., *Jesuit Relations*, 1896 – 1901, vol. XLIII, p. 205 (Iroquois); O'Callaghan, ed., *Documents*, 1855, vol. 9, p. 129.

1687. Stearn and Stearn, *Effect of Smallpox*, 1945, pp. 32 – 33; O'Callaghan, ed., *Documents*, 1855, vol. 9 pp. 460 – 61, 490 – 92; 1854, vol. 4, pp. 194 – 95; Ewers, "Influence of Epidemics," 1973, p. 108; Bolton, ed., *Spanish Exploration*, 1908, p. 388.

1696 – 99. Stearn and Stearn, *Effect of Smallpox*, 1945, pp. 33, 129; Duffy, *Epidemics*, 1953, pp. 23, 74, 244; Giraud, *History*, 1974, vol. I, pp. 56, 78.

1701 – 1703. Stearn and Stearn, *Effect of Smallpox*, 1945, pp. 36, 133; Blasingham, "Depopulation," 1956, p. 383.

1706. Ewers, "Influence of Epidemics," 1973, p. 108.

1715 – 21. Stearn and Stearn, *Effect of Smallpox*, 1945, pp. 37 – 38, 128 – 29; Duffy, *Epidemics*, 1953, pp. 55, 76 – 77; Ewers, "Influence of Epidemics," 1973, p. 108.

1729 – 33. Stearn and Stearn, *Effect of Smallpox*, 1945, pp. 37 – 38; Blasingham, "Depopulation," 1956, p. 384; Thwaites, ed., *French Regime*, Vol. II, *1727—1748*, 1906, p. 175; Duffy, *Epidemics*, 1953, p. 81; Perceval, *Journal*, 1962, pp. 57, 59.

1738 – 39. Stearn and Stearn, *Effect of Smallpox*, 1945, pp. 17, 29; Ewers, "Influence of Epidemics," 1973, p. 108; Duffy, *Epidemics*, 1953, p. 23.

1746 – . Stearn and Stearn, *Effect of Smallpox*, 1945, p. 42.

1750 – 52. Ibid., 42, 133; Ewers, "Influence of Epidemics," 1973, p. 108.

1755 – 60. Stearn and Stearn, *Effect of Smallpox*, 1945, pp. 43, 129; Duffy, "Smallpox," 1951, p. 336; *Epidemics*, 1953, pp. 86 – 87; Ewers, "Influence of Epidemics," 1973, p. 108; O'Callaghan, ed., *Documents*, 1855, vol. 10, pp. 408, 438, 580.

1762 – 66. Stearn and Stearn, *Effect of Smallpox*, 1945, pp. 42, 44 – 45, 129 – 30; Duffy, *Epidemics*, 1953, p. 98; Ewers, "Influence of Epidemics," 1973, p. 108; Gibson, *Aztecs*, 1964, p. 451; Cook, *Extent and Significance*, 1937, p. 25;

Wheeler-Vogelin, "Anthropological Report," 1974, vol. 36 pp. 150–51; Hyde, *Pawnee Indians*, 1951, p. 52; Portlock, *Voyage*, 1789, p. 271.

1779–83. Dobyns, "Estimating," 1966, pp. 440–44; Stearn and Stearn, *Effect of Smallpox*, 1945, pp. 42, 46–49, 129–34; Gibson, *Aztecs*, 1964, p. 451; Mooney, *Aboriginal Population*, 1928, p. 12; Treitlein, trans., *Sonora*, 1949, pp. 217–18.

1785. Stearn and Stearn, *Effect of Smallpox*, 1945, pp. 49, 133.

1788. Aberle, Watkins, and Pitney, "Vital History," 1940, p. 170.

1793–97. Cook, "Smallpox Epidemic," 1939, pp. 937–79.

1799. Stearn and Stearn, *Effect of Smallpox*, 1945, pp. 51–52.

1801–1802. Ibid., 73–76, 130; Ewers, "Influence of Epidemics," 1973, p. 108; Mooney, *Aboriginal Population*, 1928, p. 12; Hyde, *Pawnee Indians*, 1951, pp. 84–85; Howard, *Ponca Tribe*, 1965, p. 26; Mallery, "Calendar," 1877, p. 11; Gipson, ed., "Moravian Indian Mission," 1938, vol. 23, p. 133; Sibley, "Historical Sketches," 1832, vol. IV, pp. 721–22: Martin, "Wildlife Diseases," 1976, p. 57.

1810–11. Praus, *Sioux*, 1962, p. 10.

1815–16. Stearn and Stearn, *Effect of Smallpox*, 1945, pp. 78, 130; Ewers, "Influence of Epidemics," 1973, p. 108.

1828. Stearn and Stearn, *Effect of Smallpox*, 1945, pp. 78, 131–32; Ewers, "Influence of Epidemics," 1973, p. 108; Aberle, Watkins, and Pitney, "Vital History," 1940, p. 170; Mooney, "Calendar History," 1898, p. 274; Kessell, *Kiva, Cross, and Crown*, 1979, p. 378; McGee, "Siouan Indians," 1897, p. 194.

1831–34. Stearn and Stearn, *Effect of Smallpox*, 1945, pp. 79, 131; Fonda, "Early Wisconsin," 1868 (1907), 264–65; Le Baron, *History*, 1878, p. 415; Wishart, "Dispossession," 1979, p. 387; Lawson, *History*, 1908, p. 371; Hudson, *Southeastern Indians*, 1976, p. 462; Denig, *Five Indian Tribes*, 1961, pp. 169–70.

1843–46. Stearn and Stearn, *Effect of Smallpox*, 1945, pp. 91–92.

1848–50. Ibid., 91. Krech, "disease, starvation," 1978, p. 714.

1852–53. Stearn and Stearn, *Effect of Smallpox*, 1945, pp. 95–98, 130–32.

1860–67. Ibid., 99–100, 102, 130–31; Ewers, "Influence of Epidemics," 1973, p. 109; de Laguna, *Under Mount Saint Elias*, 1972, p. 178; Bean, *Mukat's People*, 1972, p. 17; Browne, *Tour*, 1869 (1950), p. 52.

1876–78. Stearn and Stearn, *Effect of Smallpox*, 1945, pp. 103–105, 133–35; Ewers, "Influence of Epidemics," 1973, p. 109.

1896–99. Stearn and Stearn, *Effect of Smallpox*, 1945, pp. 109–11, 132–33; Commissioner of Indian Affairs, *Annual Report*, 1899.

Table 2

1531–33. Ashburn, *Ranks of Death*, 1947, pp. 90–91; Dobyns, "Outline," 1963, pp. 497–99.

1592–93. C.O. Sauer, *Aboriginal Population*, 1935, p. 11, and later discussion in the present study.

1602. C.O. Sauer, *Aboriginal Population*, 1935, p. 11.

1633–34. Stearn and Stearn, *Effect of Smallpox*, 1945, pp. 22–28; Drake, *Old Indian Chronicle*, 1867, p. 27; Hosmer, ed., *Winthrop's Journal*, 1908, vol. 1, pp. 114–15, 118; Jameson, ed., *Narratives*, 1909, pp. 139–41; Schlesier, "Epidemics," 1976, pp. 136–38; Newcomb, *Culture and Acculturation*, 1956, p. 11; C.C. Hall, ed., *Narratives*, 1910, pp. 126–27.

1658 – 59. Bushnell, "Menéndez Cattle Barony," 1978, p. 419; Gibson, *Aztecs*, 1964, p. 450.

1692 – 93. Blasingham, "Depopulation," 1956, pp. 384, 404; Richards, *Oneida People*, 1974, p. 33.

1713 – 15. Duffy, *Epidemics*, 1953, p. 166; Blasingham, "Depopulation," 1956, pp. 383 – 84; Thwaites, ed., *French Regime*, Vol. I, *1634—1727*, 1902, pp. 323 – 34.

1727 – 28. Gibson, *Aztecs*, 1964, p. 450; Stearn and Stearn, *Effect of Smallpox*, 1945, pp. 37 – 38, 128, 133; T.G. Corbett, "Population Structure in Hispanic St. Augustine, 1629 – 1763," 1976, p. 275; Milanich, "Western Timucua," 1978, p. 73.

1748. Cook, *Extent and Significance*, 1937, pp. 23 – 24.

1759 – 60. Stearn and Stearn, *Effect of Smallpox*, 1945, p. 43.

1768 – 70. Gibson, *Aztecs*, 1964, p. 451; Cook, *Extent and Significance*, 1937, pp. 26 – 27; Arricivita, *Cronica*, 1792, p. 416.

1776 – 78. Stearn and Stearn, *Effect of Smallpox*, 1945, pp. 45 – 46, 129 – 30; Ewers, "Influence of Epidemics," 1973, p. 108.

1803. Ibid., 108.

1819. Bishop, *Northern Ojibwa*, 1974, p. 160.

1837. Mahon, *History*, 1967, p. 157.

1887. *Mohave County Miner*, March 19, June 4, 1887.

1892. Ewers, "Influence of Epidemics," 1973, p. 109.

Table 3

1559. McNeill, *Plagues and Peoples*, 1976, p. 209; Gibson, *Aztecs*, 1964, p. 449.

1647. Duffy, *Epidemics*, 1953, p. 186.

1675. Ibid., 198. In May 1676 New England militiamen were sent home to recover from a respiratory malady despite King Philip's War. The disease spread to the hostile tribes and by late June their alliance had dissolved. Hubbard, *Narrative*, 1677, pp. 84 – 84 verso; Boyd, "Enumeration," 1948, p. 188.

1698. Stearn and Stearn, *Effect of Smallpox*, 1945, p. 33; Duffy, *Epidemics*, 1953, pp. 23, 74, 244.

1746. Stearn and Stearn, *Effect of Smallpox*, 1945, p. 42.

1761. Bancroft, *History*, 1883, vol. III, p. 756; Cook, *Extent and Significance*, 1937, p. 23; Blasingham, "Depopulation," 1956, p. 384.

1779 – 83. Martin, "Wildlife Diseases," 1976, pp. 53 – 54.

1889 – 90. Ewers, "Influence of Epidemics," 1973, p. 109.

1892. Ibid., 109.

1918. Crosby, *Epidemic and Peace*, 1976.

Table 4

1545 – 48. Gibson, *Aztecs*, 1964, pp. 448 – 49; Bancroft, *History*, 1883, vol. 3, p. 756; Mendieta, *Historia*, 1945, p. 174; Zinsser, *Rats, Lice*, 1934, p. 256.

1576. Bancroft, *History*, 1883, vol. 3, p. 756; Gibson, *Aztecs*, 1964, p. 449; Mendieta, *Historia*, 1945, p. 174; Zinsser, *Rats, Lice*, 1934, p. 257.

1612 – 19. Gibson, *Aztecs*, 1964, p. 449; Bushnell, "Menéndez Cattle Barony," 1978, p. 416; C.O. Sauer, *Aboriginal Population*, 1935, p. 11; H.H. Williams, "Epidemic," 1909, p. 34ff.; Hackett, ed., *Historical Documents*, 1937, vol. 3, p. 108; Williamson, *History*, 1832, vol. I, p. 216.

1707. Giraud, *History*, 1974, p. 85, noted direct transmission from Santo Domingo to Mobile.

Table 5

1601–1602. Gibson, *Aztecs*, 1964, p. 449; C.O. Sauer, *Aboriginal Population*, 1935, p. 11.
1659. Prine, *History*, 1845, p. 99.
1735–36. Leikind, "Colonial Epidemic Diseases," 1940, p. 376.
1784–87. Gibson, *Aztecs*, 1964, p. 451.
1880s. Krech, "disease, starvation," 1978, p. 714.

Table 6

1586. Dobyns, "Outline," 1963, pp. 504–505; Lorant, ed., *New World*, 1946, pp. 272–73; Quinn, ed., *Roanoke Voyages*, 1955, vol. I, p. 306; Boyd, trans., "Expedition," 1937, pp. 6, 16, 20.
1611. C.O. Sauer, *Aboriginal Population*, 1935, p. 11.
1720. Speck, *Naskapi*, 1935, p. 29.
1742. Cook, *Extent and Significance*, 1937, pp. 23–24; Clavijero, *Historia*, 1970, Libro 4, III p. 197; Sales, *Observations*, 1956, pp. 57–58; Rowland and Sanders, eds., *Mississippi Provincial Archives*, 1932, vol. 3, p. 769.

Table 7

1832–34. References are in the chapter text for the initial cholera invasion. For the 1834 recurrence, see B.O. Williams, "Survey" and "Shiawassee County," 1880, vol. 2, pp. 469–70, 488; Nevile, Martin, and Martin, *Historic Green Bay*, 1893, p. 243; López de Santa Anna, *Mi Historia*, 1905, p. 31; E. [scalante] y Arvizu, *Proclamation*, 1833; Spier, *Yuman Tribes*, 1933, p. 15.
1849. Mooney, *Aboriginal Population*, 1928, p. 13; "Calendar History," 1898, pp. 289–90, 173; Ewers, "Influence of Epidemics," 1973, p. 108; Denig, *Five Indian Tribes*, 1961, p. 19; Commissioner of Indian Affairs, *Annual Report for the year 1849*, 1850, pp. 139, 197–98, 205, 216; Bartlett, *Personal Narrative*, 1854, vol. 2, pp. 241; S.M. Hall, "Story," 1907, p. 418; Lumholtz, *New Trails*, 1912, p. 74. The owner of the calendar stick whose oral history Lumholtz published dated "painful fits and cramps" to 1851.
1867. May, *Ecology*, 1958, p. 42; O'Connor, "Narratives," 1937, pp. 65–66; Ewers, "Influence of Epidemics," 1973, p. 109; Russell, "Pima Indians," 1908, p. 52; Quebbeman, *Medicine*, 1966, p. 153.

Table 8

1637. Thwaites, ed., *Jesuit Relations*, 1896, vol. 14, pp. 9, 99; vol. XV, pp. 21, 33, 57.
1708–10. Stearn and Stearn, *Effect of Smallpox*, 1945, pp. 36–37, 132–33; Cook, *Extent and Significance*, 1937, p. 20; Warner, "Felix Martinez," 1970, p. 272; Rowland and Sanders, eds., *Mississippi Provincial Archives*, 1929, vol. II, p. 41; Clavijero, *Historia*, 1970, p. 132.
1793. Toner, *Contributions*, 1874, pp. 94–95; Michigan Pioneer and Historical Society, *Historical Collections*, 1892, vol. 20, p. 365.
1862–65. Krech, "disease, starvation," 1978, p. 714.

Table 9

1528. Bandelier, trans., *Journey*, 1904 (1922), 64; Ewers, "Influence of Epidemics," 1973, p. 108, guessed that the disease was cholera, but that ailment had not yet spread beyond the Middle East.

1535. Baxter, *Memoir*, 1906, p. 190; Bandelier, trans., *Journey*, 1904, pp. 100, 104−107, 116; Vedia, ed., *Historiadores*, 1858, tomo 22 pp. 538, 541.

1564−70. Lorant, ed., *New World*, 1946, p. 69; Lewis and Loomie, *Spanish Jesuit Mission*, 1953, pp. 77, 85, 89; R. Williams, "To John Winthrop," 1863, vol. 6, p. 229.

1711. Giraud, *History*, 1974, p. 179.

1804. Martin, "Wildlife Diseases," 1976, pp. 59−61.

1830−33. Cook, *Epidemic*, 1955, pp. 303−26.

ESSAY TWO

Population of the Native American Paradise Lost

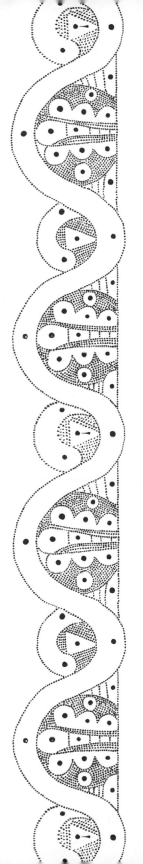

Before the invasion of peoples of the New World by pathogens that evolved among inhabitants of the Old World, Native Americans lived in a relatively disease-free environment. This fact should be clear from my lengthy enumeration of Old World pathogenic invaders. Before Europeans initiated the Columbian Exchange of germs and viruses, the peoples of the Americas suffered no smallpox, no measles, no chickenpox, no influenza, no typhus, no typhoid or paratyphoid fever, no diphtheria, no cholera, no bubonic plague, no scarlet fever, no whooping cough, and no malaria. The New World was free of a number of other Old World diseases that have not previosuly been mentioned, such as dengue, or breakbone fever, and yellow fever, which helped to make the cities on the north coast of South America Black settlements during colonial times.

The native peoples of the Americas possessed very few biological weapons with which to counter the European offensive. In the Andes, people who lived at certain altitudes in certain valleys suffered from verruga, a sometimes lethal disfiguring and debilitating disease.[1] It was geographically limited to those valleys and altitudes by the range of its sandfly vector. Consequently, it posed a threat only to a small number of Europeans who wanted to colonize the valley and the altitude range where it existed. Verruga was quite unlike malaria or yellow fever in that its insect vector proved to be a very poor colonizer. The anopheles and *Aedes aegypti* mosquitoes proved to be able to cross the Atlantic Ocean aboard sailing ships and then to spread rapidly into lowland tropical habitats in the Americas. The verruga sandfly vectors lacked that adaptability; they stayed fixed in their Andean habitat.

Ever since the Age of Discovery, Europeans have blamed first each other and then American Indians for syphilis.[2] Certainly this venereal disease spread widely through the ships' crews and seaports of Europe at the end of the fifteenth century. Historical and medical evidence that European sailors first contracted syphilis from women in the Caribbean islands and transmitted it to Europe is not so convincing as was once thought. The *Treponema* that causes syphilis cannot be distinguished microscopically from the organisms that produce yaws and related diseases.[3]

One aspect of the epidemiology of syphilis seems to have been ignored in many debates about its place of origin: the role of the disease in later decades as one of the major pathogenic contributors to the demographic decline of Native American peoples. Plainly, many native populations had never before protohistoric or historic times been exposed to syphilis, at least in the form in which it reached them via Europeans and Creoles. There is therefore good ground for advancing a mutation hypothesis. Some sailor aboard one or more ships sailing rapidly between Europe and Africa and the Caribbean may well have been the unwitting host to an early historic natural experiment in DNA exchange. That sailor may have contracted yaws in an African port and the pre-Columbian spirochete in a Caribbean port. The *Treponemas* coursing through his bloodstream exchanged genetic codes, and historic *Treponema pallidum* was created between 1492 and 1495. It was far more lethal to humans than either of its progenitors had been.

Aside from *verruga* and some form of venereal disease, almost the only biological weapons Native Americans possessed were several forms of intestinal parasites. These organisms were lethal only to children immediately after weaning, when they were likely to become infested with several worms and helminths.[4] Intestinal parasites posed no special threat to Europeans, although they caused discomfort and temporary debility during initial infestation. Several of the intestinal parasites present in Native American digestive tracts were very ancient varieties, such as pinworm, that had crossed the Bering land bridge with the original colonists of the Americas. The same varieties infested Old World populations, so that they did not threaten the homeostasis of European or African migrants to the Americas.

The near-absence of lethal pathogens in the aboriginal New World allowed the native peoples to live in almost a paradise of well-being that contrasted with their historic purgatory of disease. People simply did not very often die from illnesses prior to the Columbian Exchange. Consequently, the kind of demographic analysis that arose in Europe and applied to Colonial and later New World nations did not apply to pre-Columbian Native Americans. Thomas Malthus thought that in ancient nations, and in what he considered the "less civilized" parts of

the world, plagues and fatal epidemics had been one of the pre-
dominant checks on population increase.[5] He argued that births
"everywhere" greatly exceed deaths during plagues, epidemics, and
wars.[6] Malthus drew quantitative data from the early decennial census
reports of the United States, choosing to analyze only the data on the
white population and from sources on European regions. Thus modern
demography started off with a Eurocentric point of view, ignoring the
very different environments of pre-Columbian Native American
peoples and inhabitants of the Old World.

The very great impact that Malthus had on later population analysts
and politicians makes it important to understand his Eurocentrism.
Methodologically, Malthus's defense of the frightening conclusion for
which he became best known was curiously flawed. He used figures on
the rate of increase of only the white inhabitants of the United States
from 1790 to 1820 to calculate that under favorable "political" conditions
human population doubled every twenty-five years, a rate of increase
that he labeled geometric.[7] Malthus failed to mention the contribution
to the food supply and living standards enjoyed by this white group
that was made by Black slaves and free individuals and by Native
Americans from whom whites obtained food supplies, additional arable land, and capital from the large-scale trade in fur and peltries. As a
matter of fact, although he wrote about geometric increase of people on
a limited terrain, Malthus omitted mention of the actual territorial
expansion of the United States between 1790 and 1820. During that
thirty-year period, no fewer than ten states were admitted to the Union:
Vermont (1791), Tennessee (1796), Rhode Island (1790), Kentucky
(1792), Ohio (1803), Indiana (1816), Mississippi (1817), Illinois (1818),
Louisiana (1812), and Alabama (1819).

Despite the defects in his procedure, Malthus did correctly identify
birth and death rates as the fundamental analytical ingredients of demography. Still, he and many later demographers ignored the fact that
for millennia the Native American population had increased because
birth rates had exceeded death rates. The latter remained relatively low
because infectious diseases in the New World were scarce. In other
words, the size of the Native American population on the eve of the first
continental smallpox pandemic in 1520 reflected a long period of population growth. That growth had begun perhaps 40,000 years earlier
when a band of hunters followed glacial-age big game animals across
the relatively narrow land bridge that connected Siberia and Alaska at a
time when the sea level was lowered by immense quantities of water
frozen in continental ice caps.[8]

FOOD COLLECTOR-HUNTER-FISHERS

For most of the period of time after the initial peopling of North America until 1520, Native Americans hunted, fished, and gathered wild plants for food. They eventually increased in numbers to the limit imposed by their technological food-gathering ability. Cultural geographers have calculated the population densities achieved by peoples in various parts of the world who exploited natural resources with different economic systems. They found that the density of hunting-gathering peoples living in historic disease environments in non-Arctic areas tends to stabilize at about 0.386 persons per km^2.[9]

Such estimates appear to understate the technological ability of native North Americans inhabiting even the least favorable environment. A slightly higher density of 0.43 persons per km^2 has been demonstrated for the natives living in the arid central desert of the peninsula of Lower California. This density was calculated, moreover, from missionary records, indicating that the figure was valid at the time when Roman Catholic missionaries began to convert the peninsular Native Americans.[10] The mission period followed a century and a half of Colonial pearling along the coast of the peninsula. Pearlers who sailed across the Gulf of California almost certainly transmitted lethal Old World diseases to the peninsular peoples for decades before any missionaries arrived there.[11] Thus the pre-Colonial population in even the bleakest part of Lower California was greater than the number—somewhat more than 0.43 persons per km^2—encountered by the missionaries.

This population density figure holds a fundamental importance for understanding the size of the North American population immediately prior to the European discovery of the continent. The pre-Colonial population generally cannot be assumed to have been fewer than 0.43 persons per km^2 in the non-Arctic portions of the continent. If the northern two-thirds of Canada and Alaska are consigned to the Arctic category, it encompasses some 6,648,222 km^2 of Canada plus 1,010,421 km^2 of Alaska.[12] An ethnohistorian recently calculated that 5,400 Kutchin occupied 300,000 km^2 of this colder region, which would mean a population density of 1.7 persons per 100 km^2,[13] (throughout Arctic Canada and Alaska) only 130,197 persons. In other words, the size of the Eskimo and Native American populations that had culturally adapted to exploit Arctic resources must be determined separately from the size of the Native American population of the rest of the continent.

The remaining third of Canada and Alaska contains 3,829,323 km^2, the contiguous forty-eight United States 7,824,631 km^2;[14] and the two-thirds of Mexico north of the territory of the pre-Conquest Meso-american empires and kingdoms about 1,308,744 km². These areas may be assumed to have supported at least 0.43 Native Americans per km² in prehorticultural times. Thus the density figure for hunting-fishing-gathering peoples indicates a minimum population of 5,573,965 Native Americans in 12,962,709 km².

Many areas afforded their inhabitants resources far richer than those of the central desert of the Lower California peninsula. Many peoples possessed a far more efficient fishing and food production technology than did the peoples who had taken refuge in Lower California. Some of the tribes of Upper California reached densities of 3.86 persons per km² along rivers such as the Sacramento or San Joaquin.[15] The abundance of nutritious fish that Native Americans caught from such streams provided them with a plentiful supply of rich animal protein. When such high densities of pre-Columbian population are averaged in with others supported by distinctive economic habitats across California, the entire state appears to have sustained about 0.77 persons per km². Even the arid southern deserts are included in that average.

One ecologist estimated that 204,092 km² in California supported no fewer than 248,300 Native Americans, or a density of 1.2 per km².[16] That density was achieved without food cultivation. The minimum population that can be projected from the Lower California desert density is 87,760 persons. Thus the estimated figure for Upper California exceeds the minimum estimate by 160,540 individuals. Adding that difference to the minimum estimated for the continent, we obtain a revised figure of 5,734,505 Native Americans living in sub-Arctic areas in prehorticultural times.

The rich salmon fisheries of the rivers of Washington, Oregon, and British Columbia sustained population densities that were greater than those in California.[17] An ecological anthropologist calculated a density of 1.16 persons per km² for the Klamath Province of the culture area.[18] If the whole area was equally densely populated, then it must have supported more than 500,000 persons.

An archaeologist estimated that the Chilcotin of southern British Columbia had a population density of 1.7 persons per km² in an area of 32,944 km².[19] Such a figure suggests that British Columbia, with its populous coastal zone, contained a peak Native American pre-Colonial population of more than 1 million individuals. The province contains some 948,601 km²,[20] so a density of 1.7 persons per km² would mean a populace on the order of 1,612,622 persons, or 1,204,728 more than 407,898 minimum estimate for a density of only 0.43 persons per km².

Adding 1,204,723 to the already revised prehorticultural total yields a new revised estimate of 6,939,228 Native Americans.

When the richness of the natural resources of the Great Lakes fisheries and the abundant wild rice harvest of that area is taken into account, one can easily hypothesize that the population of North America should have exceeded 7 million persons in prehorticultural times. Such a figure stands in marked contrast to the estimates anthropologists offered for many years of the immediate prehistoric, barely pre-Columbian population of the continent. For many years, U.S. anthropologists[21] estimated the pre-Colonial population of the continent as only about 1 million persons. Either Malthus and later demographers are wrong, and human populations do not tend to increase to the limits imposed by their available food supplies under preindustrial conditions, or James Mooney, his editor John R. Swanton, and Alfred L. Kroeber greatly underestimated the numbers of Native Americans inhabiting North America. Furthermore, if we turn from the question of prehorticultural numbers to the matter of pre-Columbian peak population, we cannot disregard the fact of frequently very intensive Native American horticulture. Food growers inhabited much of the continent, as indicated on map 1.

The sub-Arctic part of North America composing the California, Basin, and Plateau regions and the Great Plains grasslands north of the limits of aboriginal horticulture amounted to some 6,447,264 km². This area inhabited by hunting-gathering and fishing-hunting-gathering peoples must have been at least as densely populated as the central desert of Lower California. Thus we should postulate a minimum Native American population of 2,772,323 for the large area between the Arctic specialists and the horticultural peoples. To that figure we must make several additions to account for zones of locally much denser nonhorticultural populations.

As indicated above, we should add about 160,540 persons to the total for the California culture area. We may then perhaps treat the 1,204,723 persons estimated for British Columbia as approximately the corrective required for the Northwest Coast culture area.

Native American peoples residing on the interior plateau of northern Mexico and the Tamaulipas-Coahuila-south-Texas region also did not produce food. Assuming that their natural resources and technology were as productive as those of the central desert of Lower California, northeastern Mexico may have held about 311,000 people early in the sixteenth century. The figures just mentioned give a total of perhaps 4,448,586 nonhorticultural Native Americans, and if we allow for the

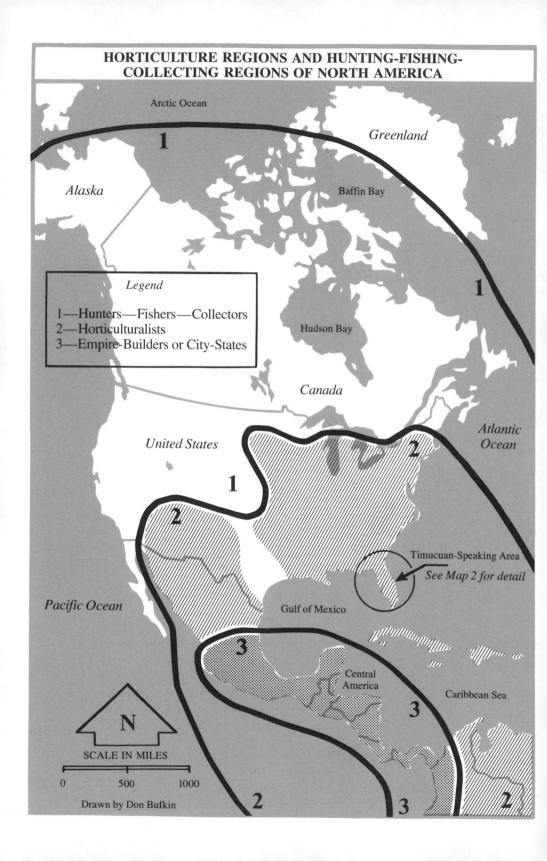

HORTICULTURE REGIONS AND HUNTING-FISHING-COLLECTING REGIONS OF NORTH AMERICA

Arctic Ocean

Greenland

1

Alaska

Baffin Bay

1

Legend

1—Hunters—Fishers—Collectors
2—Horticulturalists
3—Empire-Builders or City-States

Hudson Bay

Canada

Atlantic Ocean

United States

2

1

2

Timucuan-Speaking Area
See Map 2 for detail

Pacific Ocean

Gulf of Mexico

3

Central America

Caribbean Sea

3

N

SCALE IN MILES

0   500   1000

Drawn by Don Bufkin

2

2

3

rich Great Lakes fisheries and the wild rice harvests, the estimate of nonhorticultural Native Americans becomes approximately 5 million beings early in the sixteenth century.

FOOD PRODUCERS

Many Native American peoples in southern North America did more than hunt, fish, and gather wild plants. They cultivated maize, squash, beans, sunflowers, and other minor food crops that enabled them to increase in population. Cultural geographers regard "beginning agriculturalists" as growers able to support from 10 to 24.7 persons per km² with food they produce.[22] Native Americans may not have reached such densities, because they continued to rely on wild game and fish to supply animal protein in their diet and they lacked plows and draft or milk animals. As a result they treated plains, meadows, and savannahs as uncultivated hunting and gathering territory. Nevertheless, Native American horticulturalists in various places equaled or exceeded the population densities reached by Pacific Coast fishermen.

Native Americans along the southern shore of the Great Lakes and even in southern Ontario apparently tripled the Northwest Coast population density. The tribes living there cultivated summer crops. They also harvested plentiful wild rice from lakes, ponds, and streams. They caught an abundance of several types of spawning fish.[23] The lacustrine-riverine area is here estimated to have sustained more than 3,800,000 Native Americans at an average density of 3.86 persons per km².

The southwestern portion of the continent was thickly populated,[24] with highest densities on and near the coast. The shores of the Gulf of Mexico from the Attakapa people east through the Apalachee may have supported as many as 4.6 persons per km², for a total of about 1,100,000 individuals. The Timucuan chiefdoms, the Calusa, and smaller groups inhabiting peninsular Florida numbered perhaps 697,000 persons, with an average density of 5.72 persons per km². The Atlantic coastal plain from Florida to Massachusetts afforded a favorable habitat to about 2,211,000 Native Americans. Records of early historic population and land-management patterns suggest that pre-Columbian population density rose to as many as 13.77 people per km² in southern New England.[25] The Virginia-Maryland tidewater region was still another area of dense Native American settlement.[26] Population densities might appear as high elsewhere in North America were the documentary record equally detailed for earlier Colonial years.

In the Southwest, horticultural Native Americans for the most part depended upon crop irrigation in riverine oases, supplementing their produce by hunting and by collecting wild plant foods from vast tracts ranging from semiarid to arid. Consequently, their overall population density may have no more than matched California's 0.85 person per km². It may be asked whether aboriginal horticulture failed to spread to Californians because it could not, at least during an initial transitional phase, yield harvests larger than those made of grass seeds, acorns, cactus fruit, and so forth.[27]

Farther south, in present-day Mexico, Sonoran Desert population density averaged perhaps 1.5 individuals per km²; about 277,400 Native Americans lived there.[28] Still farther south and east lay the rim of Mesoamerican civilization. There population density rose to approximately four persons per km². Some 928,000 Native Americans lived from Nayarit east to San Luis Potosí.

The great Mississippi River valley, its major Missouri, Ohio, Kentucky, Tennessee, and Red River tributaries, and their affluents drained an area of more than 2 million km². Horticultural peoples estimated to include 5,250,000 individuals lived there, averaging 2.53 persons per km².

CONCLUSIONS

Two kinds of estimates of pre-Colonial Native American population yield the figures that I have summarized. One procedure rests on the Malthusian theorem that human beings tend to increase to the limits imposed by key food resources. Especially in the comparatively disease-less environment inhabited by pre-Columbian Native Americans, such population growth would indeed have occurred, and human numbers may be calculated on the basis of quantities of crucial foodstuffs. The other procedure uses population densities of historic populations enumerated, or closely estimated, by literate colonials. Such sample densities projected across the cultural/natural areas outlined above yield a continental estimate of approximately 18 million Native Americans living north of civilized Mesoamerica in the early years of the sixteenth century.

The 18 million figure implies an average density of about 1.15 Native Americans per km² overall, or about 1.4 persons per km² outside the Arctic region. This density is almost double the figure of 0.77 persons per km² that the U.S. Census Bureau used late in the nineteenth century to define the frontier of Euroamerican rural farm settlement.[29] Thus these estimates of Native American population call into question the accuracy of the ultranationalist interpretation of U.S. history embodied in the frontier thesis.[30] The frontier of European/Euroamerican settlement in North America was not a zone of interaction between people of European background and vacant land, nor was it a region where initial farm colonization achieved any "higher" use of land as measured in human population density. It was actually an interethnic frontier of biological, social, and economic interchange between Native Americans and Europeans and/or Euroamericans.

Not long after initial European colonization on the Atlantic Coast, the trading post was a more typical frontier institution than the farm was. The true frontier settlement was a composite one: in what later became Middle America, a settlement such as The Glaize contained traders of British and French ancestry, Native Americans of several tribal backgrounds, their Black and White captives, European refugees who preferred life among tribesmen to townsmen, and mixed-blood offspring of European men and Native American women.[31] After all, only on such an interethnic frontier of intergroup interaction could Europeans and their descendants see Native Americans dying from biological invasion by Old World pathogens. The Puritans saw skeletal bones of New England's natives who had perished in the severe plague of 1616–1619 scattered in depopulated villages and weedy old fields. They saw Massasoit and other survivors of the catastrophe suffering and dying from diseases that the newcomers had transmitted. Had they not seen these things, the Puritans could not have concluded that their deity had favored them by clearing the native proprietors from the landscape for the special benefit of colonists.[32] Native American depopulation enabled Puritan true believers to base their justification for their invasion of widowed land on Christian Scripture. The key passage came from the Book of Genesis: "Multiply and replenish the earth."[33] This crucial injunction and rationalization spread from Puritans to other Atlantic coastal colonists and persisted through time. Interethnic frontiersmen observed repeatedly the high mortality rate suffered by Native Americans during epidemics of Old World diseases, and devout Christians among them made the same frequency interpretation as did Puritans.[34]

Had Native American numbers in North America not been originally on the order of magnitude estimated in this essay, the aborigines collectively could not have survived the numerous epidemic episodes that I have outlined. Then, too, had Native Americans not been so numerous early in the sixteenth century, they could not have persisted, eventually to increase again and to create the ecological and social pressures that emerged in the United States and Canada after the Second World War.

NOTES

1. Lastres, *Historia*, 1951, vol. III, pp. 305 – 309; Anderson, ed., *Pathology*, 1953, pp. 309 – 11.
2. Crosby, *Columbian Exchange*, 1972, pp. 123 – 41.
3. Ibid., 144.
4. Payne, Gonzáles Mugaburu, and Schleicher, "Intestinal Parasite Survey," 1956, pp. 696 – 98.
5. Malthus, "Summary View," 1830 (1960), 41.
6. Ibid., 45.
7. Ibid., 17.
8. Cohen, *Food Crisis*, 1977, pp. 159 – 69; Dumond, "Archaeology," 1980, pp. 984 – 91.
9. Petersen, *Population*, 1961, p. 322; Hawley, *Human Ecology*, 1950, p. 151.
10. Aschmann, *Central Desert*, 1959, pp. 145 – 80.
11. Holmes, *New Spain*, 1963; Bancroft, *History*, 1886, vol. II, p. 422. Conquistador Fernando Cortés dispatched an expedition to discover Lower California in 1534, and pearling began not long thereafter.
12. Delury, ed., *World Almanac*, 1979; Canada = 3,851,809 square miles (p. 497); Alaska = 586,412 square miles (p. 459).
13. Krech, "disease, starvation," 1978, pp. 711, 718.
14. Delury, ed., *World Almanac*, 1979, p. 454.
15. Baumhoff, *Ecological Determinants*, 1963, pp. 155 – 235.
16. Ibid., 227, table 18, converted to metric system.
17. Kroeber, *Cultural and Natural Areas*, 1939, pp. 155 – 56.
18. Baumhoff, *Ecological Determinants*, 1963, p. 227, table 18.
19. Casteel, "Two Statis Maximum Population-Density Models," 1972, p. 30.
20. Delury, ed., *World Almanac*, 1979, p. 499. British Columbia = 366,255 square miles.
21. Mooney, *Aboriginal Population*, 1928, p. 33; Kroeber, *Cultural and Natural Areas*, 1939, pp. 143 – 44.
22. Petersen, *Population*, 1961, p. 323; Hawley, *Human Ecology*, 1950, p. 151.
23. Kroeber, *Cultural and Natural Areas*, 1939, pp. 88 – 89; Jenks, "Wild Rice Gatherers," 1900, pp. 1013 – 1137; for the fishery see Catlin, *Letters and Notes*, 1841 (1973), vol. 2, pp. 161 – 62.
24. Hudson, *Southeastern Indians*, 1976.
25. Jennings, *Invasion*, 1975, pp. 26 – 29; P.A. Thomas, "Contrastive Subsistence Strategies," 1976, pp. 1 – 18.
26. MacLeod, *American Indian Frontier*, 1928, pp. 176, 546. Truly pre-Colonial population densities in Tidewater Virginia and Maryland may have been from 4.9 to 6.8 per square kilometer.
27. H.T. Lewis, *Patterns*, 1973.
28. C.O. Sauer, *Aboriginal Population*, 1935, p. 5.
29. Porter, *Compendium*, 1892, pp. xlv – xlviii.

30. Turner, *Frontier*, 1920; Jacobs persuasively attacked Turnerian nationalism in *Dispossessing*, 1972. Elsewhere I urged clarification of institutional concepts in historical analysis of frontier institutions ("Study," 1980, pp. 5 – 25).

31. Tanner, "Glaize," 1978, pp. 15 – 40, is a charmingly written description of the true interethnic frontier.

32. Segal and Stineback, *Puritans, Indians,* 1977, p. 32, make the point that "without the epidemics" (and consequent depopulation), Puritans would have been left with "drastically" weaker justifications for their invasions. One was purchase from Native Americans, or a "gift." The other was "lawful war."

33. John Cotton, a leading Puritan divine in 1630, stated the explicit rationalization: Genesis 1:28 authorized a descendant of Adam or Noah to "come and inhabit" without purchase or permission "where there is a vacant place" (*God's Promise*, 1896, p. 6).

34. Erasmus, *Man Takes Control*, 1963, explains this concept of frequency interpretation.

The Food Resource Potential of Florida under Aboriginal Native American Management

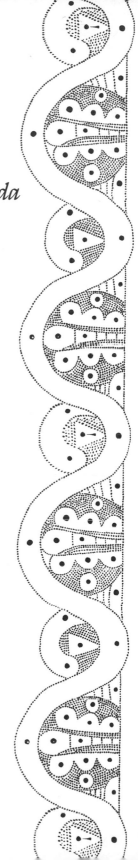

I have used population densities achieved by peoples with different technologies to estimate Native American populations in general terms for various regions of North America prior to the initial smallpox pandemic. I will now discuss the specific resources involved in sustaining populations on such a scale. To keep the analysis manageable, I will focus on an area smaller than the whole of North America.

Such analysis involves a kind of examination of the relationships between a specific environment, its flora, its fauna, and its human population. This essay, then, illustrates the thesis that to relate human carrying capacity to the gross area of a polity, as some social scientists have done,[1] is scientifically indefensible. Gross political territory is not an analytically meaningful unit. More relevant than political boundaries are the resources available to sustain human life. Thus the population density on arable and pasture land is significant in a modern nation whose people are fed by farming and animal husbandry. The regions of arable soil, and especially of high-yield irrigated cropland and even pasturage, are environmentally circumscribed.[2] The difference between territory of sovereignty and productive terrain is easily illustrated. Using Peru's total sovereign area, one calculates a density of only eight persons per km²,[3] but this figure is almost totally misleading. By determining the amount of land actually used for food production, including extensive pasturage, one discovers that Peru's population density is very different: it is a high 483 persons per km².[4] This density figure is ecologically, technologically, and socially significant.

In a pre-Columbian Native American polity, wild game, fish, and plant resources fundamentally determined the human carrying capacity of any area. For peoples with a food-producing technology, soils cultivable with human energy, given adequate precipitation or irrigation technology and water sources, established an area's capacity to sustain

48

human life. To see how these factors operated let us consider one sample area, the modern state of Florida.

I have chosen Florida for several reasons. First of all, the relation of the Gulf Stream to the peninsula made the region important to Spanish authorities as soon as pilots discovered that sailing ships could gain several knots per day by returning to Europe in the Gulf Stream. Captains and pilots thereafter depended on the Gulf Stream, but because of seasonal storms and because the peninsula and islands known as Keys lay low, many ships went aground. Other European powers eager for a share of the precious metals that Spain was shipping from New World mines quickly began to seize Spanish ships sailing in the Gulf Stream. Spain therefore colonized the peninsula in 1565 in order to deny other countries—particularly France—a port for ships that could easily prey on Spanish fleets homeward bound. The new Spanish colony had the secondary benefit of permitting the empire to ransom some survivors of many shipwrecks on the coast and Keys. As a result, at least some written records about the port of St. Augustine and its Native American hinterland exist from an earlier date than for any other portion of North America outside the heartland of New Spain. This documentation permits the ethnohistorian to discover details about the Native American population in Florida that cannot be reconstructed for native peoples living elsewhere on the continent during protohistoric times.

Moreover, the Floridian environment differs to some extent from that of any other portion of North America. The peninsula projects about as far south as the southern Rio Grande valley portion of Texas. Both sides of Florida are coastal, however, so that its climate is largely marine rather than continental. The climate and nearly flat peninsular topography foster a fairly distinctive vegetation and native fauna.[5] Comparatively abundant rainfall, inland lakes and streams, and a very long coastline have resulted in a fairly even distribution of major natural resources save in the extensive swampy areas that contrasts with the often very unequal distribution of natural food resources in much of North America. Consequently, understanding Native American population distribution in North America requires a specific analysis of the special Florida case.

PREVIOUS POPULATION ESTIMATES

Because Florida was colonized earlier than the rest of North America outside Mexico, and because it became a major vacation area after its annexation by the United States, much attention has been paid to the history of the peninsula, and a number of authors have estimated the size of the Native American population in the area.

In the mid-nineteenth century, Daniel G. Brinton reasoned that the aboriginal population of the peninsula at no time greatly exceeded 10,000 persons.[6] Brinton reasoned very much as Robertson, Bandelier, Kroeber, and Angel Rosenblat have. Chroniclers' accounts that de Soto's marauders had faced 10,000 warriors under one chief Brinton dismissed as hyperbole. From his specialized analysis of Timucuan ethnography, W.W. Ehrmann set a slightly different estimate of between 10,000 and 12,000 people on the peninsula.[7] The standard recent history of Florida fixed the aboriginal residents of the state at 25,000 persons at the beginning of the sixteenth century,[8] the period with which this discussion is mainly concerned. A military historian employed that same figure of 25,000, but for 1663, about a century and a half later.[9] The anthropologist whose findings many later authors uncritically accepted estimated that there were 24,000 Native Americans in Florida.[10]

Historians of Spanish Colonial Florida have published somewhat higher estimates of Native American numbers. The Spanish Borderlands historian Herbert E. Bolton stated that the missions of Florida once provided 30,000 Native Americans with religious instruction.[11] Still, that figure did not encompass unconverted natives and so must be regarded as understating the total Native American population. A historian of Spanish Colonial ranching estimated that these were never more than 20,000 native Americans under colonial rule during the seventeenth century and that another 15,000 conceivably had "at least some contacts with Christianity."[12] The combined total of 35,000 was still short of the actual population by at least 10,000 if Bolton was correct about the number of mission Indians.

The anthropological authors of a theoretical analysis of the Calusa estimated that this group numbered more than 4,000 individuals but fewer than 7,000. These writers clearly viewed the Calusa population as static, however, rather than as fluctuating in response to historic influences. At least one Colonial Spanish chronicler estimated Calusa numbers at 10,000 persons.[13] That figure may have referred, moreover, only to the ruler's principal settlement, where a Spanish visitor reported finding more than 4,000 people during a European intrusion in 1566.[14] In 1570, the Spaniard López de Velasco reported not only 10,000 Calusa, but also 20,000 Apalachee, 6,000 Tocobaga, 1,000 Mocoso, 1,040 Key Indians, and 80 Tekesta[15]—more than 38,000 Florida Native Americans quite apart from the populace in the Timucuan-speaking chiefdoms.

Most recently, two regional archaeologists, perhaps influenced by my own work, have set a significantly higher figure. In their textbook on Florida prehistory, Jerald T. Milanich and Charles H. Fairbanks placed the aboriginal population at a minimum of 100,000 persons, conceding that the actual population might have been several times that number.[16] It is thus worth considering whether the food resources of Florida were of a nature to support a large human population.

FLORIDA COMPARED TO LOWER CALIFORNIA

As I noted earlier, it cannot reasonably be assumed that any non-Arctic portion of North America supported fewer Native Americans than did the arid central desert of the peninsula of Lower California. A cultural geographer who carefully analyzed Catholic mission records found that the central desert supported at least 1.12 persons per mi.^{2},[17] and a population of such density existed long after Spanish pearlers and pearl traders must have transmitted Old World pathogens to—and diminished the numbers of—the peoples of Lower California.[18] We must therefore regard 1.12 people per mi.^{2}, or 0.43 persons per km^2, as a minimal population density for Native Americans.

Florida contains 58,560 mi.^{2} Projecting the state's native population using the Lower California central desert minimum density of 1.12 persons per mi.^{2} yields a very minimal estimate of at least 65,587 Native American inhabitants early in the sixteenth century. Thus previously published estimates of the early sixteenth-century Native American population (except for the 1980 figure of Milanich and Fairbanks) can be discarded as clearly much too low.

Early twentieth-century anthropologists and historians showed a pronounced (and unjustified) tendency to regard Colonial population reports as uniformly exaggerated,[19] as some analysts of Spanish-Indian relations in Florida have noted.[20] In historiographic perspective, such writers aligned themselves with the Robertson-Bandelier-Spores view that aboriginal Native Americans were few in numbers and thus were capable of only minimal levels of sociocultural integration.[21]

NOTES

1. Masering, "Carrying Capacities," 1977, pp. 484–89, table 3.
2. Carneiro, "Theory," 1970, pp. 735–36, stated the concept of "environmental circumscription" and its consequences. The quality of irrigation water and crop-producing and grazed lands as well as their quantity critically influence

the level of production achieved (Singer et al., "Bad News," 1980, pp. 1296 – 1303).

3. Masering, "Carrying Capacities," 1977, table 3.

4. Dobyns and Doughty, *Peru*, 1976, p. 308.

5. Laessle, "Study," 1944, p. 155.

6. Brinton, ed., *Notes*, 1859 (1969), 112.

7. Ehrmann, "Timucua Indians," 1940, p. 173.

8. Tebeau, *History*, 1971, p. 16.

9. Mahon, *History*, 1967, p. 2.

10. Mooney, *Aboriginal Population*, 1928, p. 8.

11. Bolton, "Mission," 1917, p. 45.

12. Arnade, "Cattle Raising," 1961, pp. 116 – 17.

13. Goggin and Sturtevant, "Calusa," 1964, p. 209, following López de Velasco, *Geografía y Descripción*, 1894.

14. Goggin and Sturtevant, "Calusa," 1964, p. 186, following Solís de Merás, "Memorial," 1894, vol. 2, p. 164. The chief's house could hold 2,000 men without crowding (Connor, trans., *Pedro Menéndez*, 1923, 145) and more than 4,000 men and women were in the chief town (ibid., 149), seemingly excluding children. Among the latter, 5,000 between the ages of 10 and 15 years sang at the windows of the chief's house during the reception for Pedro Menéndez de Avilés (Kerrigan, trans., *Pedro Menéndez*, 1965, p. 87; Barrientos, *Vida y Hechos*, 1902, p. 92).

15. Goggin and Sturtevant, "Calusa," 1964, p. 209.

16. Milanich and Fairbanks, *Florida Archaeology*, 1980, p. 18.

17. Aschmann, *Central Desert*, 1959, p. 178, table 7.

18. Venegas, *Natural and Civil History*, 1759 (1966), vol. 1, p. 180, thought that Spaniards began sailing to Lower California to barter for pearls between 1606 and 1615 and continued to cross the Gulf until colonization began.

19. Kroeber, *Cultural and Natural Areas*, 1939, p. 180.

20. Ehrmann, "Timucua Indians," 1940, p. 173; Pearson, "Spanish-Indian Relations," 1974, p. 273.

21. Borah, "Historical Demography," 1970, p. 184, felicitously suggested labeling one extreme view of Native American population size the "Robertson-Bandelier" and the other the "Clavijero-Prescott." One could easily add Angel Rosenblat to the Robertson-Bandelier category, and Spores (*Mixtec Kings*, 1967) also qualifies for admission.

SECTION ONE
Edible Wild Plants

My examination of the wild plant food resources of Florida uses two approaches. First, in a general way I follow an analytical path marked out by Paul Thompson, who estimated the range of population of the aboriginal Chipewayan by calculating the number of caribou available to that group.[1] Unlike Thompson, however, I do not focus upon a single critical resource. Florida's most important characteristic was probably the very wide range of food resources that it afforded its inhabitants, much of which aboriginal peoples must have exploited. Second, I use a method of controlled comparison that has yielded excellent results in social anthropology. One of my aims is to formulate statements about the conditions of existence of quite dissimilar social systems. My procedure therefore differs from that of social anthropologists who seek to compare, say, familial institutions varying narrowly in regions of "relatively homogeneous culture."[2] Rather, my own evaluation employs terms of controlled comparison as a means to contrasting the food resources of the peninsulas of Florida and Lower California. Instead of controlling for ecological factors, that is, I contrast them in order to note concomitant variations in population and social structure.

That the complexity of Native American social structure in Florida and Lower California differed markedly has long been recognized. The Calusa sociopolitical hierarchy contained at least four levels and probably five. A Headchief led the Calusa. Various status symbols set him apart: a gold forehead ornament, special leg bands, a dais, and obeisance from subjects. Local Townchiefs sent tribute payments to the Headchief's capital settlement. There were "principal men" and followers, or commoners.[3] During the sixteenth century, at least, shipwrecked Spaniards became Calusa slaves. Moreover, the Calusa chiefdom then incorporated not only European slaves but also Cuban Native American commoners in an ethnically diverse society.[4] Similarly, each Timucuan chiefdom was led by its Headchief, who was carried on a litter and bore many other symbols of rank. Townchiefs were frequently, if not always genetically related to the Headchief. They sent to the Headchief tribute that they collected from the commonality.[5] In contrast, the natives of Lower California were almost completely egalitarian; no very visible symbols set chiefs apart from followers. Europeans had to ob-

serve Lower Californian aboriginal behavior closely in order to perceive patterns that differentiated leaders from their followers.

As a result we find a true paradox. On the one hand, anthropologists
recognize that Native Americans in aboriginal Florida lived in complex,
hierarchically organized chiefdoms, whereas aboriginal Lower Californians lived in structurally simple societies. On the other hand, anthropologists prior to Milanich and Fairbanks consistently credited
aboriginal Florida with fewer inhabitants than Lower California! Sherburne F. Cook estimated that areas missionized by the Jesuits held
41,500 aboriginal Lower Californians,[6] with another 10,000 in the
Dominican mission zone.[7] Thus while Lower California had 51,500
aboriginal inhabitants or more, Florida for many years was considered
to have had but 24,000 or 25,000. This essay examines the question of
whether even the recent Milanich-Fairbanks estimate of 100,000
aboriginal inhabitants of Florida is ecologically and culturally reasonable.

My evaluation begins by contrasting the plant food resources of the
two peninsulas. Surprising though it may seem, Florida supported
some of the same plants that arid Lower California did. Although
Florida receives more rainfall than Lower California, precipitation is
very seasonal, so Florida's plants must be able to withstand or avoid
droughts that may last for months.

SOURCES OF SUGAR AND STARCH

Cactus Fruits

Native Americans in both Lower California and Florida had access to
sweet fruits of *Opuntia* cacti, usually called prickly pears in English. An
English ship's captain in 1709 reported that the Pericú near Cape San
Lucas had a fruit that grew "on the prickle Pear-tree"; he thought that it
tasted like gooseberries.[8] A Jesuit historian credited all of Lower
California with a "great plenty" of these *tunas*, as they are known in
Spanish.[9] A pioneer botanist who rode some 500 miles on horseback
along the mountainous spine of Lower California reported 14 species of
Opuntia growing there. These included *Opuntia tuna* Mill., the Mexi-
can domesticate, cultivated by small populations at Comondú and
Purísima late in the nineteenth century. *Opuntia engelmannii* grows on
the northern part of the peninsula, as does *O. prolifera*. The former is the
most common pad-leafed, fruit-bearing form on the Sonoran Desert.
Some species bear no edible fruit.[10]

In South Florida, the Tekesta consumed prickly pear fruit in season.[11] In 1821 James G. Forbes listed the prickly pear as one of Florida's food resources. It "affords a handsome fruit, which although troublesome to gather, is pleasant to the taste when ripe, or as a preserve."[12] Daniel Coxe, writing a century earlier, distinguished between wild and cultivated varieties of the plant but wrote that east as well as west of the Mississippi River, "from the Gulph of Mexico, some Hundreds Miles up the Country, abounds with all Sorts of Tunals, or Tuna's . . . usually found in the Province of Mexico."[13]

Coxe advocated employing Native American women and children to gather cochineal insects from *Opuntia*, which were used to make a red dye when the Gulf Coast region was settled by Europeans.[14] (A cochineal species, *Dactylopius confusus*, which secretes the coloring agent carminic acid is in fact commonly found on prickly pear plants in Florida.)[15] These parasites may have been the source of the red dye that Florida's Native Americans used on tanned skins. Unlike Coxe Forbes noted that there was some doubt as to whether the cochineal insect found on Florida *Opuntia* was genuine.

Opuntia fruit production may have been equal on the two peninsulas, or Florida's crop may have exceeded that in Lower California. The most abundant source of fructose available to the Lower California peoples was the fruit of large columnar cacti known collectively as *pitahaya*, which was very sugary, contained many oily seeds, and was only briefly in season. According to missionary Jacob Baegert, only when this fruit was ripe—for eight weeks beginning in mid-June—could peninsular Californians "satisfy their appetite without restraint." The sugar content enabled some natives to "become corpulent" during the pitahaya harvest.[16] Toward the end of the nineteenth century, the various cacti growing in Lower California were "extremely abundant and the most noticeable portion of the flora north and south, often forming forests and impassable thickets."[17]

The main pitahaya species is *Machaerocereus gummosus*, which was abundant in the Cape region at the end of the nineteenth century. The sweet pitahaya (*Lemaireo cereus thurberi* Engelm.) that grows to a height of 15 feet is common throughout the southern two-thirds of the peninsula. The "Old Man" (*Lophocereus schottii*) that grows in the same area and is common near the cape bears a smaller, less abundant fruit. A giant cactus known in Spanish as *cardon* (*Pachycereus pringlei*) grows in the southern two-thirds of the peninsula and is "common in the low country" near the cape. It reaches 50 feet in height and "in some localities forms forests"; although the fruit is quite palatable, it is smaller than that of the pitahaya.[18]

The Lower California natives became infamous among colonists for their "second harvest" of undigested pitahaya seeds picked from their excrement, which were roasted and ground into a repast the natives relished.[19] Historian Miguel Venegas labeled the pitahaya the fruit that constituted "the great harvest" of the Californians.[20] Probably the "little black seed" that Pericú residents of a fishing camp near Cape San Lucas ground with stones and ate "by handfuls" in 1709 came from the pitahaya. One English visitor described pitahaya gruel as the native equivalent of bread.[21] An Englishman who came in 1721 saw the ground meal made up "in rolls."[22]

No equally massive columnar cacti grew in Florida, yet the southern peninsula and Keys did have three species botanically closely related to the pitahayas.[23] Botanists have not yet accounted for the presence of these *Cereus* species and a few *Opuntia* species on post-Pleistocene land.[24] Evidence is emerging, however, to suggest that Native Americans elsewhere transplanted or set out cuttings of favored food plants, and it is possible that human colonists brought the first cactus cuttings to South Florida.

The Native American peoples of Florida obtained sugar from several sources much more abundant than cacti. The Timucua, at least, collected honey to eat as a high-energy food while traveling.[25] Having labeled the country near the mouth of St. Johns River "the fairest, frutefullest, and pleasantest" in the world, Jean Ribaut in 1563 listed "honney" first among its resources.[26]

Yuccas

Species of yucca that produce an edible fruit grow on both peninsulas. Lower California natives consumed the flowerbuds and blossoms of *Yucca elata* and *Y. whipplei* as vegetables, as well as the fruits of *Y. valida* on the southern peninsula and of *Y. baccata* on the northern peninsula.[27] The food production of both peninsulas may have been about equal in terms of yucca, and Floridian peoples probably also used buds and petals. Lower California peoples utilized yucca leaf fibers and *Agave* leaf fibers, both called *pita* in Spanish, in weaving nets and in making their scanty clothing.[28]

The Spaniards planted "several rows of the Spanish bayonet along the ditch" that bordered the bastions and half-bastions that fortified the town of St. Augustine in Florida. When Spain ceded the province to England in 1763, these plants "formed so close a chevaux de frize, with their pointed leaves, as to be impenetrable."[29] The Spaniards of that period also employed yucca plants to form a barrier outside the moat surrounding their outlying fortification at Mosa, garrisoned by freed Black runaways from the English colonies in the 1730s.[30] While transplanting was a long-established European technique for plant propagation, the Spaniards may have learned to transplant yuccas from seeing Native Americans do so.

Grapes

Lower Californians harvested wild grapes at a few locations, a harvest that they augmented with several varieties of berries.[31] The aridity of the environment sharply limited the areas in which berries and grapes could grow in Lower California. The wild canyon grape (*Vitus girdiana* or *V. peninsularis* could grow only along streams, and Lower California had few of them. Yet this grape was not uncommon in damp canyons around Comondú, and the fruit was of good quality, fresh or dried.[32] Florida Native Americans enjoyed significantly more grapes than Lower Californians did.

Florida actually provided two types of "grapes." The dune zone around the south coast supported thickets of the so-called pigeon plum.[33] That plant (*Coccolobis grandifolia*) grows as high as 40 feet, tolerates salt, and produces small fruits. The Tekesta consumed in season the "sea grape" (*Coccolobis unifera*), a close relative.[34] Later the Seminole people also ate sea-grape fruits.[35]

On June 1, 1539, members of de Soto's expedition who rowed ashore at Charlotte Harbor to collect grass to feed horses aboard ship also picked green grapes. Reportedly the Calusa ate the fruit "very ripe" or dried.[36] Possibly de Soto's marauders picked sea grapes. The Tekesta consumed fruits of the coco plum (*Chrysoblanus* sp.) and perhaps wild figs (*Ficus* sp.) as well as pigeon plums and huckleberries.[37] The pigeon plum tree flourishes on many south Florida barrier islands and reaches considerable densities in low hammocks. Sample counts of hammocks indicate that 2,660 can grow per hectare.[38] Later consumers of coco plums included the Seminole Indians.[39]

Farther north, both near the sea and inland, grapevines grew abundantly, with Native American encouragement. The Gentleman of Elvas was impressed by the abundance of grapes throughout the Southeast.[40] In 1563 Ribaut wrote about the "hiest, greatest and fairest vynes in all the wourld with grapes accordingly, which naturally and withowt mans helpe and tryming growe to the top of the okes and other trees."[41] In 1564, a French Huguenot wrote home to his father, "The woods are so full of vines that you can scarcely walk two steps without finding quantities of grapes just now beginning to ripen."[42] That same year, René de

Laudonnière described trees "all entwined with cords of vines, bearing grapes in such quantities that their number would be sufficient to render the place habitable" on a knoll near the mouth of St. Johns River in Timucua territory.[43]

At the southeastern extremity of the peninsula, the Tekesta also consumed true grapes when they were available.[44] At the end of colonial times, Forbes reported that the wild grapevine was still "very abundant, in the woods, and has been improved. Wine has been made from the grape of tolerable food flavour."[45] By that time, Euroamericans had imported European grapes to the peninsula.

Dates

In southern Florida, the Tekesta ate fresh palmetto berries (*Serenoa repens*) and also dried them to use for food when traveling.[46] Excavation of a charred palm berry seed from an early seventeenth-century Potano village[47] shows that the Timucua also ate these dates, which are about as large as medium-sized olives. After the plants have been burned, an underground trunk starts regrowth within a few days,[48] a feature that made palmettos very well adapted to Native American frequent burning of vegetation. The saw palmetto is a palm "so uniquitous that it is difficult to be very far out of sight of [it]" in the present century.[49]

The fruits of the needle palm usually lodge in its spines, rotting before they reach the ground, and human consumption helps the plant extend its range.[50] The blue palmetto (*Sabal minor*) grows over the widest range of any palm in North America, reaching from South Florida to eastern Texas and North Carolina. Its fruits are, however, only a quarter of an inch long. The related *Sabal etonia* grows from central Florida's Lake County south and bears fruit from half an inch to an inch in diameter.[51] This date is about half the size of smaller domesticated varieties of the Old World. In the mid-sixteenth century, one island in south-central Florida reportedly produced such an abundance of fruit, "especially dates from the palms," that its inhabitants "made a good trading business from these."[52] *Sabal etonia* appears to be the native Florida palm most likely to have yielded sizable dates in large quantities on a small area.[53]

The native date is of considerable significance in helping us form an idea of the human population that Florida's wild plants could have supported. The "fresh" domesticated date contains only 20 percent water, so it is a high-energy food. A 100-gram serving contains 75.4 g of carbohydrate, or 284 calories, plus 2.2 g of protein and 0.6 g of fat.[54] In other words, a kilogram of dates would provide all the calories an active adult would require during a day. In combination with meat from fish and game, dates were an ideal foodstuff.

In contrast, Lower California supported palm trees in significant numbers only near Cape San Lucas. Some species yielded no fruit but only fiber that the natives used to make nets.[55] The endemic fan palm (*Washingtonia filifera*) grew in mountain canyons where moisture was available.[56] This palm bears as many as a dozen fruit clusters that weigh from 5 to 20 pounds. The dark blue fruit is only about the size of a pea, with a thin layer of pulp over a large seed. Native Americans in the culture area ate the fresh fruit or sun-dried it to store for later use. Dried fruit and seeds were ground into flour.[57]

Mulberries

Local Timucuans living near the mouth of St. Johns River in 1562 carried freshly washed red and white mulberries to a French exploring vessel.[58] The native red mulberry (*Morus rubra* L.)[59] occurs throughout northern Florida, although it is nowhere abundant under twentieth-century conditions.[60] The flourishing mulberry trees of Florida encouraged Colonial Spaniards to think of producing silk there, using native mulberry leaves to feed silkworms. The Gentleman of Elvas reported that mulberries were abundant throughout the Southeast in 1539–1542,[61] which suggests that changing modes of vegetation management may have resulted in a diminution of mulberries during historic times. The Timucuan practice of giving away mulberries may mean that the fruit was highly prized or that the Timucuans enjoyed a seasonal surplus.

Pawpaws, Crabapples, Cherries, and Guavas

The pawpaw (*Asimina* sp.) ranges into Florida only along the Apalachicola River in aboriginal Apalachee territory. It produces a fruit two inches long.[62] The crabapple (*Malus angustifolia*), which bears fruit an inch in diameter, ranges westward from the Suwannee River in open woods and fencerows.[63] The native black cherry (*Prunus serotina*) grows in hardwood hammocks and throughout the northern part of Florida in cutover and disturbed areas.[64] Its bittersweet fruits, nearly one centimeter in diameter, are well worth collecting. Habitat preference indicates that burning by Native Americans would have fostered the growth of both crabapples and cherries. In Lower California the islands cherry (so-called from the islands off the southern California coast) grows in tree form only in a few very deep canyons in the central mountain chain of the peninsula, at the southern limit of its range. It is a common bush over the northern two-thirds of the peninsula.[65] Another wild cherry grows in the Sierra de la Laguna, near the tip of the peninsula.[66]

South Florida's historic Seminoles consumed guavas[67]—presumably the Cattley guava, which bears fruit about an inch in diameter with a pleasantly flavored juice and matures in late summer.[68]

Plums

Native plum trees grew abundantly in natives' fields throughout the Southeast in 1539–1542, according to the Gentleman of Elvas.[69] He mentioned obtaining dried plums at Anhaica Apalache on October 25, 1539,[70] and recorded seeing two varieties in the fields around Cosa.[71] He mentioned prunes as provisions at Autiamque, where de Soto's marauders wintered.[72] The so-called Chickasaw plum (*Prunus angustifolia*) bears red or yellow fruits two to four inches long. Common throughout northern Florida, it forms thickets in openings where the trees monopolize sunlight and along fencerows and roadsides.[73] Its preference for disturbed sites suggests that the Chickasaw plum flourished under the pre-Columbian fire regime whether transplanted or not.

The American plum (*Prunus americana* var. *floridana* Sarg.) prefers rich loamy soil. It grows in Panhandle counties, especially on the floodplain of the Apalachicola River. Its fruits are about an inch long and are bluish or purplish, ripening in midsummer. The Flatwoods plum (*P. umbellata*) is a small tree with a short trunk, occasionally forming thickets. It grows even on the sand dunes along the Atlantic Coast and widely in northern Florida in open forest. Ripe fruits from one-half to two-thirds of an inch in diameter are dark purple to red (on coastal dunes) when ripe in late summer. Their astringent flavor[74] probably did not stop Native Americans from using these fruits in some way, perhaps as a sauce for meat or fish. While plum trees grew in Lower California, they were not abundant. Jesuit missionaries reported a notable number of such trees only at San Bernabé Bay.[75]

Persimmons

The common persimmon (*Diospyros virginiana*) is apparently more adaptable than any other fruit tree native to Florida. It is common and widely distributed in many habitats from beach dunes to inland forest. Fruits are as much as an inch and a half in diameter.[76] Lower Californians had one persimmon species that grew near the Cape.

Figs

Another tree, the wild fig, occurred on both peninsulas. Some trees grow at San José del Cabo in Lower California,[77] and scattered specimens appear in Florida.[78]

The Jesuit missionary Jacob Baegert reported that the Californians "reject nothing that their teeth can chew or their stomachs are capable of digesting. . . . Thus they will eat the leaves of the Indian fig-tree, the tender shoots of certain shrubs."[79] Baegert did not indicate, however, the concentration of figs or edible shrubs. The "Indian fig" seems to have been introduced to Lower California by the Spanish. The Jesuit historian Miguel Venegas gave the Jesuits credit for having introduced the domesticated fig to that peninsula.[80] The cultivated *Ficus carica* was also brought into Florida during Colonial times.[81]

Other Fruits and Seeds

In 1709, a ship's captain listed some of the wild berries consumed by the Pericú fishermen camped near Cape San Lucas. One berry resembled that of English ivy. The native Americans dried it "at the fire," and the Englishman compared it with parched peas. Another berry he described as "like a large Currant,"[82] which it might indeed have been. Early botanical collections from Lower California included two species, *Ribes tortuosum* and *R. leptanthum*, which range northward into Arizona, New Mexico, Colorado, and Utah.[83] Its pulp was white; it tasted tart, and the natives relished it. The Englishman reported that these people had "many other seeds" unknown to him.[84] Several plants found in Lower California set edible seeds.

One exploitable seed bearer is the endemic sunflower (*Helianthus niveus*).[85] In the Andes a domesticated lupine is grown for its seeds, even though they must be leached to make them edible,[86] and we may safely assume that hungry Lower Californians ate the seeds of their endemic species, even though they were small.[87] Several of the species of blazing star that grew in Lower California may have yielded exploitable seeds. The large, oval white seeds of *Mentzelia hirsutissima*[88] possibly even indicate aboriginal domestication. Native Americans in Arizona consumed the not very large seeds of *M. albicaulis*; indeed, it was a preferred food among Northeastern Pai.[89] Without doubt Lower Californians ate *chia*, the seeds of *Salvia columbariae*.[90]

A number of berries grew abundantly in Florida. Large-fruited types included blueberries (*Cyanococcus myrsinites*), blackberries (*Rubus cu-*

neifolius), and elderberries (*Sambucus simpsonii*). There were also Christmas berries (*Rhacoma elicifolia*), snowberries (*Chiococca pineto-rum*), gopher apples (*Geobalanus oblongifolius*), huckleberries (*Deca-chacna tomentosa*), and gopherberries (*Lasiococcus dumosus*).[91]

Hawthorns are one of the commoner shrubs or trees in twentieth-century Florida vegetation. Some probably would have been collected by Native Americans. These include the mayhaw (*Crataegus aestivalis*), which prefers wet woodlands and shallow ponds. Its slightly acid, yellow-fleshed fruit is a centimeter long and is sold commercially; without doubt Florida's Native Americans gathered this fruit. The dwarf haw also bears a fruit one centimeter in diameter. It grows in open woodlands from Aluchua County westward. The swamp haw (*C. paludosa*) also prefers low woodlands and pond margins from Lafayette County westward. Native Americans may have collected fruits of the Ravenal haw (*C. ravenelli*), the Leon haw (*C. leonensis*), which grows only in one Panhandle county, the weeping, or Pensacola, haw (*C. lacrimata*) in the Panhandle from Walter to Escambia County, and other species with restricted geographic distributions, such as *C. egregia* in Liberty County.[92] The sparkleberry tree (*Vaccinium arboreum*) bears fruits with a pleasant flavor that persist on the plants into the winter. Although these black berries are only a quarter inch in diameter, the tree is common in northern Florida,[93] and the scant pulp may well have entered the Native American diet.

A Florida plant that flourished under burning by Native Americans is the partridge pea (*Chamaecrista* spp.). Pine-oak vegetation in north-central Florida burned during the first week of January 1958, and by April the green cover consisted mostly of sprouting turkey oak, chinquapin, fern, poison ivy, and partridge pea seedlings. These were 10 to 20 times as abundant in the burned area as in an unburned control zone.[94] The abundance of the partridge pea and its seeds may have encouraged their collection and direct consumption by Native Americans. In any event, the burning-stimulated seed production of the partridge pea contributed indirectly to Native American subsistence, inasmuch as the plant nourished bobwhites, other upland game birds, and perhaps animals as well. Partridge pea seeds bulked larger than any other bobwhite food in the crops of 200 birds taken statewide at all seasons, accounting for 18.47 percent of total volume. Milkpeas (*Galactia* spp.) came next, with 13.38 percent. In a flatwoods habitat, crops contained 16 percent partridge peas in the spring and 14 percent in the fall but nearly 64 percent during the winter. In a sandhills habitat, the contents of crops were 16 percent partridge pea in the fall and almost 23 percent during the winter.[95]

The vegetation of humid Florida afforded a greater abundance and variety of fruits and berries than was available in Lower California. To Baegert and other Jesuits, Lower Californians seemed perpetually hungry. No such impression of Florida's populous peoples emerges from the sixteenth-century civil and clerical accounts of them written by the Spaniards.

SOURCES OF STARCH

Wild Rice

One of the earliest scientific observers of the independent Seminoles in their South Florida refuge area reported, "all the rice they need they gather from the swamps."[96] The refugee population was small enough in numbers to have placed little pressure on wild rice stands. The importance of nineteenth-century Seminole wild rice harvesting lies in its implications for use of the grain by the earlier Calusa and Tekesta. The Seminoles must have acquired ricing technology from the Calusa. Harvesting, for example, involves paddling or poling a canoe carefully through stands of maturing grains so as not to dislodge the ripe grains and using a flail to knock them into the watercraft. When the Seminoles retreated into the South Florida Everglades, however, they were not a canoe-using people. They had become very successful cattle raisers in northern Florida and rode on horseback. Their adjustment to the swampy South Florida environment seems to have been quite rapid, suggesting that they did not have to invent independently the technology that they employed in mid-nineteenth century and later. It seems probable, in other words, that Seminole refugees absorbed some Calusa individuals and learned from them how to survive in the exotic peninsular environment. Wild rice seems likely to have been a staple of the ancient Calusa and Tekesta, and the grain must have been a significant source of starch for the South Florida population early in the sixteenth century.

Native Americans dried wild rice for storage. The dried gain retains only about 8.5 percent water, so 100 g contain more than 75 g of carbohydrate plus more than 14 g of nutritious protein. It furnishes 364 calories;[97] 687 g would provide an adult with 2,500 calories, or enough for a day's energy expenditure.

Kunti

In addition to its other bounty for Native American inhabitants,

Florida produced several plants with tubers containing abundant starch. *Zamia*, known as *kunti*, or *coontie* in Seminole,[98] grew abundantly throughout the peninsula. Preparation involves freeing the edible starch, which is generally done by grating the tuber and using water to dissolve the starch away from the fibers.[99] A southern species, *Z. integrifolia*, adapted admirably to the Everglades environment of South Florida.[100] Another species, *Z. pumila*, grew farther north and afforded almost as high caloric yields per surface unit of area. *Zamia* species which grew on many Caribbean islands and on the adjacent mainland were widely exploited by aboriginal groups. Spanish observers agreed that the Calusa living in southwestern Florida relied heavily on such roots.[101] Clearly *Zamia integrifolia* was one of the several "roots" exploited; presumably it was dried and pounded into the flour from which white bread was made. The Tekesta on the Atlantic Coast north of the Keys also relied extensively on its tubers.[102]

The end product of kunti tuber processing was almost pure starch. Indeed, starch was commercially manufactured from the tubers during the nineteenth century. Dried to a 12 percent water content, starch contains 87 g of carbohydrate per 100 g, furnishing 362 calories,[103] so 691 g of processed flour would provide 2,500 calories, enough for a day's intake for most adults.

Smilax

Known commonly in English as "bamboo briar," "cat briar," "greenbriar," or "China briar," *smilax* was another starchy-rooted plant that grew over a range in the Southeast wider than Florida alone. Kunti and *Smilax* could both be harvested the year around except when high water inundated the stands in the Everglades.[104] The Timucua evidently relied to some extent on both starchy roots. In 1597, Gov. Gonzalo Méndez de Canzo asserted that the Saturiwans of Cumberland Island "sustained themselves the greater part of the year" on "the roots of herbs" along with shellfish and acorns.[105] With tubers furnishing starch, oils from nuts, and animal protein from shellfish, the Saturiwan diet would have been fairly balanced, given the addition of fresh fruits and berries.

Manioc

Missionary reports of Lower Californian tuberous foods are ambiguous in that they may not distinguish between plants used before and after the mission period. Baegert noted that "among the roots eaten by the Californians may be mentioned the Yuka, which constitutes an important article of food in many parts of America . . . , but it is not very abundant in California." Yuca was cultivated in much of lowland tropical America, but Lower California groups did not cultivate food prior to mission times. Baegert knew that yuca was usually made into a form of bread, but the natives in Lower California would have found processing the tuber too "tedious," Baegert wrote, so they "simply roast the Yukas in a fire like potatoes."[106] The report indicates that missionaries introduced this cultivar but not the associated processing technology. Fortunately for the Lower Californians, the Europeans seem to have introduced a "sweet" variety of yuca that did not have to be leached to be safe for human consumption. Jesuit historian Miguel Venegas described the general processing technology used by Lower Californians. He wrote that they cut "large thick" yuca roots into slices from which they pressed the juice before shaping the residue into "broad thin cakes."[107] Venegas may have referred to a group different from that observed by Baegert or may have seen the same people at a later period, when processing technology had diffused to the Lower Californians. The Jesuit historian described several domesticated plants that members of his order had introduced to Lower California, of which yuca was only one. Even as an introduced cultivar, however, yuca was not very abundant in Lower California,[108] whereas *Zamia* and *Smilax* grew widely and abundantly in Florida in pre-Columbian times.

Potatoes

Nineteenth-century Seminoles depended to a considerable extent on a wild potato, "a small tuber found in black swamp land," as well as on kunti tubers.[109] Most likely Seminoles learned from remnant Calusa how to identify the edible wild potato and where to locate its tubers in the swampy South Florida environment. This tuber was no doubt one of those that furnished starch to the early sixteenth-century Calusa.

At high elevations in the mountains near the tip of Lower California a pioneer botanist found plants that he considered to be the domestic potato. They were not common[110] and again seem to have been post-mission introductions.

Yams

An English ship's captain who visited a Pericú fishing camp near Cape San Lucas in 1709 reported that the group had "some Roots that eat like Yams."[111] These Pericú presumably had not been brought under missionary influence, so nonhorticultural Lower Californians may have consumed at least one starchy root of an uncultivated plant. Pearl traders might already have introduced tuber cultivation to the Pericú. Venegas listed *camotes*, sweet potatoes, among the three tubers consumed by mission-period Lower Californians.[112] Inasmuch as the Jesuit historian described mission conditions, sweet potatoes were apparently a postcontact cultivar introduction. Just what the English visitors to the cape settlement saw in 1709 that resembled yams remains uncertain.

Jicama

Less uncertainty exists with regard to the *jicama* that Venegas listed as a third tuber consumed by Lower Californians. On the one hand, the term refers to another cultivar with a very large tuber that is grown in New Spain. It was most likely introduced to Lower California, inasmuch as *Ipomoea mexicana* still grew in the San José del Cabo region toward the end of the nineteenth century.[113] On the other hand, the name also refers to a plant indigenous to Lower California, *Ipomoea jicama*. This is a woody species that climbs other plants and was much sought after even by late nineteenth-century inhabitants of the peninsula because of its "fine flavor and watery juice." By that time, many little holes in the ground near plants growing close to trails testified to earlier removal of tubers by humans. Late nineteenth-century tubers might weigh as much as two or three pounds but were usually smaller, although tradition claimed that 6- and 10-pound tubers had once been found. *Ipomoea jicama* is a member of the morning glory family and grows on barrier islands as well as on the peninsula.[114]

Cattails

Father Jacob Baegert wrote that he saw the natives of Lower California "frequently eat the roots of the common reed, just as they were taken out of the water."[115] The rhizomes of the cattail (*Typha*) contain nutritious starch and were eaten by many Native American peoples. Florida, with 4,424 square miles of inland waters, afforded its native inhabitants far more cattail roots to eat than could arid Lower California. The Native Americans of Florida enjoyed a marked advantage over those of Lower California in terms of readily available starchy tubers.

Cooked Green Starch

The Lower California peoples relied heavily on the roasted hearts of edible *Agave* plants at certain seasons. By mid-eighteenth-century mission times they were found not to "grow as plentifully as the Californians might wish and very seldom in the neighborhood of water."[116] *Agave* cutting, trimming, and pit roasting was slow and laborious,[117] requiring a relatively high expenditure of human energy for the starch yield. Aschmann attributed the local extinction of plants close to water sources to overexploitation by aborigines.[118]

Reduced exploitation following depopulation allowed *Agaves* to proliferate in Lower California. Toward the end of the nineteenth century, an *Agave* growing about 10 feet tall was the most conspicuous plant on high mesas near Comondú. Half a dozen species grew virtually all over the peninsula.[119] *Agave sullivanii* flower stalks yield sap sufficient for the distillation of mescal. *Agave sobria* grows leaves about two feet long on highlands around Comondú. *Agave shawii* is "very abundant" in the central third of the peninsula. Two other species, *A. chrysoglossa* and *A. deserti*, were very abundant in some localities on the northern two-thirds of the peninsula. Both grow leaves that reach about 50 centimeters in length.[120] Florida lacked this component of Lower California's flora.

The peoples of Florida instead had available abundant cabbage palms, so-called from the edible growing tip. *Sabal palmetto* grows as much as 80 feet tall. It is the hardiest of Florida's native palms, growing abundantly except in the extreme western Panhandle. It thrives in a wide variety of soils and tolerates both brackish water and salt spray.[121] It forms very extensive stands on the coastal plain and especially along the St. Johns River basin. It reaches high densities in periodically inundated areas.[122] The tender new growth of this palm tree serves as a "vegetable."[123] On the subtropical, well-watered Florida peninsula, cabbage palms were more abundant than was *Agave* in Lower California. It is so abundant under twentieth-century conditions that it is difficult to find any part of Florida where plants are not in sight.[124] Historian George R. Fairbanks expressed surprise that Spaniards in St. Augustine should ever have suffered hunger in view of the abundance of this "cabbage tree palm of the land" and arrowroot.[125] His skepticism about Spanish reports to superiors in distant administrative cities was quite justified.

In just one type of plant assemblage in Florida, 2,000 cabbage palms reportedly grow per hectare,[126] and this type of palm almost certainly reached greater numbers in aboriginal times, for it is one of the plants that best survive frequent burning.[127] The Timucuans and Apalachees—and no doubt other Florida peoples—set circular fires to hunt game when they burned vegetation off their fields in January.[128] Those fires and others set to keep hunting meadows open and growing forbs and vigorous sprouts of perennial plants for upland game would have favored cabbage palm production.

In sum, the Native Americans of Florida had access to edible starch in several more forms than did the peoples of Lower California. Moreover, the Florida environment supported far greater densities of starchy species than arid Lower California did.

Other Greens

The 4,424 square miles of inland waters in Florida provided an edible green vegetable not known to the desert dwellers of Lower California. This "water lettuce" was eaten by early Euroamerican settlers before the exotic water hyacinth usurped its ecological niche. At the beginning of U.S. sovereignty, even so swift-flowing a stream as the broad St. Johns River was in "parts . . . covered with the floating plants of the . . . water lettuce" (*Pistia stratiotes*).[129]

NUTS

Lower California natives harvested some acorns and pine nuts from trees that grew in a relatively small area at higher elevations.[130] Starchy pith was also obtained from pods of mesquite; the "beans" of that tree and the palo verde growing at lower elevations were ground for use. The mesquite (*Prosopis glandulosa*) sets pods as heavy as those of irrigated plants grown on equal areas. Ground pod meal could be mixed with water to make gruel or could be baked into cakes. The screwbean (*P. pubescens*) is smaller and less common, but its pods are used in the same ways.[131] Mesquite grew at intermediate elevations of the southern two-thirds of Lower California.[132] The palos verdes provided emergency rations, their pods having little pith. As their name indicates, these trees have green bark in which photosynthesis occurs (they retain few leaves during much of the year). The common *Cercidium microphyllum* grows along the eastern side of the peninsula south to about 25 degrees north latitude. It overlaps with *C. praecox* from about 28 degrees; the latter grows south to Cape San Lucas. A Lower Californian subspecies of *C. floridum* ranges from roughly 27 degrees to almost the tip of the peninsula.[133] The Florida honey locust bears a similar pod with much pulpy tissue between the seeds. It grows in moist but well-drained river bottoms and flatland hammocks in western Florida.[134] Whether Florida's native peoples made use of that pulp is not known.

One of the striking contrasts between the flora and plant food resources of the two peninsulas lies in the proportion of temperate-zone nut-bearing trees. The oaks are notably different in the two regions. Near the tip of Lower California, one small oak species grows from Miraflores to the summit of the Sierra de la Laguna and San Francisquito. A second large species grows on the western slope of the Sierra de la Laguna to near the Pacific Ocean at Todos Santos.[135] Some trees in a central peninsular canyon without acorns late in the nineteenth century may have been a relict population.[136] The ranges of all these oaks together form only a small fraction of Lower California. More important was the extension of the southern California oak assemblage into the northern portion of the peninsula.

The Florida Native Americans enjoyed distinctly greater resources per square kilometer with respect to nuts of several kinds. This almost level peninsula offered nearly 30 species of oaks, all completely adapted to the local climate and resistant to insects.[137] Timucuan consumption of acorns has already been mentioned. Acorns that Native Americans did not directly consume nourished game, particularly deer and passenger pigeons. Examinations of contents of stomachs of more than 400 deer taken in all sections of Florida in 1953–1959 indicated something about comparative abundance of oak species and/or acorn production.[138] Table 10 describes the bulk of eight major oaks found in Florida.

In central and northern Florida, Timucuans gathered a surplus of

TABLE 10

Common Oak Species Used by Man
and Deer in Florida

Common Name	Botanical Name	Acorn Size (inches)	Range	% of Deer Stomach Contents
Water	*Quercus nigra* L.	⅓ – ½	common in all N Florida	8.6
Post	*Q. stellata* Wang.	½ – ¾	Santa Fé River West	5.6
Turkey	*Q. laevis* Walt.	n.a.	common on sandhills	3.6
Diamond-leaf	*Q. laurifolia*	½ – ⅔	Marion County west	3.5
Live	*Q. virginiana* Mill.	n.a.	common on open sites	3.1
Myrtle	*Q. myrtifolia*	n.a.	sandy sites, N counties	0.61
Cow	*Q. prinus* L.	1¼ – 1⅔	wetlands in all N Florida	0.32
—	*Q. cinerea*	n.a.		1.4

Note: n.a. = not available.
Sources: Arnold, "Check List," 1938, pp. 57–58; Kurz and Godfrey, *Trees,* 1962, pp. 68–102; Harlow, "Fall and Winter Foods," 1961, pp. 23–24, table 2.

acorns for use, along with maize, as gifts to French colonists in the 1560s or as items to trade for European goods.[139] In a report to the Spanish king, Pedro Menéndez wrote that Florida could produce bacon for the Spanish market because "there is abundant supply of acorns in the oak forests."[140] In 1597, Gonzalo Méndez de Canzo thought that the Saturiwans of Cumberland Island sustained themselves for most of the year on maize and acorns supplemented with roots and shellfish.[141] Passing through former Apalachee towns in the fall of 1716, Diego Peña wrote that these *chicazas* were "rich in fruit trees." Significantly, he listed acorns along with chestnuts, plums, and Old World peach, pomegranates, and quinces as orchard remnants.[142]

Whether or not Florida's Native Americans deliberately planted acorns so as to have oak "orchards," their use of fire for hunting and for field clearing favored oaks and diminished the numbers of pines. The annual January field burning of the Timucuans and Apalachees probably caused trees near their settlements to resemble an orchard.[143] Oaks appear to have evolved in an environment where fires occurred frequently. Mature trees are fire resistant, especially when frequent burning keeps the understory small in biomass and therefore unable to generate the intense heat required to kill mature tree crowns. Smaller oaks send up new, vigorous sprouts from their roots following a burn. Species such as live oak (*Q. virginiana*) flourish in Florida even in areas burned annually.[144]

Acorns were, moreover, not the only nuts feeding the native peoples of Florida. In 1562, Ribaut noted "many walnut trees, hazeltrees and small cherytrees verry faire and great"[145] near the mouth of St. Johns River. The number of walnuts all over the Southeast impressed the Gentleman of Elvas in 1539 – 1542.[146] Excavation of charred hickory nuts in an early seventeenth-century Potano settlement confirmed their consumption by that group.[147] Although a modern experiment suggests that 100 kg of nut meat plus oil can be obtained in 277 man-hours by cracking hulls with a mortar and pestle and boiling to remove oil and meats,[148] historical evidence of Timucuan processing techniques is lacking. The Gentleman of Elvas in 1540 recorded "considerable walnut oil" as well as bear grease at Chiaha,[149] much farther north in the Southeast. It seems reasonable to conjecture that Native Americans in this culture area did crack tough nuts such as hickories and then boiled them to obtain oil, with meats perhaps almost a by-product.

Sixteenth-century Spanish chronicles indicate that the pecan (botanically considered a hickory nut) was not then grown in Florida. There are, though, almost a dozen species of hickory nut distributed on the peninsula and throughout the Florida Panhandle. The meats of some are sweet; those of others are bitter. Perhaps the most important species because of its wide availability in the numerous swamps of the peninsula is the southern water hickory. At the opposite extreme, a scrub hickory set nuts on dry, sandy soils.[150] Yield of hickory nuts in the lower Illinois River valley has been estimated at from 165,550 to 1,000,000 kg per square kilometer.[151] At least portions of Florida may have been equally productive of hickory nuts.

Because oaks and other nut-bearing trees grew widely and abundantly in aboriginal Florida, it resembled Upper California much more than Lower California in the availability of nuts. Heavy reliance on acorns as food characterized the California culture area. Martin A. Baumhoff has calculated the human carrying capacity of the acorn supply in much of that area. He found that in the San Joaquin area acorns could sustain a population density averaging 9.86 persons per square mile.[152] Baumhoff also found that in the North Coast Range of the area, acorns could sustain an average of 5.326 persons per square mile.[153] If Florida's acorn production was on a comparable scale, then one needs to think of its early sixteenth-century population in terms of a population density not of 1.12 persons per square mile, on a par with that of arid central Lower California, but equal to or greater than the 5 to 10 persons per square mile supported by the oak thickets of Upper California. Florida's 58,560 square miles might have sustained from 292,800 to 585,600 persons early in the sixteenth century, judging from the apparent abundance of acorns. The other abundant nuts available in Florida plus the other wild plant foods mentioned in this chapter— especially the starchy tubers—would have supported an even denser human population. The Florida flora was very rich in human food indeed, compared with the flora of Lower California, and was considerably richer than that of Upper California. So aboriginal Florida should have been a densely populated region.

NOTES

1. Thompson, "Estimating Aboriginal American Population," 1966, pp. 417–24.

2. Eggan, "Social Anthropology," 1954, p. 747.

3. Goggin and Sturtevant, "Calusa," 1964, pp. 188–94.

4. Quinn, ed., *New American World*, 1979, vol. 5, pp. 9, 11.

5. Ehrmann, "Timucua Indians," 1940, pp. 182–83.

6. Cook, *Extent and Significance*, 1937, p. 12.

7. Ibid., 7.

8. Rogers, *Cruising Voyage*, 1712 (1970), 231.

9. Venegas, *Natural and Civil History*, 1759 (1966), vol. 1, p. 43.

10. *Opuntia invicta* bears many flowers but probably contributed little to the food supply. *Opuntia molesta* bears inch-long fruits. Another species is the "jumping cholla" (*Opuntia bigelovii*), a danger rather than a resource (Brandegee, "Collection," 1890, pp. 163 – 65). Botanists have now identified 26 species of *Opuntia* that grow in Lower California (Wiggins, *Flora*, 1980, pp. 604 – 609).

11. Goggin, "Tekesta Indians," 1940, p. 283; Fleming, Genelle, and Long, *Wild Flowers*, 1976, p. 53, show *Opuntia compressa*.

12. Forbes, *Sketches*, 1821 (1964), 167.

13. Coxe, *Description*, 1722 (1976), 85.

14. Ibid., 86.

15. Eisner and Nowicki, "Red Cochineal Dye," 1980, p. 1039.

16. Rau, trans., "Account," 1872, p. 363.

17. Brandegee, "Collection," 1890, p. 124.

18. Other *Cereus* species growing in restricted areas of Lower California made lesser contributions to Native American subsistence: *C. phoeniceus* from Magdalena Island to Comondú; *C. maritimus* and *C. emoryi* around El Rosario; *C. engelmannii* and *C. cochal* on elevated mesas of the central desert region (ibid., 161 – 63; Brandegee, "Flora," 1893, pp. 140 – 41). Later taxonomists split the *Cereus* into several genuses, as indicated in the text (Lindsay, "Sea of Cortez Expedition," 1964, p. 226 and plate 12; Wiggins, *Flora*, 1980, pp. 599 – 600, 609 – 10. *C. emoryi* is now considered a monotypic genus, *Bergerocactus emoryi* (Wiggins, *Flora*, 1980, p. 593). *C. engelmannii* and *C. maritimus* are now classified as *Echinocereus engelmannii* and *maritimus* (ibid., pp. 595 – 96).

19. Rau, trans., "Account," 1872, p. 365.

20. Venegas, *Natural and Civil History*, 1759 (1966), vol. 1, p. 42.

21. Rogers, *Cruising Voyage*, 1712 (1970), 230.

22. Shelvocke, *Voyage*, 1726, p. 411. The similarity of Shelvocke's account to that by Rogers suggests either that the lack of bread and the pitahaya seed staple food among the Pericú forcibly impressed them both or that Shelvocke was influenced by reading Rogers's account.

23. Long, "Vegetation," 1974, p. 37.

24. Ibid., 44.

25. Ehrmann, "Timucua Indians," 1940, p. 176.

26. Ribaut, *Whole & True Discouerye*, 1563, p. 72.

27. Shipek, *Strategy*, 1977, p. 28; Kearney and Peebles, *Flowering Plants*, 1942, pp. 197 – 98. Brandegee, "Collection," 1890, p. 208, for *Y. valida* and *Y. baccata* ranges and for *Y. whipplei* around San Julio. Contemporary botanists recognize only three species: *Y. whipplei*, *Y. valida*, and *Y. schidigera* (Wiggins, *Flora*, 1980, pp. 834 – 35).

28. Venegas, *Natural and Civil History*, 1759 (1966), vol. 1, p. 44.

29. Fairbanks, *History and Antiquities*, 1858 (1975), 161.

30. TePaske, "Fugitive Slave," 1975, p. 7.

31. Shipek, *Strategy*, 1977, p. 28.

32. Wiggins, *Flora*, 1980, p. 822; Brandegee, "Collection," 1890, p. 139.

33. Watkins and Wolfe, *Your Florida Garden*, 1968, p. 139.

34. Goggin, "Tekesta Indians," 1940, p. 283; Watkins and Wolfe, *Your Florida Garden*, 1968, p. 101; Fleming, Genelle, and Long, *Wild Flowers*, 1976, p. 40.

35. MacCauley, "Seminole Indians," 1887, p. 504.

36. Varner and Varner, trans., *Florida*, 1962, p. 59.

37. Goggin, "Tekesta Indians," 1940, p. 283.

38. Alexander, "Observations," 1955, p. 24, table 2. The estimate of plant density is based on only six quadrants each measuring five square meters, so may not be truly representative of large areas.

39. MacCauley, "Seminole Indians," 1887, p. 504.

40. Robertson, trans., *True Relation*, 1933, vol. 2, p. 311.

41. Ribaut, *Whole & True Discouerye*, 1563, p. 72.

42. Covington, "La Floride, 1963, p. 179.

43. Laudonnière, *Three Voyages*, 1975, p. 65.

44. Goggin, "Tekesta Indians," 1940, p. 283.

45. Forbes, *Sketches*, 1821 (1964), 167.

46. Goggin, "Tekesta Indians," 1940, p. 283.

47. Milanich, *Excavations*, 1972, p. 48.

48. Pritchard, "Florida Palms," 1978, p. 18. An observer of these plants under twentieth-century fire-suppression management notes that the saw palmetto sets fruit about one year in four. If seeding is as adapted to fire as growth habit, it may be true that the saw palmetto fruits dependably only on burned stems.

49. Mozingo, "A Vegetative Key," 1954, p. 46.

50. Pritchard, "Florida Palms," 1978, p. 20.

51. Ibid., 17.

52. Laudonnière, *Three Voyages*, 1975, p. 111.

53. Saw palmetto (*Serenoa repens*) can be ruled out, inasmuch as it does not transplant well and reportedly fruits only one year in four. Probably royal palm (*Roystonea elata*), because of its great height and habitat, and needle palm (*Rhapidophyllum hystrix*), because of its spines, can be ruled out. Saw cabbage palm (*Acoelorrhaphe wrightii*) bears only pea-sized black fruits like blue palmetto (*Sabal minor*) and grows only in brackish swamps. *Thrinax morsii* and *T. radiata* grow on the Keys, and the extremely rare West Indian Sargent cherry (*Pseudophoenix sargenti*) grows on only one Key. The Keys silver palm (*Coccothrinax argentata*) grows only on Keys and spottily on the Atlantic coast of the south peninsula (Pritchard, "Florida Palms," 1978, pp. 16–24; Mozingo, "Vegetative Key," 1954, pp. 47–52; Watkins and Wolfe, *Your Florida Garden*, 1968, pp. 120–25).

54. Watt, Merrill, et al., *Composition of Foods*, 1950, p. 26.

55. Venegas, *Natural and Civil History*, 1759 (1966), vol. 1, pp. 42, 72.

56. Kearney and Peebles, *Flowering Plants*, 1942, p. 175; Brandegee, "Flora," 1893, p. 176; Brandegee, "Collection," 1890, p. 209. Brown et al., "Second Locality," 1976, p. 37, fig. 1; Henderson, "Guadalupe Canyon," 1946, pp. 4–8; "La Mora Canyon," 1950, pp. 4–8; "We Camped with the Pai-Pais," 1951, pp. 8–11; Wiggins, *Flora*, 1980, p. 847.

57. Bean and Saubel, *Temalpakh*, 1972, p. 146. During famines, the Cahuilla cut down the trees, split open the trunks, and boiled the pith for food.

58. Ribaut, *Whole & True Discouerye*, 1563, p. 71; Laudonnière, *Three Voyages*, 1975, p. 20.

59. Arnold, "Check List," 1938, p. 58.

60. Kurz and Godfrey, *Trees*, 1962, p. 121.

61. Robertson, trans., *True Relation*, 1933, vol. II, p. 311.

62. Fleming, Genelle, and Long, *Wild Flowers*, 1976, p. 20, identify it as

Asimina reticulata. Kurz and Godfrey, *Trees*, 1962, p. 132, give its range as near Marianna and, for *A. triloba*, near the Appalachicola River.

63. Kurz and Godfrey, *Trees*, 1962, pp. 165 – 66; Arnold, "Check List," 1938, p. 59, also has another Florida species, *M. bracteata*.

64. Fleming, Genelle, and Long, *Wild Flowers*, 1976, p. 38; Kurz and Godfrey, *Trees*, 1962, pp. 171 – 73.

65. Brandegee, "Collection," 1890, pp. 121, 154; Bailey, ed., *Standard Cyclopedia*, 1947, vol. III, p. 2844.

66. *P. salicifolia*, according to Brandegee, "Flora," 1893, p. 135, probably *P. serotina* (Bailey, ed., *Standard Cyclopedia*, 1947, vol. 3, p. 1842). Wiggins (*Flora*, 1980, pp. 797 – 98) gives the range of *P. serotina* as canyon floors and meadow margins between 800 and 1,000 m. throughout the peninsula. *P. lyonii* grows south to Mulege and on several islands.

67. MacCauley, "Seminole Indians," 1887, p. 504.

68. Watkins and Wolfe, *Your Florida Garden*, 1968, p. 298.

69. Robertson, trans., *True Relation*, 1933, vol. 2, p. 311.

70. *Ibid.*, 67.

71. *Ibid.*, 117.

72. *Ibid.*, 205.

73. Fleming, Genelle, and Long, *Wild Flowers*, 1976, p. 24; Kurz and Godfrey, *Trees*, 1962, p. 168.

74. *Ibid.*, 175 – 76.

75. Venegas, *Natural and Civil History*, 1759 (1966), vol. 1, p. 43.

76. Kurz and Godfrey, *Trees*, 1962, pp. 260 – 62; Arnold, "Check List," 1938, p. 63, also shows *D. mosieri* as a Florida tree. Lower California persimmon is *Diospyros californica* (Wiggins, *Flora*, 1980, p. 396).

77. *Ficus palmeri*, according to Brandegee, "Flora," 1893, p. 173 and Wiggins, *Flora*, 1980, p. 142. The latter describes the fruit as small, the pulp leathery, the seeds hard and gritty. *F. brandegeei* is a second species.

78. *Ficus brevifolia*, according to Arnold, "Check List," 1938, p. 58.

79. Rau, trans., "Account," 1872, p. 364.

80. Venegas, *Natural and Civil History*, 1759 (1966), vol. 1, p. 45. On the other hand, he (*ibid.*, 43) quoted another priest as reporting that fig trees and plums grew at San Bernabé Bay and plums at another place near the Gulf Coast.

81. Arnold, "Check List," 1938, p. 63. *F. nitida* was introduced to Lower California (Wiggins, *Flora*, 1980, p. 142).

82. Rogers, *Cruising Voyage*, 1712 (1970), 230 – 31.

83. Brandegee, "Collection," 1890, pp. 154 – 55; Kearney and Peebles, *Flowering Plants*, 1942, p. 386. Wiggins, (*Flora*, 1980, p. 641) lists 5 species: *R. viburnifolium, tortuosum, brandegeei, indecorum* and *malvaceum*.

84. Rogers, *Cruising Voyage*, 1712, 230 – 31.

85. Brandegee, "Collection," 1890, p. 173. *H. annuus* occurs in northern Lower California; *H. similis* near the Cape; *H. gracilentus* and *H. californicus* also in the north (Wiggins, *Flora*, 1980, pp. 340 – 42).

86. C.O. Sauer, "Cultivated Plants," 1949, p. 498.

87. These included *Lupinus succulentus, L. sparsiflorus, L. arizonicus,* and probably *L. concinnus, L. affinis, L. micranthus,* and *L. albicaulis* (Kearney and Peebles, *Flowering Plants*, 1942, pp. 436 – 37; Brandegee, "Collection," 1890, p. 143.

88. *Ibid.*, 159. Other possibilities include *Mentzelia adhaerens, M. aspera, M.*

micrantha, M. albicaulis, M. affinis, M. veatchiana, M. nitens and *M. obscura* (Wiggins, *Flora*, 1980, pp. 714–17).

89. Kearney and Peebles, *Flowering Plants*, 1942, p. 592.

90. Brandegee, "Collection," 1890, p. 197; Kearney and Peebles, *Flowering Plants*, 1942, p. 778; Wiggins, *Flora*, 1980, p. 431.

91. Laessle, "Study," 1944, pp. 157, 160 – 61, 165 – 66; Watkins and Wolfe, *Your Florida Garden*, 1968, pp. 297 – 98; Fleming, Genelle, and Long, *Wild Flowers*, 1976, pp. 21, 25.

92. Kurz and Godfrey, *Trees*, 1962, pp. 151 – 64.

93. Ibid., 255 – 56.

94. Arata, "Effects of Burning," 1959, pp. 95, 97, 99, 102.

95. Laessle, "Study," 1944, pp. 160 – 61, 165, table 7.

96. MacCauley, "Seminole Indians," 1887, p. 504.

97. Watt, Merrill, et al., *Composition of Foods*, 1950, p. 52.

98. MacCauley, "Seminole Indians," 1887, p. 504.

99. De Boyrie Moya, Krestensen, and Goggin, "Zamia Starch," 1957, pp. 19 – 26.

100. Sleight, "Kunti," 1953, p. 49; De Boyrie Moya et. al., "Zamia Starch," p. 18.

101. Goggin and Sturtevant, "Calusa," 1964, pp. 183 – 84. Not all the authors of sources these authors cited had observed Calusa life. Swanton, *Early History*, 1922, p. 387. López de Velasco, *Geografía y Descripción*, 1894, p. 160, wrote that the Indians of Florida made white bread like that of cassava from "some roots." His compilation is a secondary source and generalizes about all Florida natives. Zubillaga, ed., *Monumenta*, 1946, p. 356. Late in 1568, Father Antonio Sedeño, after spending perhaps one month at St. Augustine and at least four in Havana, reported that Florida Native Americans subsisted on "some roots" among other foods. He might have gained hearsay knowledge from the Calusa. Wenhold, trans., *17th Century Letter*, 1936, pp. 11 – 12. Díaz visited Timucuan, Apalachee, and Guale missions but not the Calusa. His mention of root consumption applies to the northern peoples he saw. Connor, trans., *Colonial Records*, 1925, vol. I, 1570 – 1577, pp. 40 – 41, 60 – 61. Pedro Menéndez Marquez, who testified at Madrid in 1573, had at least been to Calusa country, but he stated in general terms that the land "all along the coast" was subject to flooding, and "the Indians" (*los indios*) in general subsisted on fish and roots (40 – 41). Diego Ruíz, who testified at Madrid the same year, had spent six years at St. Augustine, San Pedro, and Santa Elena, having been only 8 to 10 leagues inland from those coastal ports (56 – 57). So from hearsay he knew that the coast was "bad" and liable to flooding from Mosquito Inlet to Tocobaga (modern Tampa Bay), and that the natives there lived on fish and roots (60 – 61). The evidence of Calusa subsistence actually rests on the testimony of Pedro Menéndez Marquez and on the retrospective memoirs of one ransomed captive (B. Smith, trans., *Letter and Memoir*, 1854, pp. 15 – 16; True, ed., *Memoir*, 1944, 1945, pp. 67 – 68; Quinn, ed., *New American World*, 1979, p. 8). After his redemption, former captive Escalante stated that the residents of small 30 – 40 person hamlets on the shores of Lake Okeechobee made "bread of roots," which was their basic food most of the year. Escalante also reported that there were other roots of many kinds, including one like the truffle with a sweet taste.

102. Goggin, "Tekesta Indians," 1940, pp. 282 – 83.

103. Watt, Merrill, et al., *Composition of Foods*, 1950, p. 47.

104. Sleight, "Kunti," 1953, p. 49; B. Smith, trans., *Letter and Memoir*, 1854, p. 15; Quinn, ed., *New American World*, 1979, vol. 5, p. 8.

105. Ibid. 85.

106. Rau, trans., "Account," 1872, p. 363.

107. Venegas, *Natural and Civil History*, 1759 (1966), vol. 1, p. 44.

108. A pioneering botanist found *Manihot carthagenensis* to be "common around San José del Cabo" toward the end of the nineteenth century (Brandegee, "Flora," 1893, p. 172). *M. chlorosticta* grows on the southern peninsula (Wiggins, *Flora*, 1980, p. 129).

109. MacCauley, "Seminole Indians," 1887, p. 504.

110. Brandegee ("Flora," 1893, p. 155) labeled the plants *Solanum tuberosum* L. var. *boreale* but gave no other indication whether they were cultivated plants.

111. Rogers, *Cruising Voyage*, 1712 (1970), 230.

112. Venegas, *Natural and Civil History*, 1759 (1966), vol. 1, pp. 44–45.

113. Brandegee, "Flora," 1893, p. 154. *I. jalapa* also then grew at San José del Cabo.

114. Brandegee, "Collection" 1890, pp. 118–19, 188; Wiggins, *Flora*, 1980, pp. 381–82.

115. Rau, trans., "Account," 1872, p. 364.

116. Ibid.; Venegas, *Natural and Civil History*, 1759 (1966), vol. 1, p. 44, reported only that the mountains "yield" mescal and mistakenly described the cooking technique as boiling rather than pit roasting.

117. Rau, trans., "Account," 1872, p. 366.

118. Aschmann, *Central Desert*, 1959, p. 79.

119. Brandegee, "Collection," 1890, pp. 119, 206.

120. Ibid., 107–108; Kearney and Peebles, *Flowering Plants*, 1942, pp. 203–205; Wiggins, *Flora*, 1980, pp. 831–33.

121. Watkins and Wolfe, *Your Florida Garden*, 1968, p. 124.

122. Pritchard, "Florida Palms," 1978, p. 17.

123. MacCauley, "Seminole Indians," 1887, p. 504.

124. Mozingo, "Vegetative Key," 1954, p. 46.

125. Fairbanks, *History and Antiquities*, 1858 (1975), 138.

126. Alexander, "Observations," 1955, p. 24, table 2. Plant density is estimated from just six quadrants of five square meters each and may not accurately represent large areas.

127. Austin, "Vegetation, I. Pine Jog." 1976, p. 233.

128. Wenhold, trans. *17th Century Letter*, 1936, p. 13.

129. Adicks, ed., *Le Conte's Report*, 1978, pp. 35, 40.

130. Shipek, *Strategy*, 1977, p. 28; Wiggins, *Flora*, 1980, p. 80; acorns, pp. 135–37.

131. Wiggins, *Flora*, 1980, pp. 710–11.

132. Brandegee, "Collection," 1890, p. 152; "Flora," 1893, p. 132.

133. Carter, "Genus *Cercidium*," 1974, pp. 37, 19, fig. 1; p. 20, fig. 2.

134. Kurz and Godfrey, *Trees*, 1962, pp. 179–81.

135. Brandegee, "Flora," 1893, p. 173.

136. Brandegee, "Collection," 1890, p. 205. Lower California had 15 species of oak: *Quercus agrifolia, tomentella, peninsularis, devia, chrysolepis, dunnii, cedrosensis, dumosa, ajoensis, turbinell, brandegei, engelmannii, reticulata, oblongifolia, tuberculata* (Wiggins, *Flora*, 1980, pp. 135–37).

137. Watkins and Wolfe, *Your Florida Garden*, 1968, p. 109; Arnold, "Check

List," 1938, pp. 57–58; Kurz and Godfrey, *Trees*, 1962, pp. 68–102.

TABLE 11

Distribution of Minor Oak Species in Florida

Common Name	Botanical Name	Acorn Size (inches)*	Range
White	*Quercus albus L.*	¾	N and W counties
Sand-post	*Q. margaretta*	n.a.	all N counties
Overcup	*Q. lyrata*	1	W of Suwannee River
Chinquapin	*Q. muehlenbergii*	⅓–¾	W of Apalachicola
Bluff (bastard white)	*Q. austrina*	½	Marion to Jackson
Sand Live (Twin live)	*Q. geminata*	1	most common in evergreen scrub
Chapman's	*Q. chapmanii*	½–¾	sandhills, ridges
Laurel	*Q. hemisphaerica*	n.a.	common N counties
Willow	*Q. phellos*	⅓	Duval to Escambia
Blue jack	*Q. incana*	½	N counties
Leopard	*Q. shumardii*	¾–1	W of Marion
Blackjack	*Q. marilandica*	¾	dry, open woods
Arkansas	*Q. caput-rivuli*	½	only Okaloosa
Black	*Q. velutina*	⅔–¾	uncommon
Dwarf live	*Q. minima*	n.a.	all N counties
Spanish	*Q. falcata, var. falcata*	½	N counties

Note: n.a. = not available.   *Diameter

138. Harlow, "Fall and Winter Foods," 1961, pp. 23–24, table 2.

139. Laudonnière, *Three Voyages*, 1975, pp. 114, 125.

140. Kerrigan, trans., *Pedro Menéndez*, 1965, p. 141. The Spanish *Porq ay muchos montes de bellotas* (Barrientos, *Vida y Hechos*, 1902, p. 148) may also be translated, "because there are many oak thickets with an abundance of acorns."

141. Quinn, ed., *New American World*, 1979, vol. V, p. 85.

142. Boyd, "Diego Peña's Expedition," 1949, p. 18.

143. Wenhold, trans., *17th Century Letter*, 1936, p. 13.

144. Austin, "Vegetation," 1976, p. 233.

145. Ribaut, *Whole & True Discouerye*, 1563, p. 74.

146. Robertson, trans., *True Relation*, 1933, vol. 2, p. 311.

147. Milanich, *Excavations*, 1972, p. 48.

148. Limp and Reidhead, "Economic Evaluation," 1979, p. 71.

149. Robertson, trans., *True Relations*, 1933, vol. 2, p. 104.

150. Murrill, "Florida Hickories," 1946, pp. 116–22. Sweet-meated species include the pallid hickory (*C. pallida*), redheart (*C. olalis*), which is rare in northern Florida, and mockernut (*C. tomentosa*), which protects its nut meats with shells a quarter to a third of an inch thick (Kurz and Godfrey, 1962, pp. 39, 45, 48, 50). Bitternut (*C. cordiformis*), water hickory (*C. aquatica*), and hammock hickory (*C. magnifloridana*) have bitter meats and are worthless.

151. Limp and Reidhead, "Economic Evaluation," 1979, p. 71.

152. Baumhoff, *Ecological Determinants*, 1963, p. 219, table 16.

153. Ibid., 199, table 9.

Sources of Animal Protein

Wild plant foods provided only a fraction of the food consumed by Florida's Native American inhabitants in the early sixteenth century. The often fragmentary surviving records in which European explorers and colonists described the subsistence activities of these peoples are not sufficiently detailed to define that fraction with any precision. The existing documents do make clear that fish and game provided a large proportion of the native diet of Florida's peoples. Consequently, any estimate of the early sixteenth-century human population potential of Florida that is based on wild plant food resources alone will understate the area's carrying capacity. Meat provided Florida's native peoples with vital amino acids, salts, minerals, and calories, and comparison of the fish and game resources of the Florida and Lower California peninsulas is instructive.

Native Americans on both peninsulas lacked domesticated birds or animals other than the dog.[1] Sixteenth-century Spanish explorers reported that dogs were reared for food in the Southeastern culture area.[2] They may have been important as converters of meat scraps and offal into tender flesh with a distinctive flavor. Peoples in Florida and Lower California depended both directly and indirectly, therefore, upon hunting and fishing to obtain the animal protein in their diets. The natives of Florida enjoyed a very considerable advantage over those of Lower California.

DEFINITION OF GAME

Lower Californians consumed a very wide variety of fish, birds, mammals, reptiles, and insects that they evidently perceived as "fair game." Jacob Baegert generalized that "Californians eat, without exception, all animals they can obtain." He specifically mentioned

> owls, mice and rats; lizards and snakes; bats, grasshoppers and crickets; a kind of green caterpillar without hair, about a finger long, and an abominable white worm of the length and thickness of the thumb, which they find occasionally in old rotten wood, and consider as a particular delicacy.

The Jesuit regarded "snakes, especially" as "a favorite sort of small game, and thousands of them annually find their way into the stomachs of the Californians."[3] Historian Miguel Venegas credited the Lower California peoples with killing more big game than did Baegert. He described mountain sheep and listed mountain goats, deer, rabbits, and hares as plentiful, even though the natives "kill great numbers in their huntings."[4]

MINOR GAME

Insects

The Lower Californians attracted attention from Catholic Colonial missionaries by eating insects such as locusts, grasshoppers, and wood grubs. Such practices suggest that the resources of deer, mountain sheep and goat, small game, fowl, fish, mollusks, and crustaceans were insufficient to satisfy the craving for animal protein and perhaps even the need for calories. Admittedly, locusts were an abundant source of protein in Lower California. When George Shelvocke anchored his ship off the tip of the peninsula in mid-August 1721, "they came off to us in such abundance that the sea about us was strewed with their dead bodies." He reported that these yellow locusts flew in clouds during the day and stripped the trees of every green leaf.[5]

There is a lack of emphasis on insects in documents describing native foods in Florida. This is not, of course, conclusive proof that Native Americans there did not consume insects, but it does suggest that resources of big and small game, fish and shellfish, and reptiles were adequate to satisfy the protein appetite of whatever population Florida's peoples did reach. Immediately to the north, a Choctaw origin-migration legend recorded in 1823 – 1825 referred to insect consumption only as famine-period behavior during migration into the Southeastern environment.[6] The Timucua reportedly did eat "bugs, worms, roots, and even dirt or clay" in the winter "or at times when the regular food supply was exhausted."[7] As I have noted, roots, at least, were a staple source of starch rather than an emergency ration. It seems reasonable to speculate that specific insects and "worms" or grubs may also have furnished a regular dietary component because of taste preference rather than because of hunger.

If a regular dietary practice in Lower California was strictly famine behavior in the Southeast, the difference in cultural patterns indicates that Florida supported a larger and better-fed early sixteenth-century population than did Lower California. Again, if one assumes that human populations grow to the limits of the resources available in their environments, then the peoples of Florida should have been considerably more numerous than those of Lower California.

Snakes

The illustrations of Timucuan life that de Bry engraved after paintings by the French artist Jacques Le Moyne are not always absolutely accurate ethnographic views.[8] They do nevertheless provide at least some very good clues about the eastern Timucuan way of life. De Bry's view of two Timucuan men engaged in drying "meat, fish, and other food" may not be true to life in all its detail, but it furnishes analytical leads. The wooden drying rack of a pole grating resting on four forked corner posts may be generally accurate, as may the fanning of the smoking fire below the rack, even if the fan may not accurately represent the Timucuan fan. For present purposes, the fauna being dried hold our analytical interest. Almost certainly the picture is inaccurate in that all fish and game shown is depicted whole. Deer and alligators are much too large to smoke or dry whole. Big game would have been butchered and selected cuts smoked. Other North American peoples split fish and spread the two halves apart for drying, so it seems most likely that Timucuans also smoked split fish carcasses. Recognizing that the engraving does not depict the smoking process with complete accuracy, one can infer that the artist sacrificed ethnographic precision in order to convey to European viewers something of the diversity of the fish and game Timucuans caught and killed. By painting whole or nearly whole fish and animals, Le Moyne was able to depict several species and to demonstrate his skill as a naturalist-artist. The drying rack shown supports a snake complete with head and extended tongue—not a realistic representation of a dead reptile. The snake shown is equal in length to an alligator, and its tail disappears in smoke, so that no rattles are visible. Yet the pattern engraved in dark and light contrast on the back leaves little doubt that the artist painted a good likeness of a large diamondback rattlesnake; Le Moyne must have included rattlesnake meat in the category of "other food" smoked for Timucuan winter stores.[9]

In the twentieth century, Polk County reputedly ranks third in Florida in abundance of rattlesnakes. Yet a herpetologist looking for reptiles tends to see only half a dozen a year, and the large snakes do not seem to be very abundant. In the mid-sixteenth century and earlier, diamondback rattlers may have been more common. De Bry's engraving of Le Moyne's painting suggests that some of them reached very large size—enough to leave a lasting impression on the French artist. A diamondback rattler (*Crotalus adamanteus*) a few inches longer than seven feeet can be 15 inches in circumference.[10] If the diamondback rattlesnake was not big game for Timucuan hunters, it was certainly "medium" game, definitely worth the chase in terms of animal protein yield per kill.

If Le Moyne sought to indicate in his painting of eastern Timucuan meat smoking the variety of fish and game taken, the scene may well overrepresent species only seldom killed and may underrepresent those more frequently caught. On its face, the scene with the drying rack suggests that diamondback rattlesnakes might have constituted one-thirteenth of the eastern Timucuan game and fish take suitable for smoking for storage. It would have constituted an even smaller fraction of the total catch or kill, inasmuch as many fish and reptiles and mammals were consumed fresh and some species did not preserve well.

BIG GAME

The arid environment of Lower California afforded its Native American inhabitants three big game animals: deer, mountain goats, and mountain sheep, with perhaps antelope to the north. The sheep and goats were limited to the slopes of the mountains. The frequency with which Californian peoples managed to kill big game animals is unknown.

The moist environment of Florida afforded its inhabitants four, perhaps five, big game animals in great abundance: deer, bear, alligators, manatees, and possibly bison. Moreover, the canoe-harpoon-marine hunting technology of the peoples of South Florida enabled them to kill large marine mammals that Lower Californians apparently did not know how to hunt. The quarry included whales, porpoises, seals, and sea turtles.

Deer

English captain Woodes Rogers visited a camp of some 300 Pericú on the coast near Cape San Lucas in 1709. He observed these people fishing and, seeing their buckskins, inferred that they hunted deer at some season.[11] In 1721, George Shelvocke drew the same inference.[12] Still, the Pericú might have obtained buckskins by trade rather than by hunting; in the same culture area but just north of the peninsula, Native Americans hunted deer as their major land source of mammalian meat.[13] The sparse vegetation of Lower California could, however, support just a few deer. Baegert concluded that deer and rabbits furnished "only a small portion of a Californian's provisions."[14]

Excavation indicates that deer (*Odocoileus virginianus osceola*) constituted one of three major sources of meat in the diet of Potano Timucuans.[15] The Saturiwan Timucuans could kill enough deer to trade venison to French colonists in the 1560s.[16] The Timucuans wore tanned deerhides with heads and horns when they stalked deer to facilitate approach to bow-and-arrow range.[17] It has been thought that the South Florida Tekesta depended on venison as their major meat supply.[18] Even inhabitants of the Keys regularly consumed venison[19] of the Key deer.[20] In fact, Spanish captives expressed surprise at finding the deer "many" on the islands; the animals apparently "up to the very town."[21]

The rich natural vegetation of Florida, periodically burned over by Native American hunters, certainly supported a larger number of deer per unit of area than did arid Lower California.[22] Even in the Keys, areas frequently burned over remain as prairie or "open pineland," where fire improves the "growing condition" of species on which deer browse.[23] Fires that burn a swamp peat bed during a very dry period kill even large trees and convert portions to lakes or prairies.[24] In a cypress dome, fire kills about 95 percent of invading pines and from about 80 to 98 percent of hardwood trees, compared with 18 to 22.5 percent of the cypress.[25] Hurricanes periodically reduce the number of tall pine trees in the cover,[26] as do tornadoes. Prevention of fire for 18 years doubles the number of pine trees, but almost all the young ones grow to between 4 and 12 feet,[27] too small for seed production but often too high for deer to browse.[28]

Changes in vegetation during a period when no burning occurs lead deer to concentrate browsing on food plants other than pines. From 1951 to 1969 deer in a Key study zone (table 12) had browsed large *Erithalus* plants as high as they could reach; small ones had been cropped so closely that they were difficult to identify. During half a century, broad-leaved West Indian species displaced pines on Keys kept free from fire.[29] Thus Native American fire drives such as those described by Bishop Díaz Vara Calderón in the 1670s not only harvested deer but also encouraged those plants that nourished deer, upland game birds, and other animals. Burning by Native Americans selectively killed plants upon which deer could not browse or which did not produce mast.

In central and northern Florida, deer consume mast as about 40 percent of their total food intake. Deer competed with Native Americans for nuts and berries but also converted them into venison for human consumption. Dates from the palmetto (*Serenoa repens*) ac-

TABLE 12

Changing Density of Deer Food Plants During an
Eighteen-Year Fire-Free Period on a Florida Key

Plant	Density per Acre		Index[a]
	1951	*1969*	
Silver palm *(coccothrinax argentea)*	2,628	1,604	0.610
Randia aculeata	1,350	276	0.204
Pithecollobium guadalupense	1,002	1,060	1.058
Pinus elliotta var. densa	523	1,045	1.998
Key thatch palm *(Thrinax microcarpa)*	218	704	3.229
Conocarpus erecta	102	58	0.569
Erithalis fructicosa	102	44	0.431
Acacia peninsularis	29	7	0.241
Jacquinnia keyensis	15	—	0.0
Torrubia longifolia	15	14	0.933
Totals	5,984	4,812	0.804

[a] 1969 ÷ 1951.

Source: Alexander and Dickson, "Vegetational Changes," 1972, p. 87, table 1; p. 88, table 2; p. 92, table 4.

counted for 8.9 percent of the stomach contents of 423 deer studied at mid-twentieth century, the greatest volume of any single food. Next most abundant were acorns of water oak (8.6 percent), post oak (5.6 percent), turkey oak (3.6 percent), diamond-leaf oak (3.5 percent), live oak (3.1 percent), *Sabal palmetto* dates (2.1 percent), and *Quercus cinerea* (1.4 percent).[30]

In 1563 Ribaut wrote of "the sight of the faire medowes . . . full of herons, corleux, bitters, mallardes, egerts, wood-kockes and of all other kind of small birdes with hartest, hyndes, buckes."[31] In other words, Ribaut saw hunting meadows that the Timucua kept burned off to stimulate upland game production and wetland-edge game production.[32] Native Americans in northern Florida continued to use fire drives as a means of harvesting deer toward the end of the seventeenth century, well into Colonial times.[33] In 1564, Laudonnière confirmed the vegetative pattern the Timucua maintained when he "noticed a large number of deer gamboling across the open spaces."[34] in the high pine trees. Pedro Menéndez de Avilés also documented Native American maintenance of hunting meadows in a report to King Philip. Menéndez wrote that Colonial Florida could export hides, wool, and dried beef to Spain because it had "numerous" freshwater rivers "as well as extensive meadow lands for the grazing of cattle and sheep."[35] That deer flourished even in moist South Florida appears in a statement that later Seminoles ate venison "at any time."[36]

Florida's vegetation has at no time during U.S. sovereignty contained a mixture of plants of the same quality and quantity that it did under early sixteenth-century Native American management. Fire was then the principal tool for influencing vegetation and the game dependent upon it for food and shelter. Maximization of deer and other game was a principal result of burning, whether or not it was a conscious goal. Late historic deer populations therefore cannot be assumed to indicate the numbers present under Native American management. Deer numbers declined so that twentieth-century populations are almost surely not as dense as those extant at the beginning of the sixteenth century.

It is logical to suppose that deer habitats may have changed least in those large swampy areas where burns occurred infrequently during major droughts and where vegetation has altered least. Significantly, aerial surveying disclosed a density of one deer per 86 acres in the Big Cypress Swamp early in the 1970s, more deer than were found in any other South Florida area similarly surveyed at the time (the entire region studied had only one deer per 236 acres).[37] Unlike deer elsewhere in Florida, the Everglades animals subsist mostly on herbacious material, which accounts for two-thirds of the volume of their food, and woody plants, which compose more than one-fourth of the volume. Hydrophytic forbs constitute more than half of the volume.[38] Deer in this semiaquatic environment serve as very efficient concentrators of hydrophytic vegetation unsuited for direct human consumption.

Not many years earlier, two different surveys of deer populations in South Florida estimated one animal per 120 acres and one for each 113 acres.[39] It would be conservative, therefore, to estimate that burning by Native Americans maintained a deer population averaging approximately one deer per 100 acres. The modern state contains 37,398,400 acres, so Native American management practices suggest herds totaling some 373,984 deer.

Undoubtedly the actual numbers fluctuated in aboriginal times, as they have historically. The present policy of harvesting older bucks allows an annual kill of 14.5 percent of deer numbers with prompt replacement. Native Americans adhering to such a kill/harvest rate could have slain 54,228 full-grown deer annually. Live weight probably averaged 64 kg,[40] and the carcass dressed out at perhaps 14 percent protein, or 9.1 kg. Thus, 54,228 deer would have provided 502,575 kg, which is to say 502,575,000 g of animal protein annually. In other words, such a kill would have furnished ½ kg (500 g) of protein for 2,754 persons all year round.

Bears

That Timucuans ate bear meat is indicated by bones excavated from an early seventeenth-century Potano mission visitation settlement in central Florida.[41] Le Moyne did not include a bear in his painting of eastern Timucuan meat smoking for storage, yet the eastern Timucuans killed bears frequently enough to be able to offer the French Huguenots bear meat in trade in the 1560s, along with venison and wild turkey.[42] Eastern Timucuan willingness to trade bear meat to strangers might indicate that hunters could easily kill more bears than were required for immediate subsistence or that bear meat was not as much liked as other game. Timucuans needed bearskins to use as mattresses on their wooden slat beds.[43]

Nineteenth-century Seminoles killed bears in South Florida,[44] and this big game animal was also available to the Calusa and Tekesta. Bears have now so diminished in number that twentieth-century counts probably are no indication of early sixteenth-century populations.[45] If bears are assumed to have been a tenth as numerous as deer, then Florida's native groups might have killed 542 annually without depleting the stock. If those animals averaged 80 kg live weight and butchered out at 40 percent meat, each would have yielded 32 kg. The kill-dressed weight would have amounted to 17,344 kg, sufficient to feed 95 people 500 g of bear meat per day all year around.

Alligators

The French artist Jacques Le Moyne painted eastern Timucuan hunters killing alligators (*Alligator mississippiensis*) by thrusting a ten-foot-long pole down their throats, after which the hunters, who had waited in a blind for the alligator to come to shore, flipped the reptile over on its back. They then killed it by shooting arrows into its soft belly and by beating it with clubs.[46] Le Moyne emphasized Timucuan respect for the large reptiles which, he reported, sometimes attacked swimmers. His painting of an eastern Timucuan meat drying/smoking rack made clear that these Native Americans preserved alligator meat for winter use. In his drying-rack scene, Le Moyne showed one alligator on the rack and one attendant holding another carcass under his right arm.[47] The two reptiles represent two-thirteenths of the individual kills indicated in the painting, implying that alligators were the big game animal most often slain and/or smoked or dried. The kill ratio of alligator to deer implied by the scene is two to one, for whatever quantitative inferences the painting may be worth. Recovery of alligator bones from remains of a seventeenth-century Potano settlement shows that western Timucuans also hunted and consumed these reptiles.[48]

Alligators have survived perhaps as successfully as deer. Intensive hunting of alligators for hides materially reduced their numbers in the mid-twentieth century. A relatively brief period of protection against hide hunters led to prompt and rapid recovery in alligator numbers and biomass. In 1972, Florida reportedly supported more than 250,000 alligators.[49] The pre-Columbian alligator stock may be assumed to have been much larger.

Native American use of fire fostered an increase in alligator biomass just as it encouraged upland game productivity. A study of burned wetland shoreline found 20 alligators living along burned shore, as compared with only one on an equal length of unburned shore.[50] The burning of dead vegetation fostered rapid growth of all elements of the food chain, so the reptiles benefited from the concentration of their prey and its food in the affected area. There was one alligator per 13.65 meters of shore after the burn. Florida's many streams, lakes, marshes, and wetlands furnish millions of meters of shoreline that would have been productive alligator habitat under a regimen of fire.

The 27 major rivers in Florida afford even at straight-line measurement of their courses 6,793,443 m of shore,[51] which would support 497,688 alligators at the density found after the study burn. Florida's 19 major lakes with 10 mi.[2] or more of surface area can be estimated to have at least 7,554,098 m of shore line,[52] enough to support 553,414 alligators when periodically treated by fire. Thus the major waters alone could have supported more than 1,051,102 alligators. It appears that Le Moyne's representation of two dried alligators to one dried deer for Timucuan storage could have been accurate.

Alligators must be ranked as big game inasmuch as adults are about six feet long.[53] If Jacques Le Moyne's memory did not greatly mislead him, his painting of eastern Timucuan alligator hunters implies that they killed large animals. Timucuan hunters probably stood about 6 feet tall, and their prey ranged from 12 to 18 feet long.[54] The average live weight of an adult alligator would have equaled that of a white-tailed deer. With a tail that was large relative to body length, an alligator would yield somewhat more meat than a butchered deer would. A six-foot reptile that weighed more than 64 kg alive may be assumed to have yielded about 10.25 kg of protein.

Alligators hatch more young annually than does bear, so reptile reproduction is faster than mammalian. The pre-1520 alligator hunters could have killed perhaps 30 percent of the adults annually without depleting stocks. One can estimate that Native Americans killed 315,331 mature alligators annually. These reptiles were far more abundant in the freshwater streams, lakes, marshes, and wetlands of Florida than were mountain sheep and goats in the arid ranges of Lower California. The animal protein productivity of fresh waters made Florida's human population potential significantly greater than that of Lower California. Indeed, Florida's alligators may be considered equal in food value to Upper California's elk and antelope in terms of Native American subsistence and population.

An annual alligator harvest of 315,331 animals yielding 10.24 kg of protein apiece would provide some 3,228,989 kg, or enough to feed 500 g daily the year around to 17,693 people. Alligator biomass was apparently larger than that of any other big game animal in Florida.

Manatees

At least one major Florida warm spring received its modern name because of western Timucuan hunting. Early English-speaking explorers found manatee bones beside the spring pool that attested to Native American's former consumption of the flesh of this water-dwelling mammal, and the place was named Manatee Spring. It is one of the sources of the Suwannee River, which empties into the Gulf of Mexico, and one of the warm springs in which manatees winter.

In the twentieth century, manatees have been sighted in Manatee Spring, farther up the Suwannee River, and in the Caloosahatchee River, Estero River, Imperial River, and western Everglades on the Gulf Coast. They have been seen in Blue Spring, in the St. Johns River downstream near its mouth, at St. Augustine, in Matanzas River, in Ponce de Leon Inlet, and in Sebastian River, St. Lucie Inlet, Miami River, and Biscayne Bay on the Atlantic Coast.[55]

The manatee is a herbivorous mammal that provides several hundred pounds of meat per kill. Native Americans could kill it with weapons no more advanced than the spear and a knowledge of the beasts' seasonal movement into fresh waters and need to surface for air.

Spaniards claimed that the South Florida Tekesta took their canoes to sea to hunt for "sea cows" in the winter. "When he discovers a sea cow he throws a rope around its neck, and as the animal sinks under the water the Indian drives a stake through one of its nostrils and no matter how much it may dive, the Indian never loses it, because he goes on its back."[56] It seems unlikely that the Tekesta would have gone to sea in pursuit of manatees during the very season when those mammals sought shelter in freshwater tributaries of the ocean and especially in the warm springs of the peninsula. The account does indicate, however, that South Florida Native Americans had developed a specialized technology for killing big marine game, including the manatee.

This skill set the Floridians in marked contrast to the peoples of Lower California. Only north of that peninsula and south of Santa Barbara did any Californians sail well and fashion deep-water gear. Elsewhere California natives completely failed to exploit the pelagic fishery.[57]

Whales

The most striking contrast between the marine mammal-hunting technologies of Native Americans in Florida and those of Lower California seems to have been the ability of the Key inhabitants—Tekesta or Calusa—to take whales. In hunting whales they reportedly employed the same technology used for hunting manatees at sea, driving wooden plugs into the blowholes so as to asphyxiate the air-breathing mammals.[58] The Tekesta dried whale meat for storage.[59]

Porpoises, Seals, and Rays

Lower Californians were reportedly able to substitute teamwork and swimming ability for canoes and specialized gear so as to take at least a few large fish. An early eighteenth-century sailor's account of Pericú swim-fishing teamwork describes the natives as "driving" onto a beach a large ray sighted sunning itself close inshore.[60] Tekesta of South Florida consumed the flesh of the stingray, as attested by recovery of bones of this large fish from their kitchen middens.[61] Florida's Native Americans did not have to go to sea to hunt rays, inasmuch as these fish (Dasyatis sabinus) frequent freshwater rivers and springs, where they are fairly visible and thus may easily be speared.[62]

Excavated bones of porpoises document Tekesta success in hunting that large marine mammal.[63] A sixteenth-century Spanish captive among the Key natives credited them with taking seals to obtain their meat.[64]

Sea Turtles

One of the larger marine animals that provided Florida's Native Americans with nourishing meat was easily killed in season. Sea turtles nested on the long stretches of sandy beaches of the peninsula's barrier islands. Females were quite vulnerable during the period when they were out of water, laboriously crawling up the beaches, scooping out nests, laying eggs, and returning to the sea. To harvest the turtles Native American hunters had to compete with the peninsular bears. The Tekesta were particularly well located to take advantage of the sea turtles' nesting pattern.[65]

The 39-mile-long barrier island north of Jupiter Inlet at the end of Colonial times was still the annual destination of female loggerhead turtles, which swam there "in vast multitudes, to lay their eggs" in caches that wild bears were often quick to plunder.[66] In earlier days, when Native Americans kept the bear population smaller, hunters would have been able to collect more turtle eggs from the island themselves and to capture many adult turtles.

The Spaniards at St. Augustine consumed turtles and turtle eggs as well as shrimp and clams.[67] The native peoples of Florida would not have neglected turtles. Thus the Saturiwan Timucuans can be inferred to have hunted sea turtles and to have collected their eggs just as did the later Seminoles.[68]

Big game marine turtles occurred seasonally in some abundance in areas inhabited by the Calusa, Tekesta, and Ais and secondarily by the eastern Timucuan chiefdoms. A single mature leatherback would provide a hunter with about 118 kg of food,[69] serving 236 persons with 500 g of rich meat apiece. Another 18 kg of gelatinous fat and 16 kg of neck, heart, liver, and kidney would be available to make soup. Tekestas feasted when a marine turtle was caught. Modern experience suggests that most of the Native Americans' catch in nets would have consisted of Atlantic green turtles. The green turtle (*Chelonia mydas mydas*) ranges worldwide. The Caribbean subspecies, now greatly reduced in numbers, nests from Cape Cañaveral to Palm Beach but probably once deposited eggs along more of the coast of the peninsula from May through August. Mature females weigh from 113.6 to 129.5 kg.[70]

In one year toward the end of the nineteenth century, 42 Cedar Key fishermen using 43 nets placed from 28 boats caught 2,651 turtles weighing 48,914 kg.[71] The turtles averaged only 18.5 kg, therefore, and must have included a high proportion of juveniles, reducing the efficiency of the fishery. Available information does not indicate whether Florida's Native Americans also netted turtles of all sizes or whether they only speared mature animals. Inasmuch as turtles must breathe air, they drown in nets.

If 1895 Cedar Key turtle netting was not much different technologically from earlier Native American turtle taking, one may infer that two pre-1520 fishermen in a canoe tending two nets might land about 1,747 kg of live turtle in the course of a year. Such a harvest would yield some

699 kg of meat plus 96 kg of fat plus organ and neck meat for soup, sufficient meat to supply 500 g per day to 3.8 persons the year round, not including the soup. Historical accounts do not indicate that Florida's Native Americans had occupational specialists who devoted their time fully to the netting of turtles; more likely they caught turtles in the course of fishing and deliberately speared them only occasionally.

Historic projections based on the late nineteenth-century catch of professional fishermen from another culture could be misleading. Still, the figures on sea turtle landings in Florida shown in table 13 provide some basis for estimating possible Native American catches. The late nineteenth-century landings clearly index overfishing that depleted sea turtle stocks and resulted in greatly reduced catches for several decades. Whether Florida's Native Americans also overexploited sea turtles when the human population peaked early in the sixteenth century is unknown. Quite possibly natives did deplete the sea turtle stock for a period of perhaps two decades from 1500 to 1520, most critically by eating too many eggs. After 1520, declining numbers of Native Americans almost certainly allowed the sea turtle population an opportunity to increase until the nineteenth century.

The 1971 landings of more than 68,182 kg (live weight) of Atlantic green and loggerhead turtles occurred after the sea turtles had been depleted and after long stretches of beach where they had once nested had been abandoned. A Native American turtle catch on the order of 136,364 kg in live weight might well not have depleted the stock of turtles nesting on all the beaches that they once used. The sea turtle stock may not have been depleted until after 1884 if this reasoning is correct. An annual Native American catch of such magnitude would have yielded 54,545 kg of meat plus 7,500 kg of fat and organs for soup. Such a quantity of turtle meat would provide 500 g per day year round for 340 persons, counting the nourishing soup.

Bison

Native Americans in northwestern Florida, at least in the late seventeenth and eighteenth centuries, hunted a big game animal much larger than any in Lower California. Some buffalo (*Bison bison*) ranged into this portion of Florida during those two centuries. Buffalo may then have lived as far east as the St. Johns River. If not, bison meat appears to have been packed that far. The ruins of Fort Pupo, a historic defensive establishment on the west bank of the river in modern Clay County, yielded a bone that has been identified as a bison humerus.[72]

The earliest description of western Timucua and Apalachee hunting

TABLE 13

Sea Turtle Landings in Florida

Year	Total Weight (kg)	Green	Loggerhead
1880	81,818	—	—
1884	136,364	—	—
1890	212,844	—	—
1895	186,364	—	—
1896	236,364	—	—
1897	311,189	—	—
1918	32,827	—	—
1925	24,636	—	—
1936	8,500	—	—
1938	4,091	—	—
1940	14,492	—	—
1950	—	4,455	—
1951	—	2,864	1,909
1955		610	96
1956	—	385	798
1960	—	9,867	4,475
1963	—	23,625	3,662
1965	—	11,325	1,545
1967	—	68,929	914
1969	—	5,620	306
1970	—	190,380	11,768
1971	—	57,138	11,639

Note: Figures for years before 1950, for 1950, and for years after 1950 are not completely comparable. Available figures show trends.

Source: Rebel, *Sea Turtles,* 1974, pp. 11–13, tables 13, 14, and 15.

bison appears to date from 1674 or 1675. Cuban Bishop Gabriel Díaz Vara Calderón wrote to the crown in 1675 that Christianized Florida natives hunted bison with bows and arrows in thickets.[73] In 1686, Marcos Delgado reported seeing buffalo in what a modern scholar took to be Jackson County, near the town of Marianna,[74] which is part of the Panhandle. The Spanish explorer sighted buffalo during September.[75]

Spanish explorations of the Pensacola region in 1693 resulted in additional reports of Pensacola and Apalachee bison hunting. Exploring Santa Rosa Island, Spaniards saw bison hoofprints. They found bison tripe stewing in a Pensacola settlement, a bison head, hair, and a sash woven from its hair.[76] A missionary sent from the outposts in Apalachee territory toward Pensacola reported that bison showed the travelers where to cross one stream, possibly Yellow River. He noted crossing a creek at a bison ford and recorded that his party killed several animals, perhaps at Blackwater River.[77]

In 1716, following the depopulation of Apalachee and western Timucuan territory by Carolina militia and their Native American allies, bison ranged widely in northwestern Florida and in the Chattahootchie River basin in Georgia. Diego Peña left San Agustín on August 4, 1716, traveling west on the long-established but recently abandoned trail to the Potano and Apalachee mission settlements. On August 13 his Native American companions killed two bison on the grasslands of the former La Chua Ranch, within twentieth-century Alachua County.[78] On August 20 the party killed three bison and half a dozen deer while camped at an abandoned settlement within two or three miles of Itchetucknee Spring. Encamped on the west bank of the Río de San Juan de Guacara (Suwannee), Peña's group killed two bison and four deer on August 24. The explorers also caught many fish.[79]

The Spanish explorers killed bison on August 25, two among "many buffalo" on the next day, and two bison plus three deer on August 27. Despite a drenching storm on August 28 that kept the party from advancing, members killed two bison and half a dozen deer. Remaining encamped during a severe storm on August 29, the party settled for 16 deer. Marching five or six miles the following day, the explorers slew three bison.[80]

Passing through former settlements at Tomole and La Tama on September 7, the explorers killed three bison. The day after, the travelers feasted on parts of no fewer than 5 bison, 2 cows, and 11 deer. The party killed a bison again on September 12, along with two cows. The next day Peña's command crossed Flint River. Having moved well to the north up the Chattahootchee River, Peña's group slew six bison on September 24.[81] Clearly bison abounded along with deer, competing successfully with feral cattle for meadow and savannah pasturage.

Documentary evidence thus establishes that bison ranged over northwestern Florida during the latter seventeenth century and well into the eighteenth. It does not establish that bison ranged there during the sixteenth century. Given the documented Timucuan and Apalachee use of fire drives for hunting, we may suppose that northwestern Florida had extensive grassland prairies or savannahs between heavily vegetated stream floodplains. A suitable habitat for bison probably existed during the sixteenth century. Yet Spanish explorers during that century did not report encountering bison in Timucuan or Apalachee territory. Colonial writers did not report bison in Florida Timucuan territory until the 1670s.[82] It therefore appears unlikely that late pre-Columbian Florida natives found bison flesh available to fuel their final population growth. In fact, bison seem to have been able to invade Timucuan territory only after hunting pressure declined, when the native population fell to less than a fifth of its early sixteenth-century size.[83] Timucuan and Apalachee hunters continued to burn vegetation, however, thus fostering growth of savannah grasses and forbs upon which expanding bison herds grazed during the seventeenth century.

MIDDLE-SIZED GAME

Euroamerican hunters classify game animals as big and small. How Florida's Native American hunters categorized game is not known. The size-weight characteristics of the Florida fauna suggest that an intermediate category for middle-sized game is appropriate. The French artist Jacques Le Moyne suggested some such category in his depiction of eastern Timucuans smoking and drying meat for preservation. Le Moyne's scene was painted many years after his visit to Florida, probably from memory, without the aid of sketches made in situ. It shows one deer carcass on the smoking-drying rack; carcass configuration and hooves clearly identify the animal. A second mammal carcass on the rack is smaller than the deer and has paws rather than hooves and a long muzzle.[84] This carcass conceivably represents a dog, but Timucuans would have had no reason to smoke dog meat inasmuch as they could slaughter dogs at any time. It seems more likely that Le Moyne, handicapped in remembering after many years what he had seen in Florida, meant to portray a smaller game mammal than deer. The bobcat (*Lynx rufus floridanus*)[85] and raccoon both appear to be possible.

Bobcats

What the translator took to be "wildcats" furnished part of the fresh meat eastern Timucuans traded to the French Huguenots in 1564.[86] If Le Moyne accurately remembered relative carcass sizes, the smaller animal may have been a panther (*Felix concolor*) rather than a bobcat. The twentieth-century south Florida panther population is only one animal per 10 square miles.[87] or 5,856 in the state, but panthers may have been much more abundant in aboriginal times.

Raccoons and Oppossums

Bones excavated from an early seventeenth-century Potano mission visitation settlement attest to western Timucuan consumption of raccoon (*Procyon lotor*) and the oppossum (*Didelphis marsupialis*).[88] While neither animal dressed out to as much meat as an antelope or mountain sheep, both were medium-sized rather than small game. It is possible that Le Moyne's pawed carcass on the drying-smoking rack represented his memory of a raccoon, distorted by the passage of time. The inhabitants of the Keys ate raccoons.[89] Seminoles killed oppossums in South Florida during the nineteenth century.[90] These marsupials ranged there in earlier times, and Tekesta and Calusa hunters can be assumed to have bagged them from time to time.

Whatever medium-sized game animal Jacques Le Moyne intended to portray, it may be regarded as representing the entire category. In other words, I infer from his picture that some medium-sized game animal was slain and smoked for storage for every deer that was smoked for storage. Given the uncertainty as to whether Le Moyne's painting is quantitatively representative of the eastern Timucuan kill/storage rate, this assumption may be quite erroneous. Yet it gives at least some basis for approximating the contribution of medium-sized game animals to the Native American diet in Florida.

The Florida panther is larger than the bobcat, raccoon, or oppossum, but all four medium-sized game animals may be considered to average 21 kg in live weight. If they butchered out at 14.5 percent meat, each carcass yielded 3 kg of meat, so 54,228 middle-sized game animals would have provided 162,684 kg of meat during the course of a year. That quantity would have fed 891 persons 500 g of panther-bobcat-raccoon-possum meat daily the year around.

Turkeys

At least one upland game bird, the wild turkey, was abundant in Florida and may be assigned to the medium-sized game category on the basis of weight per kill. Its range apparently did not extend into Lower California. The Timucuans hunted turkeys with considerable success; they are known to have traded turkey meat to French colonists in 1564 – 1565.[91] Timucuans and Apalachees took turkeys with circular fire drives, especially when they burned off their fields in January.[92] The nineteenth-century Seminoles bagged turkeys in South Florida,[93] so those birds were probably also taken by earlier Tekesta and Calusa.

The wild turkey is not as pudgy as the domesticated bird; an average weight of about 14 lbs., or 6.4 kg, may be assumed. The dressed carcass may have yielded 20 percent meat, or about 1.28 kg per bird. Assuming that turkeys were as numerous as deer in Florida, there would have been about 373,984 early in the sixteenth century. Turkeys reproduce faster than deer, so that a kill of one-third of the birds should have left adequate adults to reproduce the next year. If the kill amounted to some 124,661 turkeys, 1.28 kg of meat per bird would yield a total of 159,566 kg. That quantity would have provided 500 g of turkey meat daily the year around for 874 persons.

Geese

Migratory geese should also be rated as a medium-sized game bird. They were seasonally numerous on 27,680 square kilometers of lakes, ponds, streams, swamps, marshes, and "wet prairies" in Florida, whereas they were scarcer in arid Lower California. Evidence as to the frequency with which Florida Native Americans killed geese is lacking.

Tortoises

The land tortoise called "gopher" (*Gopherus polyphemus*) was probably considerably more abundant in Florida than was the related desert tortoise in Lower California. The gopher tortoise digs underground burrows in sandy soils. The late historic Seminole consumed its flesh, like pork from the hogs they raised, "whenever they want it."[94] Although the Seminoles were few in numbers, the ease with which they caught tortoises implies that stock was abundant. Excavation of bones of this reptile from a seventeenth-century Potano village indicates that the Timucua also ate gopher tortoise meat.[95]

Herpetologists interested in the gopher tortoise estimate that the present population may number 1,200,000 individuals. This number is only about 30 percent of the earlier tortoise population, estimated at about 4 million. Even after decades of habitat loss, the gopher tortoise has survived in such numbers despite heavy hunting pressure. Poachers may load 300 tortoises onto a pickup truck, although Florida's legal bag limit is only 5 per day.[96] The land tortoise reaches a weight of as much as 4.5 kg, so it may be considered one of the middle-sized game animals.

Modern gopher tortoises flourish in forest where selective cutting allows sunlight to reach the soil and promotes growth of the grasses on which it feeds. Consequently, gopher tortoises probably responded positively to Native Americans' burning of vegetation. Its numbers may have been greater than 4 million individuals in pre-Columbian times. About half the modern population lives in north-central Florida, so half the pre-1520 population may be assumed to have lived in Florida. Under modern conditions, these tortoises successfully hatch young about one year in five.[97] Thus if the same rate obtained prior to 1520, Native Americans should have been able to kill 10 percent of the stock annually without depleting it.

An annual tortoise kill of 400,000 individuals might have yielded 1,360,000 kg in live weight if the reptiles averaged 3.4 kg. The harvest would have been about 476,000 kg of meat if the tortoises dressed out at 35 percent meat, or about 5 percent less meat than turtles would supply. There would have been, in other words, meat enough to provide 500 g daily the year around to 2,608 persons. If the gopher tortoise achieved a significantly higher hatching rate under a program of fire, the population and possible annual kill could have been greater than this estimate.

Beavers

Like the bison, the beaver was once thought not to have been native to Florida. Yet native beaver (*Castor canadensis*) persisted in Florida until late in the nineteenth century. Earlier Native Americans killed and consumed beaver. Skeletal elements have been recovered from Native American settlement sites in Jackson and Wakulla counties in the Panhandle and from Volusia, Seminole, and Brevard counties on the central-southern peninsula.[98] It may be assumed, therefore, that early sixteenth-century peoples in Florida ate beaver whenever they could.

A mature pregnant female beaver trapped in Florida in the 1960s weighed 20.7 kg.[99] The beaver may therefore be considered medium sized, and perhaps we should even regard it as big game. The relative scarcity of beavers in Florida during later historic times suggests that they did not contribute a very significant amount of food to the early sixteenth-century Native American population. Indeed, hunting pressure during that period may have depleted the beaver stock.

SMALL GAME

The willingness of Lower Californians to eat a wide variety of small birds, mammals, reptiles, and insects may mean that they consumed more species than did Florida's aboriginal population. Besides the game already mentioned, Venegas reported that turtles, herons, quail, pheasant (an evident misidentification), geese, ducks, and pigeons (actually doves) served "for the table" among Lower Californians.[100] At least on the northern portion of the peninsula, Lower Californians took wood rats, ground squirrels, quail, doves, ducks, and other birds.[101] Small game animals and birds available in Florida in some instances weighed more per kill than the Lower California analogues, and several animals and birds were very abundant and easily taken.

Rabbits

Lower California had rabbits and hares—the cottontail rabbit and jackrabbit of modern English terminology.[102] Baegert claimed that these small mammals furnished just "a small portion" of the native food intake.[103] On the basis of his 1562 visit to part of Florida, Ribaut considered it to have "cunys, hares, guynia cockes in mercelous numbre, a great dele fairer and better than be oures."[104] Florida had the Florida cottontail (*Sylvilagus floridanus floridanus*), eastern cottontail (*S. floridanus mallurus*), Carolina marsh rabbit (*S. palustris palustris*), and Florida marsh rabbit (*S. palustris paludicola*).[105]

Bones of rabbits excavated from an early seventeenth-century Potano settlement attest to historic Timucuan consumption of rabbit meat.[106] Although a single rabbit carcass furnished much less meat than one deer, rabbits reproduce much more rapidly than deer, so that they are much more plentiful. These small mammals are particularly vulnerable to mid-winter fire drives of the sort employed by the Timucua and Apalachee. Cuban Bishop Díaz Vara Calderón wrote that the Christianized natives of Florida burned the "grass and weeds" from their fields in January, "surrounding them all at one time with fire." Consequently, the rabbits that fled the fire "fall into their hands."[107] Nineteenth-century Seminole success at rabbit hunting indicates that the Calusa and Tekesta ate rabbits, too.[108]

The contribution that rabbits made to early sixteenth-century Native American subsistence is difficult to estimate because of a paucity of relevant information. A simple calculation is offered here. Each of Florida's 37,398,400 acres is assumed to have yielded one rabbit per year that weighed 1 kg alive. If we assume dressed weight to have been one-fourth of live weight, or 250 g per carcass, 51,231 people could have eaten 500 g of rabbit—two carcasses—daily the year around.

Squirrels

The abundant oak groves and other nut trees of Florida supported a class of arboreal edible fauna that was scarce in Lower California. Florida in the twentieth century abounds in squirrels, and surely it did so in pre-Columbian times as well. Excavation of early seventeenth-century Potano settlement remains revealed that the Timucuan residents ate at least two species of squirrels. These were the fox squirrel (*Scurius niger*) and the gray squirrel (*S. carolinensis*).[109] In South Florida, Seminoles killed squirrels in the nineteenth century.[110] Earlier Calusa and Tekesta no doubt also killed some Everglade gray squirrels (*S. carolinensis extimus*)[111] to eat. No attempt is made here to estimate how much meat squirrels contributed to Native Americans' subsistence.

Skunks and Other Small Animals

Although the skunk possesses musk odoriferous enough to dissuade some predators, its beautiful pelt and edible flesh make it prey to man. I have seen pelts being dressed in an Andean mountain village where the flesh is not disdained. That Florida's Timucuans ate skunk flesh (*Mephitis mephitis*) is known from the bones found in a seventeenth-century Potano settlement. Excavation has also revealed the bones of the cotton rat (*Sigmodon hispidus*) and the round-tailed muskrat (*Neofiber alleni*).[112] The cotton rat appears to be one animal that would have been discouraged by the natives' practice of burning. None was trapped in a burned-over turkey and oak pine habitat where 11 had been taken in 150 trap nights prior to a fire.[113] I will not attempt to estimate the dietary importance of such game.

Ducks

Nineteenth-century Seminoles took ducks and other wild fowl as well as quail in the South Florida wetlands.[114] No doubt the Calusa and Tekesta had done so before they arrived. Florida's 27,680 square kilometers of freshwater rivers, lakes, swamps, marshes, and wet prairies gave its Native American inhabitants a considerable advantage over Lower Californians in terms of wildfowl resources. In the twentieth century, Florida winters from a sixth to a fourth of the Atlantic Flyway duck population.[115]

The St. Marks National Wildlife Refuge recently had some 118,500 waterfowl on its 14,800 hectares. The burning, fluctuating water and salinity levels, and planted food plots of this preserve probably approximate conditions in Florida's wetlands during aboriginal times. Protection of birds against hunting may attract some to the area. The seasonal six birds per hectare suggests, given historic depletion of migratory waterfowl stocks, perhaps a minimal estimate of such birds in aboriginal times. Euroamerican duck hunters using shotguns typically kill mostly American widgeon (*Anas americana*), Ring-necked duck (*Aythya collaris*), green-winged teal (*Anas crecca*), blue-winged teal, shoveler (*A. clypeata*), pintail (*A. acuta*), lesser scaup (*Aythya affinis*), and ruddy duck (*Osyura jamaicensis*). These are species abundant in the flocks wintering on the coastal waters of the peninsula and on the Gulf Coast of Florida.[116] The Native American population early in the sixteenth century probably hunted much the same ducks.

If Native American hunters achieved a 5 percent kill, they could have taken 830,400 ducks annually, if the St. Marks Refuge figure of six ducks per hectare may be regarded as representative of all 2,768,000 hectares of Florida waterfowl habitat; the total would be 16,608,000 birds. If each duck yielded 500 g of meat, 2,275 persons could have consumed that quantity daily the year around.

Bobwhites

Probably two races of bobwhites[117] were more abundant in Florida than quail in Lower California. Savannah habitat in central Florida supports a reported 54 bobwhites per square kilometer and bird biomass increases rapidly from January to June largely because of reproduction by these large-bodied upland game birds.[118] The savannah is precisely the habitat Native Americans fostered with frequent fires, and it may be estimated to have accounted for one-fourth of Florida, or about 3,783,731 hectares, during the early sixteenth century. Such an area would, therefore, support some 204,321,474 bobwhite the year around —and sixteenth-century savannah habitat may have been more favorable than contemporary savannah. Perhaps half the birds (about 102,160,737 individuals) could be trapped, netted, burned, or shot by small boys with bows and arrows. Three studies arrived at different weights for bobwhites: 186.77 g for 108 Ohio birds,[119] 181.6 g for 61 birds weighed beginning in April and ending in October (to show seasonal variation in weight),[120] and an average of 152 g for two males in Georgia and South Carolina.[121] Therefore 160 g may be near enough the weight of average Florida bobwhites if they are indeed smaller than more northerly birds. Allowing a dressed weight of 25 percent meat, or 40 g, then 25 birds yield 1 kg of meat. The estimated annual kill would thus provide some 4,046,429 kg, or enough meat to supply 22,172 persons with 500 g daily the year around. Bobwhites in the rest of Florida increased the bird's biomass, but the present estimate is limited to an assumed savannah environment area.

Pigeons

One major difference between the two peninsulas related to availability of the passenger pigeon. A "great flock of doves" spent seven weeks near the Frenchmen forted up at the mouth of St. Johns River early in 1565. The Europeans shot more than 200 every day.[122] Florida's Native Americans could easily net this very abundant migratory bird, which was rich in oil. They could also use poles to knock the birds off their perches at night, stunning them so that they might be caught.

The passenger pigeon may have averaged 400 g live weight, yielding about 100 g of dressed meat.[123] Perhaps one-fourth of Florida supported oak thickets, which the pigeons sought for their acorns. A six-week hunting season when pigeons were roosting could likely be expected each year. French Huguenot hunters probably did not venture very far into the woods around their fort because the Saturiwan Timucuans were not friendly at the time. One may suppose that they shot 200 pigeons daily in an area of 4,400 hectares, walking out a radius of a league, or about four kilometers. The oak thicket area would have consisted of 860 zones of like size. If each provided 200 pigeons daily for six weeks, Native Americans could have consumed 7,224,000 pigeons each year. That 722,400 kg of meat (allowing 100 g per bird) would have been enough to furnish 500 g daily the year around for 3,958 persons.

Small Birds

The energy Florida's Native Americans may have expended hunting or trapping smaller birds is not known. They are known to have traded woodpecker scalps to northern groups and would not have wasted the meat of birds killed for their feathers. Certainly several smaller birds would have been abundant in Florida, given the Native American fire treatment of vegetation. During six months following the burning of wetland vegetation, the number of birds found inhabiting burned shoreline averaged 3.2 times as many as were counted in an unburned control.[124] Several bird species that clearly prefer the rapidly growing green biomass, seeds, and insects in a burned area are large enough to furnish significant amounts of meat if killed in quantity. Some of the waterbirds are absolutely large. Birds preferring a burned-over habitat at a statistically significant level are listed in table 14, with average weights, to indicate the available species that Native Americans might have hunted or trapped.

Smaller birds probably contributed only a minor portion of Native Americans' meat consumption. The little blue heron can be used to illustrate probabilities. Skilled bowmen very likely could easily kill herons, or could stun them long enough for capture, as the birds stalked food in shallow wetlands. The 27 major Florida rivers and 19 major lakes have an estimated 14,347,541 of shoreline. Assuming a heron habitat 3 m wide at water's edge consisting of frequently burned-over habitat, the 154 m² per heron found in a modern study would suggest 279,498 birds at the edge of major waters. A 10 percent kill of 27,950 mature herons weighing 350 g would yield about 2,436,875 g of meat (at 25 percent of

TABLE 14

Florida Birds That Prefer Burned-Over Wetland
Shore Habitat to Unburned Dead Biomass

Species		% Increase over Unburned	Density[a]	Weight (g)
Egret	Casmerodius albus	440	44.8	n.a.
Cardinal	Richmondena cardinalis	700	28.5	38
Crow	Corvus brachyhynchos	n.a.	20.4	427
Gallinule	Gallinula chloropus	313	50.9	260+
Great blue heron	Ardea herodias	n.a.	16.3	700±
Little blue heron	Florida caerulea	457	65.1	350
Redwinged blackbird	Agelaius phoeniceus	227	305.3	57
Mourning dove	Zenaidura macrowra	2,600	52.9	125
Robin	Turdus migratorius	n.a.	75.3	73
Snipe	Capella gallinago	1,600	32.6	n.a.
Purple gallinule	Porphyrula martinica	611	223.9	210

Notes: All increases are statistically significant except that for the blackbird. Great blue heron weight is estimated. The Pensacola used cardinal feathers as plumes in ceremonial costume (Leonard, trans. Spanish Approach, 1939, p. 161; Siguenza y Góngara, Documentos, 1963, p. 70) and were not likely to have wasted the meat of birds killed for their feathers. Light weight would prevent cardinals from contributing much to the total diet, but they are abundant in north Florida vegetation and exhibit little fear of man.

[a]Density = birds per hectare.

Sources: Percent increase and density are from Vogl, "Effects of Fire on Plants and Animals," 1973, pp. 337 – 38, tables 1, 2. Weights are from Norris and Johnston, "Weight," 1958, pp. 116 – 18 (male-female average), and from P. A. Stewart, "Preliminary List," 1937, p. 326, table 1.

live weight), or 2,436.9 kg. On an annual basis, such a small quantity would feed 500 g of meat per day to only 13 people. Inasmuch as actual shoreline was very much longer, the figures I have just provided no doubt underestimate the number of herons. Nevertheless, it seems unlikely that any of the smaller birds constituted a major food source.

The woodstork inhabits much the same wetlands environment as herons. An adult stands three feet tall and weighs about 3.2 kg. Euroamericans reportedly consume only the breast meat, soaking it overnight in salt water before frying it. Native Americans, who made flutes of the stork's leg bones, may have eaten more of its flesh. The weight of long, heavy bill, long legs, and wings means that a Woodstork breast would not butcher out at more than about 14 percent of live weight, or about 445 g. The remnant population breeds only in Florida and south Georgia, consisting of 4,500 pairs in 1980, down from 10,000 pairs in 1960.[125] Assuming that aboriginal Florida had twice as many breeders, Native Americans might have killed 10 percent of them each year without depleting the stock. A 4,000-bird kill would have provided only some 1,780 kg, or 500 g per day for not quite 10 persons (9.75) the year around.

FRESHWATER FISH

Florida's Native Americans enjoyed a very great advantage over those of Lower California primarily becuase of the abundance of fish, and of game, in inland fresh waters. In mid-1975, Florida contained 4,424 square miles of inland water, even after extensive drainage of the Everglades and some lake construction,[126] or 7.55 percent of the state's total surface area; I have used this figure in this chapter. Such waters produce more flesh than dry land does, and Florida's fresh waters were —and are—very productive.

Crustaceans

Thousands of square miles of freshwater lakes and streams provided an abundance of crustaceans, including easily caught crayfish.[127] These creatures lack endoskeletons that would survive as do mammal bones in soil beneath former Native American settlements. One cannot, therefore, expect to find archaeological evidence for their consumption. It seems unlikely, however, that Native Americans would have neglected so accessible and rich a food resource.

Fish and Mollusks

More than 100 species of fish are found in the fresh waters of Florida, including many marine fish that enter freshwater streams and lakes,[128] and many were used for food by Native Americans. An early seventeenth-century Potano mission village near Orange Lake yielded upon excavation shells of freshwater mussel (*Ellipto* spp.) and bones of bowfin (*Amia calva*), catfish (*Ictalurus* spp.), garfish (*Lepisosteus* spp.), eastern shellcracker (*Lepomis microlophus*), black bass (*Micropterus salmoides*), and other unidentified species.[129] Orange Lake is in the center of the peninsula. No mere list of these shellfish and fish can indicate the amount of animal protein which they provided Native Americans.

Mussels.　　　One mussel provides only a small amount of protein. Nearly 500 mussels of one marine species are needed to meet an adult's daily requirement of 40 g.[130] The heavy shell weight and high water content of mussels make collecting them relatively unrewarding labor.

Garfish. Garfishes yield a large amount of meat per fish taken. The Florida form of the eastern longnose gar (*Lepisosteus osseus osseus* Linn.) attains a length of about four feet and is "robust in build." The Florida gar (*L. platyrhineus*) yields a good deal of meat per catch, although it is smaller than the eastern longnose gar.[131] The Florida spotted gar was still "common" in Orange Lake at mid-twentieth century.[132]

Shellcracker. Garfish compete with human fishermen for the much smaller panfish (*Lepomis*) on which it feeds. Even so, the eastern shell-cracker (*Lepomis microlophus microlophus*), Florida's largest sunfish, is "highly regarded" by twentieth-century anglers.[133] It is still "quite common" in Orange Lake as of mid-twentieth century. It is "not un-common" for this lake to produce black crappie (*Pomoxis nigramacula-tus*) that weigh almost 1.4 kg. Largemouth bass are also "common" in Orange Lake.[134] The unidentified fish bones excavated from the historic Potano settlement probably include remains of bullhead (*Ameiurus nebulosus marmoratus*), which is "taken quite commonly," pickerel (*Esox niger, E. americanus*) and bream, or brim (*Lepomis mac-rochirus purpurescens*), probably the most abundant panfish in mid-twentieth-century Orange Lake.[135]

Bowfin. The bowfin (*Amia calva*) is not as large as the massive garfish, yet a mature specimen can provide a full meal for several people. Individuals attain weights in excess of 4.5 kg.[136] In the mid-twentieth century, sport fishermen frequently caught bowfins weighing 4.5 to 5.45 kg in Orange Lake.[137]

Catfish. The southern channel catfish (*Ictalurus lacustris punctatus*) attains in Florida a weight of more than 18 kg, four times the weight of bowfins. The white catfish (*I. catus* Linn.) is smaller.[138]

Sturgeon. The diversity of species present in Florida during aboriginal times has diminished because of pollution, heavy selective fishing of certain species, and other factors. Perhaps the largest fish available to early sixteenth-century Native Americans on the Atlantic Coast of Florida is now rarely taken in St. Johns River. This is the Atlantic sturgeon (*Acipenser oxyrhnchus*). Adult females average eight feet in length and weigh from 91 to 159 kg, depending on how much roe they are carrying. A female 14 feet long and weighing more than 364 kg has been recorded in this century. Adult male sturgeon average from six to seven feet long and weigh as much as 91 kg. The crucial behavior of sturgeon in terms of Native American fishery is that it is anadromous (females ascend freshwater streams to spawn).

The Gulf subspecies (*A. o. desotoi*) no longer ranges to Tampa Bay, yet it is commercially fished in the lower Suwannee River and appears not to have decreased during a 20-year period of exploitation.[139] Sturgeon "several feet in length" have been caught in Homosassa River, which flows nine miles from Homosassa Springs to the Gulf, as late as the mid-twentieth century.[140]

A typical mature female entering a Florida freshwater stream to spawn would average about 125 kg, of which 41.6 kg would be highly nutritious roe and 91 kg fish. The carcass would yield fillets of about 30.450 kg. Thus each fish would provide about 64.5 kg of protein—30.4 kg of meat and 34.1 kg of roe—so that only three such fish would provide more than 500 g for one person annually. Any estimation of the number of sturgeon taken by Native Americans early in the sixteenth century must be highly speculative. There are many more than 90 streams flowing from Florida into the sea or estuaries behind barrier islands, up which sturgeon may have swum to spawn. If sturgeon actually ascended only a third of those streams, and if Native Americans speared or trapped 100 fish per stream, the annual catch would have been 3,000 fish. That is about 193,500 kg of meat and roe, or enough to provide 500 g daily for 1,060 individuals each year.

Freshwater Turtles

Edible freshwater turtles abound in lakes and streams in Florida and have been considered part of the fishery. Here it seems appropriate to add evidence of Native American consumption of these reptiles. Some middens left by earlier inhabitants of the edge of the Everglades indicate that the occupants "made great use of the terrapin and other turtles in their diet." The middens are composed more of turtle carapaces than of all other bones.[141]

One Florida pond turtle still flourishes sufficiently in a state with a current population of more than 9 million inhabitants to appear as "cooter" (*Chrysemys* spp.) on the menu at certain restaurants. This and other freshwater turtles, including the snapping turtle (*Chelydra serpentina osceola*), softshell turtle (*Trionyx ferox*), and box turtle (*Terrapens carolina*), provided, together with venison and fish, the "largest portion" of meat eaten by early seventeenth-century missionized Potano Timucuans.[142]

The large contribution turtles made to the Native American diet in Florida stemmed from both their abundance and their comparatively large size. Hard-shelled turtles (*Pseydymys floridana peninsularis*), also known as "cooters," caught in Lake Panasoffkee during a modern fisheries study averaged about 3.6 kg each.[143] The Suwannee cooter (*Chrysemys concinna suwanniensis*) grows to 16 inches.[144] Snapping turtles are common in Lake Shipp, for example, yet the largest taken from that body of water during one herpetological survey weighed 7.273 kg.[145] The much larger alligator snapping turtle (*Macroclemys temmincki*) grows to weigh more than 50 kg, and sometimes more than 100 kg. It occurs only in rivers flowing into the Gulf from the Suwannee to Alabama. It tends to walk on the bottom[146] and so may seldom have been taken by Native Americans. In contrast, the Key mud turtle (*Kinosternon bauri bauri*) grows to only about four inches.[147]

Catches

Studies of twentieth-century fishing indicate how plentiful fish are and were in historic times and earlier. The commercial fishing that the state allows in the waters of Lake Okeechobee is probably not more effective than pre-Columbian weirs and traps. It is normally limited to wire traps, trotlines, and pound nets. Some 275 fishermen caught channel and white catfish amounting to slightly more than 3 million pounds in dressed weight during one calendar year studied. That figure amounted to 2.2 pounds or one kilogram per surface acre annually. Fisheries experts consider the haul about 5 percent of the potential harvest because Lake George has yielded in rough weight 28 kg of catfish per surface acre.[148] That representative catch amounted to an average of 4,959 kg per commercial fisherman annually. At about the same low level of efficiency, only 275 Native Americans fishing Lake Okeechobee full time could have caught enough channel and white catfish to feed 4,981 people 500 g of meat daily for a year.[149]

Florida's Native Americans did not live on catfish or other fish alone. Around Lake Okeechobee the aboriginal Mayaimi supplemented fish with turtles, birds, deer, opossums, snakes, and alligators.[150] Mid-twentieth-century commercial fishermen seeking catfish incidentally catch an average of 4,658 kg of turtles from Lake Okeechobee without really trying.[151] That is a bonus of 17 kg per year for each commercial fisherman. Native Americans seriously seeking turtles could have taken greater weights per fisherman per year.

Commercial fishermen are legally restricted to catching species not sought by sport fishermen. Lake Okeechobee supports at least 43 fish species,[152] several of them of large size and abundant. These include the bowfin, Florida gar (no individual shorter than eight inches has been collected in two study years), gizzard shad (*Dorosoma cepechanum*), threadfin shad (*D. petenense*), redfin pickerel (*Esox americanus*), largemouth bass, black crappie, bluegill (*Lepomis macrochirus*), redear sunfish (*Lepomis microlophus*, called shellcracker in northern Florida), migratory saltwater striped mullet (*Mugil cephalus*), and snook (*Centropomus undecimalis*).[153] Most of these species provided food for early sixteenth-century Native Americans.

Information about the comparative abundance of different fishes in Florida's freshwater lakes and streams has not often been collected, and truly accurate comparisons of the yields of various bodies of water therefore cannot be made. At mid-twentieth century, the state Game and Fresh Water Fish Commission's rough fish control unit used a haul seine with a minimum mesh of three inches to sample fish populations in seven lakes. Being made at different seasons, the catches from the lakes were not directly comparable. Still, the unit's discoveries furnish approximate indications of freshwater fish resources, inasmuch as Native Americans probably did not distinguish between rough and game fish as Euroamerican anglers do.

Channel catfish (*Ictalurus punctatus*) made up 41.6 percent of the weight of the catch from Lake Ashby, with a surface area of 1,192 acres of 1.86 square miles.[154] The shellcracker (*Lepomis microlophus*) was second most abundant, making up 21 percent of the weight of the sample catch. Channel catfish also dominated the Johns Lake catch, weighing 43.7 percent of the total, followed by gizzard shad, with 24.4 percent of catch weight.[155]

Gizzard shad made up most of the catch weight from lakes in the St. Johns River drainage system. Lake Harney in the upper reaches of that stream did not yield heavy catch weights when sampled in the summer. The shad composed 36.6 percent of the catch weight, followed by the largemouth bass at 21.4 percent and channel catfish with 15.6 percent. At 8.73 square miles, or 5,558 acres of surface, Lake Harney is one of the peninsula's larger bodies of fresh water. Lake Monroe is even larger, with 13.77 square miles, or 8,814 acres.[156] The sample catch there consisted (by weight) of 50.7 percent of gizzard shad, with largemouth bass second at 9.6 percent and channel catfish third with 7.8 percent of the weight.

Lake Jessup is connected to the St. Johns River by a short channel on its eastern end. Sampled from late August to early October, it yielded much higher weights per seine haul than the two lakes directly in the St. Johns River flow. Gizzard shad comprised 48.3 percent of the catch weight, followed by white catfish at 22.2 percent and bluegill with 11.1 percent of the catch weight.

Lake Panasoffkee drains into the Withlacoochee River. Extensive cypress marshes surround its 7.32 square miles, or 4,685 acres, of surface. April-May sample seine hauls caught high poundages. The longnose gar constituted 34.9 percent of the catch weight, followed by gizzard shad at 30.5 percent and shellcracker with 16.3 percent.[157] Black Lake is only about a mile east of Johns Lake and has only 408 acres in surface area. The longnose gar made up 73.5 percent of a single seine-haul weight, followed by channel catfish at 13.8 percent and gizzard shad at 7.3 percent.[158]

The seining results of the Florida Game and Fresh Water Fish Commission's unit at six peninsular lakes are summarized in table 15. The reported seine-haul catch weights for nine species of fish and all turtles reported are directly comparable in this table, being expressed as average grams per haul per surface acre of water. The fish species and turtles are shown in rank order of abundance by weight. This recalculation of the unit's reports indicates that the gizzard shad probably is, and was in historic and prehistoric times, the most abundant single species. It is a major source of food for bass and crappie[159] but probably was not for Native Americans.

Additional evidence that the principal species makeup of Florida's fresh waters is fairly uniform is presented in table 16 and 17. Lake Apopka is Florida's fourth largest lake, now eutrophic. The weight of fish that died off in 1963 was estimated, so that a range appears in the table, but that range is consistent with the range in the six lakes that have been studied with greater precision.[160]

From May through September 1976, a state specialist sampled species assemblages 173 times in Lake Conway's 728 hectares. Because he did not report weights, his catches cannot be directly compared with those summarized in tables 15 and 16. In terms of species frequency, 173 samples included bass in 53.8 percent of the cases, bluegill in 47.3 percent, Seminole killifish (*Fundulus seminolis*) in 46.8 percent, and the shellcracker/redear in 33.5 percent.[161] Bowfins, Florida garfish, and crappie also inhabit this lake system.[162]

During a 10-year sampling period, Lake George commercial fishermen caught an average 28 kg per surface acre of catfish.[163] From July 1952 through February 1953, fishermen seine-netted an average 4.5 kg of fish per surface acre, not counting largemouth bass or chain pickerel.[164] Removal of millions of pounds of fish did not affect the abundance. That is a catch rate of 54.5 kg of fish per surface acre per year. The modern inland freshwater area of 4,424 square miles is an acreage of 2,831,360. Assuming that all waters were more or less equal in catfish production to Lake George, as the comparisons above indicate, then

TABLE 15

Average Grams of Fish and Turtles per Seine-Net Haul per Surface Acre at Seven Florida Lakes

Species	Lakes							Total (78,245)	Average
	Ashby (1,192)	Harney (5,558)	Monroe (8,814)	Jessup (7,922)	Panasoffkee (4,685)	Johns (2,714)	George (47,360)		
Gizzard shad	8.8	15.0	16.0	64.2	102.0	88.0	473.0	767.0	110.0
Channel catfish	76.6	6.4	2.4	6.8	0.9	158.0	217.3	468.5	67.0
Black crappie	7.2	1.9	2.0	2.2	8.0	13.0	284.8	319.0	45.6
White catfish	9.1	0.2	0.3	29.5	0.1	14.6	237.9	292.0	41.7
Bluegill	11.4	2.0	1.7	14.8	18.0	45.5	184.7	278.0	39.7
Shellcracker (redear)	38.5	0.9	1.5	1.5	54.2	0.5	103.7	201.0	28.7
Turtle	79.7	7.4	1.5	1.1	78.0	1.2	—	169.0	28.1
Longnose gar	8.4	4.0	1.1	3.4	116.6	16.9	13.5	164.0	23.4
Black bass	11.4	8.8	3.0	3.5	10.6	14.9	109.4	162.0	23.1
Florida gar	7.2	0.2	0.3	0.6	9.4	5.7	5.3	28.6	4.1
Totals	258	47	30	128	398	358	1,630	2,849	411

Note: Parenthetical figures in column headings indicate surface acres. Column totals have been rounded to the nearest tenth of a gram.

Sources: Derived from Moody, "Adult Fish Populations," 1954, pp. 150, table 1; p. 154, table 2; p. 156, table 3; Lake George from Moody, "Exploited Fish Populations," 1961, p. 5.

TABLE 16

Proportions of Two Classes of Fish in Florida Lakes

Fish	Lake Ashby	Lake Harney	Lake Monroe	Lake Jessup	Lake Panasoffkee	Lake Johns	Lake Apopka
Rough	190	33	22	106	307	284	146.591 to 293.182
Game	69	14	8	22	91	74	65.909
Total	259	47	30	128	398	358	212.500 to 359.091

Note: Figures are average seine-net hauls in grams per surface acre (calculated from English weights reported) except for lake Apopka, for which the figure provided is estimated 1963 die-off in kilograms per surface acre. Rough fish = shad, catfishes, and garfishes. Game fish = bass, crappie, bluegill, and shellcracker.

Sources: Ashby, Harney, Monroe, Jessup, Panasoffkee, and Johns Lake data are from table 15, derived from Moody, "Adult Fish Populations," 1954, pp. 150, 154, 156. Lake Apopka data come from Walker, "lake apopka," 1978, pp. 13–14.

TABLE 17

Percentages of Rough and Game Fish in Florida Lakes

Fish	Lake Ashby	Lake Harney	Lake Monroe	Lake Jessup	Lake Panasoffkee	Lake Johns	Lake Apopka
Rough	73.4	71.1	72.3	82.7	77.2	79.4	69 to 81.6
Game	26.6	28.9	27.7	17.3	22.8	20.6	31 to 18.4

Note: Percentages are calculated from English weights reported.

Sources: Ashby, Harney, Monroe, Jessup, Panasoffkee, and Johns Lake data are from table 15, derived from Moody, "Adult Fish Populations," 1954, pp. 150, 154, 156. Lake Apopka data come from Walker, "lake apopka," 1978, pp. 13–14.

79,406,777 kg of catfish might have been caught annually in aboriginal Florida. Such a catch would supply 26,442,456 kg of fillets, or 500 g of catfish per day the year around for 144,890 consumers—a very full meal of meat.

Six of the lakes listed in table 15 had lower catfish yields than Lake George, but other waters are even more productive, at least under twentieth-century conditions. State fisheries researchers estimated the average weight of seinable fish caught per surface acre by one net haul. Lake George yielded 25.9 kg and Lake Crescent a lower 16.4 kg, but the upper St. Johns River 54 kg and the lower river 66.4 kg. Baiting catfish presumably contributed to the high downriver catches, and Native Americans can be presumed to have known how to bait for them.[165]

A notable discovery of the Game and Fresh Water Fish Commission's research was the relative abundance of turtles, a characteristic also indicated by the frequent catches of Lake Okeechobee commercial fishermen. The turtle catch weight averaged 55.3 percent of the combined catfish weights from six lakes from which the turtle catch has been reported.[166] Assuming that Florida's Native Americans speared, trapped, or hooked turtles about as often relative to catfish as do twentieth-century commercial fishermen, they could have landed on the order of 43,911,947 kg of turtles annually. That weight of live turtles at 40 percent yield would provide 17,564,778 kg of dressed meat, or 500 g for 96,245 consumers daily all year.

The longnose gar and Florida spotted gar together made up 25.3 percent of the catch weight of catfishes in the seven sample lakes. The figure suggests, using the Lake George catfish catch 10-year record, that Native Americans might have landed 20,089,914 kg of gars each year. A garfish catch of such magnitude could have meant 6,689,941 kg of fillets, or 500 g of fish for 36,657 consumers daily throughout the year. Fisheries researchers consider the Florida spotted gar to be "the most abundant large fish" in fresh waters south of Lake Okeechobee, so it might have bulked larger in Calusa catches.[167]

Black crappie composed 59.8 percent of the catch weight of catfish in the seven sample lakes. Based on the 10-year catch of catfish at Lake George and assuming equal distributions, Florida's Native Americans might have caught, trapped, and netted some 47,485,253 kg of these fish annually, for 15,812,589 kg of fillets, or 500 g of dressed fish for 86,644 consumers annually every day.

Bluegill made up 36.6 percent of the catfish catch weight from the seven sample lakes. If species distribution is more or less the same in Florida's fresh waters, the 10-year catfish catch from Lake George suggests that Native Americans might have netted and trapped 29,062,880 kg of bluegills annually. Such a catch would have yielded 9,677,939 kg of fillets and would have given 53,030 people 500 g of dressed-out meat daily all year around.

Shellcrackers (redears) in seven sample lakes accounted for 26.4 percent of the catch weight of catfish from the same bodies of water. Assuming that they were representative of all fresh waters in Florida, the 10-year catch of Lake George catfish implies that Native Americans could have trapped and netted some 20,963,389 kg of these panfish each year. That catch would have provided 6,980,809 kg of fillets, or 500 g daily the year around for 38,251 people.

The black bass sample from the seven lakes studied came to 21.3 percent of the total catfish catch weight. Thus, if that modern game fish were equally abundant in earlier times, the Lake George catfish commercial landing record implies that Native Americans could have trapped and speared about 16,913,643 kg of bass per year. Such a weight would fillet out at 5,632,243 kg and would feed 30,862 consumers 500 g daily all year. The Seminole may have relied on black bass for a significant part of their fish intake in the nineteenth century,[168] as in an earlier native occupation.

Minor fish species less common than the nine listed in table 15 would have afforded the peninsular Native American population little meat in their total diet. The estimates just made are summarized in table 18 to emphasize the great importance of Florida's freshwater fishery in Native Americans' subsistence. The estimated possible annual catch of eight principal freshwater fish and turtles amounts to 257,433,803 kg. Such a catch could have meant 1 kg in live weight of fish or turtle for 705,298 persons every day during the year. An edible third of live weight would have provided 500 g of fish and turtle flesh to 486,579 individuals daily the year around. This figure is not an estimate of actual population; it merely indicates the high approximate meat yield of Florida's freshwater lakes and streams.

TABLE 18

Estimated Possible Yields of Principal Food Fish and Turtles
From Florida's Fresh Waters and Human Feeding Capacity

Species	Estimated Annual Catch (lbs.)	Possible Consumers[a]	Estimated Annual Catch (kg)	Estimated Dressed Meat (kg)
Catfish	174,694,910	478,616	79,406,777	26,442,456[b]
Turtle	96,606,285	264,675	43,911,947	17,564,778[c]
Black crappie	104,467,556	286,212	47,485,253	15,812,590[b]
Bluegill	63,938,337	175,174	29,062,880	9,677,939[b]
Shellcracker (redear)	46,119,456	126,352	20,963,389	6,980,809[b]
Garfish	44,197,812	121,090	20,089,914	6,689,941[b]
Bass	37,210,016	101,945	16,913,643	5,632,243[b]
Totals	567,234,372	1,554,064	257,833,803	88,800,756

[a]Number of people who could consume one pound in live weight daily all year round.
[b]33 percent yield.
[c]40 percent of live weight.

SALTWATER FISH

Recent years have witnessed a burgeoning interest by anthropologists in the technological, sociological, and demographic adjustments that humans make to exploit marine environments. Curiously, however, a major review article on maritime hunter-gatherers completely ignores both the Lower California peoples and the South Florida Calusa and Tekesta.[169] The present chapter contributes, therefore, to our understanding of a worldwide cultural phenomenon.

No point on the Lower California peninsula lies more than a two-day journey on foot from the sea coast. Consequently, Lower California peoples could and did regularly visit the seashore. There women collected crustaceans and mollusks, while men dove into the sea to spear fish and sea turtles.[170] Baegert asserted that they did not employ nets or hooks.[171] The clerical historian Venegas credited them with maguey fiber nets.[172] The Jesuit historian relied on missionary reports, so the fishing nets he described may have been a postcontact innovation imitating European practice. The peninsular native fishery contrasted with that of the Diegueño at the northern edge of the culture area. Diegueño trapped, netted, and hooked onshore fish from dugout canoes. In the northern portion of the culture area, people allocated each settlement coastal fishing and collecting sites.[173] They were, in other words, relatively sedentary and carried out what has been labeled "central-place foraging."[174]

Most Lower Californians employed only balsas, "little rafts made of reeds" or from "the thin stem of a palm tree," as craft from which to catch fish and turtles.[175] Those near Cape San Lucas and Cedros Island on the Pacific Coast used log rafts to put to sea. Those were the only peninsular localities where trees grew that yielded enough wood to form rafts.[176]

The question of fishing technology is of critical importance in comparing food resource potentials of the two peninsulas. The Florida natives could take fish and marine mammals from dugout canoes, much sturdier craft that allowed crewmen to specialize and to form hunting teams. This vessel allowed Floridians to obtain far more protein for a given expenditure of energy, because a marine mammal carcass yielded a large amount of meat. If the Lower Californians indeed lacked nets, then even their saltwater fishery was by no means nearly as efficient as that of the Florida peoples, for the eastern Native Americans captured an abundance of estuarine fish in nets cast, set, and tended from canoes.

Mollusks

Florida Native Americans enjoyed much the same ease of access to saltwater crustaceans, mollusks, and fish near shore as the Lower Californians. At the end of the sixteenth century, Florida's Governor Gonzalo Méndez de Canzo believed that Timucuans of Cumberland Island sustained themselves most of the year on shellfish supplemented by maize, acorns, and roots.[177]

Oysters.   Spanish observers emphasized the importance of oysters served raw, boiled, or roasted.[178] The Calusa chief served oysters as well as roasted and boiled fish to Pedro Menéndez de Avilés in 1566.[179] Later Seminoles also consumed significant quantities of oysters taken from the same environment.[180]

Even half a century after the United States assumed sovereignty over Florida, a federal survey of 130 square miles of St. George and St. Vincent sounds and Apalachicola Bay located 40 productive oyster bars of 7,135 acres. Two-thirds of that productive area yielded an average of 368 bushels of marketable oysters per acre[181] on the coast of Apalachee territory. There are 13 to 14 dozen three-inch oysters in a bushel. Therefore, if the Apalachee were able to harvest 10 percent of the oysters in their major sounds, they could have gathered 262,753 bushels, or 3,415,789 dozen large oysters. At that rate, 9,358 persons could have enjoyed a dozen oysters every day the whole year around. These figures apply only to part of the Apalachee coast, and oysters were abundant in Timucuan territory and elsewhere in Florida's estuaries.

The oyster's only nutritional drawback is low yield. The shell weighs far more than the animal, and the raw shellfish is 80.5 percent water. Consequently, 100 g of shucked oysters contains only 9.8 g of protein, 5.6 g of carbohydrates and 2.1 g of fat, yielding 84 calories.[182]

The huge shell mounds on which Calusa lived testify to the importance in their diet of not only oysters but also clams, conchs, scallops, and other mollusks.[183] Inhabiting much the same environment, the Tekesta relied less on shellfish, although conch and oysters were available to them in Biscayne Bay.[184]

Conches.   Much boneless meat is furnished by the conch (*Busycon* spp.), and it evidently contributed importantly to the Calusa and Key Indian diet. The conch is undoubtedly the "snail" that, according to the Spanish captive Escalante, the Key inhabitants ate at mid-sixteenth century.[185] Adult animals contain a kilogram of meat.[186] The size of the temple and platform mounds the Calusa used into historic times attests to well-organized leadership and numerous workers to construct them and their auxiliary works.[187] Many of the mounds consist almost wholly of millions of conch shells, all with small holes at the end where Calusa cut the muscle to free the meat from the shell.[188]

Perhaps one-eighth of Florida's 5,920 km of tidal coastline produced conches in abundance, and even more grew in the waters around the Keys. If we assume that Key production equaled peninsular, yield may be estimated for 1,480 km. If Native Americans collected a mature conch once a year from each 10 m, they would have taken 148,000 conches (148,000 kg), enough to provide 500 g of meat for 811 persons daily the year around.

Clams.   The abundance of shellfish readily available for easy human collection is an important consideration in calculating their contribution to Native American diets. So is the size of individual shellfish. Lower Californians benefited from an abundance of large Pismo clams (*Tivela stultorum*). In 1945, the state of California imported 3,035,000 kg of clam meat from the peninsula by boat and truck.[189] If it had been dug the year around, that quantity would have provided 16,630 Native Americans with 500 g of clams daily. Because poor transportation facilities limited the distance clams could be shipped to U.S. canneries, the peninsular beaches were not fully exploited in the 1940s; the pre-Columbian clammers could have collected much greater tonnages.

Mid-twentieth-century commercial fishermen using techniques Native Americans could have employed collected enough clams during a single low tide to supply the daily protein requirements of from 100 to 450 adults. Two six-year-old Pismo clams provide the minimum daily protein requirement of 40 g.[190] Small wonder that Lower Californians congregated on the coasts.

Native Americans of Florida benefited from a similar large clam, the southern quahog (*Mercenaria campechiensis*). It grows buried in the substrate of sandbars at the inner edge of barrier islands. In the upper Boca Ciego Bay portion of Tampa Bay, the largest quahog recorded weighed 2.955 kg. Farther north, the North Carolina record is 1.818 kg.[191] Assuming an average live weight of 909 g, two southern quahog clams yield 114 g of shellfish at the 8:1 ratio of live weight to shucked weight. This is a scant meal for an adult human being because water content is 80 percent. Two southern quahogs would provide 0.3 percent of the minimum daily protein requirement and only 81 calories.[192]

Florida has a reported 5,920 linear kilometers of tidal coastline, measuring bays and sounds to the head of tidewater of a width of 100 feet.[193] Perhaps half that distance can be assumed to have supported Quahog clams prior to 1520. Native Americans with digging sticks could perhaps collect a ton of clam meat per month from each linear kilometer of productive beach, so 2,960 linear kilometers exploited over a three-month season could have yielded some 8,072,727 kg, enough to provide 500 g daily to 44,234 persons for an entire year, or 176,936 persons during clamming season. A serving of 500 g would contain 64 g of protein, or more than 50 percent above the minimum daily requirement, for only 405 calories.

Crustaceans

The abundance of crabs and "Florida lobster" in Timucua country deserves mention.[194] While only the tail of the crayfish contains edible meat, that is a very rich quarter pound in a mature specimen. The Florida lobster is covered with chiton and lacks parts hard enough to survive in open archaeological sites such as shell mounds. Yet such food was available in quantity to aboriginal Floridians. In 1562, Timucuans on the south bank of the St. Johns River near its mouth served Jean Ribaut fish, crabs, and lobsters or crayfish.[195]

Fish

Among fish that inhabit shallow salt water, the densely shoaling, easily netted and trapped striped mullet (*Mugil cephalus*) and silver mullet (*M. curena*) abounded in the brackish waters of bays, rivers, creeks, and even freshwater rivers and springs.[196] Other available fish included snook, redfish, spotted sea trout (*Cynoscion nebulosus*), jack (*Caranx hippos*), pompano, grouper, and mangrove snapper (*Lutianus griseus*).[197] Ancestral Native American coastal residents knew how to catch, by whatever techniques, at least 20 species of fish even before the Christian era. Identified bones excavated from a midden at Fort Walton Beach dated to 300 B.C. showed that jackfish made up 61 percent of the known "catch"; these were blue runner (*C. crysos*) and the crevalle jack (*C. hippos*). Sea catfish (*Galeichthys felix*) made up 11.6 percent, shad (*Brevoortia* spp.) 9.8 percent, and sheepshead (*Archosargus* spp.) 5.6 percent. Mullet composed only 2.8 percent, spotted sea trout another 2.3 percent, and flounder (*Bothidae*) was 1.9 percent. Other fish taken less often were the bullshard (*Carcharchinus* spp.), bowfin, lady fish (*Elops saurus*), gafftopsail catfish (*Bagre marinus*), snook, kingfish (*Menticirrhus* spp.), drum (*Pogonias cromis*), pinfish (*Lagodon* spp.), barracuda (*Sphyraena* sp.), another flounder (*Paralichthys* sp.), and toadfish (*Opasanus* sp.).[198]

The gentle slope of beaches, estuaries, and rivers enabled the Timucua to build large reed fish traps "with so manny tourns and crokes, as yt
is impossible to do yt with more cunning or industry."[199] No point in
Florida lies more than 60 miles from salt water.[200] Thus all of Florida's
Native Americans shared the ease of access to saltwater fish, mollusks,
and crustaceans that was enjoyed by Lower Californians. The St. Johns
River Timucua speared or trapped mullet, trout, flounder, turbot, and
many New World species not recognized by Frenchmen in the 1560s.[201]

The abundance of mullet in Florida's sounds between the peninsula
proper and its barrier islands and in the lower reaches of its rivers was so
great that this species might be considered approximately equivalent in
food value to the annual salmon run on the Northwest Coast and
California culture areas. Florida's coastal sounds and its principal rivers, at least, probably supported a pre-1520 population consuming
largely fish, crustaceans, and mollusks approximately as dense as that
which, according to the calculations of Martin A. Baumhoff, lived on
the Sacramento and San Joaquín rivers of central California. He estimated that those tribesmen averaged 10.40 persons per square mile,
judging from the salmon fishery.[202] While a hard and fast judgment is
difficult to make without more details about the diets of aboriginal
Native Americans in Florida, it appears from scattered references that
for the coastal villagers, at least, fish was the most important staple food
in their annual economy, as it was for the most populous tribes of
Upper California.[203] Unlike the Lower California natives, the peoples
of coastal Florida made large dugout canoes that they paddled rapidly
along the estuaries behind barrier islands and on lakes and rivers.[204]
Frequent use of canoes is an important subsistence difference, inasmuch as migratory bluefish may literally leap into a boat in a frenzy of
feeding[205] and are easily caught with simple equipment.

Faring out to sea, the Tekesta sought large fish as well as marine
mammals. They succeeded in taking sharks and sailfish in addition to
rays, as bones in their middens attest.[206] Florida's fishery during historic times became an export industry. In 1772, British surveyors reported that six fishing schooners based at Havana turned a $2,000 profit
per trip, drying their catches on the shores of Tampa Bay.[207] Ten
species of fish furnished almost 98 percent of the individuals netted
during a year-long study of the piscine population of the littoral of the
barrier islands that separate Tampa Bay from the Gulf of Mexico. They
are two kinds of kingfish (*Menticirrhus littoralis, M. focaligor*) plus
*Harangula jaguana, Anchoa hepsetus, A. cubana, A. Mitchelli, Mendis
beryllina, Opisthonema oglinum, Trachinotus carolinus,* and *T. falcatus.*
Three of these species—*H. jaguana, Mendis beryllina,* and *Menticirrhus*

littoralis—were found during all months of the year.[208] Thus Florida's Native Americans could strive to catch a wide diversity of saltwater fish and would take some species the year around.

Florida has 8,426 linear miles of coastline measuring to the head of tidewater with a width of 100 feet. Assuming that the estuary between the barrier islands and peninsula is on average a quarter mile wide— some embayments are much broader and some channels quite narrow—then estuarine surface may be calculated as 2,106.5 square miles. The real water surface fluctuates markedly with tides, but an approximation gives at least a basis for estimating catches. The calculated 2,106.5 square miles of estuarine surface would equal 1,348,160 acres.

Inasmuch as the lower St. Johns River yielded 66.364 kg of fish per acre per seine-net haul, an estimate that Native Americans could trap and net 45.455 kg of fish per acre of estuarine water seems conservative. At such a catch rate, they could have landed 61,280,000 kg of estuarine fish annually. That weight would dress out at about 20,426,667 kg of fillets, enough to feed 500 g daily to 111,927 people the year around.

WILD FOOD RESOURCES

The Everglades, although seasonally inundated, provided an ideal habitat for fish, turtle, alligator, water mammal, and even upland game. The environment resembles that of the seasonally inundated delta of the Sacramento River. The southern tip of Florida can be assumed to have supported a pre-1520 population on the same order as that found in the fish-rich, mammal-rich, waterfowl-rich confluence of the Sacramento and San Joaquín rivers in California. There the population density exceeded 10 persons per square mile. A South Florida estimate on the order of a dozen Native Americans per square mile subsisting on wild fish, mollusks, crustaceans, marine mammals, upland game animals and birds, waterfowl, and wild plant foods might not be much wide of reality and would imply about seven people per square kilometer. If South Florida's greater density averaged out at about 10 persons per square mile in all of resource-rich Florida, then the pre-1520 population was on the magnitude of 585,600 people.

Florida more nearly resembled Upper than Lower California in nut and big game resources. In estimating the human carrying capacity of big game in California, Baumhoff appears to have considered primarily deer, elk, and antelope[209] and by implication smaller game in the same habitats. Baumhoff calculated that game sustained an average of 3.65 persons per square mile in the San Joaquín area[210] and an average of

4.177 persons per square mile in the North Coast Range area.[211] The two or three upland, two riverline/lacustrine, and three marine big game animals and reptiles of Florida, plus its medium-sized and small game animals and upland game birds, plus migratory waterfowl, apparently exceeded comparable resources in California. Such food supplies may be estimated to have been capable of sustaining more than five persons per square mile, or more than 292,800 individuals within Florida's 58,560 square miles.

Another view of Florida's probable early sixteenth-century Native American population is provided by table 19. There the dressed meat yield that has been estimated for the highest-yielding fish and game types is summarized along with the calculated number of people for whom the estimated catch/kill would supply 500 g of meat daily the year around. The estimate of 749,407 daily servings of 500 g of meat falls

TABLE 19

Quantities of Fish and Game Annually Available to Sustain
Native Americans in Early Sixteenth-Century Florida

Fish or Game	Dressed Weight (kg)	Feeding Capacity[a]
Catfish	26,442,456	144,890
Estuarine fishes	20,426,667	111,927
Freshwater turtle	17,564,778	96,245
Black crappie	15,812,589	86,644
Bluegill	9,677,939	53,030
Rabbit	9,349,600	51,231
Quahog clam	8,072,727	44,234
Shellcracker	6,980,809	38,251
Garfish	6,689,941	36,657
Bass	5,632,243	30,862
Bobwhite	4,046,429	22,172
Alligator	3,228,989	17,693
Passenger pigeon	722,400	3,958
Deer	502,575	2,754
Gopher tortoise	476,000	2,608
Duck	415,200	2,275
Sturgeon	193,500	1,060
Middle-sized game	162,684	891
Turkey	159,566	874
Conch	148,000	811
Sea turtle	54,545	340
Total	—	749,407

[a]Number of persons who could be fed 500 grams of meat daily all year.

short in that it does not include offshore fish, manatees, whales, seals, and a number of small game species and shellfish that each contributed small amounts to the total kill. No doubt the weight of such additional catches and kills would bring the estimate in table 19 to significantly more than 750,000 daily servings of 500 g of meat the year around.

The implication of the figure just stated for Florida Native American population early in the sixteenth century is that the area could at least theoretically have sustained more than 750,000 human beings. Every serving of 500 g used as the unit of calculation in table 19 would provide more than the minimum adult daily requirement of animal protein (40 g). Clams, the least efficient major food source, would provide 40 g of protein in 313 g of flesh despite the high water content. Only 200 g of raw bluefish contain more than 400 g of protein, so 500 g would double the daily requirement, even allowing for shrinkage during cooking. That amount of bluefish would provide fewer than a fourth of the calories that an adult would burn during a day.[212] The wild plant foods, and especially nuts, discussed in the last chapter therefore contributed crucially to the Native American diet. Nuts and starch from roots are high-calorie foods that provided the energy for Native Americans who were clearly able to catch and kill plenty of fish and game to sustain a population of 750,000 individuals in Florida. Because of the need for carbohydrate sources, cultivated foods, discussed in the next essay, formed a crucial component of Native American's meals in Florida.

NOTES

1. Ehrmann, "Timucua Indians," 1940, p. 174.
2. Robertson, trans., *True Relation*, 1933, vol. II, pp. 79 – 81, 215. Some groups in the Southeast reportedly did not eat dogs, although they had hundreds of the animals (p. 102).
3. Rau, trans., "Account," 1872, p. 364.
4. Venegas, *Natural and Civil History*, 1759 (1966), vol. 1, pp. 36 – 37.
5. Shelvocke, *Voyage*, 1726, p. 401.
6. T.N. Campbell, "Choctaw Subsistence," 1959, p. 13.
7. Ehrmann, "Timucua Indians," 1940, p. 175.
8. Hulton, ed., *Work of Le Moyne de Morgues*, 1977; "Images," 1979, pp. 196, 208, mentions baskets and gardening tools as having been based on European models.
9. Lorant, ed., *New World*, 1946, p. 83.
10. Telford, "Herpetological Survey," 1952, p. 183.
11. Rogers, *Cruising Voyage*, 1712 (1970), 231.
12. Shelvocke, *Voyage*, 1726, p. 411.

13. Shipek, *Strategy*, 1977, pp. 28 – 29.

14. Rau, trans., "Account," 1872, p. 364.

15. Milanich, *Excavations*, 1972, p. 123.

16. Ehrmann, "Timucua Indians," 1940, p. 174; Laudonnière, *Three Voyages*, 1975, pp. 107 – 109.

17. Lorant, ed., *New World*, 1946, p. 85.

18. Goggin, "Tekesta Indians," 1940, p. 283.

19. Goggin and Sturtevant, "Calusa," 1964, p. 184, following Escalante in True, ed., *Memoir*, 1944, 1945, pp. 66 – 67 (B. Smith, trans., *Letter and Memoir*, 1854, p. 14).

20. Sherman, "List," 1936, p. 123. *Odocoileus virginianus clavium*.

21. B. Smith, trans., *Letter and Memoir*, 1854, p. 14; Quinn, ed., *New American World*, 1979, vol. V, p. 8.

22. This inference rests on the ground-breaking research of H.T. Lewis, *Patterns*, 1973, pp. 43ff.

23. Alexander and Dickson, "Vegetational Changes," 1972, pp. 85, 94.

24. Cypert, "Effects of Fires," 1961, pp. 488 – 89.

25. Ewel and Mitsch, "Effects of Fire on Species," 1978, p. 26, table 1.

26. Alexander and Dickson, "Vegetational Changes," 1972, p. 89.

27. Ibid., 90.

28. Vogl and Beck, "Response of White-Tailed Deer," 1970, p. 272, point out that burning makes new and palatable growth available at heights deer can reach, as well as tripling forb and grass yields.

29. Alexander and Dickson, "Vegetational Changes," 1972, pp. 93, 95.

30. Harlow, "Fall and Winter Foods," 1961, p. 26, fig. 1; p. 23, table 2.

31. Ribaut, *Whole & True Discouerye*, 1563, p. 72.

32. H.T. Lewis, *Patterns*, 1973, pp. 83 – 84.

33. Wenhold, trans., *17th Century Letter*, 1936, p. 13, plate 9.

34. Laudonnière, *Three Voyages*, 1975, p. 69.

35. Kerrigan, trans., *Pedro Menéndez*, 1965, p. 141. The Spanish "Ay en la florida . . . grandes prados para ganados mayores y menores" (Barrientos, *Vida y Hechos*, 1902, p. 148) might also be rendered into English as "there are in Florida large pastures for cattle and smaller stock."

36. MacCauley, "Seminole Indians," 1887, p. 504.

37. Schemnitz, "Populations," 1974, p. 162.

38. Harlow, "Fall and Winter Foods," 1961, p. 30, fig. 2.

39. Schemnitz, "Populations," 1974, p. 163.

40. Osborn, "Comment," 1980, p. 740.

41. Milanich, *Excavations*, 1972, p. 56. The peninsula supported a single species, the Florida black bear (*Euarctos floridianus*) (Sherman, "List," 1936, p. 109).

42. Ehrmann, "Timucua Indians," 1940, p. 174; Laudonnière, *Three Voyages*, 1975, pp. 107 – 108.

43. Wenhold, trans., *17th Century Letter*, 1936, p. 12.

44. MacCauley, "Seminole Indians," 1887, p. 504.

45. Schemnitz, "Populations," 1974, p. 158, estimated 500 to 1,000 black bears in South Florida in the 1959 – 71 period.

46. Lorant, ed., *New World*, 1946, p. 87.

47. Ibid., 81, 83.

48. Milanich, *Excavations*, 1972, pp. 42, 45, 56.

49. Schemnitz, "Populations," 1974, p. 160.

50. Vogl, "Effects of Fire on Plants and Animals," 1973, p. 339.

51. Morris, comp., *Florida Handbook*, 1973, pp. 494 – 95.

52. Ibid., 492.

53. McDiarmid, ed., *Rare and Endangered Biota*, vol. III, *Amphibians and Reptiles*, 1978, p. 66.

54. Lorant, ed., *New World*, 1946, p. 87.

55. Moore, "Range of the Florida Manatee," 1951, pp. 1 – 19.

56. Goggin, "Tekesta Indians," 1940, p. 282, following Swanton, *Early History*, 1922, p. 389.

57. Baumhoff, *Ecological Determinants*, 1963, p. 172.

58. Markham, *Observations*, 1878, p. 157.

59. Goggin and Sturtevant, "Calusa," 1964, pp. 184 – 85. Atlantic right whales swim slowly and do not fear human beings. The right was one of the few species that could be hunted prior to the invention of engines. South Florida natives hunted whales in shallow water where they could not dive deeply using the wooden-plug technology (Larson, *Aboriginal Subsistence Technology*, 1980, pp. 151 – 56). A 20-foot right whale calf might weigh 12 tons. If a third of live weight was edible meat, it would yield 3,671.712 kg, enough to furnish 201 persons 500 g daily the year around (or the dried equivalent of 500 g fresh meat). Thus, ten such calves would feed 2,012 persons of whale meat daily the year around, and 100 would provision 20,119 persons in the same measure all year.

60. Shelvocke, *Voyage*, 1726, pp. 414 – 15, reported that 15 or 16 people drove a ray about 15 feet wide to the beach.

61. Goggin, "Tekesta Indians," 1940, p. 282.

62. Herald and Stickland, "Annotated List," 1949, p. 101.

63. Goggin, "Tekesta Indians," 1940, p. 282.

64. Goggin and Sturtevant, "Calusa," 1964, p. 184, following Escalante in True, ed., *Memoir*, 1944, 1945, pp. 66 – 67; Quinn, ed., *New American World*, 1979, vol. V, p. 8.

65. Goggin, "Tekesta Indians," 1940, p. 283.

66. Forbes, *Sketches*, 1821 (1964), 95.

67. Chatelain, "Spanish Contributions," 1941, p. 237; Fairbanks, *History*, 1858 (1975), 138.

68. MacCauley, "Seminole Indians," 1887, p. 504.

69. The leatherback is assumed to butcher out at 40 percent meat, as is the green (Rebel, *Sea Turtles*, 1974, p. 97), although figures in Rebel's table 9 indicate that Atlantic green turtles actually butcher out at 50 percent meat, including major organs.

70. McDiarmid, ed., *Amphibians and Reptiles*, 1978, p. 23.

71. Rebel, *Sea Turtles*, 1974, p. 113.

72. Sherman, "Occurrence of Bison," 1954, p. 228; Goggin, "Fort Pupo," 1951, pp. 176 – 77.

73. Swanton, "Notes," 1938, p. 379, following Wenhold, trans., *17th Century Letter*, 1936, p. 13. She had hunters "enter the forest in pursuit of bears, bison and lions." Bishop Díaz Vara Calderón gave a native term for hunting with fire drives and wrote that after the January hunt, when fields were fired, "that finished, they enter the densest thickets for the bear, bison and lion hunt" (plate 10). He evidently had no accurate knowledge of bison habitat.

74. Boyd, "Occurrence of American Bison," 1936, p. 203.

75. Boyd, trans., "Expedition," 1937, pp. 7, 23.

76. Swanton, "Bison in Florida," 1941, p. 322, following Leonard, trans., *Spanish Approach*, 1939, pp. 157, 161, 270 – 71, and Siguenza y Góngara, *Documentos*, 1963, pp. 67, 70, 76.

77. Leonard, trans., *Spanish Approach*, 1939, pp. 270 – 271.

78. Boyd, "Diego Peña's Expedition," 1949, p. 14.

79. Ibid., 15.

80. Ibid., 16.

81. Ibid., 18 – 19, 21.

82. Rostlund, "Range," 1960, p. 400, following Wenhold, trans., *17th Century Letter*, 1936, p. 13, plate 10, and Leonard, trans., *Spanish Approach*, 1939, p. 81.

83. Rostlund, "Range," 406 – 407, partially following Haag, "Prehistory," 1955, p. 27.

84. Lorant, ed., *New World*, 1946, p. 83.

85. Sherman, "List," 1936, p. 113.

86. Ehrmann, "Timucua Indians," 1940, p. 174; Laudonnière, *Three Voyages*, 1975, pp. 107 – 108.

87. Schemnitz, "Populations," 1974, pp. 157 – 58.

88. Milanich, *Excavations*, 1972, p. 56.

89. Goggin and Sturtevant, "Calusa," 1964, p. 184, following Escalante in True, ed., *Memoir*, 1944, 1945, pp. 66 – 67; Quinn, ed., *New American World*, 1979, vol. V, p. 8.

90. MacCauley, "Seminole Indians," 1887, p. 504.

91. Ehrmann, "Timucua Indians," 1940, p. 174; Laudonnière, *Three Voyages*, 1975, pp. 107 – 108.

92. Wenhold, trans., *17th Century Letter*, 1936, p. 13, mistranslated *pavos silvestres* (plates 9 and 10) as "wild ducks" instead of "wild turkeys." Hunting ducks with fire would make little sense, whereas using fire to hunt heavier turkeys, which prefer running to flying, is logical.

93. MacCauley, "Seminole Indians," 1887, p. 604.

94. Ibid.

95. Milanich, *Excavations*, 1972, pp. 42, 56.

96. M. Thomas, "Gopher Tortoise," 1978, pp. 2 – 3.

97. Ibid., 4.

98. Layne and Johns, "Present Status," 1965, p. 212.

99. Ibid., 213.

100. Venegas, *Natural and Civil History*, 1759 (1966), vol. 1, p. 39.

101. Shipek, *Strategy*, 1977, p. 28.

102. Venegas, *Natural and Civil History*, 1759 (1966), vol. 1, pp. 36 – 37.

103. Rau, trans., "Account," 1872, p. 364.

104. Ribaut, *Whole & True Discouerye*, 1563, p. 73.

105. Sherman, "List," 1936, pp. 121 – 22.

106. Milanich, *Excavations*, 1972, p. 56.

107. Wenhold, trans., *17th Century Letter*, 1936, p. 13, plates 9 and 10.

108. MacCauley, "Seminole Indians," 1887, p. 504.

109. Milanich, *Excavations*, 1972, p. 56.

110. MacCauley, "Seminole Indians," 1887, p. 504.

111. Sherman, "List," 1936, p. 114.

112. Milanich, *Excavations*, 1972, p. 56.

113. Arata, "Effects of Burning," 1959, pp. 99 – 100.

114. MacCauley, "Seminole Indians," 1887, p. 504.

115. Goodwin, "Waterfowl Management Practices," 1979, pp. 123, 128.

116. Ibid., 126, 128.

117. *Colinus virginianus* and *C.* var. *floridianus* (Laessle, "Study," 1944, p. 170).

118. Hirth and Marion, "Bird Communities," 1979, p. 145, table 1; p. 149.

119. P.A. Stewart, "Preliminary List," 1937, p. 326.

120. Baldwin and Kendeigh, "Variations," 1938, pp. 440–41.

121. Norris and Johnston, "Weight," 1958, p. 116, table 1.

122. Laudonnière, *Three Voyages*, 1975, p. 114.

123. The mourning dove just north of Florida averages about 126.7 grams (Norris and Johnston, "Weight," 1958, p. 116, table 1) with Ohio birds 10 to 15 grams heavier (Baldwin and Kendeigh, "Variations," 1938, pp. 438–39, table 5). The extinct passenger pigeon probably weighed three times as much.

124. Vogl, "Effects of Fire on Plants and Animals," 1973, p. 337.

125. Meeker, "Florida-Based Woodstork," 1980, p. 6-A.

126. Tebeau, *History*, 1971, p. 4.

127. Franz and Franz, "Distribution," 1979, pp. 13–17.

128. Kushlan and Lodge, "Ecological and Distributional Notes," 1974, pp. 111, 113.

129. Milanich, *Excavations*, 1972, pp. 45, 48, 56. Some finds of articulated vertebrae indicate that catfish and crappie were filleted.

130. Lischka and Sheets, "Comment," 1980, p. 740.

131. Hubbs and Allen, "Fishes," 1943, pp. 112–15.

132. Reid, "Fishes," 1950, p. 175.

133. Hubbs and Allen, "Fishes," 1943, p. 127.

134. Reid, "Fishes," 1950, pp. 180–81.

135. Ibid., 177–78, 181.

136. Hubbs and Allen, "Fishes," 1943, pp. 115–16.

137. Reid, "Fishes," 1950, p. 175.

138. Hubbs and Allen, "Fishes," 1943, pp. 118–19. Curiously, no *Ictalurus* was taken from Orange Lake during a 14-month long study in the mid-twentieth century (Reid, "Fishes," 1950, p. 177).

139. Gilbert, ed., *Rare and Endangered Biota*, vol. Four, *Fishes*, 1978, pp. 6–7.

140. Herald and Strickland, "Annotated List," 1949, pp. 99, 101.

141. Goggin, "Tekesta Indians," 1940, p. 283.

142. Milanich, *Excavations*, 1972, pp. 45, 48, 56–57.

143. Moody, "Adult Fish Populations," 1954, p. 155.

144. McDiarmid, ed., *Amphibians and Reptiles*, 1978, p. 32.

145. Telford, "Herpetological Survey," 1952, p. 184. This lake is 0.6 miles by 0.7 miles (p. 175).

146. McDiarmid, ed., *Amphibians and Reptiles*, 1978, pp. 69–70.

147. Ibid., 30.

148. Agar, "Commercial Fishery," 1972, pp. 221, 223–34. During a 10-year period, Lake George provided an average 10.7 pounds of bream and 4.8 pounds of crappie per acre annually in addition to catfishes (222, table 3). Thus, total catch of just these three fishes averaged 77.2 pounds per surface acre per year—more than 35 kilograms.

149. Twentieth-century cooks consider half the live weight of a fish to be inedible, and fillets amount to one-third the live weight. Thus 1,363,636 kg in dressed weight yield 409,091 kg of fillets.

150. Goggin and Sturtevant, "Calusa," 1964, p. 184, following Escalante in True, ed., *Memoir*, 1944, 1945, pp. 67 – 68.

151. Agar, "Commercial Fishery," 1972, p. 220, table 1.

152. Agar, "Fishes," 1971, p. 53.

153. Ibid., 54 – 56, 59 – 61.

154. Moody, "Adult Fish Populations," 1954, p. 149.

155. Ibid., 157.

156. Ibid., 149, 151.

157. Ibid., 152 – 53.

158. Ibid., 158.

159. Reid, "Fishes," 1950, p. 176.

160. Walker, "lake apopka," 1978, pp. 13 – 14.

161. Guillory, "Species Assemblages," 1979, pp. 159, 161.

162. Ibid., 160.

163. Agar, "Commercial Fishery," 1971, p. 222, table 3.

164. Moody, "Exploited Fish Populations," 1961, pp. 2, 5.

165. Ibid., 4 – 5.

166. The channel and white catfish catches were 0.6711 pounds per surface acre from the six lakes, or 304 g, and turtles weighed 0.3714 pound per surface acre, or 169 g.

167. Kilby and Caldwell, "List," 1955, p. 202.

168. MacCauley, "Seminole Indians," 1887, p. 504.

169. Yesner, "Maritime Hunter-Gatherers," 1980, pp. 727 – 35, 743 – 50.

170. Rogers, *Cruising Voyage*, 1712 (1970), 230, reported that he saw Pericú near Cape San Lucas "dive to admiration." He saw no nets or hooks in use.

171. Rau, trans., "Account," 1872, p. 364.

172. Venegas, *Natural and Civil History*, 1759 (1966), vol. I, p. 78.

173. Shipek, *Strategy*, 1977, pp. 27, 29.

174. Yesner, "Maritime Hunter-Gatherers," 1980, p. 730, following Orians and Pearson, "On the Theory," 1979, p. 156.

175. Rau, trans., "Account," 1872, pp. 360, 379.

176. Elsasser, "Indians of Lower California," 1977, p. 10; Rogers, *Cruising Voyage*, 1712 (1970), 208; Shelvocke, *Voyage*, 1726, pp. 388, plate between pp. 404 – 405, 410) described the Pericú log raft as five light logs joined by pegs and propelled by a double-bladed paddle.

177. Quinn, ed., *New American World*, 1979, vol. V, p. 85.

178. Goggin and Sturtevant, "Calusa," 1964, p. 184, following Connor, trans., *Pedro Menéndez*, 1923 (1964), 148; Zubillaga, *Monumenta*, 1946, p. 356.

179. Kerrigan, trans., *Pedro Menéndez*, 1965, p. 88; Connor, trans., *Pedro Menéndez*, 1923 (1964), 148.

180. MacCauley, "Seminole Indians," 1887, p. 504.

181. Dacy, "His Succulency," 1925, pp. 30 – 31. The beds located held an estimated 2,627,534 bushels of oysters more than three inches long (32).

182. Watt, Merrill, et al., *Composition of Foods*, 1950, p. 36.

183. Goggin and Sturtevant, "Calusa," 1964, p. 184, following Goggin, "Cultural Occupation," 1949, pp. 66 – 67. Nine-tenths of this huge midden consists of oyster shell; other shellfish consumed were *Arca ponderosa, Melongena corona, Strombus pugilis, Murex* sp., *Fasciolaria gigantea, F. tulipa, Macrocallista* sp., and *Pecten* sp., besides clams and conches.

184. Goggin, "Tekesta Indians," 1940, p. 282.

185. Goggin and Sturtevant, "Calusa," 1964, p. 184, following Escalante in True, ed., *Memoir*, 1944, 1945, pp. 66 – 67, as inaccurately translated by Buckingham Smith (*Letter and Memoir*, 1854, p. 14). The curving conch shell resembles a snail shell. Quinn, ed., *New American World*, 1979, vol. V, p. 8, does not correct the translation.

186. Milanich and Fairbanks, *Florida Archaeology*, 1980, p. 244.

187. Goggin and Sturtevant, "Calusa," 1964, pp. 196 – 97.

188. Milanich and Fairbanks, *Florida Archaeology*, 1980, p. 244.

189. Aplin, "Pismo Clams," 1947, p. 31.

190. Lischka and Sheets, "Comment," 1980, p. 740, following Aplin, "Pismo Clams," 1947, p. 33, who found that fishermen dug from 80 to 240 pounds shucked weight per tide, meat being one-eighth live weight; and Tomplinson, "Mortality, Growth," 1968, pp. 100 – 107.

191. Sims, "Large Quahog Clams," 1964, p. 348.

192. Watts, Merrill, et al., *Composition of Foods*, 1950, p. 22.

193. Goodwin, "Waterfowl Management Practices," 1979, p. 23.

194. Ehrmann, "Timucua Indians," 1940, p. 175.

195. Ribaut, *Whole & True Discouerye*, 1563, p. 81.

196. Herald and Strickland, "Annotated List," 1949, p. 108.

197. Goggin and Sturtevant, "Calusa," 1964, p. 185; Herald and Strickland, "Annotated List," 1949, pp. 105, 107, 109.

198. Wing, "Animal Remains," 1967, p. 57.

199. Ribaut, *Whole and True Discouerye*, 1563, p. 71

200. Tebeau, *History*, 1971, p. 4.

201. Ehrmann, "Timucua Indians," 1940, p. 175, following Laudonnière, *Three Voyages*, 1975, p. 20.

202. Baumhoff, *Ecological Determinants*, 1963, p. 219, table 16.

203. Ibid., 169.

204. Connor, trans., *Pedro Menéndez*, 1923 (1964), 139, 143 – 44, 151.

205. Bowles, "Area Bluefish," 1980.

206. Goggin, "Tekesta Indians," 1940, p. 282.

207. Forbes, *Sketches*, 1821 (1964), 118, quoting June 3, 1772, report.

208. Saloman and Naughton, "Fishes," 1979, p. 90.

209. Baumhoff, *Ecological Determinants*, 1963, p. 176.

210. Ibid., 219, table 16.

211. Ibid., 199, table 9.

212. Watt, Merrill, et al., *Composition of Foods*, 1950, p. 15.

SECTION THREE
Plant Foods Cultivated by the South Florida Calusa

My discussion in the last two sections focused on wild game, fish, mollusks, crustaceans, and wild plants. I compared the Native Americans of Florida with nonhorticultural peoples of Lower and Upper California in order to emphasize the relative abundance of natural food resources in Florida. Still, any realistic estimation of early sixteenth-century Native American population in Florida must take into account an additional very important cultural characteristic of that population. Most of the Native American inhabitants of Florida early in the sixteenth century were horticulturalists who engaged in intensive crop production.

Historians and anthropologists alike have long recognized that the Apalachee and various Timucuan-speaking chiefdoms of central and northern Florida and southern Georgia cultivated the soil very productively.[1] On the other hand, the Calusa and their neighbors are usually considered to have lacked horticulture.[2] This section summarizes clear documentary and archaeological evidence that the Calusa in fact grew a significant quantity of their carbohydrate food intake.

CALUSAN HORTICULTURE

Escalante Fontaneda, a long-time Spanish captive among the Calusa, wrote after his release that Calusa—and he may have meant to include Ais and Tekesta—lived in "many towns on the shores of Lake Mayaimi" (Okeechobee). "They make bread of roots, which is their common food the greater part of the year."[3] Escalante Fontaneda compared another edible root with the European truffle and reported that the Calusa consumed other roots, although they preferred meat. Short though it is, Escalante Fontaneda's report is significant.

It must be borne in mind that Spanish Colonial accounts of the Calusa are few and fragmentary in their description of native culture. No modern ethnologist ever had an opportunity to study Calusa culture. Then, too, Europeans clearly failed until the twentieth century to recognize deliberate burning of vegetation by Native Americans as a major strategy of resource management.[4] It seems, therefore, quite probable that the few Colonial observers among the Calusa failed to recognize *Zamia* field preparation. Because the plant was quite strange to Europeans, they may well have been unable to distinguish between self-propagated and cultivated specimens. The principal difference in modern times seems to be that the cultivated plant thrives by comparison with the self-propagated one. The genus grows equally well in sand, loam, and limestone and shell.[5] If the Calusa deliberately or even accidentally replanted immature tubers while harvesting large ones, they would have ensured themselves a stable or augmented *Zamia* tuber supply. Spanish observers culturally more accustomed to sowing small grains and garden vegetables that mostly produced edible leaves or seeds could easily have overlooked so simple an action as the reburying of immature tubers during harvesting.

The *Zamia* plant may, in fact, have been introduced into Florida by the ancestors of the historic Calusa from a source area in the Caribbean islands.[6] While Native Americans have been known to transplant wild food plants,[7] they would have been more likely to transport a highly valued cultivar than wild tubers on a canoe journey from Cuba to Florida.

Indirect evidence that the Calusa cultivated crops appears to have existed as late as the middle of the eighteenth century. Bernard Romans carefully surveyed South Florida and noted that "at Sandy Point, the southern extremity of the peninsula, are large old fields, being the lands formerly planted by the Caloosa savages."[8] In the South of that period, "old fields" was a term consistently used to refer to horticultural sites formerly cultivated by Native Americans but later more or less taken over by weeds and shrubs. It is doubtful whether Romans could himself have seen any surviving Calusa cultivating crops at Sandy Point, so his identification of old fields there was evidently inferential. Yet Romans certainly should have been competent to recognize old fields when he saw them. His association of old fields at the southern tip of the peninsula with the Calusa known to have occupied that area during Spanish Colonial times seems quite logical, and today one can only agree with the inference.

Archaeological discoveries within historic Calusa territory indicate that pre-Columbian horticulture of a relatively intensive sort was practiced there. Excavation has recovered maize pollen.[9] It appears unlikely that Native Americans would have abandoned maize cultivation in South Florida unless disease had wiped out their strain. Moreover, excavators have uncovered ancient soil ridges of the sort widely distributed in tropical America that evidence intensive horticulture.[10] Finally, wooden pestles recovered in a state of good preservation from Key

Marco resemble nothing so much as Southeastern Native American maize-processing—pounding—utensils.[11]

The best evidence of Calusa maize cultivation, speaking methodologically, comes from early sixteenth-century Spanish reports. Yet chroniclers' references to maize grown by Calusa have been misattributed to the Tocobaga Timucuans. The source of this error has been inadequate understanding of the chronology of European exploration of the west coast of Florida. Anthropologists analyzing the Calusa have assumed, like several historians, that the Narváez and de Soto expeditions landed at what is today called Tampa Bay. In fact, those expeditions landed at Charlotte Harbor, in the heart of Calusa territory.

Not until 1566 did Calusa pilots guide Spaniards to the present Tampa Bay. Following his victory over French Huguenot would-be colonists on the Atlantic Coast of Florida, Pedro Menéndez de Avilés sailed in search of a safe water route through the peninsula. He traveled up the St. Johns River hoping to find a passage west into the Gulf of Mexico.[12] Later, he began to explore the Gulf Coast of the peninsula, seeking a passage eastward. Menéndez began, naturally, in the southwestern part of Florida that had been known to the Spaniards since early in the sixteenth century. He learned that Charlotte Harbor, the Calusa estuary of that period, did not connect to any passage of the sort he sought. The Calusa told Menéndez that he would find a "suitable waterway" near the village of the chief known as Tocobaga, which was 50 leagues away. A Calusa pilot steering by the North Star guided Menéndez's small ships to anchor directly off the dwelling of Tocobaga one hour before dawn. The Calusa-Spanish expedition completely surprised the village.[13] Menéndez did not find a passage from what is now known as Tampa Bay across the peninsula, but he and his biographer thought that he had made an important geographical discovery, and indeed he had.

After making a detailed analysis of sixteenth-century maps, David O. True concluded that earlier Spanish expeditions to Florida landed at Charlotte Harbor. He pointed out that Narváez and de Soto could not very well have landed at modern Tampa Bay, because Spaniards in the 1520s and 1530s simply did not know that it existed.[14]

If we place the Narváez and de Soto landings at Charlotte Harbor, we have conclusive proof of maize horticulture among the Calusa. Late in April, 1528, a scouting party that included Alvar Núñez Cabeza de Vaca set off along the shore of the bay. These Spaniards captured four natives and showed them kernels of maize "to find out if they knew it" inasmuch as the intruders had not yet found any. The captives somehow "told" the scouts that they would lead the Spaniards to a place with maize. In fact, they led the scouts to what the Spaniards took to be their own village, "at the end of the bay nearby." There the Calusa showed the Spaniards some maize "that was not yet fit to be gathered."[15]

On the last day of April 1528, Alvar Núñez Cabeza de Vaca set out from the bay with a Spanish patrol led by Calusa guides. The guides led the Spaniards 10 or 12 leagues to a 15-house village "where there was a large cultivated patch of corn nearly ready for harvest, and also some that was already ripe." The patrol spent two days at that settlement,[16] one of the inland Calusa villages.

In 1539, Hernando de Soto spent several weeks at the principal Calusa settlement, where he landed his army before he headed inland. A local historian who knows the terrain and has minutely compared the four primary sources of information about de Soto's expedition concluded that the town of Ocita was located near the head of Caloosahatchee Bay.[17] On July 15 de Soto finally led his forces out of Ocita to travel inland.[18] De Soto's marauders followed the south side of the Caloosahatchee River past a shallow lake drained during the nineteenth century to a prairie that they reached on July 17.[19] The next day, on July 18, de Soto's men found maize plants with roasting ears on "the Plain of Guasoco."[20] Diego Escalante Fontaneda, whom the Calusa held captive later in the sixteenth century, described this town of Guasaca located on Lake Mayaimi (Okeechobee) as the terminus of Calusa territory.[21]

Thus there are at least two sixteenth-century Spanish reports of Calusa maize cultivation at three locations ranging from the Gulf Coast to the prairie northwest of Lake Okeechobee. This is rather conclusive evidence that the Calusa grew maize. They may be assumed to have interplanted squash and beans with their maize, like other Native American maize growers. The analyst of sixteenth-century Spanish chronicles must remember that chroniclers often did not mention that with which they were already familiar, and intercropping maize, beans, and squash was already known to Alvar Núñez Cabeza de Vaca and his companions and to the members of the de Soto expedition.

Another archaeological discovery within historic Calusa territory documents horticultural activity that aimed to maximize the fishery catch. At a large ceremonial and living center on Key Marco, Frank H. Cushing toward the end of the nineteenth century recovered fragments of gourds still attached to fish nets. The Calusa were skilled canoeists, and cordage and gourd floats partially preserved under water at Key Marco attest to their technological skill as fishermen as well as to their economic enterprise. Hugh C. Cutler of the Missouri Botanical Garden identified most of the preserved gourd specimens recovered at Key

Marco as *Lagenaria siceraria*. These Key Marco specimens were even a bit larger than examples excavated at Huaca Prieta on the Peruvian Pacific Coast, which were clearly used as floats on fishing nets. The rest of the Key Marco gourd fragments were *Cucurbita pepo* var. *ovifera*.[22]

Both plants are cultivated. Consequently, one can interpret the gourd remains found at Key Marco in only two ways. The Calusa could have traded for gourds grown in Cuba or northern Florida, or they could have grown their own gourd floats. If we bear in mind (a) archaeological evidence of maize pollen in the Calusa area, (b) documented sixteenth-century commerce in *Zamia* flour that implies its cultivation, and (c) documented maize cultivation at several settlements, it seems most likely that the Calusa grew their own gourd net floats. Not only were the Calusa horticulturalists, in other words, but they grew some variety of food and utensil crops. They were sophisticated and, as ridged fields indicate, intensive gardeners.

Yet another kind of indirect evidence that the Calusa grew crops seems to have been ignored by those anthropologists who have labeled the Calusa nongardeners. One of the Spaniards whom French Huguenots rescued from captivity among Florida's Native Americans in 1565 told René Laudonnière that the Calusa sacrificed human beings in an annual fertility rite. The Calusa believed, as Laudonnière reported the conversation, that their "king's" "sorceries and spells" caused the earth to bring forth "her" fruit.[23] Once Spanish ships began to run aground on his coasts, the wise King Calos kept rescued Spaniards specifically to sacrifice "every year at the time of harvest."[24]

Simple hunting and gathering peoples did not typically celebrate harvest festivals. The White Knife Shoshoni are an illustrative example. The camps were unable to gather as a group. At most only about 300 of these people could meet for no more than five days and a half of dancing, gaming, and praying.[25] This limited social scale stands in stark contrast to the opulent and sedentary life of the Calusa.

Complex horticultural societies do celebrate harvest festivals. The annual ripening of cultivated food crops with their seasonal abundance psychologically calls for celebration, as the brief maturation of a variety of wild plant foods that collectors gathered through the year does not. The existence of seasonal, annual harvest rituals among the Calusa should have alerted anthropologists to their horticulture.

DEMOGRAPHIC IMPLICATIONS

The demographic implications of my discussion thus far may now be converted into estimates of Florida's pre-1520 Native American population. The Calusa, the Tekesta, the Ais, and possibly some smaller polities not clearly identifiable in the historic record may be considered to have occupied one-third of the area of the state, or 19,520 square miles. The richness of the wild plant, game, fish, mollusk, crustacean, and marine mammal resources of South Florida require estimating a population equal to that of the Sacramento-San-Joaquín river delta area of California, or 10 persons per square mile for nonhorticultural peoples. That figure implies 195,200 persons in South Florida prior to 1520.

For present purposes, the Tekesta, Ais, and perhaps smaller polities may be considered to have occupied the eastern half of South Florida, or some 9,760 square miles. As presumably nonhorticultural peoples, they should have numbered in the aggregate approximately 97,600 individuals prior to 1520. The large surface area of Lake Okeechobee differentiates the environment of South Florida from that of the Sacramento-San-Joaquín river system, so half the California population density, or about 48,800 persons, may be a reasonable estimate for the fisher-hunter-collector Tekesta, Ais, and perhaps other minor groups.

In the western half of South Florida, the Calusa were more numerous. The evidence that the Calusa engaged in maize and root crop production and raised gourds to increase the efficiency of their fishery requires estimating a denser Calusa population larger than that of the nonhorticulturalists in spite of the large lacustrine surface. For present purposes, lacking a more precise calculation of the food value of tuberous starch and maize and the quantities actually available to the Calusa, I assume a doubling of numbers attributable to gardening. In other words, apparent Calusa horticultural efficiency and consequent intensification of fishery may be assigned a population value of five persons per square mile. With an area of about 9,760 square miles, then, the Calusa in density at least equaled the population in the Sacramento-San-Joaquín river delta region. Thus the early sixteenth-century Calusa may be estimated to have numbered about 97,600 persons.

POPULATION AND SOCIAL STRUCTURE

A pre-1520 Native American population density on the order just estimated in South Florida would go far toward explaining a cultural phenomenon that anthropologists have considered an anomaly—the well-documented social stratification of the Calusa population.[26] The Spaniards in the mid-sixteenth century perceived the Calusa ruler as a king. He collected tribute from subject settlements in the form of mats, feathers, fruits, roots, and other foods as well as in gold, silver, and buckskins.[27] The pattern very much resembled that of the Aztecs and Incas, although Calusa society was smaller in scale than either the Mesoamerican empire or the Andean. Moreover, Calusa society was stratified into several classes. The top rank consisted of the capital town chief and chief priest. A priest "captain" occupied the second rank. A third hierarchical level contained headmen of the forty or so settlements. The principal men of those towns made up a fourth rank. At the bottom of the hierarchy, at least during historic times, were shipwrecked Spaniards held as slaves.[28] Presumably the Calusa kept Native American slaves during pre-Columbian times. Calusa society was historically ethnically diverse, inasmuch as it included not only nativeborn Calusa and Spaniards but also refugee Native Americans from Cuba. The degree to which Calusa society was ethnically diversified during pre-Columbian times is, of course, not known. The facility with which Calusan rulers absorbed foreign ethnic enclaves during the sixteenth century suggests, at the very least, that the Calusa polity was a conquest chiefdom that had emerged during the fifteenth century and had then incorporated diverse sociopolitical groups.

If the population estimate based on South Florida resource potential and Calusa horticulture is approximately correct, it accounts for Calusa social complexity in terms of high population density on a finite base of dry land. Like other societies with marriage between full siblings—in Bali, Guanche, Hawaii, Inca, Malagasy, and Mixtec[29]—the Calusa polity was a "little state" that politically integrated more than 10,000 persons and almost as many as 100,000.[30]

The other societies with marriage between full siblings obtained abundant food supplies by practicing horticulture or agriculture. The Calusa southwest Florida environment must have been rich, indeed, to sustain from natural food resources so large and dense a population as to require its documented complex social structure. The very complexity of Calusa social structure ceases to appear anomalous the moment one perceives that it organized the distribution of foodstuffs and other commodities among horticulturalists tending tubers, maize, gourds, and orchards and exploiting rich freshwater and saltwater fishing waters.

NOTES

1. Ehrmann, "Timucua Indians," 1940, p. 174; Swanton, *Early History*, 1922.
2. Goggin and Sturtevant, "Calusa," 1964, p. 183.
3. B. Smith, trans., *Letter and Memoir*, 1854, p. 15; Quinn, ed., *New American World*, 1979, vol. V, p. 8.
4. O.C. Stewart, "Fire," 1956, pp. 115–33.
5. H.G. Smith, "Ethnological and Archaeological Significance," 1951, p. 241.
6. Ibid., 242.
7. Florence C. Shipek, personal communication (Diegueño), 1979; Darrell Posey, personal communication (Kayapo), 1979.
8. Romans, *Concise Natural History*, 1775 (1962), 289. Forbes in 1821 (1964) accepted Romans' conclusion by incorporating it (without attribution) in his *Sketches*, at p. 100.
9. Sears and Sears, "Preliminary Report," 1976, pp. 53–56.
10. Denevan, *Aboriginal Cultural Geography*, 1966, pp. 84–96, 121–27; Parsons and Denevan, "Pre-Columbian Ridged Fields," 1967, pp. 92–100.
11. Gilliland, *Material Culture*, 1975, p. 69, plate 26A; p. 70, plate 27A; p. 68, plate 25.
12. Kerrigan, trans., *Pedro Menéndez*, 1965, pp. 115–19.
13. Ibid., 128–29.
14. True, "Some Early Maps," 1954, pp. 82–83.
15. Bandelier, trans., *Journey*, 1904 (1922), 12, "costeamos la bahía que habiamos hallado; y andadas cuatro leguas, tomamos cuatro indios, y mostrámosles maíz para ver si lo conocían; porque hasta entonces no habiamos visto señal de el. Ellos nos dijeron que nos llevarían donde lo había; y asi nos llevaron a su pueblo, que es al cabo de la bahía, cerca de allí, y en el nos mostraron un poco de maíz, que aún no estaba para cogerse" (Vedia, ed., *Historiadores*, 1858, p. 519).
16. Bandelier, trans., *Journey*, 1904 (1922), 13–14. Bandelier rendered "maíz sembrado, que ya estaba para cogerse, y tambien hallamos alguno que estaba ya seco" (Vedia, ed., *Historiadores*, 1858, p. 519) as "nearly ready for harvest, and also some that was already ripe." The Spanish could also be translated "that was ready to pick, and also we found some that was already dried out." Núñez could have meant that he saw either dried maize stalks in a field or dried kernels in storage. Núñez saw a small planting of immature maize at the south end of the bay a few days earlier, as noted above.
17. Schell, *De Soto*, 1966, pp. 37–38. The site is modern East Fort Myers.
18. Ibid., 48; Varner and Varner, trans., *Florida*, 1962, p. 102; Ranjel in Bourne, ed., *Narratives*, 1904, vol. II, p. 63; Robertson, trans., *True Relation*, 1933, vol. II, pp. 51–52.
19. Schell, *De Soto*, 1966, p. 51 (map); pp. 42–54; Robertson, trans., *True Relation*, 1933, vol. II, p. 52; Bourne, ed., *Narratives*, 1904, vol. II, p. 64.
20. Schell, *De Soto*, 1966, p. 54; Ranjel in Bourne, ed., *Narratives*, 1904, vol. II, p. 64.
21. B. Smith, trans., *Letter and Memoir*, 1854, p. 15; Quinn, ed., *New American World*, 1979, vol. V, p. 8, where the town name is spelled *Guacata*. Schell, *De Soto*, 1966, p. 55, quotes Escalante; see his map (51).
22. Cutler, "Appendix D," 1975, p. 255.

23. Laudonnière, *Three Voyages*, 1975, p. 110.

24. Ibid., 111.

25. Harris, "White Knife Shoshoni," 1940, p. 53.

26. Goggin and Sturtevant, "Calusa," 1964, pp. 189, 191.

27. Ibid., 188 – 89. Juan Rogel wrote in 1568 that the Calusa Headchief received tribute in feathers, mats, fruits, and other foodstuffs (Zubillaga, *Monumenta*, 1946, p. 278). Subject towns sent women to a crown prince or new ruler to symbolize their fealty or to create affinal kinship relationships (ibid., 310). Escalante slightly later wrote that Lake Okeechobee hamlets paid tribute in food, roots, buckskins, and other articles to the Calusa Headchief (B. Smith, trans., *Letter and Memoir*, 1854, p. 16; Quinn, ed., *New American World*, 1979, vol. V, p. 9).

28. Goggin and Sturtevant, "Calusa," 1964, pp. 190 – 91.

29. Ibid., 204 – 205.

30. Ibid., 206, following Murdock, "World Ethnographic Sample," 1957, p. 674.

Timucuan Maize Cultivation

The conclusion that Calusa grew maize and other food plants is sufficient to require us to revise markedly upward previous estimates of their early sixteenth-century population. While anthropologists and historians have generally recognized that the Timucuan-speaking peoples who inhabited most of the rest of Florida cultivated food crops, scholars have assumed that Timucuan numbers were relatively small, as I have indicated. It is therefore germane to analyze evidence in sixteenth-century chronicles relating to the productivity of Timucuan horticulture.

One major factor in Timucuan population growth was the quantity of maize—plus interplanted beans and squash—that these peoples grew. Horticultural production results from what modern agricultural scientists call "inputs." Land is a fundamental input. In Florida, the peninsular climate usually ensures summer growing-season rains. The land area sown to a crop determines the amount of solar energy available to convert soil nutrients, water, and genetic potential into edible maize kernels. Horticulturalists put seed into the ground, and the amount of seed planted typically governs the area cultivated.[1] In general, therefore, the area planted in a maize crop determines the amount of food harvested. Other factors or inputs are, however not always equal. Maize responds positively, for example, to fertilizer, and it suffers when competing with weeds for moisture and nutrients in the soil and for solar energy. Maize produces better when weeded than not, so maize growers usually remove competing plants to minimize competition for sunlight, water, and nutrients. Maize also produces better when the soil around its roots is stirred to interrupt capillary action and to conserve moisture, and most maize growers therefore cultivate.

Available evidence suggests that Timucuans were both intensive gardeners and extensive maize planters. Clues to their horticulture from sixteenth-century chronicles yield "a picture that is impressive if not astonishing."[2] Timucuans cultivated their maize fields with handled implements that Europeans perceived as hoes, which had blades made of stone, oyster, or mussel shells and wood or fishbones.[3] The engravings of eastern Timucuan cultivators made by de Bry from Le Moyne's paintings have been criticized as ethnographically inaccurate. The handled hoes shown are thought to represent European tools rather than

Timucuan versions.[4] Certainly Timucuan maize growers planted in hills, as other Native Americans did, and not in European furrows of the sort engraved by de Bry, so the hoe form shown is suspect.

However inaccurate his painting may have been in detail, Le Moyne did see eastern Timucuans hoeing their fields and tried to describe that activity. Moreover, one of the women shown in his painting of tilling and planting—a temporally unlikely scene—is using a digging stick that is so labeled in the accompanying caption.[5] Whether or not Timucuan women in the posture indicated gouged holes in which to drop seeds at planting time, the digging stick itself is a simple implement widely used in the Americas. The visual and textual records of the mid-sixteenth century make clear that the Timucuans used at least two major horticultural implements, one for digging or gouging and another for hoeing. They employed a variety of hoe blades, depending perhaps merely on availability of suitable materials but perhaps also on cultural definitions of tasks to be performed. One can infer, at any rate, on the basis of hand tools used, that Timucuan horticulture was to some extent intensive.

Another horticultural input is crop seed. Maize growers can increase their harvests by planting more seed per surface unit to the limit imposed by availability of nutrients, moisture in the soil, and incoming solar energy.[6] Sixteenth-century chronicles appear not to yield information on the density of planting among the Timucuans, but they do indicate that Timucuans practiced an alternative means of crop intensification on a given surface area. Cultivators in many parts of the world where temperatures and precipitation allow the practice plant a given plot of land twice during a single growing season. Previous analysts of Timucuan horticulture have already claimed that these Native Americans double-cropped their fields each year.[7] Double-cropping was environmentally feasible. At the beginning of British sovereignty over Florida, William Roberts claimed that the soil of the peninsula was "remarkably rich and fruitful, frequently producing two or three crops of *Indian* corn in the year."[8] His statement derived more from Colonial Spanish than from pre-Colonial Timucuan horticulture, so it is not very good evidence for aboriginal cropping, although it has been so interpreted.[9] It is good evidence that double-cropping was feasible.

Timucuan double-cropping would have drained soil fertility even more rapidly than single-cropping if some means of restoring nutrients to the plant root zone had not been employed. It would have produced more maize for human consumption than a single crop only if soil fertility had been maintained during the longer growing season. By the late seventeenth century, Colonial policies had clearly changed Timucuan cultivation practices. In October they sowed winter wheat, an Old

World cultivar, harvesting in June. The missionized Timucua and Apalachee began to plant maize, beans, and squash in April, after burning off weeds and dead cultivars in January.[10] Wheat (grown no doubt at Spanish insistence) competed with maize, beans, and squash for fields. April-planted maize could still have been followed by a second planting. The mission-era farming practices may have reflected missionary influence and/or functional requirements of successively planting wheat and maize in the same fields.

Evidence of pre-Columbian Timucuan cultivation patterns must be sought in pre-Colonial times, which is to say in sixteenth-century chronicles. Sixteenth-century European reports do seem to depict summer double-cropping prior to conquest, but more than half a century after initial Timucuan contact with Europeans. René Laudonnière wrote in a general description that the coastal Saturiwa sowed in March and June maize that matured in three months, replanting in the same soil.[11] March was the end of the winter frost season at the latitude of the St. Johns River mouth. In his narrative, however, Laudonnière reported that the Saturiwa Timucuans planted "all seeds" during May and early June in 1565.[12] Farther inland, up the St. Johns River, maize was already ripening among the Utina in early June.[13] Desperate French Huguenots were able to collect foodstuffs among the Utina for nearly a week before July 27, 1565.[14] Saturiwa village maize crops ripened during the latter half of July.[15]

In mid-May of 1528, members of the Narváez expedition found maize ready to harvest at whatever distance north of Charlotte Harbor they had managed to travel in two weeks.[16] On June 20, 1539, Baltasar de Gallegos rode inland from Calusa territory into southern Timucuan country. He discovered it to be "cultivated with fields of Indian corn, beans, pumpkins, and other vegetables, sufficient for the support of a large army."[17] On the basis of that reassuring finding, de Soto himself moved inland and thereby launched an invasion of Southeastern North America that lasted several years. After advancing farther north, de Soto's forces gathered a three-month supply of ripe maize from the fields of the Ocali polity in late July and early August.[18] On August 11 they found "plenty of corn" at Itara, one day's march north or northwest from Ocali.[19]

Jacques Le Moyne seemingly implied that the eastern Timucua planted in December.[20] That would not have been very practicable at the mouth of St. Johns River because of winter frosts. If Le Moyne traveled farther south than his surviving account suggests, on the other hand, the French artist might have seen maize planted in a frost-free zone in December. The roasting ears or mature ears that Alvar Núñez

Cabeza de Vaca reported near Charlotte Harbor in Calusa fields in mid-May of 1528 must have been planted at least two to three months earlier, in either February or March.[21] The dry stalks, if Alvar Núñez saw stalks rather than dried kernels, could have been residue from a crop planted even earlier or evidence of the last planting the previous summer.

The few protohistoric references to maize planting and roasting ears do suggest that the Timucuan peoples planted at least one crop as early in the spring as their respective geographic locations permitted. Those references also suggest that the Timucuans could and probably did double-crop maize and associated beans and squash. In view of evidence from the sixteenth century that the Powhatan Confederacy villagers triple-cropped maize much farther north,[22] such may well have been general practice among Native Americans in the Southwestern culture area.[23] Three maize, bean, and squash harvests would support a larger population than a single harvest. Intensive cultivation of these staple cultivars may be a major reason why Southeastern peoples were able to increase to relatively dense populations.

The area that residents of the Timucuan chiefdome planted with maize and associated food crops is not known, although some clues in sixteenth-century Spanish chronicles suggest that fields were extensive. The most explicit description of extensive cultivation in Florida is Garcilaso de la Vega's word picture of fields at a frontier Apalachee chiefdom settlement. Fernando de Soto's marauders advanced westward through the Florida Panhandle late in the summer of 1539. On its first night in Apalachee-inhabited territory, de Soto's force encamped at a "small village that marked the beginning of the fields and settlements." At dawn, the Spaniards started off toward Apalachee Town. They crossed two leagues of "great fields of corn, beans, squash and other vegetables." Those "great fields" lined both sides of the "road" the army traveled. It ran for two leagues from the frontier settlement to a ravine. On both sides, the "great fields" "spread out as far as the eye could see," with dwellings scattered about the cultivated plain.[24] A maize field that Europeans accustomed to extensive farming of broadcast-sown small grains perceived as large must have been extensive indeed.

Two leagues translates into from four to five miles of roadway, and the Spaniards probably could see for a couple of miles to either side of the road. De la Vega's description, based on the reports of members of the expedition, indicates an area of 16 square miles of cultivated fields, or 10,240 acres.

Sixteenth-century chronicles mention large quantities of dried maize kernels stored in Timucuan towns. They furnished no other clues as to field productivity per unit of area. Resorting to ethnographic analogy, one can suggest possible production. On Yucatecan limestone soils, Mayan swidden cultivation obtains from 430 to 655 kg of maize per acre the first season after forest fallowing. Quantity varies with soil quality and precipitation. Yield decreases in later years, the first-year 655 kg per acre falling to 465 kg the second year[25] and as low as 210 kg a third year.[26] To be conservative, a low Yucatecan yield may be used to suggest Florida productivity. Thus, 430 kg per acre on some 10,240 acres described as growing crops at just one Apalachee frontier town would yield 4,403,200 kg of shelled maize from a single planting. Modern Mayas subsist on about 260 kg of maize per person annually, enough cornmeal to provide 2,527.5 calories every day.[27] Such a quantity of maize would constitute an ample caloric ration for an active, large-bodied Apalachee or Timucua when combined with abundant fish and game sources of animal protein and supplemental calories. In short, 4,403,200 kg of shelled maize could support some 16,935 persons for a year.

Double-cropping Timucuan fields would have increased each growing season's harvest from a given field area by an unknown amount. On the other hand, consumption of roasting ears would have diminished the harvest of matured ears of both plantings. Consequently, double-cropping might be assumed to have allowed Timucuans to enjoy many roasting ears and still to harvest sufficient dried kernels to last for the rest of the year.

De la Vega's words about Timucuan chiefdoms' fields are less explicit than his portrait of the Apalachee frontier town's field area. Perhaps one or more of his informants for some reason remembered that particular stretch of cultivated fields, or de la Vega may have simply happened to write about it in more specific detail than he did about other cultivated zones. Still, what de la Vega did write about Timucuan cultivation gives the same general impression as his explicit picture of that Apalachee frontier town. That is, de la Vega reported that de Soto's marauders struggled through swamps and across rivers or marched through savannahs of hunting and gathering territory between the inhabited core lands of each chiefdom. The Spaniards consistently found a frontier settlement at the edge of the inhabited zone that was cultivated in all or at least in large part. The unanswered question is whether the inhabited core zones were as solidly planted as the fields on the Apalachee frontier appear to have been.

Marching north from the Acuera chiefdom in July, de Soto's forces reached the southern border of the Ocali chiefdom on July 26 or 27. A settlement they called *Uqueten* guarded the southern frontier, facing a parklike open forest or savannah 10 or 20 leagues wide with walnut, pine, and other kinds of trees.[28] Veterans of the expedition told de la Vega that they had traveled seven leagues through inhabited country from Uqueten to Ocali Town. A few houses were scattered throughout this "countryside."[29] The half-Inca author reported that Ocali Town consisted of 600 houses abandoned by the chief and all of his people. The Spaniards found a "great store of corn and other grains" when they moved into the vacant dwellings. Ocali very clearly was the central place in its subsistence territory.[30] Its residents transported food there from the immediate horticultural hinterland and from the more distant hunting and gathering savannahs on the borders with other chiefdoms.

A major river immediately north of Ocali Town marked either the northern boundary of the chiefdom or the "countryside." It no doubt afforded access by canoe to other hunting and gathering areas and possibly to additional cultivated fields. Thus the area possibly cultivated from Uqueten to Ocali Town extended from 14 to 17.5 miles on the road axis, depending on the actual length of the league de Soto's chroniclers counted. If the "countryside" were equally broad on the east-west axis, then its inhabited area was approximately 196 square miles, or about 125,440 acres. Such an area would at the Yucatecan low-yield figure grow 53,939,200 kg of dried maize at a planting, or enough at 260 kg per person to feed 207,458 individuals for a year. There is no reason to suppose that the Ocali chiefdom was so populous, and it appears that the cultivated zone either was not as wide as just assumed or was not all planted. Fields may have been scattered with dwellings, or they may have been arranged in a relatively narrow north-south belt rather than in a squarish zone.

Relying on verbalized memories of members of de Soto's forces, de la Vega described two similar settlement patterns between Ocali Town and Apalachee. His place names or chiefly sobriquets may be out of the temporal order of march of de Soto's army. Nonetheless, the descriptions are consistent with the two already summarized. Probably they apply to the Yustega chiefdom, the westernmost of the Timucuan-speaking polities. De Soto marched into the border town de la Vega called *Ochile* at dawn, with trumpets, fifes, and drums playing to frighten the inhabitants. The Spaniards captured many curious natives who came out to find out the cause of what was to them a strange racket. Once the Spaniards occupied the border town, they discovered that beyond it lay a "beautiful valley" with houses scattered in clusters of four and five.[31]

Again, when de Soto's forces marched into what de la Vega called

Osachile, they encountered scattered settlements "not arranged as villages." These were spread out over four leagues from the beginning of fields of maize, beans, and squash to Osachile Town.[32] The description clearly implies that the inhabited zone near the principal or central town was cultivated. If the inhabited area was as broad as it was long by the trail the Spaniards traveled, it contained from 64 to 100 square miles, or from 40,960 to 64,000 acres. A conservative estimate would allow two-mile leagues, or eight miles traversed by the expedition, and two miles visible on each side of the trail, for a total of 32 square miles, or 20,480 acres. That surface would grow 8,806,400 kg of maize kernels at the Yucatecan low-yield rate, or enough to feed 33,871 people for a year at 260 kg per person, providing more than 2,500 maize calories daily.

The people of both the Apalachee and western Timucuan chiefdoms seem to have lived in a similar pattern of settlement within extensively and intensively cultivated zones. In each polity, one central town functioned as political capital, with numerous outlying smaller settlements or, most likely, extended family farmsteads. These settlements occupied core habitation zones planted to food crops. Such plantings took up a solid expanse of more than 10,000 acres at one Apalachee town, but probably crops grew in scattered fields in the other Timucuan polities. Sixteenth-century chronicles described, in any event, maize planted on a scale more than sufficient to sustain thousands of residents of each polity on roasting ears and dried kernels. Timucuan society seems to have been based upon a relatively extensive maize horticulture that provided an abundance of carbohydrate to augment wild fish and game and plant foods.

The chroniclers' clues regarding maize cultivation and population in the Ocali chiefdom may be employed to illustrate the potential of Timucuan maize production. Figure 1 shows a hypothetical distribution of 196 square miles of fields around Ocali Town as they might have been seen by de Soto's marauders in 1539. No field would have been located more than seven miles from the edge of the presumably one-mile-square town. The 125,440-acre zone could theoretically support more than 200,000 persons—an unlikely number, as I have already noted. For purposes of illustration, the 600 houses reported at Ocali in 1539 may be assumed to have sheltered an average of 100 persons. That figure implies a chiefdom population of 60,000 if one further assumes that every family in the policy had sleeping quarters in Ocali Town. In other words, the houses scattered about the fields are assumed to have been field houses in which people lived during the horticultural season

Figure 1.

**A MODEL OF 196 SQUARE MILES
OF FIELDS AT OCALI IN 1539**

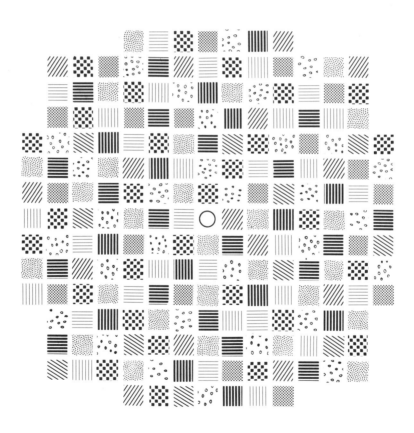

to reduce the time spent walking or canoeing between town and fields. A population of 60,000 consuming an average 260 kg of maize annually would require 15,600,000 kg.

The 125,440 acres available for maize production could produce far more than 15,600,000 kg annually. In fact, one-third of the area, or 41,813 acres, could grow 15,600,000 kg of maize by yielding only 373 kg per acre from a single planting. That estimate does not even take into account the food value of squash and beans interplanted with Timucuan maize. Yet the Timucuans could have fallowed two acres for every one planted and could still have managed to sustain 60,000 people on a relatively low yield. The documented intensity of Timucuan cultivation with double-cropping implies that yields actually were greater than 373 kg of maize per acre per year. Consequently, 60,000 Ocalans could have been fed from considerably fewer than 41,813 acres planted each year. Moreover, if adults constituted half the population (one in equilibrium), 30,000 persons or fewer (allowing for elders who did not garden) would have had to cultivate those 41,813 acres. There would have been at least 2.79 acres for each of 15,000 man-woman teams.

The logic of numbers indicates additional possibilities. If 60,000 Ocalans followed a four-year fallow cycle, then they could have cultivated 31,360 acres each year. They would have needed to achieve an average harvest of 497.5 kg of maize per acre in order to consume 260 kg apiece. That figure again ignores the squash and bean contribution to nutrition. The average would have required each of some 15,000 man-woman teams to plant and weed 2.09 acres.

If 60,000 Ocalans followed a five-year fallow cycle, then they could have cultivated 25,088 acres anew each year. They would have needed to achieve an average harvest of 626 kg of maize per acre so as to eat 260 kg per person. Such a yield is less than the 655 kg modern Mayan swidden farmers achieve. In all likelihood, therefore, prehistoric Timucuan intensive horticulturalists obtained higher yields. Each of some 15,000 man-woman gardening pairs would have had to tend but one and two-thirds acres under such a system to produce 260 kg per person in the population.

If 60,000 Ocalans followed a six-year fallow cycle, then they could have cultivated anew 20,907 acres each spring. They would have had to pick 746 kg of maize per acre in order to consume 260 kg apiece and to provide nonworkers with an equal amount. Each of the perhaps 15,000 man-woman gardening teams would have cared for only 1.4 acres of newly planted maize, beans, and squash if such were the level of Timucuan productivity. Double-cropping may have been necessary in order to enjoy roasting ears and still to harvest 746 kg of maize from slightly less than an acre and a half during each summer growing season. Some such pattern of maize cultivation appears to fit the known facts, few as they are, about Ocalan and Timucuan horticulture, with one additional proviso. Documentary descriptions of Timucuan society suggest that extended families constituted the fundamental social units, so that the man-woman or nuclear family work unit used in the examples immediately above is a purely arbitrary convention. Figure 2 shows a hypothetical model of an 18-acre extended-family farmstead—assuming that families held their fields all in the same place—supporting eight individuals. The labor force could have consisted of from two to four adults. Most likely fields actually were not held in solid blocks.

The food production on the fallowed fields would have contributed very significantly to Timucuan diet. Burning the fields encouraged fallowed areas to grow up in blackberries, blueberries, and forbs that attracted and supported dense populations of deer, rabbits, quail, doves, and other game. Hunting in the fallow fields was thus both productive and relatively easy. At the same time, Timucuans picked at least some of the berries and small fruits before the deer and other game animals and birds ate them. Significantly, if the fallowed fields did not burn each January, when the Timucuans set fire to their cultivated fields, cutting the brushy growth and burning every fifth or sixth year would have been necessary to prevent the fields from reverting to forest. To point out that the Ocali Timucuans could have grown their food crops in such a pattern is not to assert that they did so. Fallowing appears to be a reasonable hypothesis but one for which there is little direct evidence. This is a matter to which we shall return in a later essay.

NOTES

1. Mosher, *Getting Agriculture Moving*, 1966, p. 52.

2. Spellman, "Agriculture," 1948, p. 37.

3. Ehrmann, "Timucua Indians," 1940, p. 174; Ribaut, *Whole & True Discouerye*, 1563, p. 74, for stone, oyster, and mussel shell hoes.

4. Hulton, ed., *Work of Le Moyne de Morgues*, 1977, p. 210 (comment by William C. Sturtevant).

5. Lorant, ed., *New World*, 1946, p. 77.

6. Mosher, *Getting Agriculture Moving*, 1966, p. 52.

7. Ehrmann, "Timucua Indians," 1940, p. 174; Spellman, "Agriculture," 1948, p. 38. Spellman's interpretation is suspect, inasmuch as he appears not to have recognized wheat as a Spanish introduction.

8. Roberts, *Account*, 1763 (1976), B-3.

Figure 2.

**A MODEL OF 18 ACRES OF MAIZE-BEAN-SQUASH AND
FALLOW FIELDS IN A SIX YEAR CYCLE OF AN OCALI
EXTENDED FAMILY OF EIGHT PERSONS IN 1539**

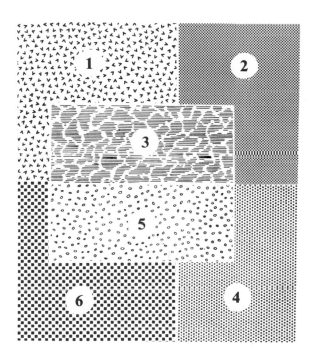

Legend

1 – 3 acres planted to maize-beans-squash interplanted in hills

2 – 3 acres of old hills fallowed, growing forbs

3 – 3 acres fallowed with yielding berries

4 – 3 acres fallowed with berries and bushes

5 – 3 acres fallowed with berries and shrubs

6 – 3 acres fallowed with tree growth beginning

9. Murphy and Hudson, "On the Problem," 1968, p. 28.

10. Wenhold, trans., *17th Century Letter*, 1936, p. 13.

11. Laudonnière, *Three Voyages*, 1975, p. 15.

12. Ibid., 130.

13. Ibid., 131.

14. Ibid., 135–37.

15. Ibid., 139–40.

16. Bandelier, trans., *Journey*, 1904 (1922), 19; Vedia, ed., *Historiadores*, 1858, p. 520; Hedrick and Riley, eds. and trans., *Journey*, 1974, p. 11.

17. De Soto, "letter," p. 8; French, comp., *Historical Collections*, 1850, pt. II, p. 91. The date comes from Bourne, ed., *Narratives*, 1904, vol. II, p. 60.

18. Robertson, trans., *True Relation*, 1933, vol. II, pp. 54–55; Bourne, ed., *Narratives*, 1904, vol. II, p. 68 (between July 26 and August 10); Schell, *De Soto*, 1966, pp. 61–63.

19. Bourne, ed., *Narratives*, 1904, vol. II, p. 69.

20. Lorant, ed., *New World*, 1946, p. 77.

21. Vedia, ed., *Historiadores*, 1858, p. 520.

22. Arthur Barlowe, 1584, in Lorant, ed., *New World*, 1946, p. 129. Thomas Hariot "heard" that the natives double-cropped the same field "in some places" (p. 246).

23. Murphy and Hudson, "On the Problem," 1968, p. 28.

24. Varner and Varner, trans., *Florida*, 1962, p. 182.

25. Erasmus, "Monument Building," 1965, p. 295.

26. Redfield and Villa Rojas, *Chan Kom*, 1934 (1962), 52, reported lowest yield as 0.5 carga per mecate and third-year plantings as yielding less than those the second year. On the other hand, Chan Kom villagers interplanted few beans that would help to sustain yields by fixing nitrogen in the soil.

27. Watt, Merrill, et al., *Composition of Foods*, 1950, p. 24. Unbolted whole ground dry white or yellow cornmeal has 355 calories per 100 g, from 73.7 g of carbohydrates.

28. Schell, *De Soto*, 1966, p. 61; Varner and Varner, trans., *Florida*, 1962, p. 121.

29. Varner and Varner, trans., *Florida*, 1962, p. 122.

30. Orians and Pearson, "On the Theory," 1979, p. 156.

31. Varner and Varner, trans., *Florida*, 1962, pp. 129–30.

32. Ibid., 169.

ESSAY FOUR

Timucuan Population in the 1560s

by Henry F. Dobyns and
William R. Swagerty

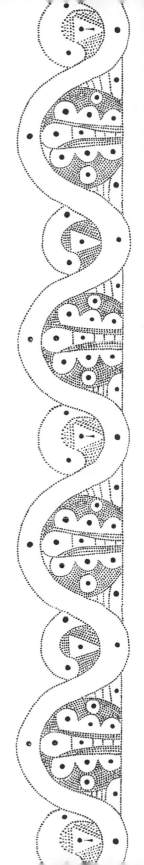

The estimates of the pre-1520 Native American population of Florida presented in earlier essays are based upon a theory as well as upon a number of facts. The theory is that human populations increase to the limits of the natural food resources available to them at any specific technological level. Where Native American groups are concerned, actuality may not always have fit that theory. Martin A. Baumhoff concluded in his analysis of determinants of California populations that certain peoples did not increase to the sustaining capacity of their natural resources. He hypothesized that slavery may have kept the Yurok population below its theoretical ecological maximum.[1] It would be, therefore, scientifically helpful to be able to cross-check the population estimates presented in earlier essays against historical descriptions of the peoples of Florida. We will now do so.

Various historic accounts deal with the population of the Timucuan-speaking peoples during one decade of the sixteenth century. We have chosen the Timucuan speakers for analysis because Europeans from three competing nations visited at least parts of Timucuan territory and left analytically useful written descriptions of settlements and social structure. The decade of the 1560s is the earliest period during which multiple descriptions of Timucuan-speaking peoples were written. That decade is as close in time to A.D. 1520 as one can come and still find documentary records useful for meaningful demographic analysis of Florida Native Americans.

TWENTIETH-CENTURY ESTIMATES

Modern scholars have made a number of statements about the numbers of Timucuan-speaking Native Americans. The estimates of the population of the Timucuan-speaking peoples who once inhabited most of Florida that have been published in the twentieth century have been conflicting (see table 20). Historians and anthropologists have arrived at different estimates of Timucuan population, partly because they have estimated that population at different or at poorly specified times. Curiously, historians seem to have been least precise about chronology. The author of the standard state history postulated that the "white man" found 14,300 Timucuans in Florida, without specifying when that discovery occurred.[2] Another historian who has published many papers about Florida's Native Americans specified no time period during which his estimated 5,000 to 8,000 eastern Timucuans might have lived.[3]

Anthropologists seem to have been somewhat more precise about the chronology of their estimates. James Mooney, who sparked twentieth-century interest in Native American population, concluded that there were about 13,000 Timucuan-speakers in A.D. 1650.[4] Archaeologist Kathleen Deagan estimated that Timucuan-speakers numbered from 15,000 to 20,000 persons in late prehistoric times.[5] These

TABLE 20

Published Twentieth-Century Estimates of
Timucuan-Speaking Native American Population

Author and Date	Population	Estimate(s)	Chronology
James Mooney (1928)	Timucua, etc.	8,000	circa 1650
	Potano	3,000	
	Yustega	1,000	
	Tocobaga	2,000	
	total	13,000	
John R. Swanton (1946)	total	13,000	circa 1650[a]
	total	10,000[b]	
John M. Goggin (1952)	total	5,000–8,000	
Charlton W. Tebeau (1971)	total	14,300 including 1,300 Tocobaga	found by the white man
James W. Covington (1975)	eastern Timucuans	5,000–8,000	circa 1560 (derived from Goggin?)
Kathleen A. Deagan (1978)	eastern Timucuans	15,000–20,000	circa 1568

[a]Restatement of Mooney.

[b]Swanton's own estimate of population at an unspecified date.

Note: Works in which the estimates were published appear in the bibliography.

numbers with their varied temporal referents do not seem to have satisfactorily pinpointed actual Timucuan numbers.

A shortcoming that is not immediately apparent mars all the estimates of Timucuan population that have been made to date. This failing relates to the inaccurate and incomplete definition of the Timucuan-speaking polities. Consequently, it is necessary initially to specify the number of Timucuan-speaking chiefdoms extant at mid-sixteenth century and earlier and to indicate at least approximately their geographic distribution.

As nearly all twentieth-century studies of Florida's Native Americans indicate, Spanish, French, and English explorers wrote most of what is known about the Timucuan-speaking peoples during the short period 1562 – 1568. We turn, therefore, to those sources to reestimate Timucuan numbers during the six-year time span. First, though, we address the problem of defining the actual number of Timucuan-speaking polities and their geographic distribution.

NOTES

1. Baumhoff, *Ecological Determinants*, 1963, p. 188.
2. Tebeau, *History*, 1971, p. 16.
3. Covington, "Relations," 1975, p. 12, included Potano, Saturiwa, Utina, and Agua Dulce in the eastern division. His figures appear to derive from the 5,000 to 8,000 Timucuan-speakers "in the sixteenth century" estimated by archaeologist Goggin, *Space and Time Perspective*, 1952, p. 29.
4. Mooney, *Aboriginal Population*, 1928, p. 8. John R. Swanton used Mooney's estimates in his *Indians*, 1946, p. 12. Swanton lowered the figure to 10,000 in his own reconstruction (map 3).
5. Deagan, "Cultures," 1978, p. 94.

Territorial Distribution of Chiefdoms

During recent decades, archaeological research has in general confirmed that some cultural differences existed between several of the Timucuan-speaking chiefdoms whose principal leaders were identified by respect titles, which Europeans treated as personal names in documents written in the 1562–1568 period. We begin, therefore, by listing the Timucuan-speaking sociopolitical entities whose early historic territories, shown on map 2, have been defined from archaeological as well as documentary evidence.

YUSTEGA

The western Timucua included, according to Jerald T. Milanich, the Yustega, Ocali, Utina, Potano, and Tocobaga chiefdoms. The Yustega were located in contemporary Madison and northern Taylor counties in Florida, between the Aucilla River frontier, with the Apalachee people on the west and the Withlacoochee-Suwannee rivers to the east.[1] Both the Narváez expedition in 1528 and the de Soto expedition in 1539 traveled through Yustega territory. The de Soto expedition chronicles relate interethnic conflicts that almost surely involved Yustegans. The chiefdom came to be identified by some approximation of "Yustega" in the 1560s. Le Moyne correctly mapped *Oustaca* between the Apalachee and Saturiwa and Utina, although he placed the creek system that the French Hugeunots used to reach the Yustega so that it appears to flow into the St. Johns from the northwest instead of from the west.[2] Le Moyne wrote that the enterprising La Roche Ferrière returned to the French fort from a sojourn among the Utina with the news that the latter had obtained all of their precious metals in wars with three Headchiefs: Potanou, Onatheaqua, and Oustaca.[3] Thus the title of a Headchief apparently became fixed on his polity, and few Europeans would forget about a chiefdom that possessed gold or silver.

UTINA

Archaeological evidence indicated that the Utina lived in an area from the Santa Fé River north into present south Georgia as far as

Map 2.

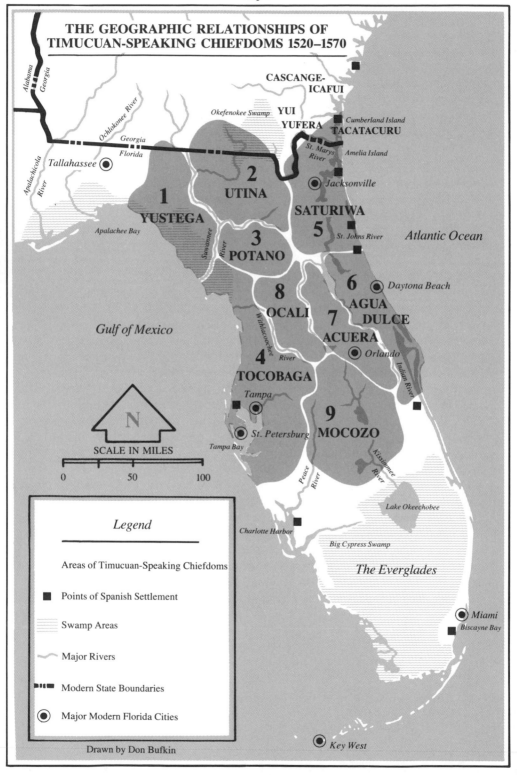

THE GEOGRAPHIC RELATIONSHIPS OF
TIMUCUAN-SPEAKING CHIEFDOMS 1520–1570

Alabama
Georgia

Ochlokonee River

Okefenokee Swamp

CASCANGE-
ICAFUI

YUI
YUFERA

Cumberland Island

TACATACURU

St. Marys
River

Amelia Island

Georgia
Florida

Apalachicola
River

Tallahassee ◉

Jacksonville ◉

2
UTINA

1
YUSTEGA

SATURIWA

Apalachee Bay

5
St. Johns River

Atlantic Ocean

3
POTANO

Suwannee River

8
OCALI

6
AGUA
DULCE

Daytona Beach ◉

7
ACUERA

Gulf of Mexico

Withlacoochee River

Orlando ◉

Indian River

4
TOCOBAGA

Tampa ◉

N

SCALE IN MILES

St. Petersburg ◉

Tampa Bay

9
MOCOZO

Kissimmee River

0   50   100

Peace River

Lake Okeechobee

Charlotte Harbor

Big Cypress Swamp

The Everglades

Legend

Areas of Timucuan-Speaking Chiefdoms

■ Points of Spanish Settlement

Swamp Areas

Major Rivers

Modern State Boundaries

◉ Major Modern Florida Cities

Miami ◉
Biscayne Bay

◉ Key West

Drawn by Don Bufkin

Valdosta. They ranged from the Suwannee River east to the edge of the coastal flatlands at the St. Johns River. Utina territory encompassed modern Hamilton, Suwannee, Columbia, Baker, Union, Bradford, and western Clay and Duval counties in Florida, plus Echols and southern Clinch counties in Georgia.[4] The Utina entered written history in the chronicles of the de Soto expedition, which may have passed through the capital town. In any event, the chronicles mentioned a settlement called variously Uri Utina, Utina Ma, or Utina Macharra.[5] In 1564 – 1565 René Laudonnière attempted to gain access to salvaged precious metals by forming an alliance between his French Huguenots and the Utina chiefdom.[6]

POTANO

The Potano people lived in modern Alachua County, Florida.[7] Potano archaeological remains are found from the Santa Fé River on the north to modern Ocala on the south and from Lake Santa Fé westward to the post-1925 boundary of Alachua County.[8] The Potano entered written history in 1539 in the chronicles of the de Soto expedition. The chroniclers recorded that de Soto marched through Potano Town between Ocali and Utina.[9]

Europeans continued to refer to this chiefdom by the same name. Le Moyne and de Bry mapped the "Potanou" upstream from the Saturiwa on a western tributary of St. Johns River.[10] Apparently the French Huguenots ascended Black Creek to reach Potano territory. French mercenaries working for the Holata Utina helped his warriors defeat a Potano army.[11] In the seventeenth century, Franciscan missionaries established Christian mission settlements of Potano during their advance westward from St. Augustine to the Apalachee people.[12] Thus the surviving Potano lay in the path of military destruction inflicted by Carolinian troops at the beginning of the eighteenth century.

TOCOBAGA

The historic Tocobaga people are known to archaeologists for having produced the physical remains of the "Safety Harbor Culture." They lived from the mouth of the Aucilla River south along the Gulf, or west, coast of the peninsula to a point south of Tampa Bay.[13] The area differs environmentally from the rest of Florida. Its saline estuaries form one of the most productive nurseries in the world for many varieties of marine life. The Tocobaga people clearly were oriented toward the estuaries and/or the open waters of the Gulf of Mexico. They were definitely not an inland people. Their very habitat indicates that the Tocobaga relied very extensively upon fish, marine mammals, turtles, and saltwater game birds for their subsistence.

In 1566, Calusa guides led Pedro Menéndez de Avilés to a major Tocobaga town on Tampa Bay.[14] After an initial burst of interest, Spanish Colonial goals and activities in Florida typically relegated To-cobaga country to a marginal role. Thus the Tocobaga escaped concentration into Christian mission settlements. In fact, the Tocobaga paddled their cypress watercraft upstream to harass some missions during the first decade of the seventeenth century. Consequently the governor of Spanish Colonial Florida in 1610 or 1611 sent troops against the Tocobaga.[15] By the 1670s, if not before, on the other hand, Tocobaga were integrated into the Colonial economy. Some worked as lightermen in the Havana-Suwannee river trade of meat, hides, and tallow.[16]

CASCANGE-ICAFUI

The main archaeological authority on the eastern Timucua reported that they consisted of five to seven tribes or chiefdoms. The Cascange-Icafui, sometimes considered separate groups, lived on the mainland of contemporary Georgia northwest of Cumberland Island, according to Kathleen Deagan. They ranged apparently from the Satilla River northward to a zone opposite Jekyll Island.[17] Theirs was not as large a territory as those of the chiefdoms previously mentioned.

YUFERA, YUI, AND IBA

The Yufera tribe lived farther west than the Cascange, apparently opposite Cumberland Island. To the west of the Yufera ranged the Yui and Iba, holding the Timucuan-speaking border south and west of the Satilla River and north of St. Mary's River. The Okefenokee Swamp formed the western border of Yui territory. A Tacatacuru group inhabited Cumberland Island off the coast.[18] The relatively small size of the territories of these northernmost eastern Timucuan-speaking groups is apparent from map 2. To the south lived more populous peoples.

SATURIWA

The Saturiwan chiefdom bore the brunt of European colonization between 1562 and 1568, so that in several respects it is the best known of the Timucuan-speaking polities. Deagan concluded that settlements of this group extended from St. Mary's River on the north to south of Spanish St. Augustine, including the lower course of the St. Johns River.[19]

The Tacatacuru Question

In attempting to estimate the number of Timucuan-speakers living in the 1560s, we will attempt to arrive at reasonable numbers for each polity so as to reach a grand total for the language group. Thus the accuracy of our estimate depends on correct identification of the polities extant in the 1560s. Our reading of the historic sources leads us to question whether the residents of Cumberland Island actually constituted an independent chiefdom. That is the "Tacatacuru Question."

The insular Cumberland Island territory of the Tacatacuru is the smallest of that of any of the Timucuan-speaking polities recognized by Deagan. The Tacatacuru exploited rich estuaries and marshes, as did the residents of Saturiba Town and Alicamani Town on the lower St. Johns River. The Tacatacuru forcibly expelled a Jesuit missionary in the 1560s, but Franciscans arrived there in 1587. In 1588, Spaniards described Cumberland Island (called San Pedro) as "thickly populated by the Indians.[20] Thereafter information about mission settlements is available; at least three were established.[21] Don Juan de Santiago had become Headchief of the Saturiwan polity by 1597 and was a staunch Christian.[22] In 1602, a Spanish mission functioned at San Pedro, the principal town, governed by a major chief with authority over the maritime towns south to St. Augustine. Also located on the island at that time were Santo Domingo, with a church for 180 Native Americans, and Santa María de Seña, with a church for 112 Christians, each situated one league from San Pedro. The missionary also worked with residents of five more small villages with few converts. These may have been remnants of five additional aboriginal towns.

The mission-period situation implied that at least five aboriginal settlements had existed and possibly more had not survived into Colonial times. On the premise that the marine-estuarine environment was rich in food resources at the St. Johns River mouth, a minimum Tacatacuru population of 7,500 during the 1560s is implied, in ways we will discuss later. If mission-period amalgamation of settlements occurred, the 1560s population would have been even larger.

The political independence of Tacatacuru from the Saturiwan chief-dom seems to us doubtful. Deagan decided that the Tacatacuru were allies of the Saturiwans.[23] As she recognized, Chief Saturiba's authority in 1567 extended to and apparently included the people on Cumberland Island. Gourgues, the leader of a French retaliatory strike against the Spanish colony, identified Chief Tacatacourou among Chief Saturiba's "kinsmen and allies."[24] In this instance, the word "allies" is not to be taken too literally. It meant that the chiefs who assembled to ally them-selves with Gourgues on his vengeance raid on Spanish outposts were town chiefs of the Saturiwan chiefdom. The identification of them, Chief Tacatacourou included, as kinsmen of Saturiba fairly conclusively placed the Cumberland Islanders within the Saturiwan polity in 1567. The date is too close to 1564–1565 for us to suppose that Saturiba had suddenly annexed a populous island. Gourgues simply provided infor-mation about part of Saturiwan territory considerably north of the lower St. Johns River where Spanish, French, and English interest and activity had focused in 1562–1565.

At the end of the sixteenth and beginning of the seventeenth century, the mission town of San Pedro on Cumberland Island had become the residence of the Headchief of the Saturiwan chiefdom, which then included the Tacatacuru and Cascange.[25] The Saturiwans probably shifted the Headchief's residence from Saturiba Town on the St. Johns River to Cumberland Island in 1567 in an effort to move the political capital away from hostile Spanish forces garrisoned at St. Augustine and the nearby San Mateo post. Gonzalo de Villaroel, commander at San Mateo during the first part of 1567, while Pedro Menéndez de Avilés sailed around the peninsula and back and forth to Havana, gave Saturiba abundant cause for migrating to Cumberland Island. Defining the Saturiwans as allies of the recently vanquished French colonists, Villaroel killed some Townchiefs and "subjects" of the Headchief. He captured and had put in chains Townchief Emoloa of the settlement four leagues upriver from Saturiba, Alicamani and one of his sons, two heirs of other town chiefs, and two of "Saturiba's chiefs."

When Menéndez returned to San Mateo from his tour of the Calusa and Tocobaga capitals on the Gulf Coast of Florida, and from a stay on Cuba, he widened the breach.[26] Menéndez summoned Saturiba to a meeting at the "port" which turned out to be a standoff. Saturiba sent representatives to talk to Emoloa, whom the Spaniards landed in chains but kept covered by twenty harquebusiers and two demiculverins loaded with small shot to fire at the chained captives should the Saturi-wans attempt to rescue them. The Headchief recognized his own per-sonal danger and stayed out of range of the Spanish firearms. In the same way, Menéndez stayed aboard ship and refused to go ashore within range of the archers, who were reported planning an ambush.

Faced with stalemate, Menéndez ordered the chained Saturiwan leaders carried back on board his vessels, and he sent a message to Saturiba that Menéndez now considered him an enemy. Menéndez threatened to order Saturiba killed to avenge Christians whom he had "treacherously" slain. The Saturiwan Headchief responded in kind that he considered all Christians—by which he meant Spaniards—his enemies.

After returning to St. Augustine, Menéndez personally led a task force of sixty soldiers on a ten-league overnight march to attack Saturiba. Unable to locate the Headchief, the task force "burned the surrounding villages, and tore up the maize fields" before returning to St. Augustine.[27] Then Menéndez sailed north to Santa Elena, and soon afterward he crossed to Spain. His death there left the colonial enterprise in Florida in considerable disarray. Menéndez and Villaroel seem to have forced Saturiba to transfer his residence from the pre-Colonial capital town on St. Johns River to Cumberland Island.

Later, the Christian mission at San Pedro may have been an attraction for Saturiwans or may have represented a compromise, a means of living at peace with Spaniards. In any event, it may be concluded that the Tacatacuru constituted one portion of the Saturiwan chiefdom, and the Tacatacuru population has therefore been included in the Saturiwan estimate below. In other words, whether there were three or eight towns on Cumberland Island in premission times, they constituted part of the towns Chief Saturiba led in the 1560s.

AGUA DULCE

The "Fresh Water," or Agua Dulce, chiefdom held the territory along the Atlantic Coast of Florida south of the Saturiwans, according to Deagan. At the beginning of the seventeenth century, the Agua Dulce group reportedly extended along the east coast of the peninsula south to Daytona Beach and west to the St. Johns River from about Palatka to Lake Harney.[28] Thus the Fresh Water people held the "middle stretches" of the St. Johns River.[29] By the early seventeenth century, however, some demographic changes may already have resulted in shifts in territories. We consider the people who lived on Mosquito Lagoon[30] to have been part of the Fresh Water chiefdom. In the 1550s, the Fresh Water head chief Oathaqua resided in a town on or near Cape Cañaveral when he suffered a humiliating defeat while escorting a daughter across Mocozo territory.[31] So Agua Dulce territory extended well to the south of Lake Harney, probably to the source of the St. Johns River.

ACUERA

The Acuera apparently lived west of the Agua Dulce people between the Ocklawaha River and the St. Johns River.[32] The Acuera dialect differed from that of the Agua Dulce.[33] Consequently, a sociopolitical distinction between the two groups seems reasonable.

In terms of historic recognition, Fernando de Soto's army marched through the "fertile" province of Acuera in 1539 en route northward from the Calusa frontier to Ocali. The conquistador left Calusa country searching for a Timucuan-speaking chief, a *Paracoxi*. The chronicles indicate that the said Paracoxi led the Timucuan-speaking polity on the Calusa frontier later called Mocozo. The Spaniards marched through his territory to the next Timucuan-speaking chiefdom to the north, the Acuera. Garcilaso de la Vega wrote that Acuera lay twenty leagues north from the Paracoxi's chiefdom.[34] Fernando de Soto was content to encamp at an Acuera maize field, in which every stalk bore three or four ears that the hungry Spaniards ate raw.

According to de la Vega, de Soto's marauders remained in Acuera territory for twenty days, but the haughty Acuera chief's warriors exacted a high toll in lives. Sensitive to Spanish ideals of chivalry because of the stresses of his own role as a Mestizo in Spanish conquest society, the half-Inca author devoted an entire chapter to the Acueran resistance to the Spaniards. Placating Spanish readers, de la Vega entitled the chapter "The insolent reply of the lord of the province of Acuera" to de Soto's demands that he meet the conquistador and cease fighting.[35] De la Vega ably portrayed the Acueran chief favorably in Spanish cultural terms. He wrote that de Soto was "astonished" at the "loftiness of spirit" and the "arrogance" with which Chief Acuera, "a barbarian," extolled his own autonomy and denigrated de Soto as a lackey of his own king. One suspects de la Vega of putting some Inca haughtiness into Chief Acuera's mouth, as did other authors at the time, when he gives two long paragraphs in quotation marks as the chief's message to de Soto. Still, Juan Ortiz, the rescued Spaniard long captive among the Calusa and Mocozo, presumably accurately translated messages brought by Acueran runners. So de la Vega's informants, impressed by the militant message familiar to them, probably remembered the gist, if not the actual wording, of the defiance.

Their memory was no doubt strongly reinforced by the actions of Chief Acuera's warriors. The native chief warned de Soto that his warriors would ambush and waylay Spaniards as long as they remained in his chiefdom. He placed de Soto on notice that his troops had orders to bring him exactly two Christian heads each week.[36] The Acueran warriors exceeded their quota, according to de la Vega. He wrote that the Acuera forces skillfully ambushed every Spaniard who strayed as little as 100 yards from camp. They carried away fourteen Spanish heads during the twenty days de Soto's marauders spent in their territory.[37] Clearly the Acuera chiefdom was powerful, and presumably it was populous.

The same polity name continued in use among Florida's Native Americans in the 1560s, so it was learned by European newcomers. Townchief Molono referred to "Acquera" in 1564.[38]

OCALI

Little has yet been discovered about the prehistoric antecedents of the Ocali chiefdom. Archaeologist Milanich considers artifacts from the region near modern Ocala to belong to the same cultural tradition as those used by the Potano.[39] Crucial information about the Ocali people comes, therefore, from the sixteenth-century documentary record of European explorations in Florida.

The chronicles of the de Soto expedition, as we have already indicated, provide a rather detailed description of at least that portion of the Ocali chiefdom that de Soto crossed in 1539. The Spanish force had to traverse uninhabited, parklike—which is to say frequently burned-over—savannah as well as swamps between Mocozo territory and the Ocali heartland. The conquistador found going difficult in some places but rode along excellent trails or "roads" in others. On July 26 or 27, de Soto rode into Uqueten, the Ocali border town on the southern frontier.[40] Clues in the chronicles of the expedition have been analyzed in the chapter on Timucuan maize cultivation and suggest that residents of Ocali had a very large productive capacity.

A paucity of archaeological research on the Ocali folk makes difficult an accurate definition of their territory. Colonial interests kept Spanish attention on other Timucuan-speakers, so that there is little documentary notice of the Ocalans in the 1560s and later. Fairly clearly, Ocali land lay south of the Potano. It was east of the Tocobaga and north of the Mocozo; the eastern frontier seems less sure. Milanich interpreted archaeological remains as indicating that the Ocali people descended from a prehistoric St. Johns culture. He thought that the Ocali moved inland from the St. Johns River seasonally.[41] On the other hand, Deagan concluded that the Acuera people "probably" lived between the Ocklawaha and St. Johns rivers.[42] If they did, then the Ocali could not have moved in a pattern of seasonal transhumance to the St. Johns River without crossing Acuera territory. We have already referred to de la Vega's reports of Acueran military effectiveness; unless the Acuera were allied with the Ocali, they seem unlikely to have permitted the latter peaceful access to their lands. We follow Deagan in assuming that the Ocklawaha River constituted the eastern boundary of Ocali territory. De Soto chronicle references to Ocali and Acuera become much less confusing when interpreted as referring to different contingents of marauders who were simultaneously in Ocali and Acuera territory on opposite sides of the Ocklawaha River.

Probably the Ocali could reach the St. Johns River by canoe from the northeastern portion of their country via the western tributaries of the lower Ocklawaha River. On the other hand, the reported size of Ocali Town in 1539 was thrice that of any other Timucuan-speaking principal town described by de Soto expeditionary chronicles. As the earlier chapter on maize productivity suggests, the Ocali appear to have been intensive horticulturalists. Consequently, it seems doubtful that the Ocali people were significantly transhumant. Certainly hunters ranged after big game animals, and foraging parties traveled into the savannahs and swamps surrounding the core of cultivated terrain. Such subsistence activities did not make the Ocali less sedentary. The permanent fish traps on the St. Johns, which may have included Ocali structures, yielded protein important in the diet.[43]

MOCOZO

At this point in our summary of Timucuan-speaking polities, it is necessary to add to the list described by Bullen, Milanich, and Deagan. Despite numerous sixteenth-century references to another, "forgotten" chiefdom, Deagan, Milanich, Bullen, and other experts on the prehistory of Florida's Native Americans appear to have overlooked the Mocozo.[44]

The Narváez expedition traveled too fast through Mocozo territory for the people to make a lasting impression on Alvar Núñez Cabeza de Vaca. Indeed, that expedition's guides may have successfully steered the Spaniards away from Mocozo settlements.[45] In 1539, however, de Soto's marauders interacted a good deal with a young chief whom they called "Mocoso." This chief must have inherited his position, inasmuch as the Spaniards estimated that he was only twenty-six or twenty-seven years old in 1539.[46] Moreover, he had evidently been a chief since he was a teenager, for Mocozo had eight and a half years before given asylum to Juan Ortiz, a Spaniard who escaped from captivity under Hirrihigua, the Calusa Townchief at Ucita on Caloosahatchee Bay or Charlotte Harbor.[47]

The proffered asylum was possibly altruistic treatment of an escaped slave. Just as likely it was Mocozo political defiance of the Calusa. In any event, when Mocozo preserved the life of Juan Ortiz, he afforded that Spanish refugee the opportunity to learn the Mocozo version of the Timucuan language. Consequently, Juan Ortiz became the invaluable and key interpreter for de Soto's marauders in 1539, when Mocozo released Ortiz to his ethnic fellows[48] in a gesture no doubt intended to cement good relationships between the Mocozo and the dangerous Spanish invaders. Appreciative of the good deed that Mocozo had performed for the Spaniards, de Soto invited the young chief to his encampment on the Gulf Coast. Mocozo made the journey, although he did not venture into Calusa territory without "many of his followers."[49]

Two days after Mocozo had called upon the Spaniards, his worried mother arrived. The Spanish officers reassured her that they had no intention of abusing Mocozo as Narváez reportedly had Hirrihigua in 1528—by cutting off his nose and turning war dogs on his mother to eat her.[50] Mocozo spent a week more among de Soto's marauders after his mother returned to their own territory. He reportedly behaved as courteously and cheerfully as though he had been reared among Spaniards.[51] The young chief was, in other words, a very skilled diplomat who had evidently questioned Juan Ortiz extensively and had learned a great deal about Spanish social structure and cultural behaviors.

Not long after Mocozo returned to his residence, de Soto's forces set out inland to seek the "principal town" of Chief "Urribarracuxi"— *Paracoxi*—in the "province" nearest the lands of Chiefs Mocozo and Hirrihigua.[52] Captain Baltasar de Gallegos led the advance contingent of sixty lancers to Mocozo's town.

A local historian concluded that de Soto ascended the Caloosahatchee River.[53] It seems equally possible that the Calusa town of Ucita was located on Charlotte Harbor, rather than on Caloosahatchee Bay, and that Gallegos's contingent rode to Mocozo's town along a "road"[54] that ascended Peace River on the direct trading path between the Calusa and their Fresh Water allies at Cape Cañaveral. Mocozo's understanding of Spanish cultural values stood him in good stead. Gallegos asked Mocozo to provide him with a guide to lead the way to the settlement of the Headchief. Mocozo was able to excuse himself on the grounds that to direct strangers against his brother-in-law could sully his honor and reputation.[55] His appeal was expressed in terms that the Spanish soldiers, meticulous on matters of personal honor,[56] could understand.

Actually, the "highway" that the Spanish advance party had traveled to Mocozo's town continued on to the Headchief's settlement.[57] In other words, both Townchief Mocozo and the Headchief of his polity apparently resided in settlements on the main trading path from Calusa to the Fresh Water chiefdom capital at Cape Cañaveral, over which the Spanish captive René Laudonnière rescued in 1564, had traveled as a courier.[58] At the end of four days, by which time Gallegos and de Soto's advance party had traveled what de la Vega reported as sixteen or seventeen leagues, the Headchief had abandoned his town along with all of the other residents.[59] Thus de la Vega's account of the de Soto expedition seems to indicate that Mocozo was Townchief of the southwesternmost border outpost of the Timucuan-speaking chiefdom adjacent to Calusa territory. The main trading path between the Calusa and Fresh Water chiefdom was a well-marked road or highway that crossed the chiefdom between. That chiefdom's capitol—possibly the *Zamia* flour and date trading center—was also located on the international roadway four days' travel for Spaniards from Mocozo's border town.

The Headchief, Paracoxi, did not return to his capitol as long as de Soto's marauders occupied it. He negotiated with Gallegos through thirty personal representatives, and the expedition's hitherto fairly pacific relations with Florida's native peoples began to sour when Gallegos seized the thirty ambassadors and put them in chains.[60]

The commander of the advance guard informed de Soto of his actions, and the expedition's leader left the Gulf Coast to march to the Headchief's town. Instead of following the well-marked road to Cape Cañaveral, de Soto ascended the Caloosahatchee River to the Calusa maize breadbasket northwest of Lake Okeechobee. From Calusa Guazoco, de Soto turned north, evidently along the same (or nearly the same) route that Narváez had taken in 1528. On July 23, 1539, de Soto advanced through a large swamp searching for a town his scouts had reported. He passed one town that the Gentleman of Elvas called *Acela*.[61] The night of July 24, de Soto's contingent slept at the town of *Tocaste*. It was located on a large lake, according to de Soto's secretary,[62] a body of water that was evidently the Lake Kissimmee of modern terminology or nearby Lake Tohopekalinga. A reported twenty leagues farther north, de Soto crossed into Acuera territory with what had become the advance guard of his forces.[63]

A generation later, during the decade of European contest for dominance over Florida's Native Americans, Diego de Escalante Fontaneda provided one version of a name for this southern chiefdom. He listed Mocoso as an independent kingdom like Tocobaga, Apalachee, and Ocali.[64] In fact, Escalante reported that the people of Apalachee were subjects of the peoples of Ocali and Mocozo.[65] Town Chief Molono told French Huguenots about a "king" named "Moqouso."[66] Jacques Le Moyne as engraved by de Bry provided still another spelling: "Mocossou." It appears on Le Moyne's map of Florida to the south of Oathkaqua, the title of the Headchief of the Fresh Water chiefdom.[67] Apparently the map location is somewhat too far east toward the Atlantic Coast of the peninsula, but it is approximately correct in terms of southward location on the borders of the Ais and Calusa.

A more accurate geographic placement of the Mocozo may be inferred from what a Spaniard rescued from captivity by French Huguenots related about interchiefdom political relationships. The Calusa ruler employed the captive as a courier to Headchief Oathkaqua of the Fresh Water chiefdom. The messenger required four to five days to make the trip between the two rulers, whom he labeled "faithful" allies. Halfway between the two capitols was a large freshwater lake called Sarrope. The inhabitants of a large "island" in it harvested large quantities of dates that they traded, and they conducted an even larger trade in *Zamia* flour.

That single island reportedly produced sufficient *Zamia* flour to feed the inhabitants of the country for fifteen-leagues around, or about thirty-three miles. The islanders sold the flour for what the Spanish captive considered a good price.[68] This island probably consisted of the area between Lake Kissimmee and Lakes Tiger, Rosalie, Pierce, Hatchineha, and Cypress, if it was not the largest island in Lake Kissimmee. The area surrounded by the various bodies of water would have seemed an island to a foot traveler. Such an active trade in a staple foodstuff implies that the "islanders" cultivated the tuberous plant that yielded their commercial flour rather than depending upon a wild plant stock. Native American trade in wild plant products is, of course, not unknown.[69] Yet the fact that a Spanish captive saw the residents of one small area trading starch, dates, and other fruits to neighboring villagers in the 1560s implies that these people actually cultivated *Zamia*, if not true manioc, and carried on some form of successful orchardry with, most likely, *Sabal etonia*. Fairly intensive cultivation would have been necessary in order to achieve on a limited land area in swampy South Florida levels of surplus food production that enabled traders to export dates, fruits, and flour. De Soto's 1539 report of extensive Mocozo maize, bean, and pumpkin cultivation and the ransomed captive's 1564 report of intensive Mocozo *Zamia* and date production together credit the Mocozo with intensive cultivation of two different crop systems at least. Evidently some Mocozo specialized in intensive *Zamia* and date palm cultivation, trading their surplus with other Mocozo specializing in extensive maize, bean, and pumpkin growing. A large and commercially active population is implied by the reports.

The date-and-flour traders were also thought to be the bravest or most belligerent warriors in the region.[70] The rescued captive related that the traders proved their bravery on one occasion by kidnapping a daughter of Chief Oathkaqua who had been betrothed to the Calusa ruler. Chief Oathkaqua escorted his daughter toward Calusa territory "with a large retinue." One may infer that the Fresh Water Headchief in fact mobilized his army to see his daughter through hostile territory to the land of his Calusa ally. Yet the traders ambushed the Fresh Water party, routed Oathkaqua and his warriors, and captured his daughter and her women attendants.[71]

The capital of the Fresh Water Headchief Oathkaqua was on or near Cape Cañaveral, according to the rescued Spanish captive. He should have known; he lived there for eight years prior to his 1564 release. The shortest route between there and the Calusa capitol skirts Lake Kissimmee either to the north or to the south. Thus the scant information from the de Soto expedition's chronicles and the 1560s fits together. The *Zamia* flour and date traders and the most belligerent warriors in South Florida were none other than the Mocozo.

Pedro Menéndez de Avilés's exploration of the St. Johns River in 1566 may have reached to Mocozo territory. At least, Menéndez's biographer claimed that the Adelantado sailed his brigantine upriver for fifty leagues to the lands of a chief called "Mocoya." Barrientos wrote, on the other hand, that this chief's power extended along the coast around St. Augustine and San Mateo and that he was allied with Saturiba.[72] Menéndez had his sailors break through a row of stakes that the natives had driven into the riverbed to try to block his passage. Soon after, the former captive among the Ais advised the Adelantado to retreat because Mocoya's country was "thick with Indians." The guide mistakenly reported that the stream emptied into Lake Maymi (Okeechobee). After ascending a final seven or eight leagues, Menéndez talked through an interpreter with a Townchief named Carabay. The latter said that Headchief Mocoya had sent him to warn Menéndez not to continue upstream.[73] Thereafter, Colonial interests turned to other Timucuan-speaking peoples.

It is quite possible that the Mocoya whom Menéndez sought was Headchief of the Acuera chiefdom and that the Adelantado did not penetrate into Mocozo country. The St. Johns River course is today considered to run for 273 miles.[74] If Menéndez accurately estimated leagues and used a league of 3.2 miles, the fifty leagues he reportedly sailed would have been approximately 160 miles, placing him about 100 miles north of the headwaters and short of Mocozo land, indicating that Mocoya was Headchief of either the Acuera or the Fresh Water chiefdom. It does not seem likely that Mocoya was leader of the coastal polity, inasmuch as French and Spanish authors alike referred to that personage as Oathkaqua.

The truth of the matter is that the Spaniards, like the English and French during the 1560s, depended on ships to move around Florida. They sailed with ease along the coasts, and Menéndez and others sailed brigantines up and down the broad St. Johns River. They easily contacted the Utina, whose easternmost settlements were on eastern tributaries of the St. Johns. Later the Spaniards pushed their missions across Potano territory along an overland trail. No one truly penetrated to the real inland empire of Mocozo, however, after de Soto's marauders passed through in 1539! The Mocozo were not forgotten by Spaniards. Europeans simply never really found out much about the belligerent warriors of south Timucualand.

CONCLUSIONS

These pages have laid considerable groundwork for an estimate of the number of Timucuan-speakers alive in the 1560s. Map 2 of chiefdom territories summarizes our interpretation of pertinent archaeological and documentary evidence. Future research on late prehistoric archaeological remains may clarify the precise locations of boundaries between several Timucuan-speaking peoples whom Europeans encountered in the sixteenth century. Meanwhile, the chiefdom territories we have been able to map suggest some intriguing questions.

A.L. Kroeber generalized that a Native American tribe living along a river uses resources of the upland environment on both sides of the stream. Kroeber based that conjecture on his studies of the Mojave tribe which inhabited a broad valley on both banks of the lower Colorado River in the arid Sonoran Desert.[75] The topography of the region is mountainous, and the Mojave people unquestionably did exploit natural resources from the river up to the crest of the mountains both east and west of their valley.[76]

The topography of Florida is much flatter than the Basin and Range Province where the Mojave live. No point on the peninsula rises more than 325 feet above sea level and none in the state higher than 345 feet.[77] In this environment, in which lakes and rivers constitute prominent features of the natural landscape, the chiefdom territories as we have mapped them indicate that Kroeber's generalization does not apply to the Timucuan-speaking peoples. In fact, major rivers appear to have served in many cases as international borders between Timucuan-speaking polities.

The western frontier of Yustega territory was reportedly the Aucilla River, and its eastern border was the Suwannee River and one of its major tributaries. Although we hypothesize that the Yustega ranged to the Gulf of Mexico for seafood, Bullen claimed that the prehistoric Tocobaga ranged to the Aucilla River along the coast.[78] If the Tocobaga held the coast, then small streams or coastal marshes divided Yustegan from Tocobagan country.

The western frontier of Utina territory was, of course, the Yustegan eastern Suwannee River border. The Santa Fé River system apparently delineated the southern Utina border with the Potano. On the northeast, the Okefenokee Swamp and upper St. Mary's River separated the Utina from the Yui. We chose to depict the southeastern Utina frontier on a low divide between the Santa Fé and St. Johns river systems. Our decision may be an error. Conceivably the Utina ranged to the west bank of St. Johns River. Given the known hostility between Utina and Saturiwa, however, it seems probable that Utina towns would not have been very safe located on tributaries of the St. Johns River within easy reach of Saturiwan war canoes.

The northern Potano frontier followed the Santa Fé River, just as the Suwannee River to the west separated Potano from Tocobaga. We may have placed the Potano eastern frontier too far east. If water formed this border, the Potano evidently stopped at the Lochloosa creek-lake system. Apparently no major stream demarcated the southern Potano frontier. The coastal swamps of the Suwannee and Waccasassa rivers appear to have been Tocobaga country, however, with the Potano ranging on drier inland terrain.

The Tocobaga appear to have culturally specialized in response to the Gulf Coast environment. They seem to have exploited coastal marshes that other Timucuan-speakers did not attempt to occupy. Swamp margins marked much of the Tocobagan frontier, therefore, with the upper Withlacoochee River apparently forming part of the Tocobaga-Ocali border. If the Tocobaga extended north only to Tarpon Springs,[79] then the Anclote River may have marked their northern frontier. Toward the south and southeast, low drainage divides may have constituted the Tocobagan frontier with the Mocozo and Calusa. We assume that the Tocobaga could dominate all of the littoral reached by short canoe trips from their Tampa Bay heartland.

The Satilla River divided the Cascange-Icafui on the north from the Yufera to the south, according to Deagan. We have less confidence in our mapping of Yufera, Yui, and Iba territory than in that of any other area. In fact, it seems quite possible that the three small groups formed parts of the Saturiwan chiefdom. If they did, the Satilla River formed its northern border, and the Okefenokee Swamp its northwestern frontier. The southwestern and southern frontiers of the Saturiwa appear to have been low drainage divides. Again, we infer that the Saturiwans dominated whatever territory they could reach in their war canoes by proceeding up tributaries of the St. Johns River. That major stream divided the Fresh Water people from the Acuera, according to Deagan. Moreover, the Ocklawaha River appears to have divided the Acuera from the Saturiwa to the north and the Ocali to the west. We infer that the Acuera-Mocozo border was a drainage divide, but this inference is supported by very few data. The western borders of Ocali land appear to have been defined by the coastal marshes of the Waccasassa River and the upper Withlacoochee River. The eastern border seems to have been the Ockloosa River and perhaps Lakes Harris and Apopka. To the north and south, on the other hand, Ocali had upland borders. The Mocozo inland empire boundaries that we have mapped are necessarily speculative. Waterways could have marked the borders of Mocozo territory rather than drainage divides.

Enough rivers, marshes, and lakes appear to have been frontiers between Timucuan-speaking chiefdoms to suggest a cultural pattern. It appears that Timucuan-speakers in many areas visualized socioeconomic and political boundaries that followed major streams and lakes and marshes. Such a notion is the precise opposite of Kroeber's conclusions with respect to the arid Sonoran Desert and California. Moreover, waterways that served as international borders suggest questions about the completeness of ethnographic information in sixteenth-century European documents. Le Moyne painted a scene captioned "How They Declare War." He wrote that a chief who declared war ordered arrows with locks of hair in the nock to be stuck in the ground along "the public ways." Moreover, the artist reported observing this behavior when the Huguenots captured the Holata Utina and escorted him through Utina settlements in order to exact provisions.[80]

Did Le Moyne make a correct inference from behavior that he observed and remembered? Even if he did, what about waterways? Did the Timucuans with common riverine frontiers use some similar technique for declaring riverine war? Were waterways neutral ground, too precious as sources of fish and turtles to be fought over? Were the fish traps that Menéndez threatened to dismantle in the St. Johns River in 1566 all within the territory of one chiefdom? Or did Timucuans perceive a midstream boundary that divided fishing rights?[81]

Effective Calusa use of war canoes against Spanish ships' crews indicates that at least the Tocobaga and Mocozo would have had to possess war canoe fleets in order to protect their settlements against Calusa raids. The apparent frequency of riverine and lacustrine chiefdom frontiers among the Timucuan-speaking peoples suggests that European accounts may have selectively emphasized upland warfare by ignoring riverine conflicts. Management of rivers and lakes may be one of the least understood aspects of Timucuan culture.

The sixteenth-century ranges of the various Timucuan-speaking chiefdoms as we have mapped them also indicate that there is more than one meaningful way in which to classify these groups. John M. Goggin's original classification of eastern, western, southeastern, and southern tribes was most useful in furthering research into the archaeological antecedents of sixteenth-century chiefdoms.[82] Directional terms are not necessarily very meaningful environmentally, however, and an ecological classification indicates clear distinctions between the dominant economic patterns of different chiefdoms.

The Tocobaga can be viewed as the significant "western," or "Gulf Coast," Timucuans, if they indeed spoke Timucuan. They found their environmental niche on the Gulf of Mexico Coast of the peninsula, which is a distinctive habitat. The Cascange-Icafui, Saturiwa, and Fresh Water chiefdoms can be classed as the significant eastern, or "Atlantic Coast," Timucuans. Their Atlantic coast environmental niche, with its St. Johns-River-St.-Mary's-River freshwater eastern margins, constituted another distinctive habitat. Between these ocean littoral chiefdoms lay the "central," or "inland," Timucuans: Yustega (if these people did not in fact range to the Gulf Coast), Utina, Potano, Ocali, Acuera, and Mocozo (we consign Yufera, Yui, and Iba to the Saturiwa chiefdom for the moment).

With this number and geographic distribution of Timucua-speaking chiefdoms defined, it is now possible to estimate their population in the 1560s, which we will do using two kinds of information.

NOTES

1. Milanich, "Western Timucua," 1978, pp. 63–69.
2. Lorant, ed., *New World*, 1946, p. 35.
3. Ibid., 48.
4. Ibid., 69–70. The Utina spoke a distinctive Timucuan dialect (Milanich, "Western Timucua," 1978, p. 61).
5. Schell, *De Soto*, 1966, p. 68; Bourne, ed., *Narratives*, 1904, vol. II, p. 70, has Ranjel's "Utina Mocharra;" translator Robertson (*True Relation*, 1933, vol. II, p. 55) has the Gentleman of Elvas's "Utina Ma."
6. Lorant, ed., *New World*, 1946, pp. 62–65; Laudonnière, *Three Voyages*, 1975, pp. 73–74, 76–77, 90–91.
7. Milanich, "Western Timucua," 1978, pp. 75–81; The Potano spoke a distinct dialect of Timucuan (ibid., 61).
8. Ibid., 35.
9. Schell, *De Soto*, 1966, p. 60; Robertson, trans., *True Relation*, 1933, vol. II, p. 55; Bourne, ed., *Narratives*, 1904, vol. II, p. 70.
10. Lorant, ed., *New World*, 1946, p. 35. The tributary was mapped as flowing from the northwest instead of the west.
11. Ibid., 61; Laudonnière, *Three Voyages*, 1975, p. 91. *Potavou* in some texts is nothing more than a misreading of "n" as "v"—not difficult because of the similarity of the two letters as handwritten by some Frenchmen.
12. Gannon, *Cross*, 1965, p. 52.
13. Bullen, "Tocobaga Indians," 1978, p. 50. This essay is seriously flawed by Bullen's erroneous conclusion that Narváez and de Soto landed on the shores of Tampa Bay. He failed to take into account True's critical analysis of pre-1566 maps showing that modern Tampa Bay simply was not known to the Spaniards. Consequently, Bullen summarized chroniclers' descriptions of the Calusa town of Ucita as though it were a Tocobaga town (53) and treated references to Calusa maize as though Alvar Núñez Cabeza de Vaca had reported Tocobaga maize. He also overlooked evidence that Townchief Mocozo lived in a chiefdom far distant from the Tocobaga (p. 52).
14. Kerrigan, trans., *Pedro Menéndez*, 1965, p. 128. Menéndez carried Headchief Carlos "and his chiefs" on the discovery voyage. The Spanish says "and other of his principal men," so all may not have been Townchiefs (Barrientos, *Vida y Hechos*, 1902, p. 135).
15. Bushnell, "Menéndez Cattle Barony," 1978, p. 416.
16. Ibid., 424.
17. Deagan, "Cultures," 1978, pp. 89–90.
18. Ibid., 90. The Icafui and Yufera spoke distinctive dialects of Timucuan (Milanich, "Western Timucua," 1978, p. 61).
19. Deagan, "Cultures," 1978, p. 90; Covington, "Relations," 1975, p. 12; Goggin, *Space and Time Perspective*, 1952, p. 28.
20. Quinn, ed., *New American World*, 1979, vol. V, p. 63.
21. Deagan, "Cultures," 1978, p. 101, following Geiger, *Biographical Dictionary*, 1940, p. 87. The Timucuan name for the island may have been *Napoyca*.
22. Quinn, ed., *New American World*, 1979, vol. V, p. 80.
23. Deagan, "Cultures," 1978, p. 102.
24. There is a significant difference in meaning between the English transla-

tion cited by Deagan and the original French. "The Fourth Voyage of the Frenchmen into Florida, under the conduct of Captaine Gourgues, in the yeere, 1567," in Hakluyt, *Principal Navigations*, 1904, vol. IX, p. 102, relates that the day after a French trumpeter had contacted "king Satourioua" there arrived "the great king Satourioua, Tacatacourou, Halmacanir, Athore, Harpaha, Melmacapé, Helicopilé, Molloua, and others his kinsmen and allies." The French reads, "le grand roy Satiroun, les roys Tacatacourou, Halianacani, Atoré, Harpaha, Helmacapé, Helicopilé, Monloua et autres; tous parens et alliaz du roy Satiroua." ("La reprinse de la Florida, par le Cappitaine Gourgue," in French, comp., *Historical Collections*, 1875, p. 275). Atoré, or Athore, is identified elsewhere as Saturiba's son, and the French construction means that all of those listed by name were, like Athore, related to Saturiba.

25. Quinn, ed., *New American World*, 1979, vol. V, pp. 80, 85; Deagan, "Cultures," 1978, p. 102, following Geiger, *Franciscan Conquest*, 1937, pp. 147–50. A change in the residence of the Headchief of the chiefdom did not require much structural change in the polity.

26. Kerrigan, trans., *Pedro Menéndez*, 1965, p. 132; Barrientos, *Vida y Hechos*, 1902, p. 139.

27. Kerrigan, trans., *Pedro Menéndez*, 1965, p. 133.

28. Deagan, "Cultures," 1978, p. 90; Goggin, *Space and Time Perspective*, 1952, p. 29. Milanich, "Western Timucua," 1978, p. 60, did not recognize that the Onatheaqua of some sixteenth-century documents were the Fresh Water people. Using only the Timucuan term, Milanich asserted that it occurs only in Laudonnière's and Le Moyne's writings and on the latter's map of Florida. Then Milanich claimed that no such tribe is referred to in north-central Florida in later documents, so he advocated omitting the chiefdom from the list of Timucuan polities. Placing Onatheaqua west of the Potano south of the St. Johns River tributary mistakenly shown flowing from the northwest is perhaps the most serious error on the map of Le Moyne and de Bry (Lorant, ed., *New World*, 1946, p. 35). In its Oathkaqua form, the Headchief's title appears very near the site of the chiefdom capitol on or near Cape Cañaveral. Admittedly, a confusing shift of terminology occurred between the French Huguenots and the Spaniards. The former consistently used Headchiefs' titles for their chiefdoms, so Onatheaqua (or Oathkaqua) is the same kind of label as Saturiwa or Utina. Spaniards in most instances followed the same practice. For some reason, however, Colonial Spaniards dropped Oathkaqua in favor of Agua Dulce. The chiefdom did exist; it was located on the Atlantic coastal littoral of the peninsula.

29. Covington, "Relations," 1975, p. 12.

30. Goggin, *Space and Time Perspective*, 1952, p. 29.

31. Lorant, ed., *New World*, 1946, p. 60; Laudonnière, *Three Voyages*, 1975, p. 112.

32. Deagan, "Cultures," 1978, p. 111.

33. Ibid., 91. Milanich, "Western Timucua," 1978, p. 61.

34. Schell, *De Soto*, 1966, p. 60; Varner and Varner, trans., *Florida*, 1962, p. 116.

35. Ibid., 117.

36. Ibid., 118.

37. Ibid., 120.

38. Laudonnière, *Three Voyages*, 1975, p. 76.

39. Milanich, "Western Timucua," 1978, p. 69.

40. Schell, *De Soto*, 1966, p. 59–62. Ranjel noted Uqueten on the frontier (Bourne, ed., *Narratives*, 1904, vol. II, p. 68). The Gentleman of Elvas telescoped many events into a short passage on the expedition's trip from Tocaste Town among the Mocozo to Cale (Robertson, trans., *True Relation*, 1933, vol. II, p. 52).

41. Milanich, "Western Timucua," 1978, p. 69.

42. Deagan, "Cultures," 1978, p. 111.

43. We infer that permanent fish traps and weirs harvested the rich St. Johns River fishery because Pedro Menéndez de Avilés threatened to destroy "fishways" on his trip up that stream in 1566 (Kerrigan, trans., *Pedro Menéndez*, 1965, p. 118, omitted the verb *derrocar* to have Menéndez threaten "to burn his village, the canoes, and the fishways." Actually, the Spanish "quemar su pueblo y canoas y deRocar las pesquerias" translates "burn the town and canoes and destroy the fish traps" (Barrientos, *Vida y Hechos*, 1902, p. 124). This is another instance of translation that significantly distorts meaning and ethnographic reality. Fish traps and weirs, being under water, could hardly be burned. They could be dismantled, however, or crushed by a Spanish brigantine.

44. Deagan, "Cultures," 1978, pp. 89–112, did not include the Mocozo among the eastern Timucua, although she did discuss the Acuera. Milanich, "Western Timucua," 1978, pp. 59–81, similarly did not include the Mocozo among the western Timucua, going only as far south as Ocali. Actually, the Mocozo and Acuera might be labeled the southern Timucua; perhaps the Ocali chiefdom should also be considered southern Timucuan.

45. Bandelier, trans., *Journey*, 1904 (1922), 19–24.

46. Varner and Varner, trans., *Florida*, 1962, p. 88.

47. Ibid., 73. Schell (*De Soto*, 1966, pp. 34–36) identified Caloosahatchee Bay as de Soto's landing place.

48. Varner and Varner, trans., *Florida*, 1962, pp. 76–77. Milanich ("Western Timucua," 1978, p. 60) claimed that there is no evidence that central Gulf Coast peoples such as the Tocobaga spoke Timucuan. The ability of Juan Ortiz to interpret verbal messages of Mocozo, Acuera, Ocali, Potano, Utina, and Yustega spokesmen is good evidence that he learned Timucuan in Mocozo Town and that all of the chiefdoms listed spoke some version of the Timucuan language.

49. Varner and Varner, trans., *Florida*, 1962, p. 84.

50. Ibid., 68.

51. Ibid., 87.

52. Ibid., 92.

53. Schell, *De Soto*, 1966, pp. 51–57.

54. Varner and Varner, trans., *Florida*, 1962, p. 93. De la Vega wrote that Mocozo came out to receive the Gallegos advance guard on "the road."

55. Ibid., 93.

56. Caro Baroja, "Honour and Shame," 1966, pp. 79–137.

57. Varner and Varner, trans., *Florida*, 1962, p. 94.

58. Laudonnière, *Three Voyages*, 1975, p. 111.

59. Varner and Varner, trans., *Florida*, 1962, p. 95.

60. Roberton, trans., *True Relation*, 1933, vol. II, pp. 50–52. Surviving chronicles leave the impression that Gallegos treated the Mocozo emissaries

with about the same regard for international protocol as was shown by the "students" who forcibly captured and imprisoned U.S. Embassy personnel in Teheran in the fall of 1979.

61. Schell, *De Soto*, 1966, p. 57; Robertson, trans., *True Relation*, 1933, vol. II, p. 52. Ranjel had *Vicela* (Bourne, ed., *Narratives*, 1904, vol. II, p. 65).

62. Schell, *De Soto*, 1966, p. 57. We disagree with Schell's identification of the "large lake" as Lake Okeechobee. We interpret the confusing chronicles as reporting that de Soto had traveled a considerable distance northward from Calusa territory.

63. Schell, *De Soto*, 1966, p. 60; Varner and Varner, trans., *Florida*, 1962, p. 116.

64. B. Smith, trans., *Letter and Memoir*, 1854, p. 19: "Tocobaga, Abalachi, Olagale, and Mogoso, which are separate kingdoms." Also see Quinn, ed. *New American World*, 1979, vol. V, p. 10. French, comp., *Historical Collections*, 1875, p. 255, "Memoir of Hernando d'Escalante Fontanedo on the Country and ancient Indian Tribes of Florida"—"Tocobajo, Abolachi, Olagale and Mogozo which are distinct kingdoms."

65. Quinn, ed., *New American World*, 1979, vol. V, p. 14.

66. Laudonnière, *Three Voyages*, 1975, p. 76.

67. Lorant, ed., *New World*, 1946, p. 35.

68. Laudonnière, *Three Voyages*, 1975, p. 111.

69. Russell, "Pima Indians," 1908, p. 93. Riverine Pima bartered with desert-dwelling Papagos for giant cactus fruit seeds and syrup, prickly pear fruit syrup, dried slabs of roasted agave plant hearts, acorns, wild piquant peppers, etc.

70. "Bravest" (Lorant, ed., *New World*, 1946, p. 58), "most belligerent of all men" (Laudonnière, *Three Voyages*, 1975, p. 111).

71. Lorant, ed., *New World*, 1946, p. 60; Laudonnière, *Three Voyages*, 1975, p. 112.

72. Kerrigan, trans., *Pedro Menéndez*, 1965, p. 117.

73. Ibid., 118.

74. Morris, comp., *Florida Handbook*, 1973, p. 494.

75. Kroeber, *Mohave Indians*, 1974, pp. 31–33.

76. Dobyns, *Hualapai Indians*, 1974, vol. I, pp. 209–50; vol. II, pp. 251–87.

77. Morris, comp., *Florida Handbook*, 1973, pp. 488, 491.

78. Bullen, "Tocobaga Indians," 1978, p. 50.

79. Bullen traced Safety Harbor archaeological remains to the Aucilla but limited historic Tocobaga to a smaller territorial range.

80. Lorant, ed., *New World*, 1946, p. 101.

81. The Northeastern Pai people visualized a "backbone of the river" in midstream of the Colorado River as constituting much of their boundary (Dobyns, *Hualapai Indians*, 1974, vol. II, pp. 288–90). There was no physical boundary in the water; the border was purely symbolic. The river itself was real enough, but the Pai regarded themselves as proprietors of half of the stream as well as of the dry land. The apparent frequency of riverine frontiers between Timucuan chiefdoms raises the question of whether Timucuan-speaking peoples held a similar perception.

82. Goggin, "Introductory Outline," 1953, pp. 4–17; Milanich, "Western Timucua," 1978, p. 60. Because Goggin did not realize that the Mocozo lived south of Tampa Bay on the Calusa frontier, his classification of "tribes" merits correction. The eastern Timucua chiefdoms were the Fresh Water and Saturiwa

(including the Tacatacuru, which Goggin made equal to Saturiwa), with Yui, Icafui, and Yufera in the group. Goggin failed to realize that the Onatheaqua of earlier documents were the Fresh Water, or Agua Dulce, of Colonial sources. The western Timucua chiefdoms were the Yustega and Tocobaga. The central, or Inland, Timucua chiefdoms were the Potano, Utina, Ocali, Acuera, and Mocozo. One might further divide the inland Timucua into a northern Utina and Potano group, regarding Ocali as central and considering Acuera and Mocozo as southern. By 1953, Goggin had correlated archaeological sites only with the Fresh Water, Potano, and Tocobaga, so that correcting his identification of chiefdoms does not alter his coordination of historic with prehistoric societies (Goggin, "Introductory Outline," 1953, p. 14).

SECTION TWO
Warriors and Population

The Colonial contest between France and Spain, with English sailors as very interested spectators, generated sincere European interest in the military prowess of the Timucuan-speaking peoples. As a result, various observers who visited Florida in the 1562–1568 period reported army sizes and other demographic information. The present reestimation of Timucuan numbers rests upon demographic clues in written European records of that decade.

In beginning with reports of the army sizes of Timucuan chiefdoms we follow the lead of Sherburne F. Cook and Lesley Byrd Simpson in *The Population of Central Mexico in the Sixteenth Century*. These authors were analyzing a population trend, which required that they establish the magnitude of the population during the Conquest period. Cook and Simpson treated estimates by conquerors and subsequent chroniclers of the size of Native American armies is one indirect means of approximating total population.[1] Recognizing that military men have been accused of exaggeration, Cook and Simpson pointed out that the two primary authors were eyewitnesses during the Conquest and were responsible fellows. They doubted that Fernando Cortés or Bernal Díaz had any motive for overstating Native American numbers, partly because neither man tended to give more credit than necessary to native allies.[2] The analysis in this chapter rests on similar methodological considerations.

SATURIWA

Surviving reports of the size of Saturiwan chiefdom armies range from a few hundred to perhaps 2,000. Jacques Le Moyne remembered that after the French commander decided to shift his allegiance from the Saturiwan Headchief to the Utina leader, the former approached French Fort Caroline "with twelve or fifteen hundred warriors."[3] That the Saturiwan chiefdom-scale mobilization mustered 1,500 warriors is also suggested by another Frenchman's observation of the Headchief in action. When the Saturiba himself tried to hold Laudonnière to his early promise of military alliance, he held a precampaign ceremony

174

within sight of the French post, together with more than 500 warriors led by ten chiefs.[4] Another European credited the Saturiba with being able to mobilize a force of many thousands.[5] These are raw demographic data from which to estimate the Saturiwan population in 1564.

The principal unknown in converting these estimates of warrior numbers into an estimate of total chiefdom population in the 1560s is the family size at that period. The Timucuan-speaking peoples had evidently been exposed to Old World contagious diseases for some years prior to 1564.[6] Consequently, Saturiwan population was probably declining during the 1560s. If it were barely maintaining itself, each man would have had a wife, and the pair would have had two children.[7] Such a situation would require multiplying the number of warriors by four in order to obtain a first approximation of population. Thus the reported Saturiwan chiefdom warrior figures would yield estimates of 4,800, 6,000, or more than 8,000 people in the families of the mobilized fighters.

Total warrior mobilization, however, must have excluded some adult males who were too old to be counted upon to fight effectively. That there were some very elderly men among the Saturiwans in 1562–1568 is clear from the European accounts.[8] Some of them, at least, would have had living wives, so that the older portion of the Saturiwan population would not be accounted for using a multiple of only four with the warrior strength.

An additional factor was the strength of the berdache institution among the Saturiwans. Although berdaches carried provisions for warriors on the march,[9] European observers presumably did not count them as warriors. Inasmuch as the berdaches assumed a female role, which by 1564 was defined to include nursing sick persons with contagious diseases, they had no wives.[10]

The cumulative total of berdaches, men past the age when they could bear arms and march to battle, plus their wives and the widows, may have been sufficiently great to justify assuming that the Saturiwan family averaged five members. In such a case, 1,200 warriors imply 6,000 total individuals; 1,500 warriors signify 7,500 persons; and more than 2,000 warriors mean more than 10,000 Saturiwans. Significantly, an observer twenty years later claimed that the powerful Saturiwan chiefdom still contained 10,000 inhabitants under a chief the Spaniards knew as Casicola.[11] If the later estimate is nearly correct and the Saturiwans had declined in population during the interval, then our preliminary estimate of the range of Saturiwan population in 1562–1568 is much too low.

YUSTEGA

The French force at Fort Caroline in 1564 – 1565 consisted of an unruly lot of noblemen who considered it far beneath their station in life to lay hand to plow, much less to hoe. Driven by dire physical necessity, they would hunt—a noble pursuit in their value system—and gather shell-fish and collect and process acorns to keep from starving.[12] When Laudonnière alienated the Saturiwan chiefdom's leader by shifting his alliance to the Utina ruler, the French forces still depended upon the Timucua to offer them maize and other provisions in trade. A Saturi-wan boycott diminished the volume of food reaching Fort Caroline, and the soldiers suffered severe hunger. Some of them in effect hired out to the Utina chiefdom as mercenaries.[13] De Groutaut, one member of this group, with a companion ventured farther westward into Yus-tega territory. When he finally returned to Fort Caroline, de Groutaut told Laudonnière that the Yustega could "muster an army of three or four thousand men."[14] This figure constitutes another estimate of army size for the westernmost group of Timucuan-speakers who faced the Apalachee across the Aucilla River frontier.

If de Groutaut's report of Yustega army numbers was as accurate as Le Moyne's report of Saturiwan army numbers, then the westerners were from 50 to 100 percent more populous than the Saturiwans. Allow-ing five persons per warrior, the Yustega numbered from 15,000 to 20,000 persons.

UTINA

When Pedro Menéndez de Avilés explored the St. Johns River by brigantine in 1566, he paid a menacing visit to the Utina chiefdom's ruler. The Spaniard sent a messenger to summon the Holata Utina, who mobilized an escort of 300 archers on very short notice.[15] The circumstances did not allow the Holata Utina time for mobilizing a chiefdom army, so the 300 may have come from his capitol.

Le Moyne drew what he called the Utinan order of march, troops "in regular ranks like an organized army," in contrast to the formation of Saturiwans, who advanced in whatever order they chose. Le Moyne depicted the Holata Utina, or Headchief, in the center of the forma-tion, in a hollow square behind his advance, followed by a rear guard, with masses of warriors marching on the flanks. Lesser chiefs sketched in the foreground block the view of the marching host. Still, the ad-vance as rendered by de Bry appears to consist of from 170 to 200 men, with the rear guard of about equal size. The right and left wings seem to contain at least 150 men each.[16] The lower estimates of the figures represented or implied in the de Bry version of Le Moyne's picture total about 700 men on the march.

The published representation may bear little resemblance to Utinan reality. Yet the apparent total force fits with demographic information Le Moyne recorded about the tightly organized Utinan field behavior. He wrote that the Headchief selected encampments. When he retired for the night, the "quartermasters" posted ten squads of ten men each in a circle around him—a select body of 100 of the bravest warriors. Then they posted ten paces farther out a circle of twenty squads, or 200 men. Then twenty paces farther came a third circle formed of forty squads, or 400 men "and so on."[17] To the point of the comment "and so on," Le Moyne arrived at precisely 700 men plus the war chief. This is an interesting and perhaps significant coincidence between Le Moyne's text and de Bry's engraving. Le Moyne may actually have observed an Utinan army of 700 men, one composed of about half the forces the chiefdom could mobilize.[18] Such a Utinan force could be mobilized relatively swiftly. When Laudonnière kidnapped the Holata Utina in the spring of 1565, the chiefdom raised overnight a force that Laudonnière estimated as 500 or 600 archers.[19]

If one pursues the arithmetical logic of Le Moyne's description of Utinan military organization, a fourth camp circle would consist of a double 80 squads of 10 men each, or 800 men, making an army of 1,500 warriors. That scale of mobilization would coincide with one report of the size of a Saturiwan chiefdom army that visited Fort Caroline. Then a fifth Utinan circle would contain 160 squads of 10 men each, or 1,600 more men, making an army of 3,100 warriors. That would be very close to the lower 3,000 figure de Groutaut reported for the Yustegan army. Le Moyne's account at least implies the fourth and probably a fifth circle for a Utinan chiefdom mobilization of from 1,500 to 3,100 warriors. Inasmuch as the Utinans were hostile to the Yustega on their western flank, to the Potano to the south, and to the Saturiwans and Agua Dulce group on their eastern frontiers, they had to be able to mobilize forces equal in number to those of their enemies in order to survive. The social scale of inimical groups must be approximately equal.[20] The aboriginal battle formation in North America was a half-moon-shaped arrangement of warriors, with each contender attempting to turn both flanks of a numerically inferior enemy force.[21] Whatever changes may have occurred in Timucuan battle tactics by the 1560s, Le Moyne's representation of a battle between armies of the Utinan and Potanoan polities shows the French mercenary gunners fighting, with the Utinan force outflanking the Potano formation. Tactics remained, therefore, traditional.

A major unknown in estimating Utinan military strength is whether this group ever had to defend two frontiers at the same time. Forces of 1,500 to 3,100 warriors clearly required widespread mobilization of men from many settlements, so a group of swift messengers must have been constantly ready for service at the chiefdom's capitol, besides a network of sentries and town runners to give an alarm. European accounts indicate that surprise attacks were launched by Timucuan polities.[22] If we conservatively assume that the Utinan chiefdom had to mobilize to meet only one enemy at a time, a conservative approximation of total population may be reached.

On the basis of overall military parity with Yustega, using de Groutaut's lower figure, we may estimate 3,000 warriors, which multiplied by five equals 15,000 Utina population. If the Utina chiefdom, whose settlements were scattered over a larger territory than were those of the Yustegan or Saturiwan chiefdoms, had to be able to mobilize enough warriors to meet simultaneous Yustegan and Saturiwan threats, then military parity demanded such numbers. Parity with Saturiwans to the east at 1,500 plus parity with half of the Yustegans to the west at 1,500 means 3,000 Utina warriors mobilized to create two frontier forces. The Yustegans can likewise be assumed to have had to keep half of their available manpower free to counter any thrust from the Apalachee on their western frontier and perhaps from their northern neighbors as well. We may therefore allow an extra 100 warriors to the Utina, implying a total population of 15,500 persons.

POTANO

Le Moyne was one of the Frenchmen who lived for a while as a mercenary among the Utina. He sketched a battle scene showing Utinan forces defeating a Potano army. As de Bry engraved the scene, the opposing forces marched in solid masses, with bowmen in the front rank of each army.[23] French harquebusiers covered both flanks of the Utinan army. Le Moyne reported that the Utinan leader was very reluctant to join battle because his shamans had predicted difficulty. In fact, Le Moyne claimed that the Utinan force would have suffered defeat had it not been for the French mercenaries. In demographic terms, the Utinan force may be inferred to have been somewhat smaller in numbers than the Potano army, if Le Moyne was not merely boasting about French prowess. Unfortunately, the right and left margins of de Bry's engraving of the battle seem to cut off the view of the armies, so no conclusions as to numbers can be drawn from the representation. Laudonnière attributed only 300 archers to the Utinans[24] but reported that the Utinan battle shaman warned the Holata Utina that the Potano lay in ambush with at least 2,000 warriors. We are left in doubt, therefore, as to the forces engaged in battle. If the shaman feared encountering a Potano army of 2,000 warriors, on the other hand, that group must have been able to mobilize such a force.

The best that can be done, then, is to employ the principle of military parity between enemies, allowing the Potano a small numerical advantage over the Utinans. Thus the Potano would have had to field at least 1,500 warriors to meet a half-strength Utinan army on equal terms. Another 100 warriors could well have provided the Potano army with the capacity to defeat the Utinan force without French help. So, 1,600 warriors multiplied by 5 equals 8,000 in total population. If the Utinan battle shaman correctly estimated the available Potano forces as more than 2,000, on the other hand, the total Potano population was more than 10,000 individuals.

At least two additional items of demographic information were recorded by members of de Soto's expedition. When the Potano Head-chief came out from his capitol to greet de Soto, 500 "noble Indian cavaliers" accompanied him arrayed in varicolored "plumage" and carrying "elegant" bows and arrows.[25] That group would appear to have been merely the Headchief's palace guard or the Potano nobility related to the ruling family; the Potano reportedly succeeded in mobilizing nearly 10,000 warriors to oppose the Spaniards. The Headchief tried to enlist native interpreters with the marauders in a surprise attack on the invaders and claimed that he had "in readiness" more than 10,000 "chosen" warriors.[26] The interpreters warned the Spaniards of the Headchief's plan, and the Spaniards prepared to cope with an assault that was no longer a surprise. The Headchief asked de Soto to inspect his host drawn up in battle formation between a forest and two lakes near the capitol. Garcilaso de la Vega's informants thought that the warriors indeed numbered "almost" 10,000.[27]

The retrospective accounts provided some confirmatory details. De Soto ordered the Headchief seized before the latter could order *him* seized, mounted his warhorse, and led the lancers' charge against the Native American ranks. The Potano army broke and fled, but "more than" 300 were lanced to death. More than 900 more warriors dove into the league-square smaller lake. The Spaniards surrounded them and fought to capture rather than to kill them. These men continued to swim and to fire their arrows until their projectiles gave out. None of the warriors surrendered until midnight, after spending fourteen hours in the water. From that time on, the weakest gradually swam to shore after listening to the blandishments of the interpreters, who promised them their lives. About 10:00 A.M. the following morning, some 200 men who had been swimming for twenty-four hours yielded in a body. Seven tough warriors stayed in the lake until 3:00 P.M., when de Soto ordered a dozen strong Spanish swimmers to haul them out.[28]

Circumstances allowed the invaders to count captives rather accurately and attracted their full attention. Some faith can consequently be placed in the reported figures. In 1539, the Potano chiefdom suffered battle casualties and men captured amounting to a total of more than 1,200 warriors. Adherents of the Robertson-Bandelier-Kroeber school of demographic thought will, of course, claim that Garcilaso de la Vega inflated the size of the Potano army to make the bravery and battle skill of the subjects of his book stand out. Alternatively, they will claim that Garcilaso's informants inflated the Potano army numbers in order to glorify in retrospect their own deeds or that they overestimated the size of the Potano force from fright. Several facts counter such arguments. First, Garcilaso actually inflated the number of Spanish lancers to 300.[29] The expedition left Cuba with 243 horses and lost 20 at sea.[30] Native Americans killed one horse on July 25[31] and another on the road between Acuera and Ocali later that month.[32] If every horse carried a lancer during the Vitachuco battle, perhaps 220 Spaniards wielded lances, so only a few had to kill more than a single Native American to achieve the reported 300 deaths by lancing. Earlier, de Soto had had mounted parties of forty and eighty men scouting simultaneously, so it is possible that about half the horses were ridden and half kept as a remount pool. In that case, each mounted lancer might have had to lance two to three Native Americans to kill 300.

Second, the number of lance fatalities claimed was actually rather low. Such a battle mortality would not have been at all unusual for the early and middle sixteenth century. At Cajamarca on November 16, 1532, Francisco Pizarro had had but some 60 horsemen in his total force of 179 Europeans. Yet those lancers killed thousands of Inca nobles and fully armed warriors in a slaughter that lasted until dark. The nobles and palace guard with the Sapa Inca Atahualpa panicked when the European lancers attacked, and those thronging the plaza of Cajamarca pushed over a wall in their urge to escape death. In the open fields, the lancers routed fully armed members of the imperial army. Not a single Spaniard lost his life that critical day.[33]

Fernando de Soto had been one of the 179 men of Cajamarca. His reinforcement of men and horses from Panamá and Nicaragua had been the crucial final component that enabled Pizarro to land at Tumbez and to initiate the conquest of Tawantinsuyu. De Soto's share of the Inca treasure converted him into one of the richest subjects of the Spanish king. The leader of the 1539 Spanish exploration of La Florida had no need to inflate battle casualty reports. He was known as one of the four best lancers ever to come to the New World from Spain.[34] There is, therefore, good reason to accept as accurate the reported 300 deaths by lancing and the capture of more than 900 warriors who dove into the smaller lake by the battlefield outside town. There is also, therefore, good reason to take "nearly" 10,000 as a reasonably accurate Spanish estimate of the size of the force mobilized by the Potano Head-chief in 1539. The Spaniards who were present and saw the total native force drawn up before the massacre could compare the total with the more than 1,200 killed and captured (warriors whom they could count with accuracy) and could project to the total.

Third, one can accuse the Gentleman of Elvas, who admitted that 30 or 40 Native Americans were lanced,[35] from a force of 400 archers in the woods near Napetuca,[36] of reducing the actual figures to make himself and the other marauders appear to have been considerably less bloodthirsty than they were. For example, Garcilaso de la Vega wrote that 900 warriors who took refuge in the smaller lake were slain about a week later when the tried to kill their Spanish owners after de Soto had condemned them to slavery and had put them in chains.[37] The Portuguese chronicler admitted to the execution of only 200 such Potano warriors by Native American captives with the marauders.[38] Interestingly, the Elvas total of 200 was the figure Garcilaso gave for the mass surrender at about 10:00 A.M. on the morning following the battle, by men who had been swimming for twenty-four hours. Thus the Gentleman of Elvas certainly can be accused of at least a selective memory.

If the Potano army numbered almost 10,000 warriors in 1539, then a chiefdom army of only 2,000 in 1562–1568 would imply that Potano population had declined by a factor of five to one during the intervening period. If population had not declined, then the Potano polity of 1539 had split, or towns of the 1539 chiefdom had been annexed by neighboring polities by the 1560s.

TOCOBAGA

After ending the French threat in Florida, Pedro Menéndez de Avilés set out to discover whether the great St. Johns River and its source lakes connected to a waterway across the peninsula to the west coast. Such a riverine-lacustrine passage through the peninsula would have afforded the colonial Spaniards important strategic advantages relative to other Europeans. In the course of his futile search, Menéndez devoted some time to courting the not very friendly Headchief of the powerful South Florida Calusa. This activity led Menéndez to sail northward along the Gulf Coast of the peninsula to Tampa Bay. There he anchored on the water's edge at the town of the Headchief of the Tocobaga realm.[39] Tampa Bay had been described to Menéndez as extending twenty leagues in from the coast, so he hoped that it might be part of the nonexistent transpeninsular passage he sought.

A general cultural pattern of assigning messengers to duty at the capital settlement is implied in the mobilization of a Tocobagan army at Tampa Bay in response to the surprise appearance of Spanish ships. Within three days of the arrival of Menéndez, more than "1,500 Indian men armed with bows and arrows arrived, in very good order."[40] This was a chiefdom army, in other words, on a par with that of the Saturiwans. The same procedure employed previously to estimate population may be followed. More than 1,500 warriors times 5 equals more than 7,500 people.

The information Spaniards reported about the Tocobaga during the 1560s is very important for our venture in historic demography. The striking similarity between French reports of Saturiwan army size and Spanish reports of the Tocobaga army size suggests a geopolitical principle. Both the Saturiwa and the Tocobaga territories had one flank on the sea coast. While this left their coastal frontiers open to attacks from war canoes, it may have freed them from marching army masses. The Yustega, according to the French, had an army twice as large as the Saturiwan or Tocobagan 1,500 and occupied an inland territory subject to attack by massed chiefdom armies on all sides. Thus the similarly situated Timucuan polities probably had populations and armies of approximately the same magnitude.

OCALI

One figure on Ocali army size appears in the published record. When de Soto's marauders prepared to leave Ocali the chief agreed to order his "vassals" to build a wooden bridge across the large river nearby. While de Soto and the chief walked along planning the structure, 500 archers attacked. The chief explained that he could not prevent the assault because "many" of his vassals had abandoned their allegiance to him once he had left his refuge and joined the Spaniards.[41] If the chief was telling the truth, then 500 archers constituted less than the full strength of the Ocali army in 1539.

What was the Ocali chiefdom's mobilization capability in the 1560s? We can only invoke the principle of numerical parity of battle forces and assume that Ocali could mobilize an army equal to that of the Potano or Tocobaga or the Agua Dulce or Acuera. Such reasoning implies that the Ocali chiefdom had a capability of mobilizing about 3,000 warriors if necessary to meet two threats simultaneously. Ocali was an inland chiefdom bordering on four other quarrelsome chiefdoms. Such an army would mean a total population of 3,000 times 5, or 15,000 persons. This estimate is significantly lower than the 60,000 people the maize field area reported around Ocali Town in 1539 could support, as noted in an earlier chapter.

FRESH WATER

The Agua Dulce group living south of the Saturiwa to Cape Cañaveral had to muster forces equal to those of the Saturiwans. At the same time, the Agua Dulce towns faced hostile Utinians across perhaps a short stretch of the St. Johns River.[42] Thus the Fresh Water people must have needed approximately 3,000 warriors to maintain military parity with the Utinans and Saturiwans simultaneously. The Fresh Water chiefdom population may therefore have reached (3,000 warriors times 5) a population of 15,000. The Acuera across a long St. Johns River border may have posed a threat like that of the Saturiwa, but the riverine border may have given Acuera-Fresh-Water relations a different cast. The Ais south of the Fresh Water chiefdom presumably posed much less of a threat than other Timucuan-speaking polities, inasmuch as the Ais were not horticultural and therefore may be inferred not to have been as populous as a Timucuan chiefdom.

ACUERA

We have found no clues in available records as to the size of Acuera population in the 1560s. The French Huguenot colonists gained the impression that the Acuera were subject to the Utina chiefdom.[43] Inasmuch as both the Potano and Ocali chiefdoms separated Utina from Acuera, it seems unlikely that the Holata Utina could have conquered the fierce Acuerans. Earlier, in 1539, de Soto's marauders may have heard a hint of some sort of tie between the Acuera and Apalachee, for Headchief Acuera threatened to cut the Spaniards who reached that polity into pieces that would be hung from trees.[44]

The Acuera Headchief spoke of himself as a "king," according to former captive Juan Ortiz, who translated his messages.[45] Garcilaso de la Vega emphasized the Hispanic-style arrogance of Headchief Acuera but made no notes regarding the size of his military forces. The Acueran ability to kill fourteen Spaniards in twenty days suggests either that the Acuerans were the most effective guerrilla fighters de Soto's marauders encountered among the Timucuans or that Headchief Acuera deployed very large numbers of warriors around the Spaniards. The expeditionary veterans whom de la Vega interviewed claimed only fifty Acueran warriors slain during the same twenty days.[46] Thus Headchief Acuera's authority was absolute enough for him to keep his troops on the battle line despite to 3.6:1 kill ratio favoring the intruders.

Once again we resort to the principle of military parity. Presumably the Acuera had to be able to meet any Ocali threat from the north, for which purpose they would need an army of 1,500 warriors. South of the Acuera chiefdom was another Timucuan-speaking polity, the Mocozo. The Fresh Water chiefdom lay east across the St. Johns River. The Tocobaga ranged to the west. The pattern of warfare between Timucuan-speaking polities during the sixteenth century requires us to assume that the Acuera had to be able to mobilize a second army in the event of a simultaneous attack by two hostile chiefdoms. On that premise we estimate that the Acuera needed to mobilize some 3,000 warriors in two armies during the 1560s. Thus we obtain an estimate of 15,000 people in the chiefdom during that decade.

MOCOZO

The dual role of the Mocozo as renowned traders and aggressive, brave fighters poses something of a dilemma when one undertakes to estimate their population. Was the islanders' trade in *Zamia* flour and dates, which extended for fifteen leagues around, limited to the Mocozo chiefdom, or was it international in scope? If the traders exchanged their food products for Calusa commodities, one must assume that the Mocozo and Calusa were at peace or, if they were at times hostile, had social techniques for trading. Fairly clearly the Mocozo did not hesitate to challenge militarily the Fresh Water chiefdom by kidnapping the Headchief's daughter, so they must have been able to meet an Agua Dulce army of about 1,500 men on equal terms and even better. Moreover, the aggressive Acuera who exacted a notable toll of lives from de Soto's marauders in 1539 lived immediately to the north of the Mocozo. It is difficult, therefore, to avoid inferring that the Mocozo had to be able to mobilize at least 3,000 warriors in the 1560s, in two armies in case of simultaneous attacks by hostile neighbors in two directions. The alliance between the Fresh Water Timucuan-speakers and the Calusa indicates that the latter were probably at least occasionally hostile to the Mocozo on their northern border.

The military parity principle provides a basis, then, for estimating total Mocozo population. Using the figure of five persons per warrior yields an estimate of about 15,000 people in the chiefdom during the 1560s.

CASCANGE-ICAFUI, YUFERA, and YUI

The Cascange-Icafui, the Yufera, and the Yui and Iba occupied relatively small territories northwest of the Saturiwa chiefdom. So little appears to be known of these groups that we here consider them as equivalent to a single chiefdom in military terms. We assume that they had to be able to mobilize sufficient warriors to counter any threat from the 1,500 Saturiwan army. Possibly the huge Okefenokee Swamp protected the western flank of these groups from enemy attack. On the other hand, the swamp waters may have offered the Utina an ideal route for war canoe assaults on these small groups. We will here infer that the swamp provided protection.

There remained the Guale to the north in modern Georgia. During the sixteenth century, the Guale demonstrated that they could be formidable foes. So the small Timucuan-speaking peoples probably had to be able to mobilize as many warriors to counter any attack from the north as for defense on their southern frontier. Consequently, using the principle of military parity, I estimate a combined force of 3,000 warriors during the 1560s. Using the factor of five persons per fighter yields a population estimate of 15,000 individuals.

CONCLUSIONS

European records of Timucuan chiefdom army sizes permit the estimation of the number of Timucuan-speakers inhabiting northern Florida and southeastern Georgia in the 1562–1568 period. The information available about the number of mobilized warriors in four or five Timucuan-speaking chiefdoms constrains us to estimate a range of

probable population. One estimate is calculated on the basis of reported minimal army sizes plus estimated army sizes using the multiple
of five. The resulting population estimate is 130,500 persons. The higher
estimate of 144,000 individuals is based on three somewhat higher
estimates of army size.

The many uncertainties involved in arriving at the population estimates presented in this essay are, no doubt, abundantly clear. We close
with a methodological note that may indicate how conservative are our
estimates based on army size reports. One consideration of Central
Mexican population on the basis of size of armies reportedly involved in
the Spanish Conquest concluded with an estimate of about 8,950,000
persons in A.D. 1519.[47] Later estimates of Central Mexican population
projected from records of tribute payments indicated 25,300,000 as the
most likely population in 1519.[48] Consequently, we do not present our
estimates of Timucuan population based upon army sizes, summarized
in table 21, as other than minimal approximations; they can, after all, be
no better than the information on which they are based. The Central
Mexican calculations suggest that projections from army size may underestimate true population. The Central Mexican estimate derived
from reported army sizes proved to be only 35 percent of the figure
obtained from taxation data. If the Timucuan situation was parallel,

TABLE 21

Estimates of Timucuan Chiefdom Populations
During the 1560s, Based on Reports of Army Size

| Chiefdom | Army Size | | Population |
	Reported	Estimated	
Saturiwa	1,500–2,000	—	7,500–10,000
Yustega	3,000–4,000	—	15,000–20,000
Utina	3,100	—	15,500
Potano	2,000+	3,200	10,000–16,000
Fresh Water	—	3,000	15,000
Acuera	—	3,000	15,000
Tocobaga	1,500+	—	7,500+
Ocali	—	3,000	15,000
Mocozo	—	3,000	15,000
Cascange-Icafui, Yufera, Yui, Iba	—	3,000	15,000

Note: The figures reported in the table suggest total army size of between 26,100 and 28,800
and total population (warriors multiplied by five) of between 130,500 and 144,000.

then the true population may have ranged from 372,857 to 411,429 persons.

NOTES

1. Cook and Simpson, *Population*, 1948, p. 22.
2. Ibid., 23.
3. Lorant, ed., *New World*, 1946, p. 42; de Bry, *Brevis Narratio*, 1591, p. 9.
4. Laudonnière, *Three Voyages*, 1975, p. 83.
5. Le Moyne remembered that subordinate chiefs told the newly arrived Frenchmen in the summer of 1564 that Saturiba could mobilize "an army many thousand strong" (Lorant, ed., *New World*, 1946, p. 38; de Bry, *Brevis Narratio*, 1591, p. 7). We take multiple thousands to mean at least 2,000. Soon after Laudonnière arrived in June 1564, Saturiba marched to Fort Caroline with (according to Le Moyne) 700 to 800 men, after having sent ahead a chief with 120 men to prepare a bower for the Headchief (Lorant, ed., *New World*, 1946, pp. 36, 38; de Bry, *Brevis Narratio*, 1591, pp. 7–8).
6. The 1559 influenza pandemic was one example (McNeill, *Plagues and Peoples*, 1976, p. 209). This topic is explored in some detail in a later chapter.
7. This situation corresponds to a hypothetical stationary population model in which the number of live births to females in one generation is counterbalanced by postnatal mortality. Helm ("female infanticide," 1980, pp. 177–78) charted this model to illustrate intergenerational consequences of female infanticide.
8. Laudonnière described the father of one presumed town chief as "one of the oldest persons on earth" and reported that his lineage included six living generations. He attributed 250 years to the next eldest male member (Laudonnière, *Three Voyages*, 1975, pp. 64–65).
9. According to Le Moyne (Lorant, ed., *New World*, 1946, p. 69; de Bry, *Brevis Narratio*, 1591, plate XVIII). Laudonnière (*Three Voyages*, 1975, p. 117) added women and boys to the military train.
10. Milanich and Sturtevant, eds., *Francisco Pareja's 1613 Confessionario*, 1972, p. 39. Pareja's guide contains questions for "sodomites," indicating the seventeenth-century survival of Timucuan male homosexuality.
11. Deagan, "Cultures," 1978, p. 94. This information came from a Frenchman whom Francis Drake in 1586 took to England from St. Augustine ("The relation of Nicholas Burgoignon, alias, Holy, whom sir Francis Drake brought from Saint Augustine also in Florida, where he had remayned sixe yeeres, in mine and Master Heriots hearing"; Hakluyt, *Principal Navigations*, 1904, vol. IX, p. 113).
12. Sparke, "Voyage," 1878, p. 54, wrote that the Frenchmen gathered acorns, pounded, and leached them and that they consumed "sundry times rootes" of which they found "many" which were wholesome. Among the latter were, no doubt, roots of *Zamia pumila* cultivated by the Saturiwans (H.G. Smith, "Ethnological and Archaeological Significance," 1951, pp. 238–44). Yet some of the Frenchmen "would not take the paynes so much as to fish in the riuer before theyr doores, but would haue all thinges put in theyre mouthes," wrote Sparke.

13. Laudonnière put the best face he could on the situation. He wrote that he sent two shallops to explore up the St. Johns River because he did not wish his men to be idle (*Three Voyages*, 1975, p. 114; Lorant, ed., *New World*, 1946, p. 62; de Bry, *Brevis Narratio*, 1591, p. 19). Utina "received them hospitably," asking them to stay. Six did so. Sparke (*Voyage*, 1878, p. 54) wrote that having consumed all the maize they could purchase, the Frenchmen "were driuen certeine of them to serue a king of the Floridians against other of his enemies for milk and other victuales." *Milk* is a misprint for *mill*, the term Sparke employed to refer to cultivated amaranth (see the discussion in a later section).

14. Laudonnière reported de Groutaut's estimate of Yustega army size as 3,000 to 4,000 (*Three Voyages*, 1975, p. 116). Le Moyne remembered de Groutaut's report as 4,000 warriors (Lorant, ed., *New World*, 1946, p. 56; de Bry, *Brevis Narratio*, 1591, p. 19).

15. Connor, trans., *Pedro Menéndez*, 1923 (1964), 207–208; Solís de Merás, "Memorial," 1894, vol. I, p. 157.

16. Lorant, ed., *New World*, 1946, p. 63; de Bry, *Brevis Narratio*, 1591, plate XIV.

17. Lorant, ed., *New World*, 1946, p. 63; de Bry, *Brevis Narratio*, 1591, plate XIV. Laudonnière (*Three Voyages*, 1975, p. 119) wrote that he sent the Holata Utina 30 gunners and that the Utina army numbered 300 warriors. He also wrote that the Utina squads numbered six warriors. Le Moyne, the eyewitness and participant in the battle, may be assumed to have been the more accurate of the two men.

18. That this task force included only about half the warriors Utina could muster appears from Laudonnière's report (*Three Voyages*, 1975, p. 120) that to help celebrate victory the Holata Utina sent for 18 or 20 Townchiefs—that being less than half of the more than 40 towns.

19. Laudonnière, *Three Voyages*, 1975, p. 128.

20. Dobyns ("Estimating," 1966, p. 401) states this principle. Goggin (*Space and Time Perspective*, 1952, p. 29) already concluded that the Utina "must have been at least as large" as the Saturiwa, inasmuch as the former group was reported to be military more powerful that the latter.

21. Secoy, *Changing Military Patterns*, 1953, p. 10, for Caddoans in the Southeast culture area.

22. See Le Moyne's representation of a fire-arrow attack on an enemy palmetto-thatched settlement (Lorant, ed., *New World*, 1946, p. 97; de Bry, *Brevis Narratio*, 1591, plate XXXI). No defending force is visible outside the defensive palisade.

23. Lorant, ed., *New World*, 1946, p. 61; de Bry, *Brevis Narratio*, 1591, plate XIII. Laudonnière, *Three Voyages*, 1975, p. 119, was not present but heard about it and wrote sooner than did Le Moyne. He reported that each Utinan warrior was an archer.

24. Laudonnière, *Three Voyages*, 1975, pp. 119–20.

25. Varner and Varner, trans., *Florida*, 1962, p. 137.

26. Ibid., 140.

27. Ibid., 145.

28. Ibid., 148–50.

29. Ibid., 147.

30. Ranjel in Bourne, ed., *Narratives*, 1904, vol. II, p. 55.

31. Ibid., 67.

32. Ibid., 68.

33. Lockhart, *Men of Cajamarca*, 1972, pp. 10–11.

34. Varner and Varner, trans., *Florida*, 1962, p. 147.

35. Robertson, trans., *True Relation*, 1933, vol. II, p. 60.

36. Ibid., 59. Ranjel also placed the battle at Napetuca (Bourne, ed., *Narratives*, 1904, vol. II, p. 73).

37. Varner and Varner, trans., *Florida*, 1962, pp. 148–50.

38. Robertson, trans., *True Relation*, 1933, vol. II, p. 63.

39. Barrientos, *Vida y Hechos*, 1902, p. 135; Kerrigan, trans., *Pedro Menéndez*, 1965, p. 129.

40. Barrientos, *Vida y Hechos*, 1902, p. 137: "dentro de 3 dias binieron mas de mill y qui.os indios de muy buena disposicion con sus arcos y flechas," which is to say that more than 1,500 very well-ordered Indian men came with their bows and arrows within three days. Translator Kerrigan (*Pedro Menéndez*, 1965, p. 130) renders "de muy buena disposicion" as "very well behaved." That they were, in the sense of being well led and obedient to orders, so that their appearance roused Spanish fears of an attack. The Tocobaga army impressed the Spaniards with its good organization, in other words.

41. Varner and Varner, trans., *Florida*, 1962, p. 123.

42. At least, Le Moyne identified the Yustega (Oustaca) and the Potanou and Fresh Water (Onatheaqua) as hostile to the Utina (Lorant, ed., *New World*, 1946, p. 48; de Bry, *Brevis Narratio*, 1591, p. 12).

43. Deagan, "Cultures," 1978, p. 112, following "The second voyage unto Florida, made and written by Captaine Laudonnière, which fortified and inhabited there two Summers and one whole winter," in Hakluyt, *Principal Navigations*, 1904, vol. IX, p. 21.

44. Varner and Varner, trans., *Florida*, 1962, p. 120.

45. Ibid., 120.

46. Ibid.

47. Cook and Simpson, *Population*, 1948, pp. 22–30.

48. Borah and Cook, "Conquest and Population," 1969, pp. 177–83.

SECTION THREE
Settlement Demography

Our estimate of 1560s Timucuan population based on European reports of army sizes suffers from a paucity of data about the armies of several Timucuan-speaking chiefdoms. It is also likely to be lower than the true 1560s population, if we consider that a figure for Central Mexican population based on army sizes is lower than the figure indicated by tribute records. Our estimate needs cross-checking against figures derived from other demographic information. Sherburne F. Cook and Lesley Byrd Simpson had records of Native American baptisms in Central Mexico,[1] but missionaries arrived too late and accomplished too little in Florida for the number of baptisms to bear meaningfully on the question of 1560s or earlier population. Historians and anthropologists have tended to cite numbers of baptized converts during the seventeenth and eighteenth centuries as though such figures bore some relationship to pre-Conquest population size. We must state clearly that they do not. Projecting Colonial numbers of converts backward in time without adjustment for losses to disease, Colonial wars, and other causes is methodologically unsound. In fact, such projections are responsible for quite unrealistically low estimates of early sixteenth-century Timucuan-speaking numbers. Fortunately for our attempt to understand the true population dynamics of the Native American peoples of Florida, nonmilitary demographic data exist to enable us to cross-check our estimates of population derived from incomplete reports of warrior numbers.

SATURIWA

The French would-be colonists managed to obtain a reliable statement of the number of Saturiwan towns. An Utina Townchief the Frenchmen called "Molona" told Vasseur that Saturiba governed thirty towns through subordinate chiefs.[2] The Utina Townchief said that ten of the thirty Saturiwan Townchiefs were Saturiba's brothers. It seems to us likely that the Headchief led the chiefdom as head of a noble elite like the Incas in Tawantinsuyu. Missionary data later indicated that Timucuan society was hierarchically organized.[3] In those terms, the leader's ten "brothers" may well have been classificatory siblings in the

Timucuan kinship nomenclature who would have been classified as "cousins" in English terminology.[4] The other twenty Townchiefs were probably also related to the ruler as nephews, or more distant cousins, or perhaps in-laws.

Knowing the number of Saturiwan settlements, we must have some means of estimating the population each held in order to make another estimate of total population. This procedure has been the key to arriving at accurate estimates of 1519 and later populations in Central Mexico.[5] The English naval leader John Hawkins in the early summer of 1565 sailed up the Atlantic Coast of Florida from 26 degrees north latitude to above 30 degrees north latitude in search of the French colony, which he then visited. His log keeper wrote that coastal towns visited consisted of only a few houses.[6] Not knowing what log keeper John Sparke meant by "not very many," we are only a little wiser. At least we can infer that Sparke meant that there were more than two houses per town, so that the settlements were not single communal houses such as those inhabited by some tribes.

As some writers have recommended,[7] we can turn to visual representations of Timucuan settlements for clues as to their size. Jacques Le Moyne's drawings as de Bry engraved them show one complete palisaded settlement protected by two guardhouses and a partial moat. The chief's house in the center of the settlement is shown larger than the others, oblong shaped, and gabled.[8] Thus the English description of the Timucuan house as large, and very much resembling English barns in size and construction, with stanchions and roof beams made of whole trees and roofs thatched with palmetto leaves,[9] would apply to the chief's dwelling. De Bry's engraving shows fifty-five additional structures inside the palisade. Some appear round, implying corbeled rafters, and some were apparently gabled. Perhaps twenty-nine of these thatched structures represent gabled roofs and twenty-six round construction like that of the communal storehouse, which Le Moyne also sketched.[10] Thus the engraving possibly intended nearly half of the structures within the palisade to represent storehouses. On the other hand, the engraving may convey no more than de Bry's license with Le Moyne's drawings, themselves made from memory. At least one can conclude that this representation is not at all inconsistent with Sparke's "not very many" houses per town.

Another picture by Le Moyne and de Bry shows Timucuan warriors shooting blazing arrows into the thatched roofs of houses in an enemy's palisaded settlement, with five houses in a small segment of the town under assault. A similar picture shows an equal number of houses in a small section of a palisaded town.[11] Each structure is depicted as round.

Le Moyne as engraved by de Bry seems to have indicated, then, that Saturiwan settlements in the 1560s when he saw them consisted of from possibly twenty to almost thirty residential structures—assuming that each one had its own storehouse—to as many as half a hundred dwellings if no storehouses were within the palisades. Human beings do tend to forget numbers,[12] and Le Moyne almost certainly painted from memory after many years in Europe. His hurried escape from Spanish soldiers attacking the French post left him no time to pack and carry away his portfolios of sketches and perhaps paintings, although he may have sent a few early paintings to France on ships going there. Le Moyne's compositions may have reflected artistic imperatives with regard to filling space as much as accurate depiction of true numbers of dwellings enclosed by the defensive palisade around a Timucuan settlement. The engravings by Le Moyne and de Bry are suggestive but not conclusive evidence as to the size of Timucuan towns.

Historians and anthropologists have remarked upon the wealth of ethnographic information about the Timucuans in French accounts of the short-lived Huguenot colony compared with data available from Spanish colonial records. Yet a Spanish history of the leader who ended the French threat to Spain's treasure fleet en route to Europe provides crucial quantitative information on settlement pattern. Near the mouth of the St. Johns River, the town where the head of the Saturiwan chiefdom himself resided consisted of "25 large houses in each of which live eight or nine Indian men with their women and children, because a lineage lived together. This town is called 'Saturiba' from which name the Lutherans have named the chief who is ruler of the place."[13] Moreover, across the river, right at the sand bar separating the riverine waters from the ocean, was another town called "Alicamani," which was "a town as large as Saturiba." It was located on an islet that would lie to the right of a vessel ascending the river. The next town lay four leagues upriver;[14] Emoloan (or Molona or Momolona) was its chief in 1565.

Admittedly the Spanish count of dwellings applied only to two of 30 Saturiwan towns. We assume for purposes of estimation that Timucuan settlements were approximately equal in size for two reasons. Towns near the chiefdom's borders required large populations for defense against enemy attacks, even if they only delayed hostile forces until chiefdom armies could be mobilized and could march to the rescue. Thus, 30 towns with 25 dwellings each imply a total of 750 Saturiwan houses.

In order to estimate total Saturiwan numbers, we need to know how many people lived in each dwelling. The Spanish source is not precise enough because it does not indicate how many women and children lived with the eight or nine men in each dwelling who belonged to one lineage. Happily, other sources from the period supply the requisite figures. In 1564, a French explorer reported that "about fifty Indians" came out of what he inferred to be a chief's house near St. Johns Bluff.[15] Whether men and women or only men welcomed the Huguenots is not clear. The Frenchman mentioned at least one other dwelling where the aged father of the presumptive chief lived.[16] Making the minimal assumption that fifty persons composed the entire population of the house, we may multiply the estimated 750 Saturiwan houses by a possibly unrepresentative sample house with 50 residents, arriving at an estimate of 37,500 Saturiwans.

A more reliable house population figure was given by Hawkins's log keeper, John Sparke. It is more reliable because it refers to houses the Englishmen had seen while sailing along the coast of the peninsula— including Agua Dulce chiefdom houses besides Saturiwan dwellings —and because Sparke specified house population even if he failed to specify the number of houses per town. Sparke wrote that each house was inhabited by 100 persons.[17] So 750 estimated Saturiwan houses inhabited by an average of 100 persons each implies a total of 75,000 Saturiwans in the mid-1560s.

Thus observers from all three national European groups present in the area in the 1562–1568 period provided different kinds of demographic information about the Saturiwa chiefdom settlements. English, French, and Spanish observers seem to have been interested in or struck by different aspects of Native American life. Putting together demographic clues provided by various observers, we have been able to arrive at reasonable estimates of Saturiwan population.

First of all, the multiple of five persons per warrior used to estimate total population in the last chapter must be discarded, apparently, as too low. Using the lower Spanish report of eight men living in a house containing 100 persons by English report gives an average lineage size of 12.5 individuals. Taking the higher Spanish report of nine men yields a lineage average of 11.1 persons. Thus the three recorded Saturiwa chiefdom army sizes provided total population estimates as follows:

1,200 warriors $\times$ 11.1 = 13,320, or $\times$ 12.5 = 15,000
1,500 warriors $\times$ 11.1 = 16,650, or $\times$ 12.5 = 18,750
2,000+ warriors $\times$ 11.1 = 22,200+, or $\times$ 12.5 = 25,000+

The total population of the Saturiwan chiefdom may well have been fewer than the 75,000 Native Americans we estimate. Located very close to the mouth of the St. Johns River, both Saturiba and Alicamani towns occupied one of the most productive environmental niches in northern Florida. Marine shellfish and estuarine fish traps and weirs lay only a short canoe trip away, while freshwater shellfish and fish were right at hand. The river afforded easy canoe access to gardens and upland game hunting farther inland. Consequently, Saturiba and Alicamani could have been the largest Saturiwan settlements.

The residence of the Headchief at Saturiba suggests that its population might have been larger than that of any other town in the polity. Tribute paid at Saturiba by residents of other towns could have sustained a somewhat larger population than the immediate hinterland of the settlement would have had. Whether other settlements were smaller than Saturiba and Alicamani is not indicated by the available evidence.

We have already suggested one military reason why frontier settlements should not have been much smaller than the capitol. We should also note the absence of any statement by a European observer that Timucuan settlements differed markedly in size. Le Moyne observed Utina towns while serving as a mercenary with the Utina army, so his visual representations of Timucuan settlements were based on his observation of a wider sample than just Saturiba and Alicamani. Hawkins put in his ship at a number of settlements along the Atlantic Coast of the peninsula while seeking the French colony. So Sparke's description of typical hosues was based on a sample larger than the two towns near the mouth of St. Johns River and included at least Fresh Water chiefdom dwellings. Even though the absence of evidence does not show the absence of a phenomenon, one would expect at least one of the European observers to have remarked upon town sizes had they been disparate.

There are, in fact, a few additional clues indicating that military dead reckoning can be applied generally to Native American settlements in Florida. These clues are Spanish descriptions of "council houses," as a Cuban bishop called them in the seventeenth century, or "chief's houses" that served as the assembly halls reported in the sixteenth century. When Pedro Menéndez de Avilés visited the Calusa Headchief early in 1566, his residence lay but two musket shots distant from the estuary. Observers reported that "2,000 men might gather therein without being very crowded."[18]

The Calusa Headchief's house might tell us nothing about the housing of Timucuan chiefdom leaders if the 1566 report stood alone. It is, however, significantly supplemented by the 1675 letter of Cuban Bishop Gabriel Díaz Vara Calderón. Reporting to the crown, the bishop wrote that each village in the four provinces of Guale, Timuqua, Apalache, and Apalachocoli had a council house. For a century, the

Colonial Spaniards had been trying to diminish chiefly authority, so that the bishop's terminology may have reflected political reality by 1675. He described the council houses as built of wood, covered with straw, and round in floor plan. "Most of them can accommodate from 2,000 to 3,000 persons."[19]

Council houses of such size were a real anomaly in 1675, especially in Christian Timucuan settlements. For Díaz Vara Calderón himself claimed to have confirmed only 13,152 Christianized Native Americans in all four districts.[20] There could have been few if any occasions on which 2,000 of those Christians assembled for a town council. The report holds great importance for the present analysis, however, because it reveals a Timucuan and regional model that in 1675 survived from the Native American heritage. The 2,000-person-capacity town council houses extant in 1675 either survived from premission times or had been built after Timucuan and other converts to Christianity had congregated in Colonial settlements. In many instances, they must have been built after the town-burning campaigns of the military leaders at St. Augustine late in the sixteenth century. In either case, those council houses constituted material evidence of Timucuan population trends and former settlement size.

The Timucuans and other Native Americans whom the bishop mentioned, as well as the Calusa, would hardly have gone to the great labor involved in gathering construction materials and erecting a council house to hold more than 2,000 persons if they never needed one. Wherever these Native Americans erected such a council house, there had once been a need for a 2,000-person-capacity assembly hall. "Most" of the Timucuan-speaking settlements may therefore be inferred to have held at one time at least 2,000 adults eligible to attend general meetings or religious ceremonies. Not every settlement was so populous, and some towns had by 1675 abandoned their traditional council-house model and had settled for something smaller and more in keeping with the reduced populations of mission villages of that era. The fundamental point is that the 2,000- to 3,000-person-capacity council house gave material expression to a Timucuan cultural model of the proper size of a town. That model necessarily derived from demographic reality when Timucuan-speakers reached their peak numbers.

The brief accounts of Pedro Menéndez de Avilés's visits to the Calusa capitol in 1566 do not describe Headchief Carlos's residence and polity meeting hall as being filled. Yet the estimate does imply that at that time the Spaniards saw so many Calusa that they thought the structure could be filled by the Headchief's subjects. Consequently the 2,000-person-capacity town meeting hall can be used to gain additional perspective on Timucuan numbers in the 1560s. If Bishop Díaz Vara Calderón reported that "most" villages had such large council houses in 1675 ("most" rather than "all" because some villages had then abandoned their cultural heritage), and that all Saturiwan towns had had them in the 1560s, then the chiefdom's population was approximately 60,000 persons at least.

The thirty reported Saturiwan towns could presumbably have contained a number of children, but the Spanish documents are so brief that one cannot infer whether the authors included juveniles in their estimates or not. If the children attended religious services or civil councils in the assembly halls, and the Spanish writers recognized that they did, then the 2,000-person figures are global. If, on the other hand, Timucuan children were not allowed to witness religious ceremonies or to attend meetings, and the Spaniards knew it, then the 2,000-person figure applies to adults, and total population was greater than this number indicates.

The descriptions of Townchiefs' houses or council houses are important because they provide another quantitative perspective on settlement size. As a group the assembly hall accounts confirm a Saturiwan population of between 60,000 and 75,000.

YUSTEGA

Demographic information about this group prior to the 1560s is scant at best. If the town of Osachile occupied in passing by de Soto's marauders was Yustegan, then the settlement pattern appears to have resembled that of the Potano and Ocali. Marching from the river, swamp, and forest no-man's-land between Potano and Yustega, if such Osachile was, the Europeans encountered "great fields" of growing maize, beans, and squash four leagues from Osachile Town. "Settlements" began at the edge of the fields and continued to the town, not dwellings grouped in villages, but separated and spread out over the entire distance. Osachile Town consisted of a reported 200 houses,[21] the same size as Vitachuco but only one-third that of Ocali Town.

Osachile in 1539 sounds rather like a ceremonial and administrative town in the midst of a large tributary population residing in scattered homesteads. This was a Mesoamerican settlement pattern characteristic of the Maya that is still visible in the parish administrative town of Chichicastenango, Guatemala, with its large hinterland of farmsteads holding more than 25,000 inhabitants.[22]

If Yustegan population structure was much the same as that of the

Saturiwans, their total numbers could have been a maximum of 150,000 persons. Probably their population was smaller than that number. Using the multiples of extended-family size that were reported among the Saturiwans, Yustegan population may be estimated from reported mobilized manpower:

3,000 warriors × 11.1 = 33,300, or × 12.5 = .37,500
4,000 warriors × 11.1 = 44,400, or × 12.5 = 50,000

Taking the least populous alternative, the Yustega chiefdom numbered not fewer than 33,300 individuals in the mid-1560s. If the Yustegan army actually was twice the size of the Saturiwan army, the former group could have numbered twice as many as the latter, or about 44,400 to 50,000, extrapolating from reported army size, and as many as 150,000 if we consider calculated town population. Taking a middle course, we might infer that there was a Yustega population of about 100,000.

UTINA

Between the Yustega and the Saturiwa chiefdoms lay the territory of the Utina chiefdom, the largest of the Timucuan-speaking polities.[23] This chiefdom joined more than forty towns engaged in trade southward to obtain gold and silver that the South Florida Calusa recovered from wrecked Spanish ships.[24] If 40 Utina towns were all as large as the Saturiwan metropolis of Saturiba, then total Utinan population was 100,000 Native Americans. The estimated warrior mobilization of 3,100 implies at least 34,410 people and possibly 38,740 individuals. These estimates may all be higher than reality because Utina territory was located on the peninsula away from the food-rich coasts. Lakes and rivers may not have been as productive as saline estuaries. On the other hand, Utina fields probably produced more maize and other horticultural products than the littoral fields.

POTANO

Participants in Fernando de Soto's 1539 raid through Florida left some record of Potano sociopolitical structure and settlement characteristics that indicate Potano-Saturiwa parallels. Garcilaso de la Vega described the province he called "Vitachuco" as then ruled by three brothers, the eldest leading half of the "land," a second at the head of three-tenths, and the youngest of two-tenths.[25] Thus the Headchief clearly had the same kind of kinship relationship to other Townchiefs that the Saturiba had with his Townchiefs. Ranjel called this Headchief "Aguacaley-quen" and wrote that he fell into the Spaniards' power after Baltasar de Gallegos captured his daughter.[26] The Gentleman of Elvas called him the Cacique of Caliquen.[27] Ranjel referred to him as "Uriutina."[28]

Traveling northward from Ocali, de Soto's marauders spent two days crossing forested land with streams. Then de Soto rode ahead the afternoon of the third day and all night to reach the southern frontier village called Ochile at dawn. Garcilaso wrote that Ochile consisted of fifty "large and substantially built" houses.[29] The chief's habitation was by Spanish standards "a magnificent structure," with an open room more than 120 feet long and 40 feet wide, with four separate entrance doors. "Many" rooms around the exterior that resembled apartments opened into the central hall.[30] Once the Headchief and his palace guard had surrendered to the besieging Spaniards, who penned him in the structure, the conquerers realized that there was a further "large settlement" of houses scattered in clusters of four and five (more or less) in a "beautiful valley" on the other side of Ochile Town.[31] The Spaniards marched three leagues from Ochile to encamp. The total settlement must have been impressively large to frighten the tough *conquistadores* away.

Juan Coles, one of the Spaniards with de Soto, told Garcilaso de la Vega that the Potano province stretched for 200 leagues.[32] That would be perhaps 440 miles, clearly an exaggeration. Yet the Potano appeared to have been more extensive than the Acuera and Ocali territories through which de Soto's marauders had previously passed. At least, the eldest brother and Headchief directly governed more than a single settlement, inasmuch as he ordered supplies collected at his capitol "from all the other" towns of his "estate."[33] The chiefdom capitol town contained in 1539 some 200 "large, strong houses," besides "many" smaller dwellings situated "like suburbs."[34] Thus the Potano settlement pattern resembled that of the Ocali, with a greater range of variation in number of houses in various settlements than was found among the Saturiwans.

We have not found a report of Potano settlement numbers during the 1560s. On the other hand, Le Moyne did write that the battle shaman of the Utina told his Headchief that more than 2,000 Potano warriors had laid an ambush for him. On the presumption that the shaman knew the enemy, we multiply 2,000 warriors by 11.1 to estimate 22,200 (and by 12.5 to estimate 25,000) as the Potano population. Actually, the dead-reckoning principle of military parity for inland Timucuan polities indicates that the Potano should have been capable of mobilizing 3,000 warriors in a total population of from 33,300 to 37,500 people.

OCALI

The known archaeological manifestations of aboriginal habitation near present-day Ocala appear to belong to the same "material culture tradition" as those of the Potano.[35] It is, therefore, tempting to treat the Ocali as a component of the Potano. Sixteenth-century chronicles clearly identify a populous chiefdom that was not geographically centered near modern Ocala. Diego Escalante Fontaneda, rescued from captivity in Florida, termed Olagale a distinct kingdom. He equated it with the Tocobaga, Mocozo, and Apalachee at mid-sixteenth century.[36] Having interviewed survivors of de Soto's expedition, Garcilaso de la Vega wrote a surprisingly detailed description of the Ocali settlement pattern in 1539. Leaving Mocozo and Acuera, de Soto expeditionary contingents crossed a dozen leagues of "wilderness" savannah. Then de Soto traveled seven leagues of inhabited country to Ocali Town. A "few houses" were scattered "throughout" the inhabited area, but the Spaniards saw no towns between the frontier outpost until they reached Ocali. That capital consisted of 600 dwellings. The residents decamped before the Spaniards arrived, however, so the latter had no chance to observe the full population of the place.[37] One chronicler referred to "the first village" under Ocali sovereignty as Uqueten.[38] Thus the true number of Ocali kingdom settlements is not clear, inasmuch as the Spaniards traveled but one path across its territory without exploring it.

A town of 600 houses would seem to imply at least 600 household heads or sons capable of bearing arms. The other scattered houses in the fields might have contained some additional families, although they may have been field huts for families who also possessed town houses. The surviving accounts of de Soto's visit do not indicate the size of Ocali dwellings. If they were like the Saturiwan houses of 1562–1568, a household population of 100 implies an Ocali total of 60,000 persons. As indicated in the earlier chapter on Timucuan maize cultivation, the chronicle reports of Ocali field extent in 1539 indicate that these Timucuans could easily have raised food to feed 60,000 persons. In 1539, at least some members of de Soto's marauders perceived the Ocali kingdom as more densely settled than the Acuera territory they had already crossed. Garcilaso de la Vega attributed the abundance of provisions de Soto found at Ocali to the presence of "more people to cultivate it" as

well as to soil of greater fertility by comparison with that in regions the
expedition had crossed.[39]

The best estimate of Ocali kingdom population that can be made
seems to be a minimum of 5,000 by 1562–1568, assuming that at least
two settlements like Saturiba survived. On the other hand, the dead-
reckoning principle would mean that Ocali was numerically on a par
with Potano and Acuera. That would be 3,000 warriors, or from 33,300
to 37,500 inhabitants.

ACUERA

Sixteenth-century reports of numbers in Acuera chiefdom settlements
are scarce. The Narváez expedition apparently crossed Acueran territory as rapidly as it could. Possibly a chief reported by Alvar Núñez
Cabeza de Vaca to have approached the Spaniards carried on another
man's shoulders, preceded by flute players, was the Headchief.[40] Presumably some action by members of the Narváez force alienated the
Headchief, causing him to be very hostile to de Soto's marauders.[41]

In 1539, while still among the Mocozo, de Soto expected to find a
"city" called Aquera.[42] One of the expedition's chroniclers indicated
that the chiefdom consisted of multiple settlements. Garcilaso de la
Vega wrote that de Soto avoided damaging "either towns or fields" of
the Acuerans,[43] but in his account the number of towns remains quite
unclear.

During the seventeenth century, at least two Roman Catholic missions were established bearing the name Acuera.[44] Consequently we
know that the Acuera group included at least two towns as late as the
middle of that century. If these followed the eastern Timucuan pattern
already described, they might have equaled Saturiba in population; at
least 5,000 Acuera may have lived in the 1560s.

By the principle of military parity, the Acuera of the 1560s would have
had to mobilize forces capable of meeting on equal terms, at the same
time, half the chiefdom army of the Ocali to the north and the Mocozo
to the south—that is, once again, approximately 3,000 warriors and a
total population of from 33,300 to 37,500 individuals.

MOCOZO

During the 1560s, Europeans generally referred to Timucuan chiefdoms, their capitols, and their Headchiefs by the same name. Thus,

Headchief Saturiba lived in Saturiba Town and led the Saturiba chiefdom (here spelled "Saturiwa" to try to lessen confusion). Thus the Holata Utina led the Utina chiefdom and resided at Utina Town. Most likely these were Timucuan respect titles or names of lineages or offices rather than personal names. Consequently Escalante's reference to a Mocoso kingdom[45] implies that the 26- or 27-year old Townchief of 1539 succeeded to the headchieftainship of the southernmost Timucuan-speaking polity.

Sixteenth-century chronicles provide little information about numbers and sizes of settlements in the forgotten chiefdom of Mocozo. The de Soto expedition chronicles appear to mention at least four Mocozo settlements occupied in 1539. Captain Baltasar de Gallegos followed the plain major trading path between the Calusa and Fresh Water polities to both Mocoso's border town and the capitol that for the Spaniards was four days' travel from it.[46] If de la Vega's informants remembered or ever learned the names for those settlements, they forgot them or did not relay them to the author—or he simply did not write them into his narrative.

The expedition's commander left the Gulf Coast Calusa town of Ucita some time after Gallegos led an advance guard into Mocozo country. It seems to us that Fernando de Soto pursued an obvious tactic for a gold-seeking explorer. He sent troop contingents over different routes in order to maximize the expedition's chances of locating precious metals. His logical procedure has confused historians who have attempted to combine accounts of several chroniclers who accompanied different contingents at one time or another into a single route of march. It appears that Schell correctly identified the route de Soto himself took into the interior of the peninsula. Instead of following the well-marked trading path that Gallegos had taken, de Soto ascended the Caloosahatchee River in Calusa territory to the northern border town of Guazoco.[47] This last place name is persuasive. Ranjel spelled the plain where one soldier died of thirst and de Soto's followers later found green roasting ears "Guaçoco." Escalante referred to the Calusa town of "Guasata."[48]

There de Soto turned north and crossed into Mocozo land. Ranjel named two settlements de Soto passed through. Early on the day they left Guazoco, de Soto's men reached what Ranjel called a "little village" named Luca. It was not the Mocozo capitol, inasmuch as Ranjel reported that Gallegos "came" from there to meet de Soto at Luca.[49] The small village was evidently in the general Timucuan chiefdom settlement pattern, the defensive settlement on the southern Mocozo frontier facing the Guazoco Calusa.

From Luca, de Soto moved apparently northward to a town the Gentleman of Elvas called "Acela"[50] and Ranjel called "Vicela."[51] On July 23, the commander went beyond Vicela-Acela to encamp for the night. Conceivably, Vicela-Acela was the chiefdom capital and de Soto's avoidance reflected his decision not to damage Mocozo settlements. On July 24, de Soto's contingent slept at a town called "Tocaste," situated on a large lake.[52] At that point, de Soto crossed the big trading route between the Calusa and the Fresh Water chiefdom. Tocaste was probably the Mocozo capitol. Still, Tocaste need not have been the Headchief's town that Gallegos had earlier reached via the trading turnpike. In any event, the two Spanish contingents passed through a minimum of four Mocozo settlements, and perhaps five if no chronicler named the capitol. Still, Mocozo settlements inhabited in 1539 might not all have been still occupied by the 1560s. Nor do the chronicles of de Soto's expedition provide clues to the population of Mocozo settlements, other than noting that Luca on the southern frontier was relatively small.

Our estimation of Mocozo population during the 1560s must proceed, therefore, from army size derived according to the principle of military parity. Using the projected 3,000-warrior figure and our lower warrior-to-lineage size of 11.1 yields an estimated 33,300 total population. The higher warrior-to-lineage size of 12.5 yields an estimate of 37,500 persons. On the other hand, if the Mocozo population was of the same magnitude as that of the Calusa to the southwest, that of the Acuera to the north, or that of the Fresh Water chiefdom to the northeast, then the Mocozo numbered from 75,000 to 100,000 persons.

TOCOBAGA

Modern archaeological investigation of Tocobaga territory has disclosed at least thirteen settlements with truncated, pyramidal temple mounds and adjacent plazas, some with burial mounds.[53] There is good reason to think, however, that significantly more than thirteen Tocobaga towns existed between 1562 and 1568 and that the population was roughly on par with that of the Saturiwa chiefdom.

As noted in the last chapter, Pedro Menéndez de Avilés established Spanish contact with the Tocobaga on Tampa Bay in 1566. He persuaded the Tocobaga leadership to demobilize the army that had responded to the emergency posed by Spanish ships anchored at the edge of the town on Tampa Bay and to discuss a peace agreement with the Calusa. No fewer than twenty-nine caciques, or chiefs, and "nearly 100 principal Indian men" stayed in the capitol for the negotiations. The twenty-nine chiefs can logically be viewed as Townchiefs, the principal men being lineage heads within those settlements or members of the ruling elite who normally resided in the satellite towns. Thus the Spanish history of Menéndez's activities hints that the Tocobaga chiefdom in 1566 included the inhabitants of twenty-nine towns. The largely coastal Tocobagan settlements could well have enjoyed much the same environmental advantages that enabled Saturiba Town and Alicamani Town to sustain populations on the order of 2,500 individuals. Thus a total Tocobagan population on the order of 72,500 individuals can be hypothesized by multiplying twenty-nine towns by 2,500 residents.

The reported army size of the Tocobaga chiefdom would indicate a considerably smaller population. The 1,500 or more warriors the Menéndez party saw in 1566 would imply only from 16,650 to 18,750 total population.

CASCANGE-ICAFUI

We here follow Deagan, who considered the Cascange and Icafui a single tribe. This northernmost Atlantic coastal Timucuan-speaking group inhabited no fewer than eight towns as late as the beginning of the seventeenth century. At that time, 1,100 of them paid tribute to the Saturiwan Headchief recognized by the Spaniards, who was at San Pedro on Cumberland Island.[54] That mission-period tributary relationship invites consideration of whether the Cascange-Icafui had a half century earlier been part of the Saturiwan chiefdom or whether the tributary obligation arose under missionary supervision.

The average Cascange settlement contained only 137.5 persons at the end of the sixteenth century. The typical Cascange settlement thirty-five to forty years earlier would presumably have contained a population of much the same size as did the Saturiwan towns. Even if the Cascange had not amalgamated any of their settlements by 1602, they had suffered significant loss of population. If they were roughly on a par with the Saturiwan towns at the earlier period, then they could have numbered eight towns times 2,500 inhabitants, or 20,000 individuals. The missionary policy of settlement amalgamation may well have reduced the number of Cascange settlements surviving in 1602, thus compensating for any inflation of the estimate of earlier numbers resulting from treating each one as equal in size to Satiruba Town and Alicamani Town.

YUFERA

Yufera territory seems not to have been very large, yet it contained multiple settlements into the early seventeenth century.[55] Beyond that fact, demographic data are lacking. The best that can be assumed, perhaps, is that the Yufera were on a par with the Cascange, perhaps consisting of 20,000 people.

YUI

As late as 1602, the Yui lived in five towns with a population that Colonial Spaniards reported at 700 to 800 persons.[56] Each Yui settlement then averaged, in other words, only some 140 to 160 inhabitants. The same villages thirty-five to forty years earlier presumably contained fewer residents than the coastal Saturiba Town and Alicamani Town, although the freshwater Okefenokee Swamp should have afforded the Yui abundant fish and game. Disregarding probable amalgamation of Yui settlements at the urging of Franciscan missionaries, we may credit the Yui during the 1560s with the same five towns they inhabited in 1602, with perhaps 2,000 persons per town. Thus we may conjecture, using slender evidence, that the Yui may have numbered 10,000 persons in about 1565.

CONCLUSIONS

Scattered European statements about numbers of towns in certain Timucuan-speaking chiefdoms, the number of large dwellings in sample towns, and the number of people residing in representative large houses, permit the estimation of the number of Timucuan-speakers inhabiting northern Florida and southeastern Georgia in the 1562 – 1568 period. The information available constrains us to estimate a range of probable populations. Town populations and settlement numbers imply larger populations than do extrapolations from army numbers (see table 22).

A Timucuan-speaking population of between 300,000 and 800,000 would be consistent with Pedro Menéndez de Avilés's description of "every populous country" in a letter he wrote to a Jesuit friend on October 15, 1566.[57] Florida would necessarily have been densely populated at that time to be able to call forth such a description from a high Colonial official familiar with New Spain. In 1565, Central Mexico ex-

TABLE 22

Estimates of Timucan Chiefdom Populations from Settlement
Numbers and from Populations of Sample Settlements

Chiefdom	Settlements	Population
Saturiwa	30	75,000
Yustega	?	100,000
Utina	40+	100,000
Potano	?	100,000
Fresh Water	?	100,000
Acuera	2+	75,000
Tocobaga	29	72,500
Ocali[a]	2+	60,000
Cascange-Icafui	8	20,000
Yufera	2+	20,000
Yui	5	10,000
Mocozo	?	75,000
Total	—	807,500

[a] See essay 3, section 4, for a discussion of this population estimate.

clusive of New Galicia still held some 4,200,000 Native Americans,[58] so that was the population density which Menéndez was accustomed to finding in the Colonial possessions.

Quantitative clues about Timucan town populations dating from the 1560s indicate that much the same situation existed there as in Central Mexico. That is, estimation of total population from army sizes yields figures lower than reality. Treating our lowest population estimate of 144,855 (derived from reported army sizes, allowing two warriors per lineage) as 35 percent of the true total population, we may infer that 413,871 Timucan-speakers lived in the 1560s (see table 23). Applying the same factor to our 163,125 projection from army sizes gives a reestimated total of 466,071 individuals. Using our estimates based on reported army sizes and allowing one warrior per lineage means distinctly higher projected totals (see table 24). The 289,710 figure thus recalculated suggests a total of 827,792 people, while the 300,810 figure similarly extrapolates to 859,457 total population. These last totals are higher than our town-size additive estimate for a maximum Timucan-speaking population of 807,500 people in the 1560s. Consequently we conclude that the extended family household that averaged from 11.1 to 12.5 members actually included two warriors. This conclusion indicates the best estimates that may be drawn from the data we have examined in

TABLE 23
Estimates of Timucuan Chiefdom Populations
during the 1560s: Two Warriors per Lineage

	Army Size		Population	
Chiefdom	Reported[a] (1)	Estimated[b] (2)	Army Low[c] (3)	Army high[d] (4)
Saturiwa	1,500	—	8,325	9,375
Yustega	3,000	—	16,650	18,750
Utina	3,100	—	17,205	19,375
Potano	2,000+	—	11,100	12,500
Potano	—	3,000	16,650	18,750
Fresh Water	—	3,000	16,650	18,750
Ocali	—	3,000	16,650	18,750
Acuera	—	3,000	16,650	18,750
Mocozo	—	3,000	16,650	18,750
Tocobaga	1,500+	—	8,325	9,375
Cascange– Icafui, Yufera, Yui, Iba	—	3,000	16,650	18,750
Total	26,100	27,100	144,855– 150,405	163,125– 169,375

Note: The total for column 1 sums all reported figures shown and estimated figures in remaining cases. The total for column 2 sums all estimated figures shown and reported figures in remaining cases. Columns 3 and 4 do not sum to the totals shown because the columns include "army low" and "army high" figures for both reported and estimated Potano army size.

[a]Reported = observed by Europeans except in the case of the Potano figure, which is a battle shaman's contemporary estimate.
[b]Estimated = inferred on the principle of military parity between inimical chiefdoms.
[c]Using a multiplier of 5.55.
[d]Using a multiplier of 6.25.

this analysis but yields a still considerable range of possible numbers for the 1560s.

About 130,500 persons is the absolute minimum estimate of Timucuan-speakers who could have been alive in the years 1562–1568.[59] The Timucuan-speaking population was about 372,857[60] to 413,871[61] or 466,071[62] if army sizes bore about the same relationship to total population in Florida as in Central Mexico. On the other hand, about 800,000 people appears to be the maximum estimate of Timucuan-speakers in the 1560s that we may base on information about extended-family, town, and chiefdom size. Such a large population seems unlikely to

TABLE 24

Estimates of Timucuan Chiefdom Populations
during the 1560s: One Warrior Per Lineage

	Army Size		Population	
Chiefdom	Reported[a] (1)	Estimated[b] (2)	Army Low[c] (3)	Army high[d] (4)
Saturiwa	1,500	—	16,650	18,750
Yustega	3,000	—	33,300	37,500
Utina	3,100	—	34,410	38,750
Potani	2,000+	—	22,200	25,000
Potano	—	3,000	33,300	37,500
Fresh Water	—	3,000	33,300	37,500
Acuera	—	3,000	33,300	37,500
Tocobaga	1,500+	—	16,650	18,750
Ocali	—	3,000	33,300	37,500
Mocozo	—	3,000	33,300	37,500
Cascange – Icafui, Yufera, Yui, Iba	—	3,000	33,300	37,500
Total	26,100	27,100	289,710– 326,250	300,810– 358,750

Note: The total for column 1 sums all reported figures shown and estimated figures in remaining cases. The total for column 2 sums all estimated figures shown and reported figures in remaining cases. Columns 3 and 4 do not sum to the totals shown because the columns include "army low" and "army high" figures for both reported and estimated Potano army size.

[a]Observed by Europeans, except in the case of the Potano figure, which is a battle shaman's contemporary estimate.

[b]Estimated on the basis of military parity with the enemy.

[c]Using a multiplier of 11.1.

[d]Using a multiplier of 12.5.

have survived earlier sixteenth-century epidemic diseases, which we will discuss in Essays Six and Seven.

A triad of final comments seems appropriate. First, the number of demographic clues present in the exploration reports of Spaniards, Englishmen, and Frenchmen is surprisingly large and analyzable. It seems remarkable that we have been able to estimate Timucuan-speaking numbers in the 1562–1568 period, because none of the many scholars of Florida history has previously done so using such data. Second, the Saturiwa chiefdom, whose population was best documented by European observers, numbered from at least 42 percent of the previous highest estimate of all Timucuan-speakers, to 117 percent of that figure, or possibly as much as 375 percent of it.

Third, the more or less documented Timucuan-speaking population we have estimated for the 1560s is convincingly similar in size to the number of Apalachee and Timucua estimated in earlier chapters on the basis of cultivated and wild food resources. The Apalachee have not been estimated in this chapter, and the Timucuan-speakers in south Georgia were not included in the estimation in the earlier chapters. Thus the figures are not directly comparable, but they do not need to be. The more or less documented Timucuan-speaking population that we estimate implies that as late as the 1560s, even after Old World diseases had diminished Timucuan population to some extent, population density remained nearer eighteen than fifteen persons per square mile. Documentary information about sixteenth-century Florida Native American populations tends to confirm the accuracy of estimates of human carrying capacity of the rich natural environment of Florida.

NOTES

1. Cook and Simpson, *Population*, 1948, pp. 18 – 22. Missionaries arrived at slightly higher numbers than did Cook and Simpson on the basis of army counts.

2. "Molona" (Laudonniére, *Three Voyages*, 1975, p. 86) is equivalent to "Momolona" (Lorant, ed., *New World*, 1946, p. 35), which is the same as "Emolan" (Barrientos, *Vida y Hechos*, 1902, p. 43; Kerrigan, trans., *Pedro Menéndez*, 1965, p. 41). Archaeologists have remarked that Timucuan settlements remained on the same sites for centuries. A leader of a hostile chiefdom would, therefore, have been unlikely to have been mistaken about the total number of Saturiwa chiefdom towns.

3. Milanich and Sturtevant, eds., *Francisco Pareja's 1613 Confessionario*, 1972, p. 40.

4. Swanton, *Early History*, 1922, p. 367.

5. Cook and Simpson, *Population*, 1948, pp. 49 – 165. Cook and Borah, *Indian Population*, 1960, pp. 5 – 32.

6. Sparke, "Voyage made," 1878, p. 52.

7. Ewers, "Symposium—Comment," 1961, p. 267, fig. 1; p. 268.

8. Lorant, ed., *New World*, 1946, p. 95; de Bry, *Brevis Narratio*, 1591, plate XXX. Sturtevant, ("Ethnological Evaluation," 1977, p. 73), refers to this type of house as "oval or rectangular" with a "ridge."

9. Sparke, "Voyage made," 1878, p. 52. Sparke's description of the Timucuan houses as "in strength not inferiour to" English barns belies Geiger's denigration of "crude huts" (*Franciscan Conquest*, 1937, p. 9).

10. Lorant, ed., *New World*, 1946, p. 79; de Bry, *Brevis Narratio*, 1591, plate

XXII. Sturtevant ("Ethnological Evaluation," 1977, p. 73) called the common house "hemispherical."

11. Lorant, ed., *New World*, 1946, pp. 97, 115; de Bry, *Brevis Narratio*, 1591, plates XXXI, XL. Historians who have essayed brief summations of Florida aboriginal settlement patterns have tended to beg the question of absolute numbers in Timucuan towns. Geiger (*Franciscan Conquest*, 1937, p. 10) for example, wrote that the Guale, Timucua, and Apalachee lived in towns containing "several hundred inhabitants" under a chief.

12. Cook, *Aboriginal Population*, 1956, p. 81, alludes to the "inability of old men and women to remember" what he calls "quantitative facts" over a "great span of years."

13. Barrientos, *Vida y hechos*, 1902, p. 54. Kerrigan translated this passage much the same way, *casas* as "dwellings," and "bive junta Vn linage" as "for all kin dwell together" (*Pedro Menéndez*, 1965, p. 41).

14. The map by Le Moyne and de Bry confirms the relative locations of these two Saturiwan settlements. It shows Alicamani Town on a peninsula just north of the mouth of St. Johns River (rather than on an island). Le Moyne had Atore, Saturiba's son, and Saturiba both labeling one hut on the south bank representing a town. His map shows another town jutting into the ocean labeled "Patica." The next town upstream, also on the south bank, is Fort Caroline, followed by Momolona and then Malica. Approximately opposite that town, Le Moyne placed a hut on the north shore to indicate Casti (Lorant, ed., *New World*, 1946, p. 35; de Bry, *Brevis Narratio*, 1591, facing p. 30). *Momoloua* evidently is the Spanish *Emolan* chief and town four leagues upstream from Saturiba Town and Alicamani Town (Barrientos, *Vida y Hechos*, 1902, p. 43; Kerrigan, trans., *Pedro Menéndez*, 1965, p. 41).

15. Laudonnière, *Three Voyages*, 1975, p. 63.

16. Ibid., 64.

17. Sparke, "Voyage made," 1878, p. 52, described the native houses as stout as English barns. A Spanish history of the Lucas Vásquez de Ayllón colonization attempt mentions even larger houses farther north in modern South Carolina. Oviedo wrote of houses each of which had to be considered a settlement. The people built walls with felled pine trunks in a row as long as 300 feet and 15–30 feet apart. They joined the branches and created a roof from mats, so 200 men could easily live in one (Quinn, ed., *New American World*, 1979, vol. I, p. 263).

18. Connor, trans., *Pedro Menéndez*, 1923 (1964), 145.

19. Wenhold, trans., *17th Century Letter*, 1936, p. 13.

20. Ibid., 12.

21. Varner and Varner, trans., *Florida*, 1962, p. 169.

22. Bunzel, *Chichicastenango*, 1952, pp. 12, 16–17, 181, 185–88.

23. Milanich, "Western Timucua," 1978, p. 70.

24. Laudonnière, *Three Voyages*, 1975, p. 76, credited the Utina with more than 40 towns on the authority of a Townchief.

25. Varner and Varner, trans., *Florida*, 1962, p. 129. The Gentleman of Elvas placed Vitachuca town in Apalachee (Robertson, trans., *True Relation*, 1933, vol. II, pp. 66–67).

26. Bourne, ed., *Narratives*, 1904, vol. II, p. 71.

27. Robertson, trans., *True Relation*, 1933, vol. II, p. 59.

28. Bourne, ed., *Narratives*, 1904, vol. II, p. 75.

29. Varner and Varner, trans., *Florida*, 1962, pp. 128 – 29.

30. Ibid., 130.

31. Ibid., 130 – 31.

32. Ibid., 137.

33. Ibid., 137.

34. Ibid., 138.

35. Milanich, "Western Timucua," 1978, p. 69.

36. French, comp., *Historical Collections*, 1875, p. 255: "distinct kingdoms"; True, ed., *Memoir*, 1944, 1945, p. 70: "que son Reinos por si," that is, "Tocobaga, Apalache, Olagale and Mocoso, which are kingdoms in themselves."

37. Varner and Varner, trans., *Florida*, 1962, p. 122. Mocozo spokesmen interpreted by Juan Ortiz led Fernando de Soto while he was still encamped on the Calusa coast to expect to find a "city" at Ocali. Indeed, before he left that coast, de Soto wrote that he planned to go into winter quarters there (de Soto, "Letter," 1539, p. 92). Thus the record indicates that Ocali was more urban than most Timucuan chiefdom capital towns.

38. Bourne, ed., *Narratives*, 1904, vol. II, p. 68.

39. Varner and Varner, trans., *Florida*, 1962, pp. 121 – 22.

40. Bandelier, trans., *Journey*, 1904 (1922), 21.

41. Varner and Varner, trans., *Florida*, 1962, p. 118.

42. De Soto, "Letter," 1854, p. 92.

43. Varner and Varner, trans., *Florida*, 1962, p. 121.

44. Deagan, "Cultures," 1978, p. 112, following Geiger, *Biographical Dictionary*, 1940, p. 126.

45. B. Smith, trans., *Letter and Memoir*, 1854, p. 19; Quinn, ed., *New American World*, 1979, vol. V, p. 8.

46. Varner and Varner, trans., *Florida*, 1962, pp. 93 – 95; de Soto, "Letter," 1854, p. 92.

47. Schell, *De Soto*, 1966, pp. 51, 54; Bourne, ed., *Narratives*, 1904, vol. II, pp. 63 – 64.

48. B. Smith, trans., *Letter and Memoir*, 1854, p. 24; Quinn, ed., *New American World*, 1979, vol. V, p. 8. Guaçata.

49. Bourne, ed., *Narratives*, 1904, vol. II, p. 64.

50. Robertson, trans., *True Relation*, 1933, vol. II, p. 52.

51. Bourne, ed., *Narratives*, 1904, vol. II, p. 65.

52. Ibid., 65. Schell, *De Soto*, 1966, p. 57, identified this as Lake Okeechobee, but de Soto had traveled a considerable distance away from that body of water after leaving Calusa *Guazoco*.

53. Bullen, "Tocobaga Indians," 1978, p. 51.

54. Deagan, "Cultures," 1978, p. 97. Geiger (*Franciscan Conquest*, 1937, p. 145) wrote that the Cascange district included seven villages subject to the chief of San Pedro in 1602. Geiger (150 – 51) also referred to an Ycafui district consisting of Cascange and eight unnamed villages, with 1,100 residents in the eight settlements.

55. Deagan, "Cultures," 1978, p. 99.

56. Ibid., 200. Geiger (*Franciscan Conquest*, 1937, p. 145) wrote of "the Indians of the five villages of Ubi" in 1602, when the Ybi cacique headed 700 or 800 people, adults and children, in these settlements (p. 140).

57. Ruidíaz y Caravia, ed., *La Florida*, 1894, vol. II, p. 158.

58. Cook and Simpson, *Population*, 1948, p. 16.

59. This estimate appears in table 21. It assumes five persons per warrior.

60. This figure takes 130,500 as 35 percent of the true total.

61. This figure treats 144,855 in column 4 of table 23 as 35 percent of the true population.

62. This figure takes 163,125 from column 5 of table 23 as 35 percent of the true population.

ESSAY FIVE

Reassessment of Timucuan Sedentarism

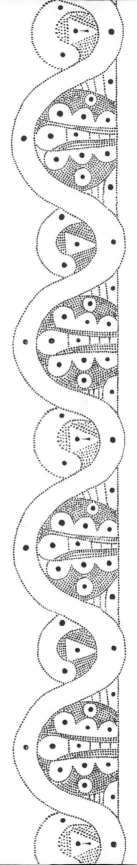

Documents Europeans wrote between 1562 and 1568 that describe Timucuan chiefdoms imply that several hundred thousand Native Americans once made a living in northern Florida. The analysis of clues in sixteenth-century documents in the last essay suggests that Timucuan population was even denser than the earlier assessment of Florida's natural resources and Native American horticulture would indicate. I now undertake, therefore, to reassess Timucuan horticulture so as to find out whether significant food factors in population growth have been overlooked.

An explanation for large Timucuan-speaking towns widely distributed over northern and central Florida cannot come, evidently, from available anthropological analyses of horticultural productivity. Anthropologists thinking in terms of only a few thousand Timucuans are already baffled by archaeological evidence of settlement permanency. Excavations have revealed that pre-Columbian settlement of not only Timucuans but also other Southeastern Native Americans were very sedentary in nature. In his summary of the Southeastern culture area, Charles Hudson[1] labeled the horticulture of the area "something of a puzzle." What mystified Hudson was that the towns and villages of the Southeast "were both large and, for the most part, rather permanent, and in the Mississippian period they had a rather complex political organization."[2] ("Mississippian" is a term archaeologists employ to refer to the late prehistoric period.) On the other hand, the main staple crop grown by Native Americans in this populous area was maize, "a seed crop which quickly exhausts the soil unless" it is renewed in some way.[3] The difficulty lies in reconciling intensive maize cultivation with sedentary settlement, for there are just two common human solutions to the problem of declining fertility of soils in horticultural fields. One is to move the field, as hypothesized in the Ocali illustration in an earlier chapter on intensiveness of maize cultivation. The other is to fertilize.[4] The Native Americans in the Southeast are not known to have fertilized their fields.[5] In fact, ethnohistorical analysis has indicated that fertilizing maize hills with dead fish was not a precontact cultural trait even in New England. The Native American individual famous in regional history for having taught Pilgrim colonists to fertilize maize in this manner apparently learned to do so while visiting Europe as a kidnapped curiosity.[6] On the other hand, the peoples of the Southeast are thought not to have practiced swidden horticulture. That is, they are thought not to have moved their fields, fallowing them for periods of years between sowings.[7] Therein lies a real dilemma for the historian.

Historic documents and ethnographic data indicate that Southeastern Native American subsistence relied heavily on maize. The maize plant is a heavy feeder that rapidly exhausts soils of nutrients such as nitrogen, phosphorus, and calcium.[8] How, then, could the Southeastern culture area peoples live in large numbers in stable settlements without moving their fields or fertilizing them? This puzzle suggests that pre-Columbian Southeastern horticulture is not yet accurately understood.

Hudson himself considered several factors that he thought helped Southeastern Native Americans to achieve relatively permanent sedentary settlement.

1. Peoples in this culture area obtained a "significant" proportion of their food by hunting, fishing, and gathering wild plant foods, diminishing their need for cultivated foods. The ratio of foods produced to foods fished, hunted, and collected remains unknown,[9] but the latter did reduce overall dependence upon horticultural products. This reasoning stems from a perception that hunting and gathering in the Southeast were "highly productive" activities. Christopher Murphy and Hudson concluded that some groups may have grown as much as three-fourths of their food, while others relied much less on cultivation.[10]

Such reasoning flies in the face of worldwide evidence that human population density rises as a consequence of food production. Many another anthropologist has argued that hunting, fishing, and wild food collection foster transhumance rather than a sedentary settlement pattern. In premission times, for example, Northern Piman peoples living in the arid Sonoran Desert shifted seasonally between riverine-oasis summer horticulture and desert-mountain-range winter hunting based on springs and seeps.[11] Timucuan acorn collecting, deer hunting, and so forth took people away from towns to oak thickets and hunting meadows. Hudson's "explanation" is thus actually part of the puzzle and not its solution.

2. Planted "in the same field," maize, beans, and squash "complemented each other," in Hudson's view. In fact, beans fix nitrogen in the soil for maize and squash to use.[12] This point is valid. Bean plants fixing atmospheric nitrogen and storing it in nodules on their roots provided the major single increment of this nutrient in Native American fields. Modern research has found, for example, that cowpeas interplanted with maize yield 100 percent more than do cowpeas planted alone.[13] Diverse crops also provide cultivators with better nutritional value per area unit than would a single crop.

These facts do not, on the other hand, account for sedentarism in the Southeast. In the first place, planting practices were not uniform within the culture area. Thomas Hariot reported that in the 1580s the Roanoke people at times sowed separately, although they more often interplanted maize, beans, "peas," pumpkins, gourds, melons, sunflowers, and amaranth.[14] In the second place, the pattern in the Southeast did not differ significantly from that elsewhere among Native American horticulturalists. All or nearly all Native Americans in North America who cultivated food crops interplanted at least maize and beans with squash in hills. Consequently they all benefited from bean plants' infusion of nitrogen into their soils and from diversified sources of nutrition. If Southeastern culture area peoples were truly more sedentary than peoples elsewhere in North America, then that sedentarism must be explained by production or by other factors that are special.

3. Southeastern Native Americans, claimed Hudson, cultivated fields in the rich bottom lands along river courses. He[15] regarded riverine land as "ideal for corn" because it was rich in nutrients, light and easily tilled with simple tools, and well drained. Periodic floods renewed fertility.

This "explanation" is an overgeneralization. The northern and central Florida habitat of Timucuan-speakers is not one of high physical relief. The rivers with permanent flow traverse relatively level terrain. The topography is quite unlike that of the Appalachian hills and valleys of the Cherokees, Creeks, and Chickasaws.[16] The soil of northern Florida is predominantly sandy—very well drained, indeed, and easily tilled with simple tools and fire—but also subject to the rapid leaching of plant nutrients down below crop root zones. In other words, Hudson's hypothesis that riverine fields accounted for the puzzling sedentarism simply does not hold for the Timucuan-speaking peoples. Their cultivated fields were certainly not limited to riverine floodplains. The large cultivated area around Ocali Town in 1539 bordered on a river, but most of its area seems to have lain well away from that stream. Yet Timucuan settlements were surely sedentary, despite some historical European statements of population movement that cannot be accepted at face value. As Kathleen A. Deagan perceived the matter, when the French Huguenots first encountered eastern Timucuans in 1562, they saw a way of life that seems to have changed very little for at least a millennium. The archaeological record shows "long continuity" in Timucuan subsistence systems until historic times.[17]

Timucuans were such enthusiastic and intensive gardeners that they integrated new crops into their ancient subsistence system very early in historic times. In 1563, Ribaut wrote that they grew "cowekcumbers, citrons, peasen," in their kitchen gardens[18] before any Spanish settlement had been established in Florida. So Ribaut's statement raises a question as to where and how Timucuans at the mouth of the St. Johns River had obtained seeds for three Old World cultivars. Conceivably Ribaut could have confused, during an observation period of only a few hours, some New World squash for cucumbers and a New World bean for peas. It is inconceivable, however, that he could have misidentified two such different cultivars and citrons or watermelons. Taken at face value, Ribaut's 1563 record documents the prior early historic diffusion of at least three plants domesticated in the Old World from the Caribbean islands or from a relatively small continental area under Spanish control by 1562 to the Saturiwa chiefdom on the Atlantic Coast of north Florida.

After European intrusions began in the 1560s, Timucuan subsistence patterns changed even more rapidly. Depopulation caused by Old World diseases, Spanish Colonial exploitation to support the military garrison at coastal St. Augustine, and missionization involving resettlement produced drastic shifts in horticulture. A diminishing Timucuan population moved from traditional settlements of considerable antiquity to new, short-lived Colonial villages. To meet the pressing demand for food to feed colonists at St. Augustine, Timucuans sowed maize more intensively and new crops, particularly wheat. Milanich[19] speculated that the new plants and cropping patterns exhausted soils faster than traditional ones.

In any event, some factor other than planting in riverine soils that were periodically flooded must have accounted for the ability of Timucuan-speaking maize growers to carry on semipermanent field cultivation. The Timucua were successful horticulturalists who "lived a life of plenty,"[20] but it is not yet clear just how they managed to do so.

NOTES

1. Hudson, *Southeastern Indians*, 1976, p. 291.
2. Ibid., 290.
3. Ibid., 291.
4. Ceci, "Fish Fertilizer," 1975, p. 28.
5. Hudson, *Southeastern Indians*, 1976, p. 290.
6. Ceci, "Fish Fertilizer," 1975, p. 27.
7. Hudson, *Southeastern Indians*, 1976, p. 290.
8. Ceci, "Fish Fertilizer," 1975, p. 27.
9. Hudson, *Southeastern Indians*, 1976, p. 526.
10. Murphy and Hudson, "On the Problem," 1968, pp. 25 – 27.
11. Burrus, *Kino and Manje*, 1971, pp. 292, 294, 297.
12. Hudson, *Southeastern Indians*, 1976, pp. 293 – 94.
13. Ward, Sutherland, and Sutherland, "Animals," 1980, p. 574, after Greenland, "Bringing the Green Revolution," 1975, p. 843, table 2.
14. Lorant, ed., *New World*, 1946, pp. 242 – 44.
15. Hudson, *Southeastern Indians*, 1976, p. 291.
16. Murphy and Hudson, "On the Problem," 1968, p. 26.
17. Deagan, "Cultures," 1978, p. 89.
18. Ribaut, *Whole & True Discouerye*, 1563, p. 73.
19. Milanich, "Western Timucua," 1978, p. 74, etc.
20. Spellman, "Agriculture," 1948, p. 37.

SECTION ONE
Diversification of Annual Food Crops

Part of the reason why Timucuans could live sedentary lives was that they were skilled gardeners who grew a wide variety of food crops. I have just mentioned their adoption of several Old World cultivars before Europeans colonized their territory. Such crop innovations demonstrated that the Timucuans maintained their populous towns in place for long periods by flexibility in food production. Timucuans grew a number of food plants besides the well-known triad of maize, beans, and squash in pre-Columbian times. First of all, Timucuans did supplement their staple maize with interplanted beans,[1] squash and pumpkins,[2] and a number of other food crops.

ZAMIA

Like the Calusa, Timucuans cultivated both seed and tuber crops. Intensive *Zamia* and/or manioc cultivation by Mocozo Timucuans has already been mentioned. The double effort to grow food extended from this southernmost to the northernmost chiefdoms. Ribaut recorded that in 1562 the Timucua near the St. Johns River cultivated "many other simples and rootes unknown unto us."[3] That record indicates that the Saturiwans cultivated *Zamia* and *Smilax*. So does the belief of the Colonial Spanish Governor Gonzalo Méndez de Canzo at the end of the century that the Cumberland Islanders depended on roots.[4]

Later events in Spanish Colonial Florida identify *Zamia* as the most probable Timucuan major root crop. Late colonial Minorcans in St. Augustine adopted *Zamia* as a kitchen garden plant.[5] The Minorcans arrived too late to have learned *Zamia* growing directly from Timucuans, so the practice may have been transmitted through either the Seminoles or Mestizos who lived at St. Augustine during the first Spanish period of sovereignty. It seems quite unlikely that people as culturally focused on plowing and broadcast sowing of small grains as were Spaniards and Minorcans would independently invent *Zamia* cultivation.

In 1821, a native English-speaking Floridian born in 1769 recorded that "Arrow-root" grew "spontaneously and in great abundance in the peninsula; it constitutes a great article of food." Forbes also noted that "the manioc is planted in trenches, about two feet and half asunder, and six inches deep." He described the plant as growing much better from "slips than from the seed it produces" and wrote that the "principal root" pushed out three or four others, independent of six or seven more roots issuing from the stem. He differentiated at least three varieties: a white that matured in eight months, the broad-leaved and red, "and other sorts," requiring sixteen to eighteen months to mature.[6]

Convincing evidence that cultivation of such root crops diffused from Native Americans to Euroamericans lay in the technology of root processing. English-speaking Floridians regarded the juice of the tuber as poisonous, and they processed it using the same technology as the Seminoles—and evidently the Calusa before them. That is, roots were peeled, then washed, scraped, and grated to the consistency of horseradish. The grated material was next placed under pressure in a cylindrical strainer to express the juice. Once dried, the tuber was grated and pounded into a flour to be cooked. This flour yielded among other things "a jelly, much used by infants and for invalids."[7] It was almost pure starch.

SQUASH

Native Americans customarily interplanted beans and squash with maize in hills. Fernando de Soto's marauders saw Timucuans following this practice in the summer of 1539. At the town de la Vega called Osachile, his informants remembered "great fields" planted in maize, beans, and "a type of squash known in Spain as Roman squash."[8] Actually, Timucuans grew more than one type of squash, and squash was at least a dual-purpose crop. The fleshy fruits provided a fresh vegetable that combined well in stews. It is not a good source of energy, being almost 89 percent water. A serving of 100 g (raw) provides only 8.8 g of carbohydrate and 1.5 g of protein, or 38 calories.[9] Other North American peoples peeled squash flesh and sliced it into long spirals to hang on poles to sun dry for storage.[10] Inasmuch as the Timucuans dried a wide variety of fish, game, and produce, they may well have dried squash. One gustatory reason for drying squash flesh is that sun drying concentrates the sugar content so that dried squash can be cooked as a sweet dish.

A second purpose of growing squash is to add to the seed content of one's diet. Native Americans generally relished squash seeds. Even in a modern Yucatecan peasant village where little but maize is planted, squash seeds were in sample years the third most frequent planting and the third most abundant harvest.[11] In extreme western Florida, the Pensacola group harvested squash seeds and kept them in baskets, as they did dried maize kernels, ready for household consumption.[12] It seems safe to infer, therefore, that the Timucuan peoples shared the same liking for squash seeds and carefully harvested them.

AMARANTH

A major new view offered here begins with one of the simple approaches of ethnohistorical analysis, the accurate translation of documents. The example employed here involves, apparently, the Mocozo chiefdom. In the summer of 1539, members of Fernando de Soto's expedition marched generally northward toward Ocali Town. Some contingents seem to have traveled west of the Ocklawaha River and some to the east in Acuera territory. The Gentleman of Elvas described the region his party traversed thus: "The land was very poor in maize, low, and very swampy, and covered with dense forests." Among his contingent, at least, "the provisions brought from the port were finished."[13] Having exhausted their supply of European or Caribbean food, the Spaniards had to live off the land until they reached the maize-rich fields around Ocali Town. The advance guard with de Soto evidently did not suffer much from hunger, for that body found "some very beautiful vales of corn" in Acuera country. Inasmuch as de la Vega characterized Acuera as a "very fertile province," and it provided an abundance of maize,[14] the zone without roasting ears must have been on the Mocozo side of the border.

In Robertson's translation of the Portuguese account, "wherever any village was found, there were some blites and he who came first gathered them and having stewed them with water and salt, ate them without anything else." The latecomers, unable to gather "blites," instead "gathered the stalks from the maize fields which being still young had no maize, and ate them." The marauders also recognized cabbage palms and began to eat that vegetable.[15] De Soto's secretary wrote that the main party ate some "herbs and roots roasted" and others "boiled without salt," not even knowing what they were.[16]

Few people are likely to know what a "blite" might be. Apparently Robertson anglicized it from the Latin botanical name for a common European cultivar, *Amaranthus blitum*. This is where the analytical technique of consulting original texts throws light upon Timucuan fields in the 1530s. The Portuguese text reads "avia algus bredos y que primeiro chegava os colbia y cozidos co sal y agoa sem outra cousa os comia."[17] In other words, "There were some pigweeds and whoever arrived first harvested them, and ate them without anything else than the salt with which they were cooked in water."

Unfortunately for those who have relied on English translations from the Portuguese, previous attempts to render the word *bredos* have been nothing if not misleading. Richard Hakluyt translated the term into English as "beetes."[18] A reprint edition edited by William B. Rye added a note that this plant probably was related to the "beetroot" and was eaten as a salad. Buckingham Smith interpreted *bredos* as cress.[19] Inasmuch as cress does not need to be cooked, and does not cook well, Smith's rendering was clearly an error.

All of these mistranslations reflect two ethnohistorical problems. On the one hand, Europeans exploring the New World during the sixteenth century still saw a vegetative landscape and Native American horticulture little modified by the early Columbian Exchange.[20] Consequently, they did not always have even a European common name to apply to Western Hemisphere plants that differed from those of the Old World. Moreover, Europeans did not always identify Native American cultivars. On the other hand, many post-sixteenth-century intellectuals translating explorers' accounts have been culturally too urban and too divorced from intimate knowledge of agriculture and field plants to translate accurately countrymen's terms from an earlier time.

Anyone who knows about the "l" to "r" shift between Spanish and Portuguese recognizes Portuguese *bredos* as cognate to Spanish *bledos*, and a French-speaker recognizes *brede*.[21] The term has the same meaning in these three Romance languages. It is best translated into English either with the botanical term *Amaranthus* or a common name, the most widely used being "pigweed."

The plant that members of de Soto's main body cooked with salt was, in other words, one with which they were familiar in their native Mediterranean habitat. There the most important amaranth has long been a domesticated plant that grows twenty-five to thirty centimeters tall. In Spain, it is cultivated for its tender leaves, eaten by humans as greens, for its rich seeds, which are fed to domestic poultry, and as green manure for fields, plowing under the entire plant.[22] No doubt peasants and perhaps gentry as well consumed the oil-rich seeds during periods of famine.

Members of the de Soto expedition who had been in New Spain had probably seen New World domesticated amaranths in the markets there. Aztecs grew amaranths and chenopods for their seeds to be employed to make special tamales to offer to the goddess Coatlatonan[23] and to feed slaves to be sacrificed during the merchants' festival,[24] to fashion edible images of mountains[25] and of the war god Huitzilopochtli on several festive occasions each year,[26] and of a man fastened to a tree-trunk for the festival of Xocotlvetzi in the tenth month.[27] Aztecs also used amaranth leaves for greens[28] and made special festive tamales from the leaves.[29] Because Catholic clergymen trying to convert Mesoamericans to Christianity perceived such use of these seeds as idolatrous activity inspired by the Devil, colonial authorities outlawed cultivation of amaranths and chenopods in New Spain. A pronounced diminution in production of both genera ensued.

The domesticated species survived in cultivation only in scattered areas. On the one hand, amaranths have been grown for food in the twentieth century in refuge areas among highland Tarahumara,[30] Warihio,[31] and Huichol.[32] On the other hand, peasant syncretism of Christian doctrine and Native American symbolism resulted in the growing of amaranths in recent years to make confections sweetened with sugar. These are sold during various local festivals in mountainous areas of the Mexican states of Guerrero, México, Morelos, Oaxaca, Puebla, and Tlaxcala.[33]

Fernando de Soto and other members of his expedition who had participated in the conquest of the Tawantinsuyu had no doubt seen quantities of both amaranths and chenopods being cultivated in the central Andes.[34] These plants seem not to have possessed pre-Columbian religious significance in the Andes, and they are still widely cultivated there. The protein-rich seeds of quinoa (*Chenopodium quinoa*) can be purchased from Native American vendors in public marketplaces from at least Otavalo, Ecuador, to highland Bolivia. Both cultivars possess the considerable advantage of yielding heavily at Andean altitudes higher than the upper limits of maize. Amaranth is often interplanted with maize at lower altitudes or is sown in a row or two at the edge of a maize field.[35]

In view of the previous experience of members of de Soto's marauders with amaranths and chenopods, there should be no doubt as to the accuracy of their identification of the crop that the Mocozo Timucuans were growing in the 1530s. To the standard Native American crop triumvirate of maize, beans, and squash must be added amaranth and possibly also chenopods as Timucuan cultivars. The motivation for growing amaranth in central Florida necessarily differed, however, from that of the peoples of the Andes, of the Central Mexican plateau, or even in the mountains of the Old Northwest of Mesoamerica.[36] Altitude could not have been the consideration in nearly level Florida.

The Timucuan motivation for growing amaranth can be inferred from the remarks of the Gentleman of Elvas. Members of the de Soto expedition simply beat the Mocozo to their own early harvest. Amaranth is a dual-purpose cultivar. On the one hand, it yields large quantities of seeds. A single plant can yield half a million tiny seeds with 200-pound-per-acre yields dry farmed and as much as 833-pound yields per irrigated acre.[37] The seeds are rich in oil. At Ocali Town de Soto's marauders in 1539 found "a great store of corn and other grains."[38] Inasmuch as Native Americans cultivated few other grains, amaranth seeds almost surely were one of the "other grains" in the Ocali Town storehouses.

On the other hand, tender amaranth leaves are also edible as tasty salad greens or boiled as a spinachlike dish. Picked tender to boil for greens, amaranth leaves have generated at least one regional Spanish term for the plant thus utilized, *quelite*.[39] As the Elvas account indicates, the Mocozo Timucuans grew maize and amaranth simultaneously, so that they were able to pick tender green leaves to consume long before slower-growing maize set and matured roasting ears. As de Soto's marauders marched northward through Florida during the summer of 1539, the Elvas chronicler reported that the main group was able to obtain green corn among the Ocali people for the first time in several days.[40] The commander enjoyed Acueran roasting ears.[41]

The Mocozo and probably the Ocali were not the only Timucuans who grew amaranth and perhaps chenopods. In May and the first half of June 1565, the French garrison of Fort Caroline in Saturiwa territory ate "roots and a type of sorrel plant" that the hungry Europeans "found in the fields."[42] That "sorrel" may have been an amaranth planted by the Saturiwa to provide fresh cultivated food precisely during an otherwise hungry season. The same European term was used by John Sparke. Coasting the peninsular barrier islands until he found the French settlement, John Hawkins discerned both marshes and meadows. "There they found sorrell to growe as abundantly as grasse, and nere theyr houses were great store of mayis and mill, and grapes of great bignesses."[43] Whether sorrel was indeed a sorrel, Sparke referred to a second cultivar growing in fields near Saturiwan towns, his "mill." The term evidently meant something like millet, a cultivar that produces small grains. Amaranth yields, it should be noted, as great a weight of grain per surface unit as does maize in the Andes.[44] It presumably did so in Timucuan fields. Thus amaranth may well have doubled edible grain production per area under cultivation. Even more important nutritionally, the grains of *Amaranthus* and of *Chenopodium* contain a significantly higher proportion of protein than do maize kernels. These grains enabled the Timucuan-speaking population to grow larger than it could have had it been limited by seasonal starvation or by acute female malnutrition every year just when labor demands for maize cultivation and weeding peaked.

The period after crops had been planted and had to be cultivated and protected, but before maize, beans, or squash yielded any fresh food, was a time of scarcity among many North American food producers. The Northern Pimans dwelling in the Sonoran Desert, for example, referred to the month before giant cactus fruits ripened as "painful month." No fresh vegetable food was yet available to them.[45] By growing amaranth, the Timucua had to gather less wild plant food during the period after horticultural crops were planted and growing but before food was available to harvest than they would had they not sown this cultivar. Possibly amaranth and chenopod cultivation combined with efficient storage of dried foodstuffs to eliminate any time of hunger among the Timucuan-speaking peoples.

One might question whether amaranth-chenopod cultivation would not have exhausted plant nutrients from sandy soils even more rapidly than simpler maize, bean, and squash cropping. Amaranths and chenopods send down fairly deep taproots and develop thick clumps of other roots. Amaranth roots reportedly raise nutrients to the zone where maize roots can reach them, so amaranth is today recommended for companionate planting by organic gardeners.[46] Without understanding the mechanisms involved, Timucuans were able to observe that maize grown with amaranth yielded better than maize planted without it. In the Timucuan horticultural pattern, the amaranths, together with beans and maize in hills, maintained soil fertility and ensured that maize plants obtained the nutrients they required.

According to French observers during the early 1560s, Timucuan field preparation involved uprooting what Frenchmen perceived as "weeds" and leaving them to dry. Europeans' identification of amaranths as weeds in Native American horticulture has consistently hindered accurate analysis.[47] When dry, the uprooted plants were burned. Although René Laudonnière wrote that the Timucuans did not "dung" their land[48]—indeed, they lacked domestic animals that would provide dung—burning of old chenopod, amaranth, and forb stalks in fact released onto the soil surface the nutrients that those plants had captured during the previous growing season, nourishing seedling maize, beans, squash, and minor crops of the new season. The specific technique differed from European green manuring with amaranth plants, but the nutritional result for seedlings was similar. While the Timucuans may not have added fertilizer from domestic animals or fish to their maize hills, they did grow amaranth/chenopods that helped to maintain nutrients near the soil surface when burned. Burning also suppressed brush and tree seedlings and thus helped to keep fields cultivable.[49] The fact that needs emphasis is that during decades and even centuries, Timucuans had only to use fire and their stone and shell tools to keep cultivated fields and hunting meadows free from shrub and tree seedlings. They did not have to "clear" mature forest growth, as some anthropologists have assumed they did, at a high labor investment cost.[50]

AMARANTH/CHENOPOD CULTIVATION IN THE SOUTHEAST

The Timucuan evidence points to the advisability of reassessing the horticultural capacity of other Native American peoples in the Southeastern culture area. There are a number of historical indications that amaranths and chenopods may have been grown rather widely in the pre-Columbian Southeast.

A young Native American from the South Carolina coast taken by slave raiders to Santo Domingo early in the 1520s later visited Spain. There he described a small grain his people called *xatha*. Carl O. Sauer thought that it might have been a chenopod.[51] He based his conclusion partly on a later Roanoke expedition record of what he took to be a chenopod under cultivation on the Carolina coast. Thomas Hariot recognized this as "an herb" known in Dutch as *melden*.[52] The historian David B. Quinn translated *melde* as referring to the spinach and beet families but identified the American plant as an *Atriplex*. That interpretation is subject to the methodological shortcomings already mentioned. Hariot reported that this cultivar grew four to five feet tall. This is the height that the cultivated *Chenopodium* reaches in the central Andes, and the author has grown a northwest Mexican amaranth cultivar equally tall. Hariot reported that the Carolina coastal Algonkians made "a thick fine-tasting broth of its seeds." Thickening soups is precisely one of the more common uses of contemporary *Chenopodium* in the Andes.

That Hariot saw a chenopod appears from the Native American practice of burning the stalk to obtain what Hariot called "salt." The ethnographic analogue is the chewing of pellets of stalk ash with coca leaves by central Andean peoples[53] as a substitute for lime. On the other hand, Hariot described the Algonkians as hoeing up "weeds" to burn in the fields before breaking ground for planting, like the Timucuans. This behavior Hariot did not interpret as conscious fertilization.[54] Hariot was ethnocentric, however, and seems to have inferred that the Carolina Algonkians burned the dead vegetation to avoid carrying it off. Lynn Ceci concluded that the beneficial effect of ashes on the soil was "incidental" to field clearing.[55] She ignored abundant ethnographic evidence that Native Americans were conscious of the result of their controlled burns.[56]

Hariot's record has been noted not only by Sauer[57] but also by William C. Sturtevant[58] and by Christian F. Feest.[59] The latter claimed that a long summer growing season allowed the Carolina natives to harvest two maize crops from the same fields between July and September. Indeed, Arthur Barlowe in 1584 had described the coastal Carolina Algonkians as planting maize in May to harvest in July, replanting in June for an August crop, and planting for a September crop.[60] Barlowe's assertions were based necessarily partly on inference. Barlowe did not arrive on the Carolina coast until early in July.[61] He returned to England in September,[62] having sailed from Carolina on about August 24 after a six-week stay.[63] Thus Barlowe could not have seen the reported May and June plantings. Barlowe evidently saw plants of different heights that he took to be maize from successive plantings. John White depicted a settlement with maize in three stages of growth in adjacent fields,[64] presumably what Barlowe also saw. White's watercolor portrayed three maize plantings but not double-cropping of a single field in one season.

The Carolina coastal peoples inhabited sandy soil habitat much like that of the Timucua. It lacked lands at elevations that would make either amaranth or chenopods useful as a maize substitute. Like the Timucua, therefore, the Carolina coastal Algonkians apparently grew amaranth and/or chenopods to solve the problems of spring hunger and of maintaining maize field fertility without fertilizers.

In another direction, eighteenth-century French accounts of the Natchez indicate that they grew both amaranth and chenopods and for the same reasons. One observer described a plant as the French *belle dame sauvage*, "which grows in all countries."[65] He contrasted its growth to as much as four feet in height with its foot-and-a-half growth in Europe. The Frenchman reported that the Natchez and other unspecified groups sowed this grain on Mississippi River sand banks after floodwaters had receded. Women and children covered the sown grain using their feet and did not cultivate it until autumn harvest. The difference in height between European and American plants indicated not only specific differences but also that the Mississippi River valley plant was domesticated. Swanton erred in identifying both grains as wild rice, which grows only in water and never on a sand bar after water leaves it high and dry.

The second grain the Natchez grew "naturally and without any cultivation" may have been an amaranth. Le Page du Pratz did not specify where the Natchez grew it, but evidently it grew in maize fields, inasmuch as he did not describe a different location, as he did for the cultivar sown on sand bars. To the European not familiar with Native American companionate planting in hills, amaranth could look like a volunteer but tolerated plant.

Thus early European accounts described several Native American peoples in the Southeast as cultivating amaranth and/or chenopods. At least the Timucuan-speaking chiefdoms, the inhabitants of Chicora, the coastal Carolina Algonkians (Powhatan Confederacy), and the Natchez and other Mississippi River groups thus intensified their horticulture. This historically documented distribution of the amaranth cultivar is broader than that known to botanists.[66]

Amaranths and chenopods belong to an "old eastern agricultural complex" of plants that were still grown in the Southeast after Mesoamerican maize, beans, and squash arrived.[67] Amaranths and chenopods continued in cultivation for several good reasons.

1. Amaranths and chenopods provided Southeastern culture area horticulturalists with fresh greens early during the summer before other cultivated plants produced edible parts.

2. Amaranths and chenopods produced grain weights equal to that produced by maize and higher in vegetable protein content than maize.

3. Companionate-planted amaranths helped to maintain fertility in continuously cropped maize fields by raising leaching nutrients to the soil surface. Nutrients became available to quick-sprouting crops when native cultivators burned dead plants shortly before sowing a new crop. The people of Chicora and the Powhatan Confederacy lived largely on a sandy coastal plain rather similar to peninsular Florida in soil characteristics, so this attribute of amaranth was significant to them and may have been for the Natchez as well.

Amaranth and chenopod cultivation was hardly unique among Southeastern peoples. Yet such horticulture appears to have contributed significantly to maintaining the fertility of maize fields in sandy, easily leached soils. I suggest that a significant part of the answer to the puzzle of sedentary settlement in the Southeast is amaranth-chenopod cultivation.

NOTES

1. Ribaut, *Whole & True Discouerye*, 1563, p. 81.
2. Ehrmann, "Timucua Indians," 1940, p. 176.
3. Ribaut, *Whole & True Discouerye*, 1563, p. 73.
4. Quinn, ed., *New American World*, 1979, vol. V, p. 85.
5. National Society of the Colonial Dames of America, *Turn Left*, 1976, p. 26.
6. Forbes, *Sketches*, 1821 (1964), 157.
7. Ibid., 158.
8. Varner and Varner, trans., *Florida*, 1962, p. 169.
9. Watt, Merrill, et al., *Composition of Foods*, 1950, p. 47.
10. Author's observations among modern Papagos.
11. Redfield and Villa Rojas, *Chan Kom*, 1934 (1962), 53, table 3.
12. A Spanish exploring expedition at the end of the seventeenth century reported finding baskets of squash seeds, among other provisions (Leonard, trans., *Spanish Approach*, 1939, p. 161; Siguenza y Góngara, *Documentos*, 1963, p. 70).
13. Robertson, trans., *True Relation*, 1933, vol. II, p. 53.
14. Varner and Varner, trans., *Florida*, 1962, p. 116.
15. Robertson, trans., *True Relation*, 1933, vol. II, p. 53.
16. Bourne, ed., *Narratives*, 1904, vol. II, p. 68.
17. Robertson, trans., *True Relation*, 1932, vol. I, p. rrrij.
18. Hakluyt, *Discovery and Conquest*, 1609 (n.d.), p. 36.
19. B. Smith, trans., *Narratives*, 1968, p. 37.
20. Crosby, *Columbian Exchange*, 1972, p. 1 ff.
21. Lefèvre, *La Grande Encyclopédie*, *S.V.* "Amarante."
22. *Enciclopedia Universal Ilustrada Europeo-Americana*, s.v. "Amaranto."
23. Sahagun, *History*, 1932, pp. 78–79.
24. Ibid., 129.
25. Ibid., 120–21.
26. Safford, "Forgotten Cereal," 1917, pp. 286–89. Sahagun, *History*, 1932, pp. 84–85; Sahagun, *Historia General*, 1955, vol. I, pp. 152, 194, 206, 218, 224.
27. Sahagun, *History*, 1932, pp. 109, 112.
28. Ibid., 105.
29. Ibid., 137.
30. J.D. Sauer, "Grain Amaranths and Their Relatives," 1967, p. 113.
31. Gentry, *Rio Mayo Plants*, 1942, p. 108.
32. Lumholtz, *Unknown Mexico*, 1902, vol. II, pp. 47–50.
33. Safford, "Forgotten Cereal," 1917, pp. 292–93; J.D. Sauer, "Grain Amaranths," 1950, p. 591.
34. C.O. Sauer, "Cultivated Plants," 1949, pp. 496–98.
35. Author's observations in Lima and Ancash departments, Peru.
36. Dobyns, "Altitude Sorting," 1974, pp. 42–48.
37. J.D. Sauer, "Grain Amaranths and Their Relatives," 1967, pp. 105, 119–20.
38. Varner and Varner, trans., *Florida*, 1962, p. 122.
39. Lumholtz, *New Trails*, 1912, pp. 131, 134.
40. Robertson, trans., *True Relation*, 1933, vol. II, pp. 53–54.
41. Varner and Varner, trans., *Florida*, 1962, p. 116.
42. Laudonnière, *Three Voyages*, 1975, p. 122.

43. Sparke, "Voyage made," 1878, p. 42; Spellman, "Agriculture," 1948, p. 43.

44. C.O. Sauer, "Cultivated Plants," 1949, vol. VI, p. 498.

45. Underhill, *Social Organization*, 1939, p. 125.

46. Cox, "Companion Planting," 1979, p. 62.

47. Dobyns, "Breves Comentarios," 1976, pp. 125 – 28.

48. Laudonnière, *Three Voyages*, 1975, p. 15; "History of the First Attempt of the French to Colonize the Newly Discovered Country of Florida," in French, comp., *Historical Collections*, 1869, p. 174.

49. O.C. Stewart, "Fire," 1956, pp. 119, 122.

50. Murphy and Hudson, "On the Problem," 1968, pp. 25, 29.

51. C.O. Sauer, *Sixteenth Century North America*, 1971, pp. 70 – 71, 288.

52. Lorant, ed., *New World*, 1946, p. 244.

53. C.O. Sauer, "Cultivated Plants," 1949, vol. VI, p. 496.

54. Quinn, ed., *Roanoke Voyages*, 1955, vol. I, p. 341; Lorant, ed., *New World*, 1946, p. 244.

55. Ceci, "Fish fertilizer," 1975, p. 28.

56. O.C. Stewart, "Fire," 1956, pp. 119 – 20, 129; Dobyns, *From Fire to Flood*, 1981, pp. 27 – 43.

57. C.O. Sauer, *Sixteenth Century North America*, 1971, pp. 260, 287.

58. Sturtevant, "Historic Carolina Algonkian Cultivation," 1965, pp. 64 – 65.

59. Feest, "Northern Carolina Algonquians," 1978, p. 273.

60. Lorant, ed., *New World*, 1946, p. 129.

61. Ibid., 129.

62. Ibid., 133.

63. Quinn, ed., *Roanoke Voyages*, 1955, vol. I, p. 320, n. 7.

64. Lorant, ed., *New World*, 1946, p. 191.

65. Le Page du Pratz, *History of Louisiana*, 1774 (1975), p. 175. The eighteenth-century translator erroneously thought that Le Page referred to buckwheat. (*Histoire de la Louisiana* [Paris: DeBure, 1758], pp. 316 – 17).

66. J.D. Sauer, "Grain Amaranths," 1950; "Grain Amaranths and Their Relatives," 1967.

67. Hudson, *Southeastern Indians*, 1976, p. 294.

SECTION TWO
Orchardry and Sanitation

Growing Amaranths and Chenopods helped Native Americans in the Southeast culture area to live in large, sedentary towns. This practice is, however, not the complete answer to the "puzzle" of sedentarism in the region. The present section of this essay discusses two additional factors in town life in the pre-Columbian Southeast.

ORCHARDRY

Amaranths could not maintain maize field fertility for long periods of time without assistance from other plants and some external sources of nutrients. While the amaranth taproot and its feeder root network penetrate much deeper into soil than do maize roots, the amaranth cannot retrieve or retain nutrients leached below a certain depth. Native Americans in the Southeast employed at least one additional horticultural technique that recycled deep-leached nutrients to the surface of maize fields. That technique was to leave and/or to plant in cultivated fields various trees yielding highly prized nuts and fruits. Orchardry contributed to maintaining long-term soil fertility.

Carl O. Sauer pointed out that European cultural practice was to clear a cultivated grain or other field of trees.[1] A tree constituted an obstacle to a plow team of animals. In contrast, Native Americans generally left standing any trees that yielded useful fruit or nuts. A tree was no particular obstacle to human beings hoeing hills who were completely unconcerned about straight-line furrows. This practice of encouraging useful trees may still be observed in Indoamerica. Moreover, archaeologists have inferred that a contemporary concentration of fifteen trees that produced fruit, fiber, bark, or resin near the center of prehistoric Mayan ceremonial sites reflects a dominant group control of such resources when the sites were inhabited.[2]

In the central Andean region, fruit- and nut-yielding shrubs and trees may be seen growing in high-altitude fencerows where they are sustained by natural precipitation.[3] On the arid coastal littoral, trees such as *pacae* are planted deliberately along irrigation ditches, where they receive an adequate supply of water.

In the Southeast, Native Americans inland from the coasts who cultivated alluvial riverine fields grew their crops in the preferred habitat of the black walnut (*Juglans nigra*). The deep roots of the walnut trees performed the same fertility maintenance function as amaranths. Tree roots penetrate deeper and raise a greater quantity of nutrients to their leaves than any annual plant. Deciduous leaves deposit nutrients on field surfaces to decompose or to be burned with "weeds" immediately prior to planting. Sixteenth-century eyewitness evidence of this technique is clear, although tree leaves are not specifically mentioned and the texts must be interpreted.[4] No one who has raked the fallen leaves of deciduous fruit or nut trees from a twentieth-century lawn will doubt that numerous such leaves were mixed with the "weeds" Timucuans burned in January to prepare fields for planting.

The chroniclers of de Soto's invasion recorded that nut trees were common in Native American fields in both the Atlantic coastal plain and Tennessee River valley.[5] The Gentleman of Elvas reported that from coastal Cofitachique to inland Creek Chiaha, mulberries, walnuts, and plum trees "grow wild in the fields without being planted or manured and are as large and vigorous as if they were cultivated and irrigated in gardens."[6] The Creeks at Chiaha in the latter valley stored a great deal of nut oil.[7] The Spaniards did not in mid-sixteenth century encounter pecan trees east of the Mississippi River. Immediately west of that stream, however, they saw many pecan trees growing in Native Americans' fields.[8] Biedma remembered that the de Soto expedition first encountered pecans at Quizquiz, a short distance east of the Mississippi River but politically subject to a ruler who lived on the west side.[9] The Gentleman of Elvas first mentioned the pecan growing "in the fields" of Aquixo, the province west of the Mississippi River,[10] or "in the open field."[11] He also recorded mulberry trees and two varieties of plum, commenting that the trees were all "as green as if they stood in orchards"[12] or all the trees "as verdant all year as if set out in gardens and in a clear grove."[13] However it is translated, the text described fruit trees growing in the midst of annual cultivated plants and showing no sign of nitrogen deficiency, if color descriptions can be trusted.

The contribution of fruit trees to maintaining maize field fertility was also reported among the Apalachee by the Gentleman of Elvas. The dried plums supplied to the de Soto expedition at Apalachee "come from trees that grow in the fields without being planted," he claimed.[14] Considering the limited opportunities de Soto's marauders had to observe orchardry, plum trees could have been deliberately planted as well as tolerated.

Whatever the degree to which Native Americans cultivated plums, it did not so genetically modify them that they could not reproduce on their own. Still, evidence of their cultivation is clear in the historic record. In 1716, for example, explorer Diego Peña reported "medlars" still growing in numbers at the former settlements of Patale, San Luís, Tomale, and La Tama in abandoned Apalachee territory in modern Leon County, Florida.[15] The Apalachee had also grown quinces, pomegranates, and peaches introduced to the peninsula by the Spaniards.

Carl O. Sauer theorized that later Anglo-American settlers on former fields of Native Americans kept plum trees they found there. Sauer thought that Native Americans had selected plums for fruit size and quality and for upright tree habit.[16] Such selection required not merely tolerating volunteer trees but planting seeds and weeding out less de-sirable seedlings and/or transplanting preferred trees. Peter Martyr d'Anglería reported on the basis of his interviews with Lucas Vásquez de Ayllón and the kidnapped Francisco de Chicora, deliberate growing of fruit trees in gardens. "They even have trees in their gardens" on the coastal plain of South Carolina.[17]

Fruit and nut tree cultivation in fields with maize and other annuals planted in hills contributed to maintaining fertility in both the upland riverine and coastal lowland Southeast. Deagan's list of Saturiwan tree crops indicates the extent to which the Timucuan-speaking peoples employed fruit and nut trees to solve the problem of fertility mainte-nance: cherries, white and red mulberries, persimmons, walnuts, chestnuts, and dwarf chinquapins.[18] In 1539, de Soto's marauders found "prunes" among the dried foods stored at Ocali Town,[19] so the Ocali evidently picked plums from trees in their seven-league-long core-inhabited zone with its summer maize fields. Stored prunes attest not only to Timucuan food-drying technology but also to Ocali orchardry on a scale at least large enough to meet tastes for fresh fruit and to permit harvest of additional plums to dry for storage. Timucuans pre-served and probably planted a variety of cultivated fruit and nut trees that recovered nutrients leached below the zone penetrated by amaranth roots. These trees raised such nutrients up to deciduous leaves that restored them to the soil surface for the benefit of the follow-ing season's maize, bean, and squash crop.

The Southeastern Native American practice of leaving or planting nut and fruit trees in fields planted to annual crops significantly influ-enced another aspect of the ecological system. The trees no doubt attracted birds, performing the same function as fencerow trees and shrubs in other agricultural regimens. Birds flying from tree to tree, and especially those nesting in the fruit and nut trees, would have helped appreciably to restrain the insect population of the cultivated fields. To the extent that birds roosted and nested in the fruit and nut trees, they would have contributed their dung to the leaf mold under those trees. Bird dung is high in nitrogen content, so that such "natural" fertilization would help to account for the healthy green appearance of the fruit and nut trees upon which early European observers commented. As the leaves of deciduous fruit and nut trees scattered over the field, nutrients captured by the trees would be recycled to the annual plants.

The fruit and nut trees in the cultivated fields would have been attractive training grounds for Timucuan boys learning to hunt with small bows and arrows. Those lads could hope to kill a dove or a fat bluejay by climbing into the branches and then waiting quietly for a bird to perch where a well-placed arrow would kill it. Such small triumphs no doubt contributed marginally to family food supplies.

Not all birds were uniformly beneficial to the Timucuan horticultural economy. Some birds posed a threat to maize and perhaps to bean and squash harvests. On June 24, 1564, René Laudonnière noted that the Saturiwans were posting sentinels in huts in a corner of their maize fields to frighten birds away from maturing grain.[20] The use of people in maize fields near harvest time to scare birds away from the ripening grains is characteristic of intensive maize cultivation.

The sixteenth-century documentary evidence for Timucuan cultivation of amaranth and perhaps chenopods, and for the interplanting of annual food crops with perennial nut and fruit trees, suggests a pair of important conclusions about pre-Columbian Timucuan and Southeastern Native American life. (1) The Timucuan-speaking peoples were more efficient horticulturalists than either historians or anthropologists have heretofore credited them with being. (2) The Timucuans had apparently solved the widespread problem of limitation of population growth imposed by annual seasonal food shortages as well as maintaining sedentary settlements based on continuous cultivation of maize fields. Thus Timucuan population may be assumed to have been denser than that of other Native Americans in similar habitats who lacked their technology and complex social structure.

Until this point, the discussion of cultivated plant distributions has been couched in terms of the Southeastern culture area. Identification of a significant amaranth/chenopod role in Timucuan horticulture and of the importance of fruit and nut trees in that economy calls for a comment about relationships with another culture area. Anthropologists have on occasion speculated that various traits of the Southeastern culture area may have originated in Mesoamerica. Maize, beans, and squash are all tropical cultivars domesticated in Mesoamerica; seeds diffused to the Southeast at some remote prehistoric time. The last chapter emphasized that amaranth and chenopod seeds must be added to the list, although the concept of horticulture may have diffused rather than actual seeds. Not just three but perhaps five domesticated plants grown by Timucuans came from tropical America. An earlier chapter stressed the importance of *Zamia* starch in the Timucuan and Calusan diets. This genus is an analogue of manioc, cultivated widely in tropical America. If ancestors of the Calusa did not import it into Florida, they or the ancestral Timucuans did something even more notable. With a manioc model in mind, they identified a Floridian plant genus that looks nothing at all like manioc and adapted it to cultivation for its starchy root. Defining a truly domesticated plant that is not grown for its seeds is frequently difficult, but the fact that contemporary ornamental *Zamia* plants do better when cultivated than when left alone identifies this plant as one significantly influenced by man.

The cultivation of nut and fruit trees and of maize, beans, squash, amaranth and chenopod in combination in the southeast resembles in pattern Mesoamerican food production practice. The perennial plants differ between the two areas, just as *Zamia* differs from manioc. Mesoamericans grow tropical species such as chonta palm (*Bactris utilis*), soursop (*Annona muricata*), avocado (*Persea americana*), the black cherry (*Prunus serotina*) that also grows in Florida, guava, or pacae (*Inga* sp.), mammee (*Mammea americana*), papaya (*Carica papaya*), sapotes (*Calocarpum mammosum*), lucuma (*Lucuma obovata*),[21] ramón, or breadnut (*Brosimum alicastrum*), and fruits known in Maya as *chiceh* (*Chrysophyllum mexicana*), *chirichojom* (*Acrocomia mexicana*), *kilim* (*Spondias purpurea*), *nance* (*Byrosonima crassifolia*), *pich* (*Enterolobium cyclocarpium*), and *subul* (*Sideroxylon gaumeri*).[22] Such tropical plants could not survive even in subtropical Florida, so the Southeastern orchard species inventory is much smaller than the Mesoamerican. Yet the overall patterns appear to be very similar—so similar, in fact, as to suggest both direct and stimulus diffusion of Mesoamerican horticultural technologies to the Southeast. The conclusion is simply stated; no attempt will be made to review here a relatively voluminous literature debating this question.

SETTLEMENT SANITATION

One other aspect of Timucuan life merits a short discussion, even though it must be mainly speculative. This is the question of sanitation in the towns. The sixteenth-century European documents do not describe the habits of elimination of the Timucuans. Did they defecate and urinate in their horticultural fields? If they did so, then their wastes helped to maintain field fertility, especially in nitrogen and phosphorus, for the human digestive tract adds these elements to foods that pass through it, making human urine and excrement excellent fertilizers. Intensive Chinese agriculture succeeded for centuries in feeding a very dense population because it recycled human wastes directly to the fields.

What little evidence there seems to be on this matter is at best indirect. That is, none of the Europeans who spent time among Timucuans in the sixteenth century seems to have written anything about Timucuan towns or houses being strikingly dirty or smelly. European household and town sanitation in that century left much to be desired by current standards, so Europeans would not have considered towns as garbage strewn and littered with excrement as their own to be out of the ordinary. Yet Europeans did on occasion complain about the odors of Native American households elsewhere in North America or about the large flea population in the beds or filth in the settlements. Whatever the state of sanitation in Timucuan settlements, it appears to have been no worse than that in European towns of the period.

The state of the documentary record raises the possibility that Timucuans were comparatively tidy around their houses and in their towns. If they had not been relatively clean, their long-occupied townsites presumably would have carried an odor strong enough to prompt Europeans to complain. It can be hypothesized, therefore, that good Timucuan manners required that adults and older children defecate and urinate outside the settlement. If that was the case, then people had a choice between cultivated fields nearby and whatever oak thickets, berry patches, or other brush or trees grew within a convenient distance from town.

The pattern of cultivating nut and fruit trees in fields planted to annual crops suggests that at least some human waste was directly deposited on the fields. In the warm, moist Florida climate, hills interplanted with maize, beans, squash, amaranth, and gourds would have to be weeded to allow domestic plants to flourish. Weeding during any Florida spring or summer is hot, tiring work. The shade of the interplanted nut and fruit trees would be a nearly irresistible attraction for tired weeders. Before or after resting in the shade of a fruit or nut tree, the weeders would tend to urinate or defecate. Probably good manners militated against soiling the shaded areas where people rested, making the field itself the logical target.

NOTES

1. C.O. Sauer, *Sixteenth Century North America*, 1971, p. 181.
2. Folan, Fletcher, and Kintz, "Fruit, Fiber," 1979, pp. 699–700.
3. C.O. Sauer, "Cultivated Plants," 1949, vol. VI, p. 542. Brush, *Mountain Field*, 1977, p. 98.
4. Laudonnière, *Three Voyages*, 1975, p. 15. Pre-Columbian weed-leaf burning survived until late in the seventeenth century (Wenhold, trans., *17th Century Letter*, 1936, p. 13).
5. C.O. Sauer, *Sixteenth Century North America*, 1971, p. 181; Varner and Varner, trans., *Florida*, 1962, pp. 328, 331; B. Smith, trans., *Narratives*, 1968, pp. 63, 70.
6. Robertson, trans., *True Relation*, 1933, vol. II, p. 103.
7. B. Smith, trans., *Narratives*, 1968, p. 70; Robertson, trans., *True Relation*, 1933, vol. II, p. 104.
8. C.O. Sauer, *Sixteenth Century North America*, 1971, p. 182.
9. B. Smith, trans., *Narratives*, 1968, p. 249.
10. Ibid., 107.
11. Robertson, trans., *True Relation*, 1933, vol. II, p. 166.
12. B. Smith, trans., *Narratives*, 1968, p. 108.
13. Robertson, trans., *True Relation*, 1933, vol. II, p. 166.
14. B. Smith, trans., *Narratives*, 1968, p. 47; Robertson, trans., *True Relation*, 1933, vol. II, p. 67.
15. Boyd, "Diego Peña's Expedition," 1949, p. 18.
16. C.O. Sauer, *Sixteenth Century North America*, 1971, p. 290.
17. Quinn, ed., *New American World*, 1979, vol. I, p. 270.
18. Deagan, "Cultures," 1978, p. 104.
19. Varner and Varner, trans., *Florida*, 1962, p. 122.
20. Laudonnière, *Three Voyages*, 1975, p. 62.
21. C.O. Sauer, "Cultivated Plants," 1949, vol. VI, pp. 523–32.
22. Folan, Fletcher, and Kintz, "Fruit, Fiber," 1979, p. 699.

SECTION THREE
Storehouses and Canoes

Other very significant factors in Timucuan sedentarism were technological and social. One of these factors, the canoe, enabled Timucuans to forage for fish, mollusks, and game and wild plant foods from a settlement central to all their foraging patches. The second factor, the chief's communal storehouse, enabled the Timucuans to centralize critical storage, processing, and consumption of cultivated foodstuffs.[1]

In the backward areas of the world where peasant agriculture persists today, one of the most severe obstacles to the commercialization of subsistence farming is the lack of storage facilities for crops. Peasant producers typically must sell directly in a marketplace or sell to middlemen at miserable prices because they cannot store their harvests.[2] Anthropologists and economists familiar with contemporary peasants tend to forget, perhaps, that the pre-Conquest Native Americans built and used many food storehouses. The royal *tambo* was a frequent feature of the central Andean landscape of the Tawantinsuyu long before the arrival of Francisco Pizarro.[3] Numerous imperial storehouses held tribute in foodstuffs, including maize, beans, peppers, pumpkin seeds, chia, and amaranth seeds, plus feathers, cotton, and other textiles, both in Tenochtitlán and in other cities in and under the Triple Alliance.[4] Clans and families also maintained their own granaries throughout civilized Mesoamerica.[5] Storing produce to carry populations through drought years or other disasters was, in fact, more typical than not of Native America.

One major factor in Timucuan sedentarism was communal warehousing of dried foods in a very Mesoamerican pattern. The Saturiwan Timucua, at least, built large, communal storehouses possibly intended to serve an entire chiefdom.[6] They dried large quantities of fish, alligators, snakes, deer, and other game on wooden racks over smoking fires.[7] They also dried maize, beans, and no doubt squash[8] and amaranth/chenopod seeds, plus nuts, berries, fruits, such as plums, and other foodstuffs. They deposited these dried stores in their communal storehouses.

Judging from the picture of one drawn by Jacques Le Moyne on the basis of his observation in 1564, the Timucuan communal storehouse possessed one characteristic very important in the present analysis. That is, storehouses were erected on or very near the banks of streams navigable by Timucuan canoes. De Bry engraved a storehouse with a canoe in view on the stream in the foreground.[9] In other words, Timucuans did not depend upon human muscles alone to move their food to storage or to remove it from a storehouse for consumption. They could move heavy cargoes of dried foods relatively long distances by canoe over both riverine and lacustrine routes. As a consequence, Timucuans did not have to plant their crops only close to their towns or only along river banks. The waterways abundant in low-lying Florida, together with the canoe, afforded Timucuan peoples the capacity to cultivate fields close to or distant from their towns. Conceivably they could engage in swidden horticulture and move their fields from one spot to another when fertility did decline despite the cultivation of fruit and nut trees and of amaranths and chenopods—while maintaining sedentary settlements. Canoes and numerous waterways, plus the social organization of communal storage and the technical skills of drying and smoking foodstuffs, all together afforded the Timucuan-speaking peoples that capability.

Timucuans relied on canoes for transporting dried foods to and from storage and also for fishing and for trade. Building their towns on the edge of the water on Tampa Bay, Cumberland Island, or on the St. Johns River, the Ocklawaha River, the Kissimmee River, the Santa Fé River, or numerous smaller streams, made canoe travel and cargo transport efficient and convenient. The location of many towns on the water's edge did not, however, mean that all or even most cultivated fields were located on riverine flood plains, as some analysts have argued.[10] To Timucuan cultivators who did harvest fields close to water, proximity to canoe transport was probably the primary conscious consideration, rather than friability of the soil or any other factor.

The canoe enabled Timucuans rapidly and regularly to scan one of the richest game habitats in their territory, the periodically burned vegetation on and near the shoreline of rivers, creeks, lakes, marshes, and wetlands. This zone abounded in alligators, several large birds, and some kinds of fish and turtles.

At least one perceptive Colonial Spaniard actually perceived the key role the canoe played in the Timucuan economy. In 1597 the Florida colony suffered several reverses. The Guale people rebelled against Christian proselytization and killed five Franciscan missionaries among them. The Ais slew a Spanish and Native American trading party that went beyond Cape Cañaveral with goods to barter for amber.[11] A long-time resident of St. Augustine, Bartolomé de Argüelles, on August 3, 1598, wrote to the king his recommendations for changes in the colonial service personnel and policies. On the basis of his experience with the native peoples, Argüelles wrote that the manner in which the Spaniards could most damage them would be for "a couple of boats and forty experienced men" to travel up and down the waterways to "take all the canoes in which they sail from one island to another to hunt and sow, and break them into pieces." To complete a scorched-earth strategy, these marauders should cut down the maize, beans, and pumpkins in the flower.[12] Thus Argüelles left no doubt that he viewed canoe transportation as vital to the functioning of a Timucuan subsistence economy based squarely on horticultural production and on animal protein obtained by hunting.

Timucuan chiefdom social structure, with rather authoritarian chiefs and considerable role specialization, seems to have facilitated the operation of communal storage facilities and food storage on a large scale. This cultural trait of Timucuan-speaking peoples, like other Timucuan characteristics, is reminiscent of the empire of Tawantinsuyu and the native states of Mesoamerica.

The very Mesoamerican aspect of Timucuan society, with centralized political management of a communal storehouse bears emphasis. Timucuan studies have consistently underestimated the contribution of horticultural products to Timucuan diet; scholars have been misled by sixteenth-century documents. Even Kathleen A. Deagan characterized the Saturiwans as horticulturalists during the warm half of the year and as hunter-gatherers for the other half.[13] She probably followed the reasoning of Ehrmann,[14] who concluded that the Timucua spent their winters living in the woods "entirely on game, fish, wild berries, nuts, and herbs." He followed René Laudonnière all too trustingly. That wily Frenchman indeed wrote that the "Indians" spent January, February, and March in the woods hunting and "living upon what they take in the chase." As is often the case with historic texts, however, one cannot afford to take at face value everything that Laudonnière wrote. Laudonnière's trading relations with the Timucuan tribes should be kept very much in mind when we interpret his descriptions of their economies. Laudonnière was not able to obtain food from the Saturiwans during the three-month period he mentioned in 1565.[15] The reason was not that the Timucua relied on what they could immediately obtain by hunting and gathering. On the contrary, the reason was that they wisely kept their dried food stores for their own consumption. They refused to trade food to the Europeans, who were the people then dependent on what they could kill, catch, collect, or obtain by trade.[16]

In fact, the Timucuans dried and stored maize—probably the longer-season variety of the Southeastern culture area tribes that matured in some fourteen weeks[17]—as well as many other foodstuffs,[18] to be consumed during the colder months. Laudonnière himself wrote that the Timucua carried all of the grain harvested into a "public granary" but claimed that they sowed enough for only a six-month supply.[19] Again, Laudonnière evidently miscalculated. The Saturiwa no doubt stored sufficient dried foods to supply themselves through a winter season. What they had not anticipated was having to feed a host of hungry Frenchmen who were producing no food! The evident importance of food storage among the Timucua indicates that a relatively large portion of their diet was composed of horticultural products. The large-scale smoking-drying of game that Le Moyne represented[20] suggests that the Timucua stored sufficient dried animal protein to tide them over emergencies. Certainly the Timucua were at no time dependent on immediate kills to survive, as Laudonnière and those who have taken some of his statements at face value implied. The Timucuan hunter might have had to kill an animal to provide fresh meat for the pot or roasting stick, but the visual and documentary evidence indicates that there was dried meat to fall back on if a hunter failed to bring game home on a particular day.

Rather conclusive evidence exists that the Timucua dried food and stored enough to sustain the population for more than a single winter. De Soto's marauders reached Ocali Town on July 26 and departed on August 22, 1539.[21] At Ocali, these European adventurers found in the 600 houses a "great store" of acorns, other nuts, raisins, prunes, maize, other grains, and vegetables.[22] Raisins and prunes quite clearly had to be stored foods, dried in 1538 or earlier and carried over from the previous winter. The 1539 acorn and nut crops had not yet ripened and fallen by July 26, so the acorns and other nuts also came from earlier harvest years. Conceivably maize and other grains could have come from a first 1539 spring planting, but the standing maize crop was just ripe enough for the Spaniards to harvest it.[23] If the maize in storage was not from an early spring 1539 planting that had been harvested and dried by late July, it, too, had been grown and processed in 1538 or earlier. Thus the food stores found in the houses consisted of dried food that the Ocali people had carried over at least one winter. The Ocali people, and by inference the other Timucuan-speaking groups, were not by any means living hand to mouth. Fernando de Soto was able to plunder the stored foods in Ocali houses just as he and Pizarro's other followers had plundered royal tambos during the conquest of Tawantinsuyu in South America.

In fact, the Timucuan society of which one learns from careful evaluation of sixteenth-century sources has a strikingly Incan cast. The Headchief possessed absolute authority. He could have a person executed.[24] He had centralized—at least among the Saturiwa—storehouses into which families reportedly conveyed their cultivated food harvests. He mobilized armies numbering thousands of warriors. Were those armies provisioned out of communal storehouses? In any event, hierarchically organized Timucuan societies were not by any stretch of the imagination living precariously on the edge of starvation. The Timucuan-speaking chiefdoms were densely populated, very sedentary, and complexly organized. The people produced a significant surplus of food beyond immediate day-to-day needs that was stored in order to provide an adequate subsistence the year around and also to furnish a balanced diet even in case of crop failure.

The other face of Timucuan society, rather Nahua-like, looked over the prow of a canoe paddled along a river, creek, or ditch or across a lake. That Saturiba Town or Alicamani Town could hold 2,500 people should not surprise anyone who stops to think that Tenochtitlán reached a population of 60,000 or 300,000, depending on how one interprets surviving evidence, immediately prior to Spanish Conquest. It did so because the city was built on causeways in Lake Texcoco and was supplied via canoe in large part. Tribute in foodstuffs remanded from conquered provinces certainly helped to sustain the dense and absolutely large population of Tenochtitlán. Much of that tribute moved into the city on human backs. Yet watercraft brought fresh vegetables and grains from Xochimilco's *chinampa* gardens to the city. Fishermen in canoes harvested fish from the lake to feed the urban populace. The importance of waterborne transport in late pre-Columbian Mesoamerican civilization is shown by one simple fact. The largest urban centers took form only around lakes. A dearth of navigable streams elsewhere restricted the substitution of watercraft for direct human transportation.[25] What the canoe did for Tenochtitlán it did also for Timucuan towns, albeit on a smaller scale.

The economic importance of canoe transportation in Timucuan life calls for a comment about a general deficiency in anthropological theory. Anthropologists appear to be in general a group of landlubbers with no perception of the functional importance of watercraft in human societies. One leading analyst of social structure, for example, devised a putatively quantitative measure of cultural complexity considering solely land transportation technology. The five classifications of land transport constitute one-tenth of all fifty characteristics in the measure. Consequently, all pre-Conquest New World Native American cultures score zero on this measure because they transported things on land "exclusively by human carriers."[26] The result of such reasoning is to underrate all New World societies that developed significant waterborne canoe transport relative to any Old World society with domesticated animals. Peoples relying on pack animals are credited with one point in the "measure," even though a cargo canoe can carry considerably greater weight than a pack animal. Moreover, the crude sled, or travois without wheels, is in this scheme scored two points, regardless of the greater cargo capacity of the large canoe. Yet these characteristics supposedly constitute a scale measuring indirectly the extent of trade between different groups of people!

The relationship between efficient techniques for moving large quantities of commodities within particular societies may be more significant than intergroup exchange. The configuration of Aztec society well illustrates such a functional relationship. The analyst of cultural complexity credited the Aztecs with four points for their high degree of urbanization—populations exceeding 1,000 persons in local communities.[27] Yet the very large urban population of the Aztec capital city of Tenochtitlán depended upon canoe transport of foodstuffs on Lake Texcoco for its existence. Tenochtitlán could not have grown to its 60,000 or 300,000 inhabitants had it had to rely solely on human land transport. The Aztecs should be credited with a canoe transport system that was functionally equivalent to Old World domesticated animals pulling two-wheeled carts, at the very least. That would be a score of three on the land transport scale devised by the would-be measurer of cultural complexity.

Pre-Conquest Inca society furnishes another illustration of the functional importance of cargo watercraft in a complex conquest state. The conquered peoples inhabiting the coastal valleys on the Pacific side of the Andes long sailed offshore to dig bird guano from islands where it accumulated and to haul it back to the mainland to fertilize their irrigated fields. The would-be analyst of cultural complexity rightly scored the Inca a maximum four on horticulture. Inca horticulture did contribute more than any other subsistence activity to the food supply and was conducted by intensive techniques, including both irrigation and fertilization with bird guano. The analyst also credited the Incas with one point because they could pack small burdens on domesticated llamas. One guano cargo raft carried as much weight as hundreds of balky llamas, however, and the fertilizer was absolutely essential for maintaining food production in irrigated valley fields that had been cropped for thousands of years.[28] Properly analyzed, in other words, the Inca should have received one or two additional points for their fertilizer-hauling raft fleet.

Perhaps the best illustration of the absurdity of a purely land-transport measure of cultural complexity is its treatment of the Huron people. The Huron were the premier intergroup traders of the eastern

Great Lakes region when Europeans penetrated that area.[29] They back-packed goods out to their most distant, scattered Algonkian-speaking woodlands customers, but they moved the bulk of their maize and other commodities by canoe. The Huron took maximum geopolitical and economic advantage of the Great Lakes and tributary rivers, lakes, and creeks over a wide expanse of territory. Light enough for one man to carry, their birchbark canoe could carry the weight of a hogshead[30] in addition to its crew. Yet the would-be measurer of cultural complexity scored the Huron zero on land transport.[31] Such a score emphasizes the fallaciousness of taking land transport as the sole indirect measure of intergroup trade. Surely the Huron should score two or three if scale of international trade is actually what one seeks to quantify and evaluate.

The characteristics of several Native American societies—Aztec, Inca, Huron, and the various Timucuan-speaking chiefdoms—high-light the functional importance of canoe transportation. The short-comings of quantitative comparison that relies solely on land transport technology show that anthropologists need to rethink their analyses of Native American cultures. Especially when peoples of the New World are compared to those of the Old, meaningful comparison occurs in terms of capability of moving heavy weights and not in terms of the specific techniques for moving them. As long as water is available on which to float it, a cargo canoe or raft is the functional equivalent of a wheeled cart. If one seeks to measure trade, moreover, one should analyze trade and not transportation systems.

NOTES

1. Orians and Pearson, "On the Theory," 1979, p. 158.

2. Mellor et al., *Developing Rural India*, 1968. The author observed the severe handicap on commercializing peasant production in Antioquia Department, Colombia, while on a research assignment for the Organization of American States in 1976.

3. Dobyns and Doughty, *Peru*, 1976, p. 56.

4. Vaillant, *Aztecs*, 1941, p. 231; Días del Castillo, *Discovery and Conquest*, 1908 (1956), 211; Sahagun, *Historia de las Cosas*, 1955, vol. III, p. 44; Anderson and Dibble, trans., *Florentine Codex*, 1955, p. 47; Bancroft, *Native Races*, 1875, vol. II, p. 349; Hernandez Xolocotzi, "Maize Granaries," 1949, pp. 159–64.

5. Vaillant, *Aztecs*, 1941, p. 115; Hernandez Xolocotzi, "Maize Granaries," 1949, pp. 164–67.

6. Lorant, ed., *New World*, 1946, p. 79; Laudonnière, *Three Voyages*, 1975, p. 174.

7. Lorant, ed., *New World*, 1946, p. 83.

8. Ibid., 81.

9. Ibid., 79.

10. Murphy and Hudson, "On the Problem," 1968, p. 27.

11. Quinn, ed., *New American World*, 1979, vol. V, p. 88.

12. Ibid., 89.

13. Deagan, "Cultures," 1978, p. 104.

14. Ehrmann, "Timucua Indians," 1940, p. 174.

15. Laudonnière, *Three Voyages*, 1975, p. 121.

16. Lorant, ed., *New World*, 1946, pp. 15–16, 94.

17. Hudson, *Southeastern Indians*, 1976, p. 293; Lorant, ed., *New World*, 1946, p. 242.

18. Spellman, "Agriculture," 1948, p. 46.

19. Laudonnière, *Three Voyages*, 1975, p. 15.

20. Lorant, ed., *New World*, 1946, p. 83.

21. Bourne, ed., *Narratives*, 1904, vol. II, pp. 67–69.

22. Varner and Varner, trans., *Florida*, 1962, p. 122.

23. Robertson, trans., *True Relations*, 1933, vol. II, pp. 53–54.

24. Lorant, ed., *New World*, 1946, p. 99. A sentry who let enemies burn a town was executed.

25. Borah, "Discontinuity and Continuity," 1979, p. 5.

26. Murdock and Provost, "Measurement," 1973, p. 381.

27. Ibid., 380, 386.

28. Dobyns and Doughty, *Peru*, 1976, pp. 33–36.

29. Trigger, *Hurons*, 1969, pp. 36–40.

30. Tooker, *Ethnography*, 1964, pp. 22, 25–27.

31. Murdock and Provost, "Measurement," 1973, pp. 381, 386.

An Outline of Florida Epidemiology

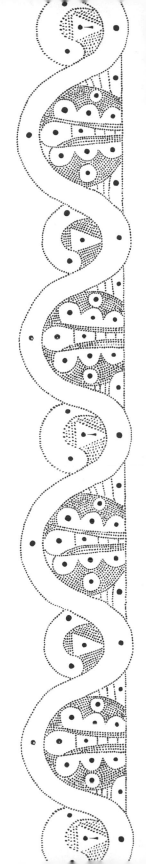

Some scholars of Florida's Native Americans have demonstrated an awareness that Old World diseases greatly thinned the area's aboriginal population. No one seems to have identified, however, nearly all of the lethal epidemics that occurred or the Old World diseases that became endemic on the peninsula. Archaeologists have tended to focus on only three seventeenth-century epidemic episodes. Briefly reporting that state archaeologists had located four Apalachee and Yustega mission sites, B. Calvin Jones stated that epidemics had taken a toll in 1613 – 1617, in 1649 – 1650, and in 1672.[1] Jerald T. Milanich also wrote that epidemics "swept through the Timucua" on the same three occasions.[2] Two of these epidemic episodes, those beginning in 1613 and 1672, had already been mentioned by an ethnohistorian of the Southeast.[3] Actually, the Native American peoples of Florida suffered perhaps eight major epidemic episodes during the protohistoric half century from A.D. 1512 to 1562. Native American numbers did not merely become thinned; biological disaster struck the inhabitants of the peninsula.

In the course of analyzing the impact of plagues on the peoples of the world, William H. McNeill pointed out that historians have seriously neglected disease in explaining human events.[4] So have anthropologists. McNeill called for a broad reinterpretation of history explicitly taking disease and epidemics into account; I will undertake to illuminate only one small area. This analysis points to evidence suggestive of seaborne commerce, message transmission, personnel transfers, and supply shipments between Caribbean islands and continental Colonial New Spain and Florida frequent enough to maintain Florida in the same epidemic region as the colonized area of the Spanish empire between 1512 and 1763.

The procedure in this analysis is simple. I identify episodes of epidemic diseases in Florida, examine the documentary record of New

Spain and the West Indian colonies, to discover whether the epidemic in Florida was apparently transmitted from the European-colonized areas, and also seek alternative sources of contagion in the documentary record. In this essay, the general summary of major epidemics presented in the initial essay is particularized to a specific portion of North America. I also amplify the record of lethal epidemics in this smaller region. Each disease is diagnosed as best it can be at this time, given the available clues.

NOTES

1. B.C. Jones, "Spanish Mission Site," 1972, p. 1.
2. Milanich, *Excavations*, 1972, p. 58.
3. Swanton, *Early History*, 1922, p. 338.
4. McNeill, *Plagues and Peoples*, 1976, p. 4.

SECTION ONE
The Protohistoric Period, 1512-1562

Certain Spanish maps indicate that explorers discovered and charted at least the southern portion of the peninsula of Florida in about A.D. 1500.[1] Documented European exploration on land began several years later, in 1513. Then French Huguenots set up a temporary settlement in 1564. Ousting the Huguenots, the Spaniards settled the first permanent town in North America at St. Augustine in 1565. Florida was, of course, inhabited by several Native American chiefdoms. They were subject to indirect transmission of Old World pathogens from the time the Spaniards conquered insular Native Americans and settled on Hispaniola and Puerto Rico. They became especially vulnerable after Spaniards colonized Cuba, because its people and the South Florida Calusa seem to have kept up regular communication. Florida's natives were also subject to direct transatlantic transmission of lethal Old World diseases from the time European ships were wrecked along the peninsular coast, and survivors were held captive by Native American chiefs. The documentary record of such biological contacts between Europeans and Native Americans, while scant, is analyzable. Consequently, the label "protohistoric" applies to the period from about 1512 to 1562, when a continuous documented record of European colonization and intermittent contact with Native Americans began. The Columbian Exchange of diseases and human genes flourished during that protohistoric period. While it is doubtful whether historians will ever be able to reconstruct the entire record of microbial invasion of Florida's Native American population prior to 1563, enough clues are available to permit the identification of some major epidemic episodes that struck Florida's Native Americans before 1565.

The brief French colonization in north Florida provided a comparative wealth of information about several Timucuan-speaking peoples. The French observer most important to the present analysis arrived at the mouth of the St. Johns River from France on June 22, 1564.[2] He was Jacques Le Moyne de Morgues. This artist observed the Saturiwa chiefdom and other Timucuans until Spanish forces overwhelmed French Fort Caroline on September 20, 1565.[3] Le Moyne painted a number of scenes showing Timucuans in a variety of roles, including contacts with Frenchmen. Moreover, Le Moyne wrote specific comments on the natives in addition to his narrative of events in the French colony. The available engravings and text provide significant information about the transmission of diseases to the Native Americans in Florida during the protohistoric period and their cultural changes to attempt to cope with those biological invasions.

One of Le Moyne's forty-three paintings shows Timucuan transvestites, termed "hermaphrodites" by Le Moyne, carrying the bodies of dead Timucua to a burial ground. De Bry's engraving of pairs of transvestites carrying bodies on European-style litters with a handle in each hand does not agree with Le Moyne's textual description. Le Moyne wrote that the transvestites fastened hide thongs to the ends of poles and supported these with their heads. The very use of a woven-reed mat-and-pole litter, however supported, suggests that a cultural change had occurred during protohistoric times. It was not common among North American peoples for bodies to be carried to interment on woven reed mats that transvestites supported by poles. Usually relatives buried their dead, or members of a paired moiety spared relatives from the sad task.

At the end of his text, Le Moyne added a single sentence of great significance. He wrote that the "hermaphrodites" looked after "those who have contagious diseases; they take the sick on their shoulders to places selected for the purpose and feed and care for them until they are well again."[4] The engraving shows in the upper left background two transvestites carrying presumably sick adults on their backs. The implications of this engraving and text appear not to have been realized by historians or archaeologists writing about the Timucua.

1. The first inference to be drawn from Le Moyne's record, brief though it may be, is that cultural change had occurred.

a. The Timucua had learned to identify at least some contagious—Old World—diseases.

b. They had also learned the concept and instituted the practice of isolating patients—placing them in quarantine—and of providing them with nursing care to aid their recovery.

c. Moreover, the Timucua assigned a specific group in the population to this risky task. High-risk nursing it was, inasmuch as truly contagious diseases would have been contracted by transvestite nurses oftener than by any other component of the population.

The Timucuan therapy Le Moyne recorded in 1564 was truly astonishing behavior for a Native American group. When the first smallpox pandemic struck the New World peoples in 1520, Native Americans lacked any cultural pattern for dealing with the contagious diseases that had evolved in the Old World. They lacked any cultural behavior identifiable as nursing. Indeed, Native American religious beliefs and practices of ritual purification dictated taking sweat baths, which increased Native American mortality from febrile, eruptive diseases such as smallpox, measles, and chickenpox. Spanish observers of Nahuatl behavior commented on the negative consequences of sweat bathing.[5] Yet Le Moyne apparently did not paint or mention a sweat lodge—a very significant omission. Almost certainly Le Moyne would have seen a sweat lodge if the Timucua had still used them regularly in 1564, and Le Moyne would almost surely have painted one; the sweat lodge was an exotic building in which practices strange to Europeans were carried out.

Instead, Le Moyne painted another scene showing Timucua utilizing the heat of fires, and the smoke of burning leaves, including tobacco, to treat patients. The scene is entirely in the open air, but patients lie on what de Bry engraved to look rather like cots. Le Moyne wrote that the Timucua built what he called "a bench long enough and wide enough for the sick person, and he is laid upon it, either on his back or on his stomach," depending on the illness. One part of a treatment that Le Moyne evidently observed and remembered consisted of burning "seeds" on hot coals placed under the face of the patient on his stomach. "This is to act as a purge, expelling the poison from the body and thus curing the disease," according to Le Moyne.[6]

Le Moyne's two sets of descriptions of Timucuan curing are not entirely mutually consistent. One painting shows men, women, and children surrounding patients being treated while lying on "cots." No transvestites are in evidence. The difference conceivably lay in Timucuan perception of contagion, so that the shamanistic treatment described dealt with what the Timucua did not regard as contagious diseases. Le Moyne specifically stated that "venereal disease is common among them, and they have several natural remedies for it." Thus it is possible that the scene portrayed Timucuan treatment of one venereal disease, among other ailments.

If Le Moyne's painting did depict Timucuan treatment of syphilis, then it provides very significant evidence of the epidemiology of that disease. Syphilis is caused by a relatively fragile spirochete that cannot survive fresh air or sunlight. It flourishes only within the body, in the bloodstream. That is why syphilis is a venereal disease—the most frequent mode of transmission is contact between penis and vagina, where the tender spirochete is protected. There is, however, an additional mode of transmission—the direct blood-to-blood transfer of spirochetes, which can and does occur in modern medical practice. First, a syphilitic pregnant woman can transmit the spirochete to her fetus. Then, too, the afflicted woman can transmit the spirochete to an attending physician during delivery, should she hemorrhage, and should the physician happen to cut a hand through a rubber glove, so that the spirochete-carrying blood flows over the cut. Finally, a nurse who handles syringes used for injecting syphilitic patients can become infected if a spirochete-contaminated needle comes in contact with an open cut.

The point of this summary is that Le Moyne depicted and described a nearly perfect mechanism for transmitting the spirochete from sick patients to well men and women. That is, Le Moyne wrote that "cutting the skin of his forehead with a sharp shell, they suck the blood with their own mouths, spitting it out into an earthen jar or a gourd. Women who are nursing or are pregnant come and drink this blood."[7] As a result any shaman who happened to have a cut or sore in his mouth and sucked blood from a syphilitic patient could contract the disease. Moreover, a woman who promptly drank the extracted blood could also contract syphilis if she had any cut in her mouth or any gum disease. The pregnant woman could then transmit the disease transplacentally to her growing child. It is thus quite probable that Le Moyne recorded major evidence as to why the Timucuan population declined with even greater rapidity than most North American native groups. Timucuan treatment provided a second direct blood-to-blood mode for transmitting syphilis to pregnant and nursing women, precisely the most vulnerable individuals, demographically speaking.

2. The second inference to be drawn from Le Moyne's pictures is that Old World contagious diseases had long since invaded the Native Americans of Florida. The Timucuan cultural change in life-support provision recorded by Le Moyne in 1564 – 1565 could have come about only through reinforcement by repeated epidemic episodes prior to that time. More will be said on this point below.

3. The concentration of evident European therapeutic traits present among the Timucuans by 1564 implies the origin of both contagious diseases and cultural knowledge of their treatment. The numerous Spaniards shipwrecked on the shores of southern Florida for some twenty years prior to 1564, many of whom were rescued and held captive by the Calusa, clearly are implicated. A high proportion of the Spanish ships wrecked off Florida had sailed more or less directly there from the port of Vera Cruz with New Spain's and Peruvian bullion shipments. Consequently, the wrecked ships had not been at sea long enough for whatever contagious diseases passengers might have been suffering to run their course before the shipwrecked survivors were rescued by the Calusa. Calusa covetousness for European goods, which kept them alert for wrecked vessels, and the basic humanitarian instinct that led

them to rescue survivors (even if some were later sacrificed to chiefdom deities), inevitably exposed the Calusa and the other peoples of Florida with whom they traded to Old World contagious diseases.

The shipwrecked Spaniards held among the Calusa would have known European techniques for nursing patients with various diseases. The European life-support techniques Le Moyne noted among the Timucua in 1564 indicate that the captive Spaniards did in fact nurse Calusa patients with some, and perhaps marked, success. The observant Native Americans copied European nursing techniques. On the record, these included (1) patient isolation, (2) assigning semioutcasts as nurses, whether slaves among the Calusa or transvestites among the Timucua, (3) the provision of life-support services, and (4) a termination of sweatbathing.

It bears emphasis that such new cultural practices were too complex to have been learned during a single epidemic episode, nor would they have been transmitted from the South Florida Calusa to the northeast Florida Saturiwa in a short period of time. Le Moyne's 1564 observations among the Saturiwans indicate, therefore, that the peoples of Florida were repeatedly attacked by Old World pathogens prior to 1564. Shipwrecked Spaniards transmitted some if not all of those pathogens to the Florida Native Americans. Shipwrecked Spaniards among the Calusa also evidently taught the natives, intentionally or not, how to nurse patients with contagious diseases. The scarcity of accounts by rescued Spanish captives and the laconic nature of the few that survive from Florida no doubt mean that all of the diseases that shipwrecked Spaniards transmitted to the Calusa will never be identified. Some probable epidemics can nonetheless be listed.

1513 – 1514

The first epidemic of Old World disease may have swept through the native peoples of Florida in 1513 –1514. Most historians of early sixteenth-century New World epidemiology have viewed the smallpox transmitted to Mesoamericans in 1520 after the outbreak on Hispaniola in late 1518 as the initial continental pandemic.[8] There is, however, rather extraordinary evidence that an earlier episode affected the natives of Florida.

During the early and middle sixteenth century, Spaniards, Cuban natives, and at least the ruling elite of the peoples of Florida all sought there a "River Jordan." There was, needless to say, no river named "Jordan" in Florida until Spaniards applied that biblical term to one stream in Apalachee and to another in Guale country. Actually, the searchers sought not a river bearing that name but one possessing the miraculous curative powers that many Christians attribute to the River Jordan in the Christian Holy Land. Many an otherwise staid Protestant pilgrim returns home bearing a vial of Jordan River water, at least hoping that it may be good for the ills of the flesh. Sixteenth-century Spaniards tended to be fanatical true believers in Christianity at the end of 700 years of warfare against Islam. They were credulous believers in miraculous cures of disease wrought by divine providence. The European pilgrimage to the Spanish shrine of St. James Major still flourished at the time—a pilgrimage that mobilized many people seeking cures to earthly ills as well as a future state of grace.[9] Moreover, those Spaniards were frustrated because in spite of repeated Christian Crusades to the Holy Land, Islamic military prowess continued to interdict Christian access to the miraculous waters of the Palestinian River Jordan. The search for a River Jordan in Florida can be understood only within that historic frame of reference of Christian belief and behavior.

The Florida River Jordan that people talked about, wrote the one-time Calusa captive Diego de Escalante Fontaneda, was "a superstition of the Indians of Cuba"[10] and did not exist. Escalante also reported that "anciently," from his perspective (he wrote in about 1575), many Cuban natives landed at Calusa ports to seek the miraculous river. Chief Sunquene, father of Calusa Headchief Carlos whom the Spaniards found in power in the 1560s, halted the searchers and formed them into an enduring Cuban settlement in his domain.[11] This apparently constituted the very first recorded historic settlement of Cuban refugees in South Florida.

Writing a generation or more after the Cuban migration, Escalante seems to have fallen into an error all too common among later ethnographers. He assumed an interethnic contact phenomenon to have been an aboriginal Native American trait. As indicated earlier, Native Americans had no need for miraculous cures until Old World diseases began to decimate them. They certainly could not refer to any stream as the River Jordan until they had learned something about Christianity. On the face of the facts, few as they are, what Escalante recorded was a Native American millenarian movement couched in terms that clearly reflected Christian teaching. Having somehow heard from Spaniards about the Holy Land River Jordan's miracloous reputation for curing, Cuban Native Americans paddled their canoes to Florida to seek waters "which did good work, even to the turning of aged men and women back to their youth."[12] The parallel with late nineteenth-century Ghost Dance Movement belief that the dead would be restored to life and game renewed by proper ritual is clear.[13] The natives of Cuba had come under such psychological stress that they sought a millennial solution to their problems. Their quest was primarily for curative waters. Unfortunately, historians picked up Escalante's probably ridiculing aside, "even to the turning of aged men and women back to their youth" and transformed it into a fictitious "Fountain of Youth."

One can also attribute part of the cause of a millenarian movement among Cuban natives to acute deprivation under harsh Spanish Colonial exploitation[14] if this series of events occurred in 1512 – 1523, for the Spaniards launched their conquest of that island in 1511.[15] During that conquest, Spanish leaders reportedly broke their pledges of peace to Native Americans who greeted them hospitably with gifts of food. Bartolomé de las Casas witnessed one Spanish massacre of 3,000 such men, women, and children.[16] Las Casas wrote that 70,000 Cuban natives perished in Spanish mines during a three- to four-month period.[17] Such an attrition rate indicates that contagious disease ran rampant, apart from Spanish treatment of Native American laborers that was wasteful rather than conservative.

On the other hand, the Florida natives who joined the millenarian search for a Jordan River were not yet subject to Colonial rule. Consequently, deprivation under Colonial exploitation cannot account for their participation. Yet "the kings and caciques of Florida" gathered information about the miraculous waters and joined the search for them, according to Escalante. "So earnestly did they engage in the pursuit, that there remained not a river nor a brook in all Florida, not even lakes and ponds, in which they did not bathe."[18] The peoples of Florida must have had a powerful motivation for seeking curative waters. The obvious explanation for the behavior of the Cubans and the Florida ruling elite is that all suffered from a serious, lethal, contagious epidemic of an Old World disease to which neither Native American population possessed any immunity. Waves of Native American refugees from Spanish Conquest may have transmitted disease to their hosts beyond the area under Colonial control. A chief known as Hatuey fled Hispaniola with many of "his people." They found temporary refuge on Cuba before the Spaniards invaded that island in 1511. Hatuey had his followers dance before a basket full of gold and jewels on the premise that this was the Spanish deity, believing that such an offering might alter the distressing course of events—certainly a religious innovation of a millenarian nature. The Spaniards captured Hatuey, however, and burned him at the stake in Cuba.[19]

Surprisingly, there is a record of direct carriage of disease to the natives of Cuba in 1512. "Certain" Europeans sailing along the Cuban coasts "left" with a chief who was already known by a Spanish name, "a certeyne poore maryner beinge diseased." That mariner soon recovered his health. He learned enough of the local language to communicate with the Cuban natives. He evidently became both a mercenary and a free-lance, nonclerical, Mariolatrous missionary. On the one hand, "he was oftentymes the kynges Lieuetenaunt in his warres ageynst other princes his bortherers." On the other hand, he wore a picture of the Virgin Mary and persuaded the chief whom he served to build a chapel and altar and to begin to pray there in memorized Spanish words. Accounts carried to credulous intellectuals in Spain described Mary performing miracles in a battlefield contest of champions.[20] Vain about their military prowess, Europeans typically went into details about battles but neglected other aspects of culture.

Native Americans viewed events very differently, as William McNeill noted. They viewed epidemic disease as divine punishment for human transgressions. During early sixteenth-century epidemic episodes, they watched adult Europeans stay healthy or recover from pathogens that killed their relatives in demoralizing numbers. They concluded, therefore, that the God about whom Christians talked in fact possessed greater power than their own.[21]

The rapid conversion of the leader of one Cuban chiefdom by a sailor put ashore while ill who recovered and then preached the miraculous powers of the Virgin appears suspiciously like the action of a chief who had just watched great numbers of his people perish from the disease that the sailor survived. The recovered lay preacher could have been the European Christian source of Cuban knowledge about the Christian concept of the River Jordan's waters as miraculously curative.

The extremely rapid decline in Native American numbers on the island of Hispaniola, where Spaniards first colonized New World territory, attests to early transatlantic transmission of Old World diseases. S.F. Cook and W.W. Borah calculated from available information about population that these numbers fell from 3,770,000 in 1496 to only 92,300 in 1508, then to 61,600 in 1509 and 65,800 in 1510, and to only 26,700 in 1512 and 27,800 in 1514, with a mere 15,600 remaining in 1518.[22] Not only the gross depopulation but also the age structure of the population attests to catastrophically disproportionate mortality among children. During the latter half of 1514, Rodrigo de Albuquerque carried out a *repartimiento*, or assignment of Native Americans for work and payment of tribute. He counted adults and in some places enumerated children and the aged.[23] Cook and Borah located 279 statements of children and found a ratio of only 141 children per 1,000 adults. That is an extraordinarily small proportion[24] and could have resulted only from disproportionately high child mortality unless Hispaniola natives were successfully hiding their children from Spanish authorities. If they hid their offspring, the question arises, who cared for them?

The dearth of children does not support Sauer's interpretation that Spanish disruption of native economic and social organization caused the precipitous decline.[25] Old World diseases are surely implicated. Cook and Borah pointed out that Columbus made his first voyage with sick men, a large proportion of Colonial Spaniards were ill at any given moment, and the Spaniards suffered steady mortality.[26]

The kind of psychological shock that mortality on the scale suffered by the aborigines of Hispaniola caused certainly could generate a millenarian response among Cubans similarly afflicted. At least one Spaniard heard natives talk about the quest for miraculous water in Florida and joined the quest. "It is a cause for merriment," scoffed Escalante, "that Juan Ponz de León went to Florida to find the River Jordan."[27] Anyone attempting to determine an epidemic chronology for the native peoples of Florida must be grateful that the conqueror of the island of San Juan de Puerto Rico did join in the quest. Juan Ponce de León sailed to Florida twice. He made his initial trip in 1513, apparently exploring at least part of the Atlantic Coast of the peninsula. He returned in 1521, when the Calusa stoutly resisted his landing. The Calusa so severely wounded Ponce de León that he sailed to Havana, where he died from his wound, probably from infection. The conditions of intergroup contact during Ponce's 1521 voyage were not very propitious for transmission of disease.

Tempting though it might be to attribute the millenarian search for miraculous curing waters to the smallpox epidemic that reached Cuba in 1519, Ponce actually became part of the quest in 1513. Peter Martyr d'Anglería mentioned the supposedly miraculous waters in his Decade 2, which was published in 1515–1516.[28] What remains in doubt is the diagnosis of the disease that stressed the peoples of Florida.

Whatever the disease that swept through the Native Americans of the Caribbean islands and sent Cubans to Florida seeking miraculously curative waters, it seems to have reached the Isthmus of Panamá. The Spaniards were still learning how to colonize the New World. Consequently, they sometimes failed to carry with them provisions sufficient to sustain them until they could raise their own food or could obtain it from Native Americans whom they conquered. Such was the situation among hundreds of Spanish colonists on the Isthmus in 1514. As a result, 700 Spaniards perished during one month from starvation and from an unidentified disease. The contagion probably spread from the Europeans to the Native American population. From 1514 to 1530, 2 million Native Americans died in the isthmus region, according to a Colonial historian who was himself present during the period of highest mortality and who buried a wife and son there.[29]

1519 SMALLPOX

The most lethal Old World disease to decimate Native American populations lacking any immunity or resistance to European and African pathogens was smallpox. Spanish ships appear to have transported persons with active cases of smallpox to the Caribbean islands in 1518. Smallpox broke out on the island of Hispaniola in December. By early January 1519, royal officials reported to the crown that one-third of the natives had died and that the epidemic continued.[30] By May 20, 1519, colonial officials on Hispaniola estimated that more than half of the Native American population was dead.[31] The epidemic had spread to the natives of Puerto Rico by the end of 1518,[32] and by mid-1519 it was sweeping through the natives of Cuba.[33] It was from Cuba that Pánfilo de Narváez sailed to the continent with a soldier suffering from smallpox that he transmitted to the Native Americans of Central Mexico.[34]

Cuba may have been the source of transmission of this epidemic disease to Florida, across the relatively narrow stretch of ocean between the island and the Florida cape. The likelihood of such transmission lay in the frequency with which oceangoing Calusa canoeists visited Cuba to trade. During his 1513 voyage, Ponce de León engaged the Calusa, who fought from double-hulled canoes.[35] Such watercraft clearly possessed considerable seagoing capacity. The Calusa traded with Bahama Islanders and with the aboriginal sixteenth-century Colonial inhabitants of Cuba.[36] The flight of Cuban natives to Calusa territory early in the sixteenth century attests both to their ability to cross the ocean between the island and Florida and to their having learned something about Florida during previous contacts. As late as the mid-eighteenth century, visits to Havana by Calusa leaders were frequent.[37]

No doubt European commodities as well as the strange behavior of colonials in Havana attracted Calusa chiefs and traders during Colonial times. The watercraft technology that the Calusa used to reach Cuba and to return was evidently aboriginal, judging from archaeological recovery of Key Marco toy double hulled canoes.[38] Consequently, if Calusa traders visited Cuba during 1519 and 1520 when the great smallpox pandemic raged there, they almost certainly contracted the disease and transmitted it to their relatives in Florida.

New Spain might also have been a source of transmission of smallpox to Florida, via a continental-margin canoe trade route. When smallpox spread through the Central Mexican empires and kingdoms and northward, Native American traders traveled by canoe on the protected waters sheltered by the barrier islands from civilized coastal ports in Mesoamerica to North America. Documentary evidence of that aboriginal trading pattern and its survival was provided to an extent by a cleric who survived a shipwreck on the Gulf Coast. The event has usually been dated as occurring in 1553,[39] but almost surely Marcos de Mena was aboard the 1554 treasure fleet. He struggled for some distance along the coast toward Pánuco. Native American canoe traders found the lone Spaniard wandering dazed along the shore and invited him to ride in their canoe. They returned Mena to the coast of New Spain, within easy walking distance of the Colonial settlement of Tampico. Wise in the ways of colonials, the Native American textile traders declined to accompany the grateful lay brother into the Spanish town.[40]

Their reluctance to expose themselves to Spanish official action indicates that a possibly still very large aboriginal-style trade in religious goods illegal and immoral in Spanish eyes flourished along what is now called the intracoastal waterway, invisible to and unknown to Spanish authorities. The rapidity of canoe travel from Mesoamerica to Native American coastal settlements on the water route east to Florida made transmission of smallpox by the crews of seagoing canoes feasible in 1520.

1528 GASTROINTESTINAL INFECTION

The Native American population of Florida was again threatened by Old World contagion no later than 1528 through 1530. In 1528, a major pestilence attacked Cuba's surviving Native American population, prompting a militant nativistic movement against the Spaniards in October 1529.[41] An estimated third of that island's Native Americans perished.[42] The Spanish dominant group "suffered" from a general shortage of subservient ethnic-group labor.[43] The Calusa propensity for visiting Cuba by canoe fostered transmission of this disease to the Native Americans of Florida.

An official with the Pánfilo de Narváez expedition of 1528 to Florida, Alvar Núñez Cabeza de Vaca, became one of its few survivors and the principal chronicler. When the expedition's members attempted to build rafts and sail around the Gulf of Mexico Coast to New Spain, large numbers were wrecked on Galveston Island. There many of the

Spaniards died. Some probably perished from starvation, some possibly from scurvy, a vitamin deficiency ailment but not an infectious one. On the other hand, one or more carriers among the Spaniards survived long enough to transmit a deadly infection to the island-dwelling Native Americans who succored the Europeans. Núñez recorded that half of the economically specialized islanders perished.[44] Núñez described their ailment as a stomach sickness. He reported that the Native Americans believed that their uninvited European guests had killed those who died. They were biologically correct.

The islanders were economically specialized, collecting shellfish and fish in the estuary and trading marine products for vegetable produce collected by inland groups. A waterborne germ or virus is therefore probably implicated in the Native American epidemic, and consequently the disease was probably self-limiting and did not spread beyond the Galveston Islanders. John C. Ewers suggested that cholera might have been the cause of the 1528 insular mortality.[45] Medical historians date the worldwide spread of cholera to the nineteenth century,[46] however, so typhoid fever seems a more likely culprit.

A more epidemic disease than typhoid fever may have been abroad in Cuba for members of the 1528 Narváez expedition to carry with them to peninsular Florida and the Gulf Coast. It is possible that the epidemic disease that further depopulated Cuba in 1528 – 1530 was the measles that a Spaniard carried to New Spain and to Central America in 1530. In Cuba, the disease was labeled smallpox,[47] but smallpox could not have caused such a high mortality so soon after the 1518 – 1520 episode; only one-third of the people reportedly survived in 1528. *Viruelas* meant no more, apparently, than "red-rash-producing disease with high fever and appreciable mortality." Thus either measles or typhoid fever could have been the disease.

What spread widely through New Spain and Peru during 1530 and 1531 was, however, identified as measles.[48] Spanish settlement in Honduras,[49] Nicaragua,[50] and Panamá,[51] generated documentary record of a rapid spread of the measles pandemic through the Native American populations of all of Central America. Measles should not have caused high mortality among Spaniards, who presumably had had childhood cases and had gained immunity. Yet members of the Narváez expedition were sick in significant numbers at least while they were in the territory of the Apalachee chiefdom before they embarked on their ill-fated rafting venture. Having traveled north and then west from their landing on Florida's west, or Gulf, coast, Narváez's men rested for nearly a month at Apalachee. Then they spent more than a week moving to Aute near the Gulf Coast. A contingent began to build rafts. The expedition's leader and many men remained at the near-coast town of Aute, where Native Americans killed ten men, and more than forty died from disease. Apparently six others had earlier succumbed to disease. The expedition suffered a mortality rate of 153 per 1,000 even before it embarked on its hastily built rafts. Most interaction between Native Americans and Spaniards was hostile, which tended to limit opportunities for the invaders to transmit their ailment(s) to the native peoples in Florida.

One point should be clarified. The forty Spaniards who died from illness at Aute did not perish from scurvy. The Spaniards found abundant unharvested crops of maize, beans, and squash in the fields around Aute, and the fresh foods would have eliminated any scurvy that might have existed among the invaders.[52] The pathogen killed adult Europeans at a 15 percent rate, a fact suggestive of typhoid fever, scarlet fever, or plague rather than smallpox, measles, or chickenpox. Núñez Cabeza de Vaca emphasized a disordered stomach as a symptom, making typhoid a likely diagnosis.

At least one additional possible mode of transmission to Native Americans of the 1528 infection running through the Narváez expedition bears mentioning. One man whom Narváez ordered to sail to Cuba for supplies and to return carried out the commander's orders. When the brigantine returned to Charlotte Harbor, the disaffected local Calusa chief managed to capture four Spaniards who went ashore. He held three captive for several days before having them tortured and killed during a ceremonial. The chief's wife and daughters pled for the life of the fourth Spanish captive, then just eighteen years of age, and he was spared.[53] Thus the Calusa were exposed to four possible Old World pathogen carriers for a period of several days and kept one enslaved for a year and a half.

The young Spanish captive, Juan Ortiz, then escaped to the town of teenaged Chief Mocozo.[54] That Townchief sent him to Fernando de Soto when the expeditionary leader landed on the Calusa coast of Florida in 1539.[55] Ortiz could have transmitted whatever contagion assaulted Cuba in 1528–1530 if he had a mild case when he returned to South Florida. If he was a typhoid carrier, Ortiz could have transmitted that disease to both Calusa and Mocozo.

1535–1538

In 1540, members of Fernando de Soto's marauding party marched into Cofitachique, a Creek settlement north of the Savannah River in modern South Carolina. De Soto's men found an abundance of what they regarded as poor-quality freshwater pearls. The Native Americans wore these pearls as bracelets and necklaces. They also bedecked the bodies of their dead leaders with pearls and stored them in chests. De Soto and his men carried off mortuary gift pearls without Native American hindrance; de Soto himself claimed the chest full of pearls. Many of these precious stones came from one or more settlements near Cofitachique Town that were completely abandoned in 1540. The various Spanish accounts of the expedition's visit to Cofitachique agreed that the abandoned towns had been depopulated by a terrible pestilence one or two years earlier.[56] That dating appears to have been reliable, inasmuch as members of de Soto's expedition provisioned themselves with dried maize from the intact maize cribs in the town that had survived the epidemic and from another town subject to the ruling family.[57] While pearls and even wooden chests holding them would have persisted for a number of years, maize would not have remained edible for many years without house and crib maintenance in the moist southeastern climate.

The distance between Central Mexico and Florida and the Savannah River was so great that an epidemic under way in southern New Spain in 1539 likely could not have spread to Native Americans on the Atlantic Coast that year. A "plague" occurred in Central Mexico in 1538,[58] reportedly smallpox,[59] causing a red rash. The mechanism of transmission by canoe trader still operated then, so that rapid seaborne transmission was possible. There is little doubt that the Creeks were significantly depopulated, implying that the Timucua and probably other Florida Native Americans were also. If canoe traders did not transmit the contagion raging in Central Mexico to the Floridians in 1539, then the epidemic disease transmitted earlier to the Central Mexicans evidently spread overland from tribe to tribe. Evidence that such an overland spread of infectious disease occurred along Native American inland trade routes is found in the narrative of Alvar Núñez Cabeza de Vaca.

In 1534, Núñez and his fellow survivors of the Narváez expedition began to travel westward across Texas toward New Spain. Núñez and the Moor gained freedom of movement by becoming curing shamans. The frequency with which they performed cures, or convinced Native Americans of their shamanistic relationship to the supernatural, indicates that one or more epidemics originating in Colonial New Spain had spread northward and eastward through Texas tribal peoples.[60] In 1535, Núñez and his companions crossed from Texas to Sinaloa. Sickness broke out among the hundreds of Native Americans accompanying them. They halted their march; more than 300 Native Americans fell ill. Many of them died.[61] Whatever killed Núñez's companions may have been the disease that reached the Creeks on the Atlantic Coast, perhaps in 1536, 1537, 1538, or 1539, depopulating entire settlements. That disease may be inferred to have spread to the peoples of Florida.

1545—1548 BUBONIC PLAGUE

In New Spain, the third massive historic pandemic struck native Americans in 1545. The disease recurred until 1548. This ailment was called *cocoliztli* in Nahuatl, and it spread widely, causing its greatest mortality in coastal peoples.[62] Patients suffered from high fever and bled from the nose, a frequent sequel of high fever. Mendieta placed Tlaxcalan mortality alone at 150,000 persons.[63] One historian estimated that five-sixths of the Native Americans died, a suspiciously high mortality rate.[64]

Hans Zinsser suspected that typhus was the disease.[65] On the other hand, the Bishop of Mexico, Fray Juan de Zumárraga, founded a hospital to treat either syphilis or bubonic plague patients in 1545 or 1546.[66] Such Colonial hospitals often were founded when an epidemic made clear the need for them. A plague diagnosis is consistent with the fact that in the central Andes, llamas suffered from the pestilence that struck people there in 1546.[67] Llamas are cameloids, so are presumably able to serve as an animal reservoir for flea-vectored bubonic plague.[68] The epidemic was termed *gucumatz* in Mayan. In Guatemala, the epidemic was termed in Spanish *peste*, which refers specifically to plague, although it also means "epidemic" in a general sense. In Totonicapán in that province, it lasted from 1541 to 1545,[69] although it ran from 1545 to 1548 in most of Mesoamerica.

The persistence of the intracoastal waterway Mesoamerican canoe trade into at least the following decade implies that the 1545—1548 bubonic plague epidemic in Mesoamerica could have been quickly transmitted to Florida by canoe crews. If the plague did not come to Florida quickly via canoe, it almost certainly came slowly overland.

A third possible mode of rapid transmission of plague, specific and general, from New Spain to Florida either began in 1545 or assumed significant proportions at that date. This was direct Spanish shipboard transmission via treasure fleet vessels that wrecked on the Keys or peninsula, some of whose passengers and crew members were saved by the Calusa. No doubt some of the rats that inevitably infested the ships also survived the wrecks and could have carried plague-vector fleas ashore to seek food and shelter in Native American dwellings and storehouses. At least one Spanish ship was wrecked on the Florida coast in 1545. A survivor who was shipwrecked twenty years prior to his rescue was ransomed from Native American hands by Pedro Menéndez de Avilés in 1565.[70] The year before, the French Huguenot René Laudonnière persuaded Florida chiefs to send to Fort Caroline two captive shipwrecked Spaniards. They told him that they had been aboard one of three ships wrecked on the Keys fifteen years earlier, or in 1549.[71] The possibility of ship transmission of disease to Florida arose when Peru and New Spain began shipping silver from the great strikes made in 1545 at Andean Potosí[72] and in 1546 at Zacatecas.[73]

1549 TYPHUS

Spaniards possibly directly transmitted one of the fever-producing diseases, perhaps "ship's typhus," to the Calusa in 1549. The *Santa Maria de la Encina* sailed from Vera Cruz early in the year, bound for Florida. The ship's pilot, Juan de Arana, found that portion of Florida then known to the Spaniards. On May 30, Dominican priest Luís Cancer de Barbastro landed on the shore near the Bay of Espiritu Santo (Charlotte Harbor). Father Diego de Toloso, or Peñalosa, a lay brother named Fuentes, and a Native American woman the Spaniards knew as "Magdalena" accompanied Cancer. The Spaniards gave presents to the first Native Americans they met, sat in a hut for a while talking to Calusa spokesmen through the interpreter, and returned to the ship for more gifts.[74] A sailor went ashore with Tolosa, Fuentes, and Magdalena.

When Cancer returned to land, his companions had disappeared. After a week's sailing along the coast, the ship spent another week entering the bay, and Cancer continued to seek the missing people. Magdalena, whom the Spaniards had brought along as an interpreter, appeared at nearly every landing, having shed her Colonial clothing. Incredibly, on June 23 a Spaniard named Juan Muñoz paddled out to the ship in a canoe. He identified himself as a member of de Soto's marauders who had been captured ten years before and enslaved. He reported that the Calusa had killed the priest and lay brother and had enslaved the sailor.[75] Cancer nonetheless went ashore on June 26, and the Calusa clubbed him to death on a mound near his landing place. The ship then returned to New Spain, and with good reason. Most of its crew was too ill with a fever to work the craft. Moreover, it was running low on water and had exhausted its store of unspoiled provisions.[76]

In other words, both Magdalena and the sailor who was enslaved could have carried ashore typhus-vectoring lice to transmit to the Florida native population. The Calusa might even have been attacked by lice from the bodies of the two slain priests and lay brother.

The Spanish plan to employ Magdalena as an interpreter is epidemiologically significant not only for the 1549 incident but also for earlier epidemics. Although she came from Cuba to Florida, once ashore among the Calusa, she assured the Spaniards that the natives belonged to "her tribe" and spoke "her" language. If Magdalena was a Calusa, at least one other Spanish ship had visited the same coast and had captured people to take to Cuba as slaves. Evidently that slaving expedition occurred long enough before 1549 for the Florida woman to acquire the reasonable fluency in Spanish that she would have needed before Cancer and his companions could consider her a suitable interpreter. If the Florida warriors managed to capture any of the slavers who were ill or were carriers of Old World pathogens, they ran the risk of another ailment besides enslavement.

If Magdalena had not been captured in Florida, she had evidently been enslaved during a Calusa canoe voyage visit to Cuba, an instance of overseas contact that exposed the Calusa to nearly every disease that Europeans transmitted to the natives of that island. If such was the case, the presence of a woman on a Calusa voyage to Cuba indicates that such trips were made rather routinely and by numbers of Calusa.

If Magdalena was a native of Cuba, then her "tribesmen" must have been the refugee Cubans whom Headchief Carlos's father settled in his territory when they came seeking the magically curative effects of a putative Jordan River. Otherwise, the Calusa must have spoken the same language as one or more aboriginal groups of Cuba. All the interpretations that can be placed on the peregrinations and reported statements of Magdalena indicate so frequent contact by such large numbers of individuals passing between Calusa and Cuba that epidemic transmission of infectious disease to the Calusa is very highly probable.

1550 MUMPS

Mumps are not often regarded as a lethal disease in modern times, but they were in Tacuba and elsewhere in New Spain in 1550.[77] There is a possibility that the infection was transmitted to Florida by Native American canoe traders.

The direct evidence for transmission of bubonic plague in 1545 – 1548, of typhus in 1549, or of mumps in 1550 from Spanish Colonial areas to

Florida's Native Americans is scant. Indirect evidence, on the other hand, is convincing. This evidence consists of a wholesale depopulation of the Southeast, accompanied by a collapse of the aboriginal way of life, between 1542 and 1559. When de Soto's marauders marched around the Southeast for three years, they everywhere found large Native American settlements. The expedition's chroniclers repeatedly commented on the populous horticultural districts along main river valleys and around the capital towns of native chiefdoms. Here and there the raiders encountered groups temporarily short of horticultural supplies, as in the Cofitachique chiefdom, where the flight of people from a frightening epidemic during the planting season of 1539 had causd them to miss a year's production. Yet the aboriginal way of life persisted over a broad expanse of territory.

Powerful chiefs reclined under canopies on large state canoes or were carried on litters on land by lower-class retainers. Some theocratic heads of chiefdoms declined even to meet Spaniards face to face, delegating that no doubt unpleasant task to "talking chiefs." The population of many native towns was large enough to impress the marauders, many of whom should not have been easily impressed, as they were veterans of the conquest of Tawantinsuyu or the Triple Alliance. The fact that de Soto's large task force successfully lived from supplies given to it by some Native American chiefs and seized from the storehouses of others attested to the continued functioning of traditional ways of life and successful food production despite pre-1539 depopulation by invading Old World diseases.

By the time Tristán de Luna attempted to colonize the Gulf Coast at Pensacola in 1559, that situation had very dramatically changed. Only twenty years after de Soto's rampage through the Southeast began, the Native American way of life his men saw had for the most part collapsed. A few chiefdoms, such as the Natchez on the lower Mississippi River and the Timucuan chiefdoms and the Calusa in South Florida, still functioned with something resembling the splendor and commodity abundance that they had known before 1539 – 1542. Search as he might, however, de Luna could not find Native American food supplies to seize to sustain his colonists. His followers almost certainly themselves transmitted epidemic disease to Native Americans that may well have interrupted planting in 1559, as had the 1539 episode among the Cofitachique.

The general collapse of the good society that Native Americans had known for centuries in the brief period of twenty years indicates that demographic catastrophe struck the peoples of the Southeast between 1542 and 1559. The scope of that disaster cannot be attributed to the loss

of a single summer's harvest in 1559. Areas that were heavily populated in
1539 – 1542 appeared virtually depopulated by 1559 – 1560. Archaeologists
have found many large "prehistoric" sites that were occupied until
approximately the 1542 – 1559 interval, as best they can be dated, and
were then abruptly abandoned.[78] I conclude that invading Old World
diseases led to rapid depopulation and a collapse of food production
because of demoralization and loss of manpower coupled with major
disruptions of traditional social organization.

The dense pre-Columbian population of Florida and the rest of the
Southeast culture area had been thinned even before de Soto's marauders devastated the region in 1539 – 1542. That much is clear from the
expedition's chroniclers' descriptions of the state of the Cofitachique
chiefdom in 1540. Consequently, there can be little doubt that the
aboriginal cultural patterns had already been weakened. The depredations of de Soto's marauders contributed to weakening the chiefdoms
even more by selective homicide against ruling elite lineages. The
simultaneous enslavement of large numbers of human carriers and concubines may have offset the high mortality de Soto's men caused among
the native elites. Removal of the numerous concubines de Soto's men
seized for their licentious binge apparently was on a scale sufficient to
depress significantly the birth rate in a number of towns in succeeding
years.

To attribute the subsequent collapse of the aboriginal way of life in
the bulk of the Southeastern culture area chiefdoms to the de Soto
expedition's depredations would be, however, to accord it too much
impact. The final blows to the aboriginal way of life occurred after 1542
and after the departure of the survivors of the de Soto expedition to
New Spain. The bubonic plague pandemic of the late 1540s was clearly
one of the culprits. The disease peaked in central New Spain in 1545, but
it was present and caused significant mortality for several years. It must
be assumed that the disease either spread through the Southeast overland through the Southwest and across the southern Great Plains or
was transmitted by canoe traders via the major waterways. If plague
recurred during the planting season of two or three summers in succession, it could have caused frightened Native Americans to flee from
permanent towns that had become infested with plague-bearing rats.
Like the Cofitachique people in 1539, they would have failed to plant.
While their food stores would carry them through one year without a
harvest, it is extremely doubtful whether food stored under the already
disrupted conditions prior to 1545 would have carried very many town
populations for two years without harvests, much less three. Moreover,
starvation could have become truly massive if bubonic plague had been

spread by hordes of invading rats that consumed stored dried foods and soiled what they did not eat. Starvation added to epidemic disease mortality would account for the demographic and cultural collapse that clearly occurred.

1559 INFLUENZA

One of the Old World diseases particularly likely to have been transmitted from Native American to Native American well beyond the populations under European Colonial rule was influenza. A major worldwide influenza pandemic struck Native Americans in Florida in 1559. The contagion was directly transmitted by sea by colonists aboard thirteen sailing vessels that left Vera Cruz on June 11, 1559. The ships carried approximately 1,500 individuals—soldiers, their wives and children, servants, Black slaves, "and a number of Florida Indians who had come to Mexico with the escaped Spaniards" and had returned. There were also 240 horses on the ships, a significant detail if the specific virus happened to be transmitted by horses.[79] This was the de Luna colony that landed near modern Pensacola. The Native Americans from Florida who returned there with the de Luna expedition provided an ideal mechanism for spreading influenza widely among Native Americans as they returned to their homes or acted as interpreters and cultural brokers between the Spanish colonists and Native Americans.

Pandemic influenza had broken out in Europe in 1556. It recurred off and on until 1560 and caused "serious demographic consequences" on both sides of the Atlantic. In England, where a number of people had begun to try to count the population, an estimated one-fifth perished.[80] The epidemic struck Spanish troops fighting Muslims in Algeria in 1558,[81] having begun in Madrid in 1557.[82] Influenza began to kill Mayanspeaking Native Americans in Guatemala a week after Easter in 1559.[83] Thus the epidemic was well under way before the de Luna expedition left Vera Cruz early in June. That the colonists carried the disease with them is indicated in the serious illness of 800 settlers who stayed at the place the Spaniards called Nanipacna, an eighty-house Native American settlement that had been abandoned when the colonists reached it.[84] The influenza virus spread also to the South American viceroyalty of Peru, causing heavy mortality in the capital city of Lima. The Spanish responded strongly, founding a new charity nursing order and a hospital.[85]

The geographic explorations by components of the de Luna colony, and frequent face-to-face contacts between those Spaniards and the

Apalachee and other tribes, made virtually certain the transmission of influenza to the natives of Florida. Intertribal trade on the peninsula and canoe trade between Florida Native Americans and Spaniards at Havana would then probably have spread the virus to all of the peninsular ethnic groups. Patients ill with influenza would have responded better when given nursing care (such as that which Le Moyne described Saturiwan tranvestites as providing in 1564), so the 1559 epidemic episode was no doubt a major experience reinforcing the new cultural pattern learned from Spanish captives. The virus was probably about as lethal among Florida Native Americans as among Englishmen.

SUMMARY

This section has examined evidence for the transmission of epidemic diseases to the Native American population of Florida during the protohistoric period from about A.D. 1512 to 1562. Available clues suggest that pathogens causing eight serious epidemics in Colonial populations could rather easily have been transmitted from New Spain and/or Cuba to the Calusa and Timucua (see table 25). Significantly, at least six different diseases are known to have been present in Cuba and/or New Spain for continental overland or seaborne ship and/or canoe transmission to Florida. These were (1) smallpox in 1519, (2) perhaps typhoid fever in 1528, or measles in 1528 – 1531, (3) bubonic plague in 1545 – 1548, (4) typhus in 1549, (5) mumps in 1550, and (6) influenza in 1559. Only the 1513 – 1514 disease—although it was most likely malaria—and the decimating pestilence of 1535 – 1539 remain unidentified. The significance of

TABLE 25
Possible and Documented Epidemic Disease Episodes
among Native Americans of Florida, 1512—1562

Date	Disease	Probability	Mortality
1513—1514	Malaria (?)	likely	unknown
1519—1524	Smallpox	nearly certain	50—75%
1528	Measles or typhoid fever	nearly certain	about 50%
1535—1539	Unidentified	documented	high
1545—1548	Bubonic plague	nearly certain	about 12.5%
1549	Typhus	very probable	perhaps 10%
1550	Mumps	possible	unknown
1559	Influenza	nearly certain	about 20%

the diversity of pathogens attacking Florida's Native Americans in 1512 – 1562 is that survivors of one epidemic gained no immunity to the next disease. Thus each pathogen could achieve maximal mortality.

French observation of disease conditions among the Timucua in 1564 made clear that venereal disease(s) was endemic at that time. Consequently, each of the epidemic episodes of a major pathogen would result in higher mortality than would have occurred in a population free from endemic ailments. Evidence from protohistoric times strongly suggests that Florida's native peoples were decimated during that period by assaults from a succession of contagious Old World diseases. Yet the functioning authoritarian political structure of the Timucuan chiefdoms reported in the 1560s suggests that Florida's peoples may have suffered less depopulation during preceding decades than did inhabitants of chiefdoms elsewhere in the Southeast.

NOTES

1. True, "Some Early Maps," 1954, pp. 77 – 80.
2. Lorant, ed., *New World*, 1946, p. 36.
3. Ibid., 30.
4. Ibid., 69.
5. Díaz del Castillo, *Discovery and Conquest*, 1908 (1956), 293 – 94.
6. Lorant, ed., *New World*, 1946, p. 75.
7. Ibid., 75.
8. Dobyns, "Outline," 1963, p. 494.
9. Rousell, *Les Pèlerinages*, 1954, pp. 37, 47, 163, etc.
10. B. Smith, trans., *Letter and Memoir*, 1854, p. 17; True, ed., *Memoir*, 1944, 1945, p. 28.
11. B. Smith, trans., *Letter and Memoir*, 1854, p. 17; French, comp., *Historical Collections*, 1875, p. 253; True, ed., *Memoir*, 1944, 1945, p. 29.
12. B. Smith, trans., *Letter and Memoir*, 1854, p. 17; French, comp., *Historical Collections*, 1875, p. 253; True, ed., *Memoir*, 1944, 1945, p. 29.
13. Mooney, "Ghost Dance Religion," 1896, pp. 777 – 83.
14. C.O. Sauer, *Early Spanish Main*, 1966, pp. 202 – 204, argued that Spanish demands disrupted Native American socio organization and demoralized the people.
15. Las Casas, *Devastation*, 1974, p. 53.
16. Ibid., 55 – 56.
17. Ibid., 57.
18. Smith, trans., *Letter and Memoir*, 1854, p. 17; True, ed., *Memoir*, 1944, 1945, p. 29. French (*Historical Collections*, 1875, p. 253) translated the Spanish: "So eager were they in their search, that they did not pass a river, a brook, a lake, or even a swamp, without bathing in it; and even to this day, they have not ceased to look for it."

19. Las Casas, *Devastation*, 1974, pp. 54 – 55.

20. Anghiera, *Decades*, 1555 (1966), 73 – 74.

21. McNeill, *Plagues and Peoples*, 1976, pp. 207 – 208.

22. Cook and Borah, *Essays*, 1971, vol. I, p. 401.

23. Ibid., 380.

24. Ibid., 383.

25. C.O. Sauer, *Early Spanish Main*, 1966, pp. 202 – 204.

26. Cook and Borah, *Essays*, 1971, vol. I, pp. 409 – 10. A majority of the Spaniards attempting to colonize the Caribbean coast of South America during the initial decade of the sixteenth century died from disease or in battle with Native Americans (Andagoya, *Narrative*, 1865, p. 4).

27. Smith, trans., *Letter and Memoir*, 1854, p. 18; True, ed., *Memoir*, 1944, 1945, p. 19. French (*Historical Collections*, 1875, p. 254) put it: "It seems incredible that Juan Ponce de León should have gone to Florida to look for such a river."

28. True, ed., *Memoir*, 1944, 1945, p. 46, n. 21E. Anghiera, *Decades*, 1555 (1966), 86 – 87 (book 10, decade 2) said many wise or fortunate courtiers in Spain believed in the existence of a spring that "maketh owld men younge ageyne." The real New World presented so many strange things to Europeans that many of them credulously believed rumors and tales of quite unreal phenomena.

29. Crosby, *Columbian Exchange*, 1972, p. 50. In 1514, Pedro Arías de Avila arrived at Darién at the end of July with 1,500 men fresh from Spain. Vasco Núñez de Balboa led some 450 men already there. This colonial population of about 1,950 men lost 700 who "died of sickness and hunger" in a single month (Andagoya, *Narrative*, 1865, pp. 2, 4, 6). Thus almost 36 percent of the colonists perished in that lethal month. Seawater had damaged the flour and other stores that Arías's ships had brought from Spain. Consequently some Spaniards who were unable to change their food habits probably did starve, and others probably died from scurvy for lack of Vitamin C that abounded in tropical fruits on the Isthmus. Andagoya (*Narrative*, 1865, p. 6) attributed at least some illness to the ecology of the Darién outpost. Its environs were "woody covered with swamps." The environment was hospitable to mosquitoes, in other words. So malaria brought by earlier Spanish pioneers may have been the disease that ran rampant in 1512 – 14.

30. Dobyns, "Outline," 1963, p. 494. Pacheco and Cárdenas, eds., *Colección*, 1864, vol. I, p. 367. B. Smith, comp., *Colección*, 1857, p. 44.

31 .Pacheco and Cárdenas, eds., *Colección*, 1864, vol. I, p. 370.

32. Ibid., vol. I, p. 368. B. Smith, comp., *Colección*, 1857, p. 45.

33. Wright, *Early History of Cuba*, 1916, pp. 86 – 87.

34. Herrera y Tordesillas, *Historia General*, 1945, vol. III, pp. 274 – 75; Clavijero, *Historia Antigua*, 1944, vol. II, p. 232; *Desertazioni Sulla Terra* 1781, p. 282; Sahagun, *Historia de las Cosas*, 1955, pp. 61 – 62; Díaz del Castillo, *Discovery and Conquest*, 1908 (1956), 293 – 94; Steck, *Motolinia's History*, 1951, pp. 87 – 88; Mendieta, *Historia*, 1945, p. 173.

35. C.M. Lewis, "Calusa," 1978, p. 20.

36. Ibid., 21.

37. Sturtevant, "Last," 1978, pp. 78, 142.

38. Gilliland, *Material Culture*, 1975, pp. 55, 123, 126.

39. Lowery, *Spanish Settlements*, 1905 (1959), vol. I, p. 352; Kerrigan, trans., *Barcia's Chronological History*, 1951, pp. 30 – 32.

40. Lowery, *Spanish Settlements*, 1905, vol. I, p. 353; Kerrigan, trans., *Barcia's Chronological History*, 1951, p. 32.

41. Wright, *Early History*, 1916, pp. 136 – 37.

42. Guerra y Sánchez, *Historia*, 1952, vol. I, p. 230.

43. Wright, *Early History*, 1916, p. 201.

44. Bandelier, trans., *Journey*, 1904 (1922), 64; Davenport, trans., "Expedition," 1924, p. 230. The *Relación* specified that "the Indians took sick with a disease of the stomach of which half of their people soon died" (n. 2). Fernandez de Oviedo (*Historia general*, 1959, vol. IV, p. 295) clearly stated: "An illness of the stomach struck the natives of the land from which half of them died."

45. Ewers, "Influence of Epidemics," 1973, p. 108.

46. May, *Ecology*, 1958, pp. 38 – 43.

47. Wright, *Early History*, 1916, p. 136; Guerra y Sánchez, *Historia*, 1952, vol. I, p. 230.

48. McNeill, *Plagues and Peoples*, 1976, p. 209; Dobyns, "Outline," 1963, pp. 497 – 99; Mendieta, *Historia*, 1945, p. 174; Steck, *Motolinia's History*, 1951, p. 88.

49. Chamberlain, *Conquest and Colonization*, 1953, p. 28.

50. Porras Barranechea, *Cartas*, 1959, p. 46.

51. Ibid., 24, 26.

52. Hallenbeck, *Alvar Núñez Cabeza de Vaca*, 1940, p. 44, discussed the 40 deaths from sickness and 10 casualties at Aute while the task force threw the rafts together, also provisions found at Aute (42).

53. Varner and Varner, trans., *Florida*, 1962, pp. 62 – 63. The Gentleman of Elvas reported that only two men landed and that the natives slew one on the spot (Robertson, trans., *True Relation*, 1933, vol. II, p. 40).

54. Varner and Varner, trans., *Florida*, 1962, pp. 70 – 71; Robertson, trans., *True Relation*, 1933, vol. II, pp. 42 – 44.

55. Varner and Varner, trans., *Florida*, 1962, pp. 76, 79; Robertson, *True Relation*, 1933, vol. II, pp. 45 – 46.

56. C.O. Sauer, *Sixteenth Century North America*, 1971, p. 167. De la Vega reported that six negotiators who met de Soto outside Cofitachique explained that there was a food shortage because people fled their town without planting during the "great pestilence" that had struck all towns in the chiefdom just one year before (Varner and Varner, trans., *Florida*, 1962, p. 298).

57. C.O. Sauer, *Sixteenth Century North America*, 1971, p. 302; Varner and Varner, trans., *Florida*, 1962, pp. 300, 325 – 26.

58. Gerhard, *Guide*, 1972, p. 23.

59. Gibson, *Aztecs*, 1964, p. 448.

60. Translator Bandelier (*Journey*, 1904 [1922], 204 – 208) mentions cures in 1534 – 35.

61. C.O. Sauer, *Sixteenth Century North America*, 1971, p. 302; Bandelier, trans., *Journey*, 1904 (1922), 147 – 49.

62. Gerhard, *Guide*, 1972, p. 23; Bancroft (*Native Races*, 1875, vol. I, p. 639), on the contrary, located the greatest havoc "in the interior, on the central plateau, and in the coldest and most arid regions, the lowlands of the coast being nearly . . . free from its effects."

63. Mendieta, *Historia*, 1945, p. 174.

64. Bancroft, *History*, vol. II, 1886, p. 553.

65. Zinsser, *Rats, Lice*, 1934, p. 256.

66. García, *El Clero*, 1907, p. 103.

67. Polo T., "Apuntes," 1913, p. 56.

68. Dobyns, "Outline," 1963, p. 513.

69. Veblen, "Native Population Decline," 1977, p. 497.

70. True, ed., *Memoir*, 1944, 1945, p. 12; Connor, trans., *Colonial Records*, 1925, vol. I, pp. 34 – 35. Menéndez reported other Spaniards had spent 15 and 18 years as captives, dating their wrecks to 1547 and 1550, partly still within the 1545 – 48 period of epidemic bubonic plague in New Spain.

71. Laudonnière, *Three Voyages*, 1975, pp. 109 – 10.

72. Dobyns and Doughty, *Peru*, 1976, p. 86.

73. Powell, *Soldiers, Indians*, 1952, pp. 10 – 12. The "rush" to Zacatecas came in 1549.

74. Gannon, *Cross*, 1965, pp. 10 – 11; O'Daniel, *Dominicans*, 1930, pp. 61 – 63; B. Smith, comp., *Colección*, 1857, p. 193 – 95.

75. Gannon, *Cross*, 1965, p. 14; O'Daniel, *Dominicans*, 1930, pp. 64 – 65; B. Smith, comp., *Colección*, 1857, p. 196.

76. Gannon, *Cross*, 1965, p. 14; O'Daniel, *Dominicans*, 1930, pp. 66 – 67; B. Smith, comp., *Colección*, 1857, p. 199; "los mas de ellos estavan con calenturas" (p. 201).

77. Gerhard, *Guide*, 1972, p. 23.

78. Milner, "Epidemic Disease," 1980, pp. 39 – 56.

79. Lowery, *Spanish Settlements*, 1905 (1959), vol. I, p. 359.

80. McNeill, *Plagues and Peoples*, 1976, p. 209.

81. Alegre, *Historia*, Tome I, Libros 1 – 3, 1956, vol. I, p. 51.

82. McBryde, "Influenza," 1940, p. 297.

83. Ibid., 294, 300.

84. Lowery, *Spanish Settlements*, 1905 (1959), 368 – 69; Priestley, *Luna Papers*, 1928, p. 103.

85. Cobo, *Fundación*, 1956, vol. II, p. 447.

SECTION TWO
The Colonial Period, 1562—1763

The historic, or Colonial, period in Florida, when literate Europeans recorded a fairly continuous, if ethnocentric, set of observations of Native American life, opened with the arrival of French Huguenot colonists in 1562. The type of documentation available altered dramatically with Jacques Le Moyne's arrival in 1564. Because Le Moyne's forty-three paintings depicted a wide range of Timucuan activities—two of them often represented within one painting—Le Moyne's record actually documented events of which he was apparently not conscious. Europeans tended to view Native Americans as unchanged by the Columbian Exchange, a cultural and biological process of which they were only marginally conscious in the 1560s, especially if the Europeans thought themselves the "first White men" to have come into contact with particular Native Americans. European observers lacked, moreover, any earlier record of observations against which they could compare their own so as to become conscious of changes among the Native Americans they saw.[1]

1564—1570

In this situation, Jacques Le Moyne actually painted and wrote evidence of a major epidemic of infectious disease among the Saturiwa Timucuan chiefdom in 1564—1565 without consciously recognizing it. The evidence for Timucuan cultural change in providing European-style nursing and life support for persons sick with Old World contagions has already been discussed in the last chapter. What should be recognized at this point is that Le Moyne could not have painted transvestites carrying sick adults off to special nursing locations and could not have written that transvestites performed this function for those ill from contagion in Timucua society *unless an episode of epidemic Old World disease had swept through the Saturiwa during the period when Le Moyne was at Fort Caroline (or among the Utina serving as a mercenary) to observe the behavior an epidemic elicited*. Had an epidemic episode not occurred between Le Moyne's arrival on June 22, 1564, and the Spanish capture of Fort Caroline on September 20, 1565, Le Moyne simply could not have learned about epidemic-period behavior by Timucuan transvestites.

Actually, the epidemic episode among the Timucuans can be other-wise dated to 1564. When Spanish Jesuits attempted to found missions among the Powhatan Confederacy Native Americans in 1570, they re-ported that the area had been "chastised . . . with six years of famine and death, which has brought it about that there is much less popula-tion than usual."[2] The Jesuit historian Francisco X. Alegre added a year, writing that "for seven years that people had been continually bela-bored by an epidemic."[3] He probably inadvertently changed "six" into "seven." Thus the Spanish Colonial record indicates that the epidemic spread widely among Atlantic coastal native populations.

The source of infection appears to have been Central Mexico. The several-year-long epidemic on the Atlantic Coast of North America most likely resulted from a variety of diseases that spread through Native American groups in a series, for "various" diseases reached epidemic proportions in the Valley of Mexico during 1563 and 1564.[4] The central Mexican mortality and consequent Indoamerican depopulation prompted a personal inspector for the Spanish crown to increase trib-utes so as to compensate Spaniards for the thinned number of tribute payers.[5]

1586 DOUBLE JEOPARDY

Late in May 1586 direct transmission of epidemic disease from English privateers to Native Americans living at and near St. Augustine may have occurred. The log of the *Primrose*, one of the ships in the war fleet led by Francis Drake, recorded: "The wilde people at first comminge of our men died verie fast and said amongest themselues, It was the Eng-lisshe God that made them die so faste."[6] The complements of Drake's ships did, in fact, carry with them a deadly contagion. Drake had sailed hurriedly from Plymouth on September 14, 1585. He put into Santiago in the Cape Verde Islands on November 17 to finish fitting for a long voyage and quartered many of his 2,300 men in the deserted town for ten days. "There was adjoining to their greatest church an hospital, with as brave rooms in it, and in as goodly order as any man can devise; we found about 20 sick persons, all negroes, lying of very foul and frightful diseases. In this hospital we took all the bells out of the steeple and brought them away with us."[7] Members of Drake's forces visiting the Black patients in the church hospital may have contracted one or more acute fevers from them. The work force removing the bells may also have caught the disease(s), and men quartered in the vacant houses of the port town may have contracted a disease transmitted by insect vectors in the houses.

Drake sailed again on November 29, and two days later epidemic disease broke out on board his ships.[8] The fleet made its New World landfall at Dominica and traded with the Indoamericans there. The contagion may have spread to them. The English war fleet sailed on to capture the city of Santo Domingo, Spain's oldest New World settlement and a wealthy one. Then Drake occupied the city of Cartagena on the northern coast of South America for six weeks, transmitting the infection his men carried to the Colonial population of South America. By that time, Drake's forces were so diminished and the survivors of the disease so weakened that he sailed for England. His fleet stopped off on its way home to capture St. Augustine, having lost some 750 men. Three-fourths of Drake's casualties were caused by the Cape Verde Island fever, which caused victims to break out with a rash of small spots as well as to suffer from a burning fever.[9] In other words, Drake's men carried an infection aboard ship that had caused a mortality greater than 25 percent among adult Englishmen and had an incubation period of one week, so that his sailors and troops could well have infected the Native Americans about St. Augustine.

On the other hand, the possibility remains that the Florida Native Americans came down with some other infectious disease from which they began by coincidence to die when the English invaders appeared. The log already cited recorded that Drake's fleet arrived at St. Augustine on May 27 and sailed on June 2. That was time enough for a disease with a week-long incubation period to break out as the Englishmen were about to depart. Yet the author of the log wrote that the "wild people" died very fast when the invaders first arrived. Thus the identity of the source of contagion remains unsure, but the ship's log did undoubtedly record a serious epidemic episode.

The epidemic that seamen with Drake witnessed at St. Augustine may well have originated among English colonists at Roanoke. Slightly more than 100 Englishmen in Raleigh's colony suffered no mortality, but Thomas Hariot's report makes clear that they transmitted at least two epidemic diseases to the Native Americans with whom they came into contact. In one dramatic passage, Hariot wrote that a few days after the Englishmen visited hostile settlements, 20 Native Americans died in some, 40 in others, 60 in some, and in one 120 perished, "which in truth was very many in respect to their numbers." The disease was strange to the natives, so that they knew neither how to cure it nor even what it was.[10] Whatever this contagious disease may have been, it appears likely to have been the cause of the epidemic episode from which Native Americans began to die at St. Augustine just when Drake's fleet occupied that Spanish outpost. If Drake's personnel then transmitted the Cape Verde Island affliction from which it suffered to the Timucua, the Florida native American peoples were ravaged by two epidemic episodes in short succession.

1596

A new royal governor, Gonzalo Méndez de Canzo, arrived at St. Augustine on June 2, 1597. Initially, at least, Méndez de Canzo wrote with some enthusiasm about a hospital then under construction in the Florida outpost. He reported that hospital care had kept "many" soldiers, Indians, and Blacks from dying the previous summer.[11] The disease that struck St. Augustine and neighboring Native Americans could have been the measles that was epidemic in Central Mexico in 1595.[12]

Another possibility is that the disease that felled Spaniards, Native Americans, and Blacks in St. Augustine during the summer of 1596 was bubonic plague. Plague appeared in London during the autumn of 1592 and reached its peak there during the summer of 1593.[13] In 1592 and 1593, *cocoliztli* as well as measles was epidemic in Central Mexico[14] and the Mixtec country and along the Pacific Coast.[15] In frontier Sinaloa, however, the 1592 – 1593 episode was labeled "a most violent pestilence of smallpox and measles."[16] Almost no one among the frontier tribes escaped the contagion. "Repulsive crusts" covered some sick people from head to foot. Others suffered as the skin peeled from their hands and feet. Burning with fever, people fled their homes. Mortality in the Sinaloa frontier area ran 25 percent among Christian converts, 1,000 of the first 4,000 baptized persons perishing.[17] This biological disaster triggered a Native American nativistic movement during which traditionalists slew the Jesuit missionary Gonzalo de Tapia.

Thus, published descriptions of later sixteenth-century Colonial Florida document epidemic disease episodes there at least thrice, in 1564 – 1570, in 1586, and in 1596. Those were years of fundamentally proprietary governance of the colony when missionary activity was just beginning.

1613 – 1617 BUBONIC PLAGUE

During the seventeenth century, epidemic mortality began, as Jones and Milanich recognized, when an epidemic struck Colonial Florida in 1613. At least half of the Christianized Native American population perished within a four-year period.[18] Franciscan missionaries reported to the king that half the natives converted to Christianity died of "plague and other contagious diseases." They used the Spanish term for plague, although such usage is not a conclusive diagnosis because, as I noted above, Spaniards also used the term to mean "epidemic." Other evidence supports the specific identification. Central Mexico was afflicted in 1613 by the disease *cocoliztli*.[19]

If *cocoliztli* meant in 1613 what it had meant in 1545, then this disease was, according to the analysis presented above, bubonic plague. That diagnosis is more consistent with the pattern of mortality distributed over four years among missionized Native Americans than a smallpox etiology. Smallpox, transmitted from person to person, spreads to all susceptible individuals in a residential population very quickly. Bubonic plague, transmitted by a flea vector from an animal reservoir (usually rats but on occasion other rodents), does not typically spread in a linear pattern to all susceptible persons in a residential population. Rather, plague typically is transmitted seemingly at random and does take a few years to spread to all of the susceptible individuals.

Franciscan missionaries then in Florida wrote to the crown at the beginning of January in 1617 that during the previous four years, half of the Native Americans there had perished of repeated episodes of epidemics and contagious diseases. The Franciscans claimed that more than 8,000 Christian converts had survived and many heathens. There were still no missions among the Apalachees, the South Carolina tribes, or the Calusa.[20]

1649 YELLOW FEVER

As Jones and Milanich noted, an infectious epidemic struck Spanish Colonial Florida in 1649. It differed from most earlier epidemics in that the pathogen killed Spaniards as well as Native Americans. Officials, such as the provincial governor, two treasury officers, and two company commanders, and many missionaries died. The contagion was directly transmitted by ship's personnel from Havana, where more than one-third of the population had died of the disease.[21] Four successive royal prosecuting attorneys died in Havana in quick succession.[22] This was an epidemic not of a domesticated European disease but of African yellow fever that broke out in Mérida and Campeche, Yucatan; San Juan de Puerto Rico; and Havana, Cuba, in 1648.[23] The population of the Caribbean ports panicked.

Yellow fever could not invade the peoples of the New World until its mosquito vector, *Aedes aegypti*, survived a transatlantic voyage and found a niche in which it could survive. It seems surprising that the mosquito had not hitchhiked across the ocean earlier, inasmuch as it is "domesticated," that is, it breeds in water in a container such as a cistern, water cask, or gourd.[24] The destination of the initial successful transatlantic crossing apparently was Barbados, where the mosquito found a fine ecological niche. Yellow fever was epidemic on that English-ruled island by September 1647.[25] By January 1648 the disease had spread to San Juan de Puerto Rico because of movements of troops and prisoners. Florida became part of its Caribbean and Gulf habitat. It recurred among the presidential troops in 1649[26] and 1650.[27] Because the disease was new, neither Europeans nor Native Americans possessed any immunity to it nor indeed any effective treatment for it.

1653 SMALLPOX

Florida's Governor Diego de Robelledo, who took office in 1655, reported that Spanish inhabitants had smallpox, as did many Native Americans, and that the Blacks had all died.[28] Settlements of the Timucuan-speaking peoples were significantly depopulated by this epidemic and during an uprising against Spanish colonial exploitation that it precipitated as well as by subsequent suppression.[29] The millenarian response to epidemic stress that began early in the sixteenth century continued among surviving Florida Native Americans.

1659 MEASLES

A lethal measles epidemic followed the earlier smallpox episode and consequent Native-American-Spanish war in Florida. The provincial governor who took office on February 20 in 1659, Alonso de Aranguiz y Cotes, reported to Spain on November 1 of that year his bad luck: following his arrival more than 10,000 Native Americans had died from the highly contagious measles.[30] Gov. Aranguiz y Cotes arrived by ship from Havana, where he had been delayed for some time. Again, the chronicle of epidemics in New Spain does not indicate that measles was epidemic there at the time. Transmission may have been transatlantic. Native Americans living near Montreal, in French Canada, "were dying . . . like flies" in 1659,[31] a circumstance that suggests direct transatlantic transmission followed by a spread among Native Americans along the Atlantic Coast.

1672

As Jones and Milanich noted, an unidentified epidemic assaulted north Florida's Native Americans again in 1672.[32] Three years later, an official enumeration of both converted and unconverted Native Americans showed that only 10,766 remained under Colonial rule. Only 13 percent of them were presumably Timucuan-speakers.[33] Overland transmission of the 1672 disease from northern New Spain appears to be a possibility. In the previous year, 1671, the Pueblo peoples of New Mexico suffered from "a great pestilence" that caused high mortality among both people and cattle.[34] Probably, therefore, influenza is implicated.

1675

In mid-1675, Capt. Juan Fernandez de Florencia wrote a report on the missions of the Apalachee and Timucua areas of Spanish Florida. Fernandez was the deputy governor in charge of the Apalachee Province and held the military rank of captain. He listed some twenty-seven mission or related populations that ranged in numbers from 40 at a St. Johns River ferry on the road to St. Augustine, to 1,400 in San Luís, the Apalachee provincial capital. The Guale and Timucuan missions were already nearly depopulated. Those among the Apalachee still had hundreds of residents. Fernandez ended with a key statement: "I have not taken a census and they die daily."[35]

No doubt Fernandez meant his statement that Native Americans died daily to be understood somewhat figuratively. Still, it is indicative of an epidemic in progress, even if Fernandez merely supposed that Native Americans died frequently, for only one-third of the settlements he reported had more than 365 inhabitants. In other words, taking his statement at face value, if the normal death rate was one person daily, two-thirds of the settlements he listed could not have survived another year (see table 26).

Of twenty-six settlements reported by Fernandez, sixteen would have disappeared entirely in less than one year with a death rate of one person per day! None of the settlements he listed could have survived such a death rate for four years. Even if Fernandez exaggerated, his remark identified the summer of 1675 as a period of pestilence and heightened mortality. Possibly smallpox was transmitted overland from northern New Spain via the Coahuiltecan tribes of south Texas.[36] Perhaps there was a direct transmission from Cuba or from Spain itself.

TABLE 26
Apalache-Guale-Timucua Settlements in 1675,
in Rank Order of Population Size

Settlement	Population	Years of Survival[a]
San Luís	1,400	3.8
San Lorenzo Ybitachuco	1,200	3.3
San Damián Acpayca	900	2.5
San Joseph Ocuya	900	2.5
Concepción Ayabale	800	2.2
San Juan Azpalaga	800	2.2
San Martín Tomole	700	1.9
San Pedro Patale	500	1.4
San Carlos	400	1.1
Candelaria	300	0.8
Asunción de Nuestra Señora	300	0.8
San Matheo	300	0.8
Santa Elena Machava	300	0.8
San Pedro	300	0.8
San Francisco Oconí	200	0.55
San Antonio Bacuqua	120	0.33
Santa Fé	110	0.30
San Nicolás Tolentino	100	0.27
San Juan Guacara	80	0.22
Santa Cruz Taragica	80	0.22
Santa Catholina	60	0.16
San Francisco	60	0.16
Santa Cruz Ytuchafun	60	0.16
Natividad de Nuestra Gracia	40	0.11
San Miguel Asile	40	0.11
Ferry	40	0.11

[a]Assuming a death rate of one person daily.
Source: Boyd, "Enumeration," 1948, pp. 184—87.

1686 FEVER

There is record of illness in 1686 among Gulf Coast inhabitants of
Colonial Florida and probably among adjacent Native Americans.
Marcos Delgado set out from Apalachee on August 28, 1686, with
twelve soldiers and twenty Apalachee auxiliaries. He visited villages of
the Creeks with the goal of reaching the Mobile. In mid-September, the
expedition's commander reported to the provincial governor that he
and half of the soldiers and Apalachee auxiliaries "fell ill with a fever."
Delgado wrote that he himself was twice attacked by fever.[37] It seems
possible that both the Mestizo soldiers and Apalachee auxiliaries suffered from malaria and that repeated acute attacks occurred as a conse-

quence of physical exertion on the march. On the other hand, it also seems possible that the travelers contracted some contagious disease of which fever was one symptom as they left Apalachee territory, so that they fell ill in the midst of the Creek villages. Typhus could well have been the culprit. That disease was reported as epidemic in Guatemala in 1686[38] and could have been widespread throughout Spanish North America.

1716

The British campaigns of 1702–1704 during the War of the Spanish Succession ended the Spanish mission system in northern Florida. South Carolina militia burned some settlements, captured thousands of Timucuans, and marched them off to slavery in South Carolina.[39] Even after the collapse of Christian convert population during the war, serious illness continued to assault the handful of surviving Native Americans. In 1716, Diego Peña led a scouting party from St. Augustine westward through the former Timucuan and Apalachee missions. Peña left the post on August 4, and five days later he encamped "because three Indians were sick."[40]

The illness may have been some chronic ailment to which Native Americans living in or near St. Augustine were subject, aggravated by the rigors of an overland journey. When Peña returned to St. Augustine in early November, Colonial officials turned out to receive him and the independent Native American leaders accompanying him. The governor himself did not greet the chiefs at the town gate but awaited them in the palace because of his own recent illness.[41] In other words, there was probably an endemic, chronic ailment such as malaria that affected both Native Americans and relatively transient inhabitants such as the royal governor.

1727

The extant historical literature appears to contain some confusion about the process of the Columbian Exchange in and around St. Augustine between 1725 and 1729. William Neill referred to an epidemic that struck there in 1726.[42] J.T. Milanich referred to a pestilence that struck the St. Augustine Timucuan town between September 1 and October 5 in 1728.[43] Historian Theodore Corbett referred to an unidentified epidemic that began in "the Indian suburbs and spread to St. Augustine" during 1727.[44]

Original sources include a letter dated September 1, 1727, that Gov. Antonio de Benavides wrote to the king, transmitting a copy of his enumeration of 1,021 Native Americans of various tribal antecedents living in sixteen ethnic settlements. Benavides stated in his cover letter that after he had carried out his inspection of the Native American rancherías, 166 recently converted native Christians had died in an epidemic,[45] a crude death rate of 163 per 1,000 people.

It is quite possible that both measles and smallpox spread to the Florida Native Americans during these years, causing lower death rates than in earlier years because some people were already immune as a result of prior infections. Smallpox reportedly spread to the missionized Native Americans of Sonora in northwestern New Spain in January of 1724.[46] The geographic extension of the epidemic episode is indicated by the death of the reigning Spanish monarch, young Luís I, from smallpox that same year.[47]

Measles is implicated inasmuch as that disease was epidemic in New Spain, and especially in Mexico City during 1727 and 1728, in January of which year the episode ended.[48] Farther south in Guatemala, measles caused epidemic mortality in 1725–1728.[49] Thus measles may have spread northward close on the heels of a widespread although perhaps sporadically distributed smallpox epidemic.

TIMUCUAN EXTINCTION

Spanish officials evacuated Florida in accord with the 1763 Treaty of Paris. British troops landed and occupied the province. The Spaniards took with them nearly all their civilian population, including a few hundred surviving Christian Native Americans. They settled the latter near Veracruz on the fever-wracked coast of New Spain.[50] A few Calusa may have remained in South Florida, never having converted to Christianity. Lower Creek towns becoming known as Seminoles, from Spanish *cimarrón* ("wild"), occupied most of the peninsula, whatever the European notions of sovereignty. In other words, by 1763, the Timucuan-speaking peoples were virtually extinct in Florida, and the Calusa may have been nearly so.

SUMMARY

At least a dozen epidemic disease episodes are known to have occurred among Florida's Native Americans from 1564 to 1727 and are listed in table 27. I have identified episodes of yellow fever, plague, measles, and smallpox and have indicated their probable or possible modes of transmission to the peninsular population. Perhaps the most important finding is that more than a third of the epidemic disease agents appear to have been transmitted directly across the Atlantic Ocean by passengers and/or crewmen on sailing ships. These are (1) the 1586 Cape Verde infectious fever that Drake's fleet carried and possibly transmitted at St. Augustine; (2) another contagion brought the previous year by English colonists on Roanoke Island; (3) the 1649 yellow fever epidemic that followed the initial 1647 transport of mosquito vector and pathogen across the Atlantic; (4) the 1654 smallpox epidemic that may have been carried across the Atlantic by Swedes or colonists other than Spaniards; and (5) the 1659 measles epidemic.

Four other Florida epidemic diseases may have been transmitted from New Spain, but the available documentation does not clearly indicate such transmission. These are (1) the 1564–1570 series of epidemic episodes occurring simultaneously in Central Mexico and in Florida and the Atlantic Coast of North America; (2) the 1613–1617 bubonic plague that spread north along the Atlantic Coast through the New England tribes; (3) the 1672 epidemic, possibly influenza spread in part by domestic animal hosts across the continent from the northern

TABLE 27

Documented and Possible Epidemic Disease Episodes
Among Native Americans of Colonial Florida, 1564–1727

Date	Disease	Probability	Mortality
1564—1570	Unidentified + endemic syphilis	documented	severe
1585—1586	Unidentified	documented	severe
1586	Vectored fever	probable	15—20%
1596	Measles	documented	about 25%
1613—1617	Bubonic plague	documented	50%
1649	Yellow fever	documented	about 33%
1653—	Smallpox	documented	unknown
1659	Measles	documented	unknown
1672	Influenza (?)	documented	unknown
1675	Unidentified	probable	unknown
1686	Unidentified (typhus ?)	documented	unknown
1716	Perhaps chronic	documented	unknown
1726±	Smallpox (?)	nearly certain	unknown
1727 or 1728	Measles (?)	nearly certain	16%

frontier of New Spain; and (4) probably epidemic smallpox, which could have come straight from Spain as well as from New Spain in 1724 or 1725, followed very quickly by measles spreading northward from Central America.

At least five and probably seven infectious epidemics struck the Native Americans surviving in Florida during the seventeenth century, instead of the three usually mentioned. The five differed from each other in the most lethal pattern. First came bubonic plague in 1613 – 1617. After a long interval possibly indicating that very few Native Americans survived in Florida, yellow fever arrived in 1649, followed in rapid succession by smallpox in 1653, measles in 1659, and probably influenza in 1672. Then came an unidentified contagion in 1675 and perhaps typhus in 1686. Each epidemic found large numbers of susceptible victims because the diseases differed. Earlier diseases conferred no immunity to later ones. Native Americans must have died in great numbers in Florida during the later seventeenth century, but particularly during the sequence of yellow fever (1649), smallpox (1653), and measles (1659). Moreover, other documents still in Spanish archives may record additional epidemic episodes.

The expanded outline of epidemic disease among Florida's native peoples during the seventeenth century still does not mean that the seventeenth century was as lethal as the sixteenth in terms of total mortality. During that initial century Old World pathogens invaded the Florida natives when they had reached their population maximum, in 1513 – 1514, 1519, 1528 – 1531, 1535 – 1538, 1545, 1549, perhaps 1550, 1559, 1564 – 1570, 1586 (two waves), and finally 1596. That was a total of one dozen epidemic episodes, half of them virtually certain. Given the lethalness of the smallpox, bubonic plague, measles, and other pathogens involved in "virgin soil" pandemics, the native population could not but have fallen rapidly during the entire sixteenth century. Consequently, there simply were not nearly so many Native Americans left to die during the seventeenth century.

A schematic reconstruction of the depopulation trend among Native Americans in Florida appears in figure 3. This chart is even more empirical and schematic than those drawn by S.F. Cook and Woodrow Borah to graph the population trend in Central Mexico during the same period.[51] Whereas Cook and Borah analyzed numbers derived from enumerations or estimates based upon records of tribute payments, figure 3, representing a different approach, presents a trend based only on best-documented epidemic disease episodes and mortality known for the various diseases involved in other Native American populations if not reported from Florida. Figure 3 intentionally emphasizes decisive

FIGURE 3
Schematic Reconstruction of Approximate
Depopulation Trend of Florida Native Americans, 1519–1617

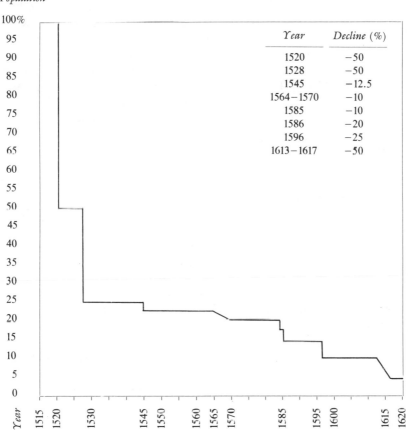

*Percent
of
Population*

Year	Decline (%)
1520	−50
1528	−50
1545	−12.5
1564–1570	−10
1585	−10
1586	−20
1596	−25
1613–1617	−50

demographic events of a kind unknown during the nineteenth or twentieth century since demography emerged as a science.

This schematic reconstruction ignores the 1513–1514 episode as unquantifiable and starts from the 1517–1519 population. The 1519 smallpox pandemic is shown as killing only half of the people. Then the population is shown as precisely in balance until each of the next epidemics struck. This is a conservative procedure, inasmuch as sequelae of smallpox and other diseases and new endemic ailments elsewhere caused Native American numbers to fall even between epidemic episodes. The 1528 episode is attributed to measles, with another 50 percent loss in population. The 1545 bubonic plague pandemic is assigned 12.5 percent mortality based on a loss of 800,000 of 6,300,000 Central Mexicans. The 1564–1570 episode is attributed an arbitrary 10 percent loss, perhaps an underestimate of mortality in view of the presence of endemic venereal disease among at least Timucuan-speaking groups. The more contagious disease that Raleigh's spies transmitted at Roanoke that apparently reached the Saturiwan Timucuans just as Drake's forces occupied St. Augustine is assigned a 10 percent mortality. That may also be an underestimate, in view of Thomas Hariot's description of village mortality farther north. The vectored fever Drake's men picked up in the Cape Verde Islands is assumed to have been transmitted to the Florida natives. The mortality rate is approximately that which his forces suffered. The end-of-the-century measles epidemic is calculated at 25 percent mortality, although this could well have been considerably higher if there had in fact been no measles in Florida since 1528 or so. The 50 percent mortality Franciscan missionaries reported occurred among Christian converts between 1613 and 1617 during that bubonic plague epidemic is taken to have afflicted non-Christians as well.

This schematic reconstruction omits the 1559 influenza epidemic, which almost certainly caused significant mortality among Florida natives, and other diseases. Nevertheless, it suggests that it is reasonable to think that the 1617 Native American population of Florida was on the order of 5 percent of the size of the 1517 population. It should be emphasized that this schematic chart shows no actual population figures. The figure is presented to stress the conclusion that Florida's Native American population decreased precipitously from at least 1519 and then rapidly until 1617.[52] This demographic trend affected social behavior and cultural patterns in fundamental ways. The demographic losses combined with psychological shock and cosmological confusion to cause the collapse of aboriginal Southeastern cultures. That collapse followed the biological invasion of probably malaria in 1513–1514, smallpox in 1519, measles in 1528, bubonic plage in 1545, and influenza in 1559. The demographic disaster was maximum because none of these pathogens conferred any immunity to any of the subsequent invaders. Consequently every one decimated a completely susceptible population.

NOTES

1. Sixteenth-century observers thought in terms of an inaccurate normative theory of cultural change, like many twentieth-century anthropologists (Steward, "Theory and Application," 1955, pp. 295–96).

2. Lewis and Loomie, *Spanish Jesuit Mission*, 1953, pp. 85, 89.

3. Alegre, *Historia*, 1956, vol. I, p. 77.

4. Gerhard, *Guide*, 1972, p. 23.

5. Mendieta, *Historia*, 1945, p. 174.

6. Quinn, ed., *Roanoke Voyages*, 1955, vol. I, p. 306; J.S. Corbett, "Discourse and Description," 1898, p. 26.

7. Ibid., 9.

8. Ibid., 12. "We had not been two days at sea but there fell a great sickness amongst our men, not in one ship alone but in all the whole fleet." Creighton, *History*, 1891, vol. I, pp. 585–86; Dobyns, "Outline," 1963, p. 504.

9. J.S. Corbett, "Discourse and Description," 1898, p. 52; Creighton, *History*, 1891, vol. I, pp. 587–88; Dobyns, "Outline," 1963, p. 504.

10. C.O. Sauer, *Sixteenth Century North America*, 1971, p. 303; Jennings, *Invasion*, 1975, p. 23; Quinn, ed., *Roanoke Voyages*, 1955, vol. I, p. 378; Crosby, *Columbian Exchange*, 1972, pp. 40–41; Lorant, ed., *New World*, 1946, p. 272.

11. Geiger, *Franciscan Conquest*, 1937, vol. I, p. 77.

12. Beals, "Acculturation," 1967, p. 461; Gibson, *Aztecs*, 1964, p. 449; Mendieta, *Historia*, 1945, p. 174.

13. Creighton, *History*, 1891, vol. I, p. 351.

14. Gibson, *Aztecs*, 1964, p. 449.

15. Gerhard, *Guide*, 1972, p. 23.

16. C.O. Sauer, *Aboriginal Population*, 1935, p. 11.

17. Karns, *Unknown Arizona*, 1954, p. 277.

18. Bushnell, "Menéndez Cattle Barony," 1978, p. 416; Swanton, *Early History*, 1922, p. 338.

19. Gibson, *Aztecs*, 1964, p. 449.

20. Pareja, et al., Oficio, 17 de enero de 1617.

21. Bushnell, "Menéndez Cattle Barony," 1978, p. 419; Ruíz de Salazar, Oficio, 14 de julio de 1650.

22. Silverio Sainza, *Cuba*, 1972, p. 300.

23. Schendel, Alvarez Amezquita, and Bustamante, *Medicine*, 1969, p. 107; McNeill, *Plagues and Peoples*, 1976, p. 213; Brau, *La colonización*, 1907, p. 455; Alegre, *Historia*, 1959, Tomo III, pp. 137–38.

24. McNeill, *Plagues and Peoples*, 1976, p. 213.

25. Creighton, *History*, 1891, vol. I, pp. 620–21.

26. Moreno Ponce de León, Memorial, 7 de setiembre de 1651.

27. Ruíz de Salazar, Oficio, 14 de julio de 1650.

28. Chatelain, *Defenses*, 1941, p. 56.

29. Swanton, *Early History*, 1922, p. 338.

30. Bushnell, "Menéndez Cattle Barony," 1978, p. 420; Aranguíz y Cotes, 1 de noviembre de 1659.

31. Campbell, *Pioneer Laymen*, 1915, vol. I, p. 213.

32. Bushnell, "Menéndez Cattle Barony," 1978, p. 425; Swanton, *Early History*, 1922, p. 338.

33. Bushnell, "Menéndez Cattle Barony," 1978, p. 425.

34. Hackett, ed., *Historical Documents*, 1937, vol. III, pp. 17, 302.

35. Boyd, "Enumeration," 1948, p. 188.

36. Ewers, "Influence of Epidemics," 1973, p. 108; Bolton, ed., *Spanish Exploration*, 1908, p. 298 (refers to perhaps an earlier episode); Sheridan and Naylor, *Rarámuri*, 1979, p. 37.

37. Boyd, trans., "Expedition," 1937, pp. 5–6, 14–16.

38. Veblen, "Native Population Decline," 1977, p. 498.

39. Boyd, Smith, and Griffin, *Here They Once Stood*, 1951, pp. 36–95.

40. Boyd, "Diego Peña's Expedition," 1949, p. 13.

41. Ibid., 11.

42. Neill, "Indian and Spanish Site," 1968, p. 112.

43. Milanich, "Western Timucua," 1978, p. 73; following Geiger, *Biographical Dictionary*, 1940, p. 136.

44. T.G. Corbett, "Population Structure," 1976, p. 275.

45. Benavides, a S. M. dando cuenta de haber hecho la visita a los indios, 1 de setiembre de 1727.

46. Campos, Libro de Bautismos, no. 1, p. 45.

47. Chapman, *History*, 1918, pp. 377–78.

48. Gibson, *Aztecs*, 1964, p. 450.

49. Veblen, "Native Population Decline," 1977, p. 498.

50. Gold, "Settlement," 1965, pp. 567–76; *Borderland Empires*, 1969.

51. Cook and Borah, *Essays*, 1971, p. 83, etc.

52. If figures are fitted to the demographic trend line reconstructed in figure 3, earlier estimates of Florida Native American population can be checked for mutual consistency with the new estimates. The 1562–68 estimate of total population in table 23 based on a multiple of 5.5 persons per warrior is here revised upward to 155,000 individuals. Population estimates and mortality estimates appear in table 28.

SECTION THREE
Estimates of the Timucuan-Speaking Population, 1517–1620

Reconstructing the historic epidemiology of a population is an important first step—albeit merely initial—toward that accurate interpretation of historic events for which William McNeill eloquently argued. In the New World, reconstructing an approximate depopulation trend such as that presented in figure 3 becomes a second and methodologically significant step toward accurate demographic analysis, for figure 3 describes decisive demographic events affecting real people in real time. The curve in figure 3 shows the magnitude of declines of population during actual pandemic or epidemic episodes. It does not disguise such decisive demographic events by mathematical manipulations.[1] Another analytical step permits the estimation of Native American numbers at several specific time periods, which may then be compared with earlier estimates of Florida population reached using different techniques.

This next analytical step is taken in figure 4. The figures in figure 4 are population estimates instead of the proportions employed in figure 3. The numerical starting point for figure 4 population estimates is a 1564 Timucuan-speaking total population rounded to 150,000 persons. This basic figure is derived from table 23; it is the population estimated from warrior counts for the chiefdoms, allowing two warriors per lineage and 5.5 per counted mobilized warrior. From that base figure, figure 4 relates population estimates to nine decisive demographic events, the earlier epidemics of 1520–1524, 1531–1533, 1545–1548, and 1559, and the later ones of 1564–1570, 1585, 1596, and 1613–1619. This is almost the ten counts that S.F. Cook and Woodrow Borah regarded as "optimal" for historic demographic analysis[2] over a comparable period of time.

The depopulation trend line shown in figure 4 implies that Timucuan population totaled about 150,000 persons for only about five years, between 1559 and 1564. Figure 4 differs from figure 3 in that the 1559 influenza epidemic has been estimated to have produced a 5 percent mortality and to have significantly disrupted horticultural activity during the summer of 1559. This change in reconstructing the depopulation trend has been introduced to help to account for the observed collapse of Southeastern aboriginal chiefdoms between the departure of the de Soto expedition in 1543 and the arrival of the de Luna colonists in 1559 and their inland explorations in 1560.

FIGURE 4
Estimate of Timucuan-Speaking Population from
A.D. 1515 to 1620 Based on Reconstructed Depopulation Trend

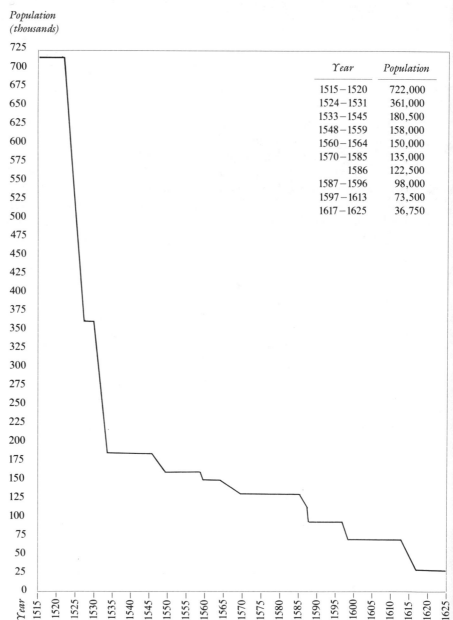

Population
(thousands)

Year	Population
1515 – 1520	722,000
1524 – 1531	361,000
1533 – 1545	180,500
1548 – 1559	158,000
1560 – 1564	150,000
1570 – 1585	135,000
1586	122,500
1587 – 1596	98,000
1597 – 1613	73,500
1617 – 1625	36,750

In other words, it is now assumed that the influenza pandemic had to contribute to that collapse along with the bubonic plague pandemic of 1545–1548 and the delayed impact of earlier pandemic diseases and the massive mortality they caused. The probable 12.5 percent mortality of the plague pandemic is regarded as an insufficient although necessary condition for the collapse of the Southeastern chiefdoms. Influenza mortality, and more importantly illness that demoralized people and kept them from planting in 1559 and further weakened the already seriously undermined authority of aboriginal theocratic leaders, are hypothesized as the final, sufficient conditions producing the collapse of the chiefdoms during the very period when the de Luna colony tried and failed to settle the Gulf Coast relying on Native American surplus food production. The estimated populations at various dates are summarized in table 28.

There are, of course, alternative explanations for the collapse of the Southeastern chiefdoms between 1543 and 1559. some of them have already been mentioned: surely selective execution of ruling elites by de Soto's marauders so weakened traditional authority as to hasten its disintegration. It is also possible that the bubonic plague caused mortality nearer the 50 percent that Franciscan missionaries reported for the 1613–1617 Florida plague epidemic than the 12.5 percent estimated on the basis of reported 1545–1548 mortality and total population in Central Mexico.

The depopulation trend reconstructed in figure 4 suggests that Timucuan speakers numbered about 158,000 between 1549 and 1559. The reconstructed trend indicates that perhaps 180,500 Timucuan speakers lived between 1533 and 1545 to suffer the depredations of de Soto's

TABLE 28
Estimated Timucuan Population Trend, 1517—1620

Chronology	Event	Mortality	Surviving Population
1517	—	—	722,000
1519—1524	Smallpox pandemic	361,000 (50%)	361,000
1528—1533	Measles pandemic	180,500 (50%)	180,500
1545—1548	Bubonic plague pandemic	22,500 (12.5%)	158,000
1559	Influenza pandemic	8,000 (5%)	150,000
1564—1570	Unidentified epidemic	15,000 (10%)	135,000
1585	Unidentified epidemic	13,500 (10%)	121,500
1586	Cape Verde Island fever	24,300 (20%)	97,200
1596	Measles (?) epidemic	24,300 (25%)	72,900
1613—1617	Bubonic plague	36,450 (50%)	36,450

marauders. Actually, a few thousand more should be added to the 1533 – 1539 estimate to allow for the direct casualties inflicted by de Soto's men. Before that, the reconstructed trend suggests that there were some 361,000 Timucuan-speakers between 1525 and 1528 and that there had been about 722,000 of them prior to 1519. The last figure can be compared with the estimate of 749,407 people who could have con-sumed 500 grams of meat daily in aboriginal Florida, according to an earlier estimate (table 19). Even if the Calusa numbered 100,000 and the Apalachee another 100,000, a Florida total population of 922,000 individuals would have been within the environmental human-life-sustaining capacity of the area. The differences between estimates reached on quite different bases are so large as to dismay a modern demographer accustomed to dealing only with modern census enumer-ations. Still, they are mutually consistent enough to suggest to the historic demographer that they lie within the correct order of mag-nitude.[3] The mutual consistency is also great enough to indicate that previously published estimates of the number of aboriginal Native Americans in Florida have definitely not been of the correct order of magnitude.

The methodological reasons for the gross underestimates of aborigi-nal population previously published appear from the depopulation trend reconstructed in figure 4. Historians and anthropologists have typically based their estimates of "aboriginal" numbers on population reports from the seventeenth century. As the figure 4 depopulation trend indicates, Colonial Florida began the seventeenth century with perhaps 70,000 to 75,000 Timucuan-speakers. Most of them had never been counted, however, because the Franciscan missionary program was then just beginning to expand inland beyond the Atlantic coastal chiefdoms. By the time the Christian conversion program achieved any significant amount of success, the Timucuan-speaking population had been halved by the bubonic plague (between 1613 and 1617). If there were about 36,750 Timucuan-speakers left alive in 1618, then the 8,000 the Franciscans claimed as converts amounted to some 21.77 percent of the total. Inasmuch as the missionaries never reached some chiefdoms, their conversion rate was considerably higher among the Saturiwa, Potano, Yustega, and Utina among whom they did work. In other words, the earlier published estimates of total Florida or Timucuan aboriginal population are quite consistent with post-1617 numbers indi-cated by the figure 4 depopulation trend. Previously published esti-mates of Florida's aboriginal population all suffered from the same basic methodological defect. They treated seventeenth-century Colo-nial population counts as reflecting numbers before the Columbian

Exchange. They failed to take into account the sixteenth-century epidemiology of Florida's Native Americans, so they ignored a whole series of decisive demographic events that caused wholesale human mortality. Thus the authors of these estimates postulated quite errone-ously low figures for pre-Columbian or early sixteenth-century Native American population magnitudes.

NOTES

1. By drawing graph lines from population count to count, through time, Cook and Borah (*Essays*, 1971, pp. 80 – 81; fig. 1 and 2) effectively mask the decisive impact of epidemic mortality. By converting population counts into their logarithms, Cook and Borah (p. 84, fig. 3; p. 86, fig. 4; p. 88, fig. 5) even more effectively masked the jerkiness that characterized the process of Native American depopulation in Central Mexico. It is possible for a historic demog-rapher to distort reality in the attempt to placate modern demographers by employing inappropriate statistical techniques. The methodological truth is that because modern demographers have not had to analyze populations suffer-ing massive mortality but not enumerated, they have had little occasion to develop tools for such analyses.

2. Cook and Borah, *Essays*, 1971, vol. I, pp. 78 – 79.

3. The difference between the estimated human sustenance capacity of Flori-da's annual protein supply of 749,407 and 922,000 is about 172,593 persons. That is about 18.7 percent, about three times larger than the 5.8 percent error that Cook and Borah (*Essays*, 1971, vol. I, pp. 74 – 75) characterized as "entirely satisfactory" when studying sixteenth- and seventeenth-century populations.

Depopulation as a Dynamic of Cultural Change

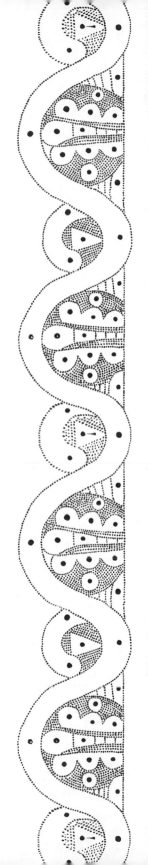

This volume makes a methodological excursion through several techniques for estimating Native American historic and aboriginal populations. Several essays present evidence that epidemic diseases caused massive depopulation of native Native Americans during the sixteenth century. The length of this methodological tour has been such that it may be well to summarize some of the major conclusions reached in its course.

PRE-COLUMBIAN POPULATION

The second essay about the lost Native American biological paradise estimated North America's pre-Columbian population as approximately 18 million. Standard modern demographic and ecological techniques indicate such a figure. Those techniques indicated that the Timucuan chiefdoms, the Calusa, and the Apalachee numbered perhaps 697,000 persons early in the sixteenth century. That population would have averaged a density of 5.7 persons per square kilometer.

Essay 3 began with a section comparing wild plant food resources in Florida and Lower California. The analysis indicated that Florida's natural resources could have sustained between 292,800 and 585,600 individuals early in the sixteenth century without recourse to horticulture. The second section analyzed fish, turtle, upland game birds and animals, and marine mammals available to Native Americans in Florida. It concluded that almost three-fourths of a million individuals could have consumed one 500-gram serving of meat daily the year round. The third section marshaled documentary evidence that the South Florida Calusa grew maize and other food crops, even though historians and anthropologists have thought that they did not. Calusa population was estimated at about 97,600 persons early in the sixteenth century. Such a large number is consistent with the known complexity of Calusa social structure and horticultural food production. The fourth section of that essay analyzed clues to the intensiveness of Timucua horticulture in sixteenth-century documents to show how a single chiefdom could easily sustain a population of 60,000 people.

In the fourth essay, William R. Swagerty and I reviewed sixteenth-century evidence for the number and distribution of Timucuan-speaking polities. The first section rescues from the oblivion of erroneously interpreted early sixteenth-century geography the southernmost Timucuan-speaking chiefdom, the Mocozo. The second section estimates the population of each chiefdom in the 1560s on the basis of reported and projected army sizes. If we use a multiple of five persons per mobilized warrior, the army figures point to a Timucuan-speaking population of from 130,500 to 144,000 between 1562 and 1568. The third section utilizes documentary reports of settlement numbers per chiefdom, number of houses per settlement, and number of residents per house to estimate Timucuan numbers in a different way. The people-house-town estimation procedure yields a maximum estimate of 807,500 individuals in 1562–1568. Combining the mobilized warrior reports with the resident-house-town data led us to reestimate the total population as between 144,855 and 150,405 persons in the 1560s. That range of numbers results from using the multiple of 5.5 persons per mobilized warrior and the premise that every reported lineage residential unit included two warriors.

The ecology of Florida and sixteenth-century documents afford much evidence that Timucuan and Calusan numbers were far larger than historians and anthropologists have recognized. Although anthropologists knew that Timucuan settlements were quite sedentary, investigators were unable to explain fully how this was possible. My own analysis consequently focused on previously unknown or overlooked Native American techniques for intensifying food production and resource management. The fifth essay began with a section describing Timucuan diversification of annual food crops. It emphasized the importance of amaranth cultivation for greens and grain. This Native American food plant is usually dismissed as a weed by Euroamericans. The second section briefly discussed the basic contribution of orchardry to food production. A third section signaled the vital roles of storehouses and canoes in food resource management.

Following some explanations for the density of early sixteenth-century Native American population, the analysis turned to the question of numbers. Essay 6 in its first section analyzed clues in sixteenth-century documents to construct a tentative chronology of decisive epidemic events in Florida during protohistoric times. The protohistoric period is viewed as the half century between 1512 and 1562. The second section used more explicit documentary statements about infectious disease to extend the chronology of decisive disease events through Spanish colonial times from 1564 to 1727. The text then illustrated how the regional chronology of decisive epidemic events serves as a tool for tracing Timucuan depopulation from 1519 to 1619. Total Timucuan numbers declined, according to the trend graphed in figure 4 and derived from reported epidemic mortality rates and known decisive epidemic events, from about 722,000 in 1517 to about 36,750 in 1618. The population before the Columbian Exchange was estimated using what might be labeled a "cumulative epidemic mortality" technique starting with a fairly firm mid-sixteenth-century population figure.[1]

The earlier analysis of fish and game resources and the discussion of sixteenth-century documentary clues as to the intensiveness and extensiveness of Florida's Native American horticulture indicate that such a peak population could have sustained itself at a good nutritional level. Thus, detailed ethnohistorical regional analysis suggests a larger early sixteenth-century population in Florida than was hypothesized in the second chapter using standard demographic/ecological techniques. Instead of 697,000 people, the early sixteenth-century Timucuans, Calusans, and Apalachee numbered perhaps 919,600 individuals, or about 6.1 persons for each of the 151,691 square kilometers in Florida. Assuming that the estimated 97,600 Calusa occupied some 12,533 km^2,[2] their population density averaged about 7.8 persons per km^2. If 722,000 Timucuan-speakers held 73,130 km^2 in Florida and Georgia, their population density averaged about 9.9 individuals per km^2.[3]

NOTES

1. Since this passage was written, Noble David Cook has published a parallel estimation technique that he calls a "disease mortality model" using a table format rather than a chart format (*Demographic Collapse*, 1981, pp. 59–74).

2. Calusa territory has been assumed to have comprised all 2,119 square miles of Collier County; 1,189 in Hendry; 1,005 in Lee; 898 in Glades; 832 in Charlotte; 320, or half of Sarasota; 325, or half of De Soto; and 280, or a fourth of Highlands County. That makes 4,839 square miles, or 12,533 square kilometers (Morris, comp., *Florida Handbook*, 1973, p. 581).

3. Timucuan territory has been calculated as comprising a total of 28,235 square miles in the following counties:

Florida (Square miles)

Madison	708	St. Johns	660	Clay	644
Taylor	1,052	Putnam	879	DeSoto (½)	326
Hamilton	515	Flagler	504	Indian River (½)	275
Suwannee	687	Marion	1,652	Lake	1,163
Lafayette	551	Volusia	1,207	Seminole	352
Dixie	709	Sumter	574	Orange	1,003
Gilchrist	348	Union	245	Polk	2,048
Levi (½)	569	Bradford	301	Osceola	1,467
Alachua	965	Nassau	671	Hardee	630
Columbia	789	Duval	840	Highlands (¾)	839
Baker	588	Brevard (⅓)	437	Okeechobee (¾)	585
				Subtotal	24,783

Georgia (Square miles)

Brooks (½)	246	Clinch (½)	399	Camden	653
Lowndes (½)	254	Ware (⅓)	455	Brantley (½)	224
Echols	425	Charlton	796	*Subtotal*	3,452

SECTION ONE
Settlement Amalgamation: A Behavioral Response to Depopulation

Earlier I discussed the flight of Cuban Native Americans from their native island to Florida in search of supposedly miraculously curative waters in a River Jordan. I interpreted this movement as evidence that those Cuban natives had been afflicted by an infectious epidemic of some Old World disease. Another aspect of that flight sets the principal theme for this section, which is the act of human migration and resettlement. Diego de Escalante Fontaneda's laconic reference to the migration of the Cubans and their resettlement among the Calusa provides few details. We do not know from how many Cuban settlements the migrants may have come. Escalante gives the impression that the Calusa ruler forced the Cubans to resettle in their own segregated village or villages somewhat apart from the Calusa themselves. Still, we know just enough to identify significant regularities in Native American behavior during the massive biological invasion by Old World pathogens.

If we attentively scan early European chronicles of New World exploration and colonization, we discover that an impressive number of Native American migrations and resettlements stimulated by epidemic disease are mentioned. In the sixteenth century not long after the Cubans evidently fled to Florida, the indefatigable overland traveler Alvar Núñez Cabeza de Vaca recorded massive movements of Native Americans during the passage through their territories of an unidentified epidemic in late 1535. Núñez and his companions traveled with an ever-changing entourage of hundreds of Native Americans from the time they reached horticultural settlements on the Rio Grande until they finally reached Colonial territory near Culiacán in the spring of 1536. Most specifically, several hundred Névomes, or Lower Pimans, accompanied the Spanish refugees from their homeland to the Colonial frontier and stayed there. Men, women, and children—"the whole pueblo of Quajo"—migrated. They founded a new Piman settlement called Bamoa, "building themselves there houses and a fort for their defense." They converted en masse to Christianity, and they and their surviving descendants stayed in Bamoa near Culiacán.[1]

In 1540 Fernando de Soto's marauders reached the chiefdom capital city and trading center on the South Atlantic coastal plain that they knew as Cofitachique. The female chief of the polity discovered the Spanish greed for pearls and sent de Soto and his followers a short distance to an abandoned settlement, where they took possession of a trunk full of fire-blackened pearls. The Spaniards were rather awed to find a complete town standing, a chest full of pearls in its temple, and cribs full of maize, which they appropriated for their own use. Grass was starting to grow in the streets. Garcilaso de la Vega's reconstruction of the reason for the abandonment of the settlement was that most of its inhabitants died during an epidemic the year prior to the arrival of de Soto. The abandonment of the town meant the amalgamation of its survivors with those of other Cofitachique towns.

Members of the Francisco Vázquez de Coronado expedition recorded evidence of the same sort of population decline and amalgamation of survivors among the Pueblos in 1540. The chronicler Castañeda in a clear statement noted that the Tiwas in 1540 occupied a dozen Pueblos but that seven others had been abandoned. Moreover, depopulation had progressed so far that the still-occupied Pueblos possessed surplus vacant rooms. Consequently when the Spaniards moved into a Pueblo, its inhabitants could simply leave and move in with friends or relatives in another only partially filled settlement. Several instances of such migration and resettlement occurred during the Vázquez de Coronado expedition's aggression against upper Rio Grande valley Pueblos.[2]

The important point is that these early sixteenth-century Native American migrations and resettlements were made of the Indians' own volition. It is true that the Cubans were influenced by a Spanish Christian quest for miracle cures. The Névomes who migrated to Bamoa in 1536 may have thought that they were escaping decimating epidemics by moving into Christian territory and accepting the Christian deity. Yet they acted on their own initiative before Colonial officials or missionaries sought to congregate Native Americans within sound of a church bell.

This point is important because it makes clear that one Native American response to demoralizing epidemic episodes was emigration, independent of Colonial policies. This behavior ties the sixteenth-century migrations and resettlements to a generalization already made about the behavior of Northern Piman-speakers. Analyzing the depopulation of two river valley oases, I stated that these people had in mind a cultural model of a proper settlement. That model specified how many people a proper settlement contained. In the eighteenth century the cultural model of a minimal settlement was approximately 200 individuals. When a settlement fell significantly below that figure, Northern

Pimans migrated to another village and amalgamated with its residents to bring their numbers above the minimum size specified in their mental model.[3] The statement of the principle of migration and resettlement in terms of a Piman cultural model of settlement size was weakened because of concurrent Colonial policies carried out by civil officials, missionaries, and even cooperative Native American leaders under the sanction of Colonial officers. With the sixteenth-century pre-Colonial instances of migration and resettlement amalgamation in mind, this principle can be clearly recognized.

Moreover, if we use Bamoa as a key analytical case, the principle can be refined. That is, as Native American population declined during epidemics and to endemic diseases, natives altered their cultural definition of a proper settlement to involve reduced numbers. It happens that Bamoa received Piman-speaking reinforcements from beyond the Colonial frontier in 1615. The mission frontier had at that time not advanced very far north of Bamoa and Culiacán and indeed would not reach the Yaqui people who intervened between New Spain and the Névomes for another two years. Yet to the delight of the missionaries, one day early in the year, some 350 Névomes arrived from their homeland to take up residence with the survivors of the original settlement at Bamoa. The migrants said that another 150 of their older people would soon follow them.[4] Thus the act of migration and amalgamation, plus the statement about the intentions of stay-at-homes, implied that early in the seventeenth century the Piman cultural model of a proper settlement called for approximately 500 inhabitants.

The immediate impulse that decided 350 Pimans to migrate south to Colonial territory appears to have been a drought that resulted in poor harvests for even horticulturalists who employed efficient irrigation techniques. The older people waited at home, hoping for a better 1615 harvest so that they would be able to make the long journey on foot in better condition than had the younger migrants of early 1615. The latter may have nearly exhausted their supplies of stored food by the time they migrated during the winter of 1614 – 1615. The immediate "push" factor of poor crop yield was only one component in the motivation of the Piman migrants.

They suffered continued mortality from Old World diseases, the experience that had motivated the earlier 1536 migration to Bamoa. This is evident in the missionary report of the number of "children" baptized soon after the 1615 migration. Father Diego de Guzmán wrote that the day after the migrants arrived at Bamoa, he "baptized all the children, who numbered 114."[5] That number is only 22.8 percent of 500 total population of the settlement, indicating differential mortality among children and perhaps impaired fertility among women of child-bearing age. The migratory Pueblo was not reproducing in the adverse disease environment of the early seventeenth century.

In that situation, the Christian message of salvation and resurrection at least held out hope, heightened perhaps by Native American desperate expectation that the God of the Christians might stay the diseases the Christians spread. The message had reached the migrants in some form before they decided to move. According to the Bamoa missionary, one of the migrants preached about the mysteries of the Holy Faith every night during the migration. This person had previously spent much time in Bamoa and had learned the Christian message there.[6] The prospect of maize rations distributed by the Jesuits, magical protection against diseases, and resurrection in case of a fatal outcome consequently pulled these Piman migrants from their northerly homeland to amalgamate with the inhabitants of Colonial Bamoa.

Their migration from a settlement inhabited by 500 people both defines the Piman cultural model for a proper settlement in 1615 and dates a beginning reduction in that number. It was not until Piman population declined in successive epidemic disease episodes that the cultural model of a proper settlement declined to a population of approximately 200, which my earlier analysis discerned in the pattern of eighteenth-century Northern Piman migration and amalgamation of settlements.

In the Southeast, the Timucuan-speaking peoples were not the only ones decimated by epidemic disease mortality. In 1540–1543, de Soto's marauders encountered a number of autonomous Native American states warring against each other on and near the Mississippi River. Some of them ceased to exist during the following century and a half.[7] In fact, the situation that the Tristán de Luna expedition found in 1559–1560 during a futile attempt to colonize Pensacola Bay indicated that catastrophic depopulation had occurred during the interval.[8]

At the end of the seventeenth century, French colonists found the Natchez still rapidly declining in numbers. A 1704 French report of the previous six years estimated Natchez depopulation during that brief period as one-third.[9] That period included a severe smallpox epidemic among the riverine groups in 1699.[10] By the time the French learned very much about the Natchez, therefore, that polity was a shadow of its former self. The authoritarian Natchez theocratic elite ruled over only some nine remnant villages. Moreover, at least four of those villages were inhabited by refugee survivors of the Tioux, Koroa, and other Tunican-speaking peoples from farther north. Natchez sociopolitical structure apparently was in the process of changing to integrate such

refugee recruits, who spoke a language different from that of the elite.[11]
The Natchez nobles accepted the Tunican-speaking refugees as commoners within their social hierarchy. Jeffrey P. Brain hypothesized that
the Natchez nobility sought to integrate the refugee peoples into their
polity by intermarriages.[12] If Brain is correct, the Natchez nobles set
about amalgamating strangers by converting them into relatives.

Brain's hypothesis is that Natchez marriage rules as well as definitions of social class changed in response to the attempted incorporation
into the polity of refugee villages speaking a distinct language. He
suggests the possibility of far-reaching changes resulting from amalgamation of multiple ethnic groups. Here, the emphasis lies on the simpler fact of amalgamation and its antecedents. Although the truly historic period did not begin in the lower Mississippi valley until the end
of the seventeenth century, earlier Spanish exploration chronicles reported a dense population fighting wars over natural resources as late as
1541 – 1543. Surviving Native Americans still fought each other at the end
of the seventeenth century. By that time they fought not for aboriginal
reasons, however, but as pawns of and surrogates for agents of European Colonial powers.

As part of their strategy for maintaining a population that more or
less fit their cultural model of a proper polity, the Natchez "adopted"
the Tioux, Grigra, and other refugee groups. The result appears to have
been a brief ethnic diversification of the Natchez polity until French
colonists dispersed the survivors. They then found refuge among other
Native Americans, whose ethnic makeup they in turn diversified. At the
same time, the process of abandonment of settlements reduced overall
economic diversity. The migration of peoples who fused with formerly
distinct ethnic groups reduced overall numbers of autonomous Native
American polities. In the course of time, the amalgamation of formerly
autonomous ethnic groups, especially through intermarriage forced by
the continual process of depopulation, with consequent scarcity of
eligible spouses, materially reduced the number of surviving ethnic
groups and no doubt lessened an earlier cultural and linguistic diversity.

MOREYS' LAW

It seems appropriate here to call attention to a special dimension of
depopulation along the lower Mississippi River. The once autonomous
and warring ministates north of the Natchez collapsed on the Natchez.
Those to the south suffered massive depopulation, according to the

written historical record. As the Natchez struggled to integrate foreign refugees into their social—and particularly their military—system, they had to cope with continual warfare carried on by powerful Chickasaw and Choctaw confederacies centered in the Appalachian highlands. As already indicated, agents of the European Colonial powers instigated intergroup warfare in the Southeast. Those agents used Native American surrogates to try to control trading areas, with an ultimate goal of territorial domination.[13] Such European meddling in Native American affairs can be ignored in a purely demographic analysis of the situation along the lower Mississippi River. The point is that the Choctaws and Chickasaws possessed the military manpower late in the seventeenth century to harass and nearly to overwhelm the Natchez and other riverine ethnic groups. In fact, they possessed sufficient manpower and sufficient access to British-made muskets, lead balls, and powder to drive the Arkansas-Quapaw off the Mississippi and up the Arkansas River.[14]

The numerical superiority of the Chickasaw and Choctaw seems to represent a significant demographic shift between 1540–1543 and the late seventeenth century. When de Soto's marauders ranged through the Southeast, they were not overly impressed with the power of the presumable ancestors of the Chickasaws and Choctaws. Even those ethnocentric Spaniards were, however, impressed by the might of the Mississippi riverine ministates they visited. The survivors of the expedition were especially impressed with the size and number of war canoes the peoples along the lower course of the river sent against their sloops when they finally sailed downstream and across the Gulf of Mexico to New Spain. By the late seventeenth century the naval power that the riverine groups had shown in the mid-sixteenth century had greatly diminished. Riverine groups abandoned their territories to the more powerful uplanders and amalgamated into multiethnic polities, such as the Natchez, to withstand the uplanders.

What had happened along the lower Mississippi River between 1543 and the 1690s was an instance of what may be termed the Moreys' Law. The law was first formulated in the form of a conclusion about what occurred historically between native peoples on the rivers of Venezuela, in nearby areas of South America, and among the peoples aboriginally inhabiting the forested areas away from major streams. Under pre-Conquest conditions, the riverine peoples grew to larger numbers, so that they militarily dominated the upland folk. Then the Spaniards and other Europeans who relied on riverine transportation whenever possible transmitted numerous Old World pathogens to the riverine peoples. The dense populations of Native Americans along the rivers became, moreover, tempting targets for European slave raids that further reduced native numbers. Hiding from hostile Europeans, the riverine intense horticulturalists necessarily neglected their gardens or returned to find their crops stolen or their plants destroyed. The riverine peoples therefore declined faster than did the forest folk.

The inland peoples traded less frequently with Europeans than the riverine groups, so they contracted fewer Old World diseases, especially the waterborne ones. Less numerous and more isolated from easy transportation by water, the backwoodsmen lost fewer people to slave raiders. They suffered less hunger from loss of crops than the riverine groups because they depended less on cultivated foods. Ultimately, the aboriginally riverine groups were almost exterminated. Eventually the backwoods peoples were able to migrate into a nearly abandoned and quite productive niche vacated as a result of depopulation.[15]

As a law of human affairs, the Moreys' conclusion, confirmed in the lower Mississippi River valley, might be phrased this way. Under historic conditions of the Columbian Exchange, depopulation occurred more rapidly and completely among aboriginally denser riverine-lacustrine horticultural peoples than among aboriginal more scattered backlanders more reliant on hunting and wild plant food collection.

Major factors contributing to the greater depopulation of riverine and lacustrine peoples were:

1. transmission to them of Old World waterborne pathogens such as typhoid fever
2. exposure to slave raids by Europeans utilizing water craft for transportation
3. disruption of horticultural production by interethnic hostilities, with consequent famine and malnutrition.

By the late seventeenth century, the lower Mississippi River riverine peoples had been so depopulated that the Chickasaw and Choctaw uplanders began to colonize their former environmental niche. The founding of English Charles Town in 1670 and the rapid movement of horseback traders west along well-established aboriginal trading paths provided Chickasaws with European weapons to facilitate their conquest of riverine territory. The founding of French Mobile before the end of the century provided the Choctaws as well with European guns to facilitate the same invasion of the riverine environmental niche. There may not be firm evidence of frequent European slave raids up the Mississippi River. There is, on the other hand, evidence for the decimation wrought by waterborne diseases. Between March 1699 and March

1700, half of the Houma died from what Iberville called "an abdominal flux,"[16] an acute diarrhea.

The same process of disproportionately great depopulation of riverine peoples seems to have extended upstream during the eighteenth century. In 1714, the French trader Bourgmond ascended the Missouri River as far as the Platte River of Nebraska. Enumerating tribes on the Missouri, he mentioned three villages of Aricaras and, farther upstream, forty villages of Caricara, presumably the same group. He called them "very numerous."[17] Literate Europeans did not return to Aricara territory until the end of that century. Meanwhile, epidemic disease depopulated the Aricara.

In 1795, Aricara oral history still recorded a time when the Aricara inhabited no fewer than thirty-two villages. Then they were decimated by three smallpox epidemics.[18] By 1785, therefore, the surviving Aricara had amalgamated into only seven villages, mustering 900 warriors. They still lived along the Missouri River.[19] A short time before, the disastrous smallpox pandemic of 1779–1783 had swept away tens of thousands of Native Americans.[20]

The few Aricara families who escaped from each of the villages joined those from the other settlements until, in 1795, only two villages with 500 warriors remained. Some or all of them migrated to live near the Mandan 150 miles upstream by 1796.[21] Thereafter the Aricara remnant migrated a number of times back and forth between the Mandan settlement and their aboriginal homeland downriver, even abandoning riverine life for a while to survive by hunting on the Great Plains. In 1837, the Aricara returned to the Missouri River at Fort Clark, and in 1838 they moved into the village the Mandan had abandoned after the smallpox had decimated them in 1837. The Aricara abandoned that settlement after Fort Clark was destroyed in 1861. They erected a new village opposite Fort Berthold in 1862. Later, they crossed the river to amalgamate with the handful of surviving Mandan and Hidatsa.[22] The once very numerous Aricara have thus since the late nineteenth century constituted but one tiny ethnic component of a Fort Berthold Reservation polity formally organized in the twentieth century as the Three Affiliated Tribes.[23]

One lesson seems reasonably clear. The military prowess of the Dakota tribes has been considerably overrated. The various Ojibwa groups were able to wrest numerous wild-rice-growing lakes and streams from the Dakotas. The Ojibwa westward movement forced the Dakotas out of their aboriginal territory onto the grassy plains. The historic availability of horses and bison that could be hunted productively from horseback may have served as a magnet attracting Dakotas toward the plains environment. These factors have been discussed many times. What has not often been explicitly recognized is that a fundamental demographic change occurred along the entire Missouri River during the eighteenth century. The aboriginal dense riverine village population was decimated by Old World diseases. At century's end, Aricara oral history recorded three devastating smallpox epidemics. The Aricara and other riverine peoples may not have realized that waterborne endemic and epidemic diseases and malaria were also critical factors in their depopulation. The Dakotas and other nonriverine peoples were probably equally exposed to viral ailments, such as smallpox. On occasion, it is true, nearby groups were differentially infected, with one group suffering less than another that diminished sharply in numbers.[24] Still, during a period as long as a century, the accidents of viral contagion should not account for the total depopulation of the riverine groups including the Aricara and for the greater survival and possibly even population growth of the Dakotas.

An additional demographic factor had to have been at work. The most likely culprit was typhoid fever. Other waterborne pathogens may have been transmitted up the Missouri River by Native American traders and travelers who had gone to visit French missions, trading posts, and villages such as St. Louis on the Mississippi River. Malaria probably was one debilitating endemic disease transmitted up the Missouri River to the sedentary Aricara and other riverine villages. Certainly malaria had reached the Illinois Confederacy settlements during the eighteenth century.[25] It was, therefore, available to spread farther up another major stream to populous native American fixed riverine settlements. The more mobile nonriverine plainsmen such as the Dakota would have been far less exposed to malaria than were riverine or lacustrine groups. Whatever combination of water-related diseases afflicted the Aricara and similiar peoples, their depopulation opened the Missouri River valley to the Dakotas and to other bison hunters.

CONCLUSIONS

A common response to depopulation has been identified in the Caribbean culture area (among Cuban groups), the Timucua and Natchez in the Southeast culture area, the Névomes and Northern Pimans in the Rancherían culture area, the Pueblo culture area, and the Northeastern Woodland salient on the northern Great Plains. That seems to be a sufficiently large sample to suggest that a very widespread Native American cultural pattern has been identified. Possibly it was universal among North American peoples.

The important features of this pattern of response to depopulation are:

A. abandonment of settlements located in marginally productive environmental niches

B. migration to environments that were more productive in terms of the basic subsistence technology of the peoples involved

C. amalgamation of survivors of abandoned settlements into a diminished number of continuing or new ones, in an attempt to maintain a number of inhabitants culturally defined as proper by each group

D. amalgamation of survivors of diverse lineage and even ethnic origins into a diminished number of polities, resulting in:

1. intermarriages, further diluting and erasing earlier ethnic distinctions

2. adoption of locally dominant group languages, reducing linguistic diversity

3. sometimes very rapid changes in many conventional understandings formerly shared, for the purpose of adjusting to the survival demands of quickly altering man-land ratios, Colonial manipulation or domination, and so forth.

Identification of the wide distribution of depopulation and consequent amalgamation of social remnants means that A.L. Kroeber was mistaken in giving Caucasians credit for repeatedly rolling up "a number of related obscure bands or minute villages into the larger package of a 'tribe.' "[26] Instead, and in fact, survivors of once-populous ministates and large tribes with numerous settlements migrated in order to amalgamate themselves into viable settlements.

It follows that Caucasians did not endow the groups that survived "with sovereign power and territorial ownership which the native nationality had mostly never even claimed," as Kroeber asserted. At least in the frame of reference of European legal concepts, the survivors of small states, such as those in the Southeast, or the Pueblos, took with them as they amalgamated their sovereignty and their property. They still possessed the territory that their ancestors necessarily exploited when population peaked early in the sixteenth century. Many of them continued to try to defend ancestral territories until their numbers fell too low to allow them to resist larger Native American groups or invading Europeans. Native American depopulation afforded Euroamericans the opportunity to seize territory by military force at a price in lives, material, and capital that was very low relative to what it would have been at the beginning of the sixteenth century.

NOTES

1. Alegre, *Historia*, 1958, Tomo II, pp. 563 – 64.

2. Winship, *Coronado Expedition*, 1896, pp. 503, 510 – 11, 561.

3. Dobyns, "Indian Extinction," 1963, p. 177.

4. Alegre, *Historia*, 1958, Tomo II, p. 565.

5. Ibid., 566.

6. Ibid., 565.

7. Brain, "Natchez 'Paradox,' " 1971, p. 220.

8. Milner, "Epidemic Disease," 1980, pp. 39 – 56.

9. Swanton, *Indian Tribes*, 1911, p. 39.

10. Shea, *Early Voyages*, 1861, p. 72.

11. Brain, "Natchez 'Paradox,' " 1971, p. 220. Swanton (*Indian Tribes*, 1911, p. 45) noted that Iberville was told of nine villages, but another Frenchman claimed there were 10 or 12. Tioux (Swanton, 334), Grigra (Swanton, 336).

12. Brain, "Natchez 'Paradox,' " 1971, p. 221.

13. Baird, *Choctaw People*, 1973, pp. 12 – 18.

14. Baird, *Quapaw People*, 1975, p. 6, 19.

15. Morey and Morey, "Foragers and Farmers," 1973, pp. 229 – 46.

16. Swanton, *Indian Tribes*, 1911, pp. 286 – 88.

17. Wedel, "Archaeological Materials," 1955, p. 77.

18. Ibid., 79.

19. Ibid., 78, following Nasatir, "Account," 1930, p. 535.

20. Dobyns, "Estimating," 1966, pp. 441 – 42.

21. Wedel, "Archaeological Materials," 1955, p. 79.

22. Ibid., 81.

23. Cash and Wolff, *Three Affiliated Tribes*, 1974, pp. 44, 50, 58, 66, 76.

24. Wissler, *Population Changes*, 1936, p. 8.

25. Blasingham, "Depopulation," 1956, pp. 382 – 83.

26. Kroeber, "Nature of the Land-Holding Group," 1955, p. 304.

SECTION TWO
The Relationship Between Epidemic
Mortality and Settlement Shifts

Knowledge of characteristic Native American response to biological and psychological stress during and after major epidemics can further the accurate dating and interpretation of archaeologically studied settlements. This section examines information about migration and settlement attrition in a culture area not previously discussed to find out whether the people there behaved in much the same pattern as those already described. The area selected is the Northeast; the language group chosen is Iroquois. Iroquois studies have disproportionately influenced anthropological thought and theory and historical interpretations of the development of economic and political institutions in North America. Thus whatever the present analysis can discover that helps explain Iroquois protohistoric-historic behavior assumes importance.

A starting point for examing Iroquois behavior under the psychological and cultural stresses of epidemic depopulation is the Seneca tribe. It migrated a number of times between the mid-sixteenth century and the destruction of Seneca villages in 1687 by a French army under Gen. Jacques-René de Brisay, Marquis Denonville. Two coexisting great villages moved no fewer than seven times during that period, even though each migration covered only a mile or two of distance.[1] It must be emphasized that the Seneca did not begin their protohistoric migrations at mid-sixteenth century. The archaeologists who determined the sequence of their movement of village locations after 1550 remained uncertain as to the identity and location of "prehistoric" Seneca settlements.

In other words, the Seneca had already migrated at least once to reach the mid-sixteenth century villages that the archaeologists were able to identify as sites where these people began a series of later moves. That pre-1550 migration—and there may have been more than one—implies that the Seneca had been affected by one or more of the pandemics of Old World contagious diseases that spread through the inhabitants of Florida. The present state of knowledge and availability of evidence does not allow precise identification of the disease or diseases that affected the Seneca prior to 1550. Some probabilities can, nevertheless, be stated. The known communicability of the smallpox virus in human populations, especially a population never before exposed to the disease, makes it almost certain that the 1520 – 1524 pandemic reached the Seneca. The earlier discussion of the Timucua indicated a probable independent introduction of smallpox into North America via Florida. So it seems quite unlikely that the Iroquois and their neighbors escaped the initial great pandemic with its high mortality.

After that, the unknown disease that Europeans spread widely in 1535 surely afflicted the Seneca. Alvar Núñez Cabeza de Vaca recorded its geographic progress northward from Colonial New Spain to the tribes of the Great Plains. Chroniclers of de Soto's marauders perhaps recorded its passage and indicated its seriousness at Cofitachique at the Fall Line in modern South Carolina. Records of the Jacques Cartier expedition on the St. Lawrence River mention French transmission of that or another disease to Iroquoian-speaking hosts in 1535. So there can be little doubt that the Seneca caught whatever disease swept over North America that year. The Cartier chronicle indicates a relatively high mortality from whatever his Frenchmen transmitted to the Iroquois.

In other words, there are enough clues in the scant written records of the protohistoric sixteenth century to indicate that Seneca village movements originated in epidemic depopulation, just as they did among the Pueblos, the Venezuelan Achagua, and the Aricara and Pimans. Recognizing depopulation by epidemic disease as both a necessary and a sufficient condition for Seneca village movement prior to 1550 also suggests an archaeological research strategy. The quest for "prehistoric" villages inhabited during the first half of the sixteenth protohistoric century should not be conducted in terms of an explicit or implicit model of a static population. Early sixteenth-century Seneca settlements were predictably more numerous than the ones surviving after 1550 or else were much larger. Knowing that the Seneca migrated seven times after 1550, and hypothesizing that they did so in the aftermath of later epidemic disease episodes, one can compare the chronology of Seneca village abandonment and building with the chronology of known epidemic episodes. Table 29 presents such a comparison. That table incorporates not only the information about historic epidemics summarized in the opening chapter but also documentary information about epidemics in New England not previously discussed. This information comes from a rather remarkable source.

Not long after initial English colonization on the coast of New England, an earthquake occurred in 1638. It worried the colonists. They wondered whether they might have ventured into a seismically unstable and dangerous region. One colonist, the redoubtable Roger Williams,

TABLE 29

Chronology of Seneca Migrations and Epidemics

Time	Disease	Florida Epidemics	New England Epidemics	Seneca Village Migration Correlated with Pandemic Diseases				Epidemics in Other Regions
1690								
1688				French Army Destroys				
1686				Rochester	Kirkwood	Boughton	Beale	
1684				Junction	Village	Hill	Village	
1682				Village		Village		
1680								
1678								
1676								
1674								
1672	Smallpox	1672						
1670			1670					1670 New Mexico
1668			1669	Dann	Marsh	Fox		
1666				Village	Village	Village		
1664		1665						
1662	Smallpox		1663					1663 Delaware
1660								
1658	Measles	1659						1658—9 Canada
1656								
1654	Smallpox	1654	1654					1654 Delaware
1652								
1650			1649					
1648				Power	Steele			
1646				House	Village			
1644				Village				
1642								
1640	Smallpox		1639					1640 New Mexico
1638	Scarlet Fever							
1636			1637					1635 New Mexico
1634	Measles		1633					
1632				Lima	Bosely	Warren	Cornish	
1630	Plague			Village	Mills	Village	Village	1630 New Mexico
1628					Village			
1626								
1624								
1622								
1620								

TABLE 29 continued

Time	Disease	Florida Epidemics	New England Epidemics	Seneca Village Migration Correlated with Pandemic Diseases				Epidemics in Other Regions
1618	Bubonic Plague		1619					
1616		1617	1617					1617 Sinaloa
1614		1613						New Mexico
1612				Dutch	Feugle	Factory		
1610				Hollow	Village	Hollow		
1608				Village		Village		
1606								
1604								
1602								
1600								
1598						Factory		
1596	Measles	1596				Hollow		1597 New Spain
1594						Village		
1592			1592+					1592
1590					Cameron			
1588					Village			
1586	Fever	1586	1586					1585 Roanoke
1584						Tram		
1582						Village		
1580								
1578								
1576								
1574	Unknown		1574					
1572								
1570		1570			Adams			
1568			1568+		Village			
1566								
1564								1564 New Spain
1562								
1560					Rich-	Belcher		
1558	Influenza	1559			mond	Village		
1556					Mills			
1554					Village			
1552								

TABLE 29 continued

Time	Disease	Florida Epidemics	New England Epidemics	Seneca Village Migration Correlated with Pandemic Diseases		Epidemics in Other Regions
1550				Rich-	Belcher	
1548	Bubonic Plague			mond Mill	Village *(cont.)*	1548 New
1546				Village		1545 Spain
1544				*(cont.)*		
1542						
1540						
1538						
1536						
1534						
1532	Measles					1533 New
1530						1531 Spain
1528	Typhoid	1528				
1526						
1524	Smallpox	1524	?			1524 Andes
1522						Mesoamerica
1520						1520
1518				Earlier Seneca		
1516				Settlements		
1514						
1512						
1510	North American Continent Apparently Free from Old World Diseases					

Key to Symbols on Table 29.

[ ] Seneca Villages (Archaeological Sites)

[▨] Pandemic Disease Period during which Senecas apparently moved from one village site to another

carried out what must be regarded as pioneering scientific research on
this question. While he may have prayed to his God to prevent future
earthquakes, Williams questioned the local experts—Narragansett
elders—about earlier earthquakes. Such research activity appears logical to a later generation accustomed to cross-cultural research. It was
not necessarily perceived that way by Williams's contemporaries.

Roger Williams discovered that older Narragansetts indeed remembered that earthquakes had occurred before. Moreover, his informants
could count years since their occurrence. For purposes of the present
analysis, what is even more important is that Williams discovered that
the Narragansetts mentally associated earthquakes with pestilence.
Consequently, Williams's earthquake chronology for New England
serves here as a chronology of episodes of epidemic disease severe
enough to be linked in memory to other phenomena and thus remembered for a long time.[2]

The comparison of the Narragansett earthquake-epidemic chronology with the documented Florida epidemic chronology indicates very
close correspondence. The earliest date that Williams obtained from
elderly Narragansetts at about 1568 falls precisely within the known
1564 – 1570 period of famine and disease that reached from Florida at
least to Tidewater Virginia, according to written records. The Narragansett 1574 epidemic has no equivalent in the Florida historic
epidemiology. It may be inferred, therefore, that an unknown contagious disease was transmitted by the crew of a non-Spanish European
trading vessel either directly to the Narragansetts or to some other New
England coastal group from which it spread to some extent.

The Narragansett-reported pestilence in 1584 falls no more than a year
earlier than the two diseases that, as we know from Thomas Hariot's
report, the English scouts on Roanoke Island transmitted to the Native
Americans there. The Englishmen could well have transmitted one of
their more contagious diseases to neighboring peoples as soon as they
established face-to-face contact with them. The log of one of Drake's
ships indicates that this contagion was already felling Native Americans
in 1586 when the English fleet captured St. Augustine. It is not surprising, therefore, to find that the Narragansett elders remembered an
epidemic at that period. It is not surprising, either, that oral history
should be a year or two off in dating the episode, inasmuch as the
Narragansett lacked writing. Whatever contagious disease the English
scouts transmitted across the Atlantic Ocean apparently spread widely
among Native Americans all along the coast from at least New England
to Florida and for an unknown distance inland. Powhatan oral history
may yield additional clues. The ruler in 1608 told John Smith that he had

thrice watched his people die.[3] If he referred to epidemics rather than wars, and counted the 1564–1570 episode as the first, then the 1585–1586 mortality was the second.

The late sixteenth-century epidemic that Narragansett elders placed about 1592 could have been another directly transmitted disease. It seems more likely that it was the measles that struck Native Americans in Colonial Florida in 1596. The earlier New England dating could mean that a European ship brought measles to the St. Lawrence estuary region on a fishing-trading voyage. The measles then spread to the Narragansetts, perhaps, on its way south to Florida. On the other hand, New Spain suffered from a series of epidemic episodes from 1592 to 1597, so that the Native Americans of Florida could have been infected by travelers from New Spain. Simultaneous 1592 transmission from Europe to two or more sections of the Atlantic coast of North America is also a possible interpretation of the record. Again, the Narragansett oral tradition could have dated the epidemic a year or so too early. Powhatan's recollection of three major decimations of his people prior to 1608 may also have referred to this measles epidemic. Devastation in the mid-1590s would have been the third such episode he mentioned to Smith in 1608.

The coincidence between the epidemic chronology in Narragansett oral tradition with documented episodes in Florida is very close. Three out of four reported New England epidemics may be interpreted as local episodes in widespread pandemics that affected many tribes along at least the Atlantic Coast of the continent.

A comparison of the two versions of the chronology of Seneca village movement and reconstruction shown in table 29 with the epidemic chronologies shows some significant parallels. Wray and Schoff and Wray consistently dated the founding of the Cameron village to 1575, within one year of the 1574 Narragansett epidemic. Wray and Schoff dated the beginning of four villages, and Wray one of them, to 1590, within two years of the Narragansett oral history date for an epidemic but six years prior its probable true date. In his later chronology, Wray placed the founding of the two villages in 1600, only four years later.

There are other agreements between the Wray-Schoff and Wray chronologies of Seneca village movement and the epidemic chronologies. There are also discrepancies. The archaeological chronologies are quite arbitrary except for the terminal date of 1687, when the Marquis Denonville's army destroyed the Seneca settlements. All of the earlier dates for migrations were placed in years ending in zero or five. Wray and Schoff were quite frank in stating that they viewed the seven known Seneca migrations as meaning that these people "must have remained from 15 to 25 years at each location."[4] In his later and somewhat different revised chronology, Wray listed "Important Dates and Events," some of which are documented and some of which are changes in trade goods reaching the Senecas.[5] Save for the Marquis Denonville's expedition in 1687, these events are not causes of Seneca settlement abandonment and reconstruction.

The real explanation for protohistoric Seneca settlement abandonment and reconstruction is, I submit, epidemic deaths. The short distance that the Senecas migrated from one village site to another suggests that fear of the ghosts of the deceased and/or melancholy associations with villages where many relatives had perished caused suvivors to abandon a site where an epidemic caused high mortality. The available archaeological record does not indicate the attrition in number of settlements that one might expect. This oddity may be an artifact of archaeological research conducted with an implicit model of stable Native American population. It may also be a result of destruction of some Seneca protohistoric village ruins by farming operations, urbanization, treasure hunting, and other later historic Euroamerican activities.

The degree to which epidemic diseases appear to have prompted Seneca abandonment of settlements, migration, and reconstruction is shown in table 29. In this table the transitional periods that Wray and Schoff placed in years ending in zero and five, like individuals who, unsure of their ages, give rounded figures to census enumerators, have been adjusted to reflect the known epidemic chronology in Florida and New England. From 1619, the New England epidemic chronology is recorded in documents. Before 1600, the table follows the Narragansett oral history chronology already mentioned. In the right column of table 29, some additional documented epidemic disease episodes elsewhere in North American are indicated to emphasize that certain diseases spread very widely across the continent.

The chronology of Seneca settlement abandonment and reconstruction presented in table 29 indicates that every Seneca migration prior to 1687 can be attributed to epidemic mortality. Moreover, after adjustment the arbitrary dates that Wray and Schoff suggested on a priori grounds only—without identifying causation—are convincingly close to the actual epidemic chronology.

Wray arbitrarily terminated his "prehistoric era" in 1500, a date that I have adjusted in table 29 to 1520 – 1524, the period of the initial smallpox pandemic. The villages at Richmond Mills and Belcher were founded then or shortly thereafter, it is suggested, by Senecas who abandoned Genesee and Bristol Valley sites as a consequence of the pandemic. Presumably these villages were then occupied until the 1564 – 1570 pandemic in eastern North America that is confirmed by Narragansett oral history and is implied by the date of 1565 for the beginning of the Tram village that Wray suggested in his revised chronology.

The village at Adams is considered here to have been started by Senecas migrating after the 1564 – 1570 episode began. It is hypothesized that it was abandoned in 1574 or thereabouts as a consequence of the more localized pestilence recorded in Narragansett oral tradition. This date is within a year or so of the time at which Wray consistently placed abandonment of this site, although the revised dating suggested here implies that occupation of the site lasted no more than a decade. The other branch of the Senecas stayed at the Tram site village, it is here hypothesized, until the 1585 contagion that the Englishmen transmitted to Roanoke Islanders had spread into the region extending from the Great Lakes to New England. Then the Senecas abandoned that village and started another at Factory Hollow.[6]

The 1596 measles epidemic occasioned the abandonment of the Cameron site village and founding of settlements at Dutch Hollow and Feugle. Significantly, yet another kind of evidence can be brought to bear on this correlation of dates. Physical anthropologist Lorraine P. Saunders generously provided me wtih very significant evidence bearing on this dating and attribution of motivation for migration. She has studied some of the skeletal remains that Wray and his colleagues excavated from Seneca cemeteries. Determining the age at death—as physical anthropologists can with great precision—of fifty-three persons from one Cameron site cemetery, Saunders found that 41.5 percent were ten years or younger and that 47.2 percent were fifteen years or younger. The excavation notes concerning another cemetery at the Cameron site suggest that just over half of the individuals buried there died in adolescence, childhood, or infancy. Not knowing the proportion of persons of different ages in the population that occupied the Cameron site village, one cannot be certain how age-selective mortality was. Clearly, children, young teenagers, and infants perished in much higher proportions at Cameron than at the earlier Adams village site. Saunders identified only 12.4 percent of the skeletons from a cemetery there as having died at age ten or younger and 20.9 percent at age fifteen or younger.

The difference in proportion of deaths of Senecas aged fifteen or less in the Cameron and Adams settlement cemeteries indicates that different diseases caused their abandonment. If the present interpretation of the chronology is correct, then the 1574 epidemic among the Narragansett, Seneca, and intervening peoples was particularly lethal among adults. Inasmuch as Saunders found only 21 percent of the skeletons in the Adams cemetery to have died at age fifteen or younger, 79 percent must have been older. Moreover, there is a clear indication that mortality increased with age in the 1574 epidemic, according to Saunders' findings for the eleven-fifteen age group in the two burial sites. At Cameron it was only 5.7 percent of the total, while at Adams it was 8.5 percent.

The epidemic disease that struck the Cameron village Seneca between 1592 and 1596 was, in contrast, mortal mainly among infants and children, who accounted for half or nearly half of the death toll. This is the pattern of mortality that measles causes in a population that has not been immunized or exposed for a period of years. The skeletal evidence cannot prove that the Seneca perished from measles, but it is quite consistent with the inference that the measles known to have spread through Colonial Spanish populations was the epidemic disease that reached the Narragansett and the Seneca. The adult mortality suggests that some older Seneca were immune but that others were not. If the 1564 – 1570 epidemic was measles, individuals more than twenty-six to thirty-two years of age in 1596 could have been immune because they had had measles as children, whereas all those born after 1570 would have been susceptible. There could not have been very many people of sixty-three to sixty-eight yeras or older who had survived the first measles pandemic in 1528 – 1533.

During the seventeenth century, European records precisely date epidemic episodes among Native Americans. The movements of Seneca villages can be matched accurately with those episodes. A bubonic plague pandemic reached Florida in 1613, extending to Sinaloa, Chesapeake Bay groups,[7] and New England peoples in 1617. It may be considered the cause of abandonment of the villages at Dutch Hollow, Feugle, and Factory Hollow. In what may have been an attempt at dispersion (alternatively, the conjecture may reflect our incomplete knowledge of Seneca archaeology), the Senecas then constructed four villages, at Lima, Bosely Mills, Warren, and Cornish. Those four villages survived only until the very lethal wave of contagious diseases directly transmitted from Europe swept through the Native American peoples of the Great Lakes and eastern Canadian region from 1633 to 1639. The first pathogen to strike in 1633 – 1634 appears to have been some form of measles.[8] The second pathogen seems to have been scarlet fever, which struck the Native Americans in 1637.[9] The third in this series of epidemics that decimated the Native Americans of the Great Lakes region in rapid succession came in 1639. It was evidently smallpox, the most lethal of all.[10]

This wave of epidemics greatly disrupted the lives of many peoples besides the Senecas. Moreover, the documentary record began to note Iroquois migratory response to epidemic disease. In 1638, a European actually wrote that the Wenro Nation refugees had migrated in that year to Huron country. The Wenro had been the easternmost of the allies of the Neutral, living adjacent to the Senecas.[11] The 1633–1634 measles and 1637 scarlet fever surely infected the Senecas, inasmuch as the diseases apparently so depopulated the Wenro as to motivate large-scale migration even before smallpox became epidemic a year later, in 1639. Thus the turmoil that the recent mortality caused among the Iroquois-speaking peoples did not entirely escape European notice. The Seneca archaeological remains indicate that both branches suffered enough depopulation to reduce the four pre-1633 settlements to two. One branch built at Power House site and the other at Steele.[12]

The next shift in Seneca village location may be dated to the five-year period between 1649 and 1654. A disease identified as smallpox struck the New England and Canadian tribes in 1649. It caused high mortality among the Hurons who had converted to Catholicism. Many had abadoned their homes and sought refuge at French Colonial settlements. There they perished of hunger, disease, or attacks by warriors of the Five Nations Iroquois. The Huron Confederacy in effect broke up in 1649, and the Five Nations adopted many survivors. Another even more widespread epidemic occurred five years later, in 1654. It was reported among Native Americans in Florida and among the Delaware as well as New England tribes. It was, therefore, more likely than the 1649 episode to have motivated Seneca village abandonment. The accretion of Hurons adopted into Seneca clans almost surely provided the numbers that enabled the Senecas to build three villages, at the Dann, Marsh, and Fox sites.[13]

The continued amalgamation of survivors of the Huron and other Iroquoian-speaking tribes may have enabled the Senecas to scatter into four villages after their next migration. That appears to have followed what was reported as yet another smallpox epidemic episode in 1669–1670.

In 1687, French Governor Brisay, Marquis Denonville, sent his army against the four villages, and his troops destroyed them. Thereafter the eastern and western Senecas apparently again concentrated into a single village each. English Colonial influence became so important among the Five Nations that their decisions about migrating may have resembled those of the Pueblos after Spanish colonization of New Mexico in 1598. The Senecas were no longer wholly autonomous; they lived under a system of indirect Colonial rule.

The analysis in this chapter leads to several conclusions. It shows that the absolute epidemic chronology of North America established from clues in historic documents provides the archaeologist with a chronology of numerous Native American migrations and settlement amalgamations. By dating widespread epidemic episodes, the chronology dates within about five years settlement shifts motivated by the psychological shock of epidemic mortality or by fear of the ghosts of deceased relatives, or by migration to maintain a culturally defined "proper" settlement size. This analysis also suggests that where abandonment and reconstruction of settlements can be approximately dated on another basis, such as from quantitative changes in trade goods, the epidemic chronology can refine the archaeological dating and cultural interpretation. Moreover, when this adjustment can be accomplished, the archaeological evidence can then indicate that specific epidemic episodes reached populations for which no documentary record exists at the time of the protohistoric biological invasion. Analysis of skeletal remains of inhabitants of short-lived settlements can also help to identify the nature of epidemic diseases that led to settlement abandonments.

The evidence that infectious epidemics occurred almost simultaneously among "index peoples" in Florida, southern New England, and the south shore of the Great Lakes has important implications. In Florida by 1564 there were Europeans who could directly transmit contagion to Native Americans there. The Narragansetts and Senecas lived, however, still far distant from Europeans, except perhaps French fur traders sailing up the St. Lawrence River. The 1564–1570 epidemic must, therefore, have spread through intervening Native American groups to the Senecas and probably to the Narragansetts. In other words, members of groups between Florida and the Great Lakes and New England interacted with each other often enough to transmit invading viruses and germs. Peoples throughout this area belonged to one social interaction network. Thus trade and other activities united them into what may be regarded as a single "social region." As a consequence, the entire Atlantic coastal region from Florida to the lakes and New England also constituted what may be termed one "epidemic region." That is, a sufficiently contagious virus transmitted to Native Americans in any part of the "epidemic region" tended to invade all of the native peoples in it. Thus an unidentified disease invaded the index peoples at the three corners of the epidemic region again in 1585–1586, and probably measles did so in about 1596, before Europeans colonized any of the Atlantic Coast north of Florida. The bubonic plague epidemic that began in Florida in 1613 apparently reached Virginia and

New England in 1617. That disease invaded Native Americans in an even larger zone, possibly including most of temperate North America.

For more than half a century following 1564, therefore, Native Americans in eastern North America maintained frequent enough intergroup contacts to spread invading Old World pathogens throughout an epidemic region of susceptible peoples. The persistence of intense social interaction in this large region despite extensive depopulation indicates that the social interaction pattern was aboriginal. It existed, logically, from pre-Columbian times, so its participants transmitted, and died from, the smallpox in 1520, measles in 1531, and plague in 1545.

After thinning of Native American numbers by plague between 1613 and 1619, the aboriginal social network may have collapsed for lack of sufficient numbers to carry on intergroup contacts to the previous frequencies. Thereafter, expanding European colonies provided multiple potential points for pathogenic invasions of Native American populations trading with colonists. The 1653–1654 smallpox epidemic spread to the widely separated index groups plus at least the Delawares. It may signal the emergence of a Colonial epidemic region apparently comparable in size to the aboriginal social and epidemic region. In 1669–1670, smallpox swept through Native Americans in New England, triggering Seneca migration. It reached Florida in 1672. The variation in epidemic dates among the distant index groups points to multiple transmissions from Europeans to Native Americans. By that time, surviving Native Americans suffered from the risk of microbial and viral invasion on not just two but many fronts.

NOTES

1. Wray and Schoff, "Preliminary Report," 1953, p. 53.

2. R. Williams, "To John Winthrop," 1863, p. 229.

3. Sheehan, *Savagism*, 1980, p. 142, following Barbour, *Jamestown Voyages*, 1969, vol. II, p. 426. John Smith reported the conversation in a war-peace context, but Powhatan more likely referred to epidemic mortality than to battle losses (*General Historie*, 1624, p. 75).

4. Wray and Schoff, "Preliminary Report," 1953, p. 53.

5. Wray, *Manual*, 1973, p. 8.

6. There appears to be additional physical evidence of lethal consequences of this epidemic episode among Susquehannocks in Washington Boro Basin in Lancaster County, Pennsylvania (Heisey and Witmer, "Of Historic Susquehannock Cemeteries," 1962, p. 99). Susquehannock settlement sequence has not been studied in sufficient detail to determine whether Susquehannocks

moved like Senecas after each epidemic episode. At the very least, they created a series of cemeteries when epidemic mortality dictated rapid burial of numerous bodies. The earliest known cemetery in the microregion is known as Blue Rock Cemetery. Bodies were interred with heads oriented apparently at random, in all directions. Later, villages reopened graves to inter bodies at "slightly higher levels," so that they were superimposed on the original burials (101). Average age at death of 31 skeletons was only 17−19 years (104), indicating epidemic deaths, but a disease to which older people were immune from previous exposure. The excavators inferred that inhabitants of the Schultz town site across the river buried their dead in Blue Rock Cemetery toward the end of the town occupation. Grave furnishings suggested to investigators that interments had been made during "a relatively short period of time" at about 1580−90 (108). The researchers explicitly recognized epidemic mortality.

Correlating their finds with the Seneca sequence, the archaeologists concluded that except for glass beads, "trait trends at Blue Rock and the Schultz site correspond closely with the Adams and Tram sites in the Seneca sequence" (117). On the other hand, the bead styles resembled those reported at "the Cameron and even the Dutch Hollow and Factory Hollow sites." One can, therefore, infer that the local Susquehannocks opened Blue Rock Cemetery during the 1570s, when they had time to dig relatively deep graves. Then Old World disease reached them along with trade goods, and 1585 mortality caused an emergency. Survivors used unconsolidated grave fill to dispose quickly of bodies of victims of the epidemic on top of skeletons of the originally interred dead. The following year, 1586, the second epidemic disease that Europeans transmitted to Atlantic coastal peoples in quick succession struck. Survivors reopened the soft grave fill and buried the third and uppermost layer of corpses in Blue Rock Cemetery.

7. Kingsbury, *Records*, 1933, vol. III, p. 92. Governor Argall (March 10,1617/18) reported "mortality far greater among the Indians" than among the colonists and a concurrent "morrain amongst the deer." About 300 Virginia colonists died in a 1619 recurrence or during the onslaught of another mortal disease that also struck "chiefly amongst the Indians" (275, 310, 319−20).

8. Thwaites, ed., *Jesuit Relations*, 1896, vol. VII, p. 87; Schlesier, "Epidemics," 1976, p. 138.

9. Thwaites, ed., *Jesuit Relations*, 1898, vol. 14, p. 99.

10. Stearn and Stearn, *Effect of Smallpox*, 1945, p. 26; Thwaites, ed., *Jesuit Relations*, 1898, vol. 20, pp. 21, 37, 41, 29; vol. 16, pp. 101, 103−11, 217−19. The scale or mortality is indicated by reference to dogs' consumption of corpses that could not be buried.

11. White, "Neutral and Wenroe," 1978, p. 409, following Thwaites, ed., *Jesuit Relations*, 1898, vol. 17, pp. 25, 27, 29.

12. There is physical evidence of mortality caused by one or more of the series of epidemics during the 1630s among the Susquehannocks. Excavators of what they called the Middle Cemetery at the Strickler site estimated that it dates to 1640−50. They concluded that offerings in graves and "burial practices correspond closely with those on the Power House and Steele sites in the Seneca sequence" (Heisey and Witmer, "Of Historic Susquehannock Cemeteries," 1962, p. 122). As shown in table 30, the present analysis dates Seneca habitation of those two villages between the 1639 smallpox epidemic and the presumed smallpox epidemics of 1649 and 1654. The Middle Cemetery at Strickler on the

Susquehanna River may, then, have contained bodies of victims of the 1639 smallpox epidemic and perhaps some from the antecedent 1637 scarlet fever and 1633–34 measles epidemics. Preservation of bone was poor, so sampling may not be representative. Approximate age determinations on 29 skeletons indicated that average age at death was 16–18 years, and a dozen children died between age 6 and 8 (120). High mortality of six- to eight-year-olds probably indicates that Susquehannocks buried victims of the 1649 smallpox epidemic in this cemetery—children who had been born after the 1639 episode and were therefore susceptible to the virus.

Whatever the epidemic in question may have done to Susquehannock settlement shifts, it clearly had a pronounced effect on ceramic production. It probably killed most experienced potters. When not found associated with trade goods, pottery such as that made and used at Strickler site village "was mistakenly considered to be older than Susquehannock wares that preceded it." The reason is that archaeologists tend to regard technologies as improving through time, and these vessels are "primitive in appearance and workmanship." The excavators wrote: "The most obvious explanation . . . is a degeneration of the ceramic craft of a native culture demoralized by a deluge of European influence" (122). Demoralized the Susquehannock no doubt were, but epidemic disease mortality contributed far more to demoralization than did direct European influence.

13. Physical evidence also attests to transmission of the viruses abroad, apparently in 1654, to Susquehannocks. Besides the Middle Cemetery at Strickler town site, two more cemeteries were required by its inhabitants. They lie southwest and northeast of the Middle Cemetery (Heisey and Witmer, "Of Historic Susquehannock Cemeteries," 1962, p. 118, following Cadzow, *Archaeological Studies*, 1936, and Futer, "Strickler Site," 1959). Trade goods were more abundant in quantity and variety in the northeast than in the Middle Cemetery (Heisey and Witmer, "Of Historic Susquehannock Cemeteries," 1962, p. 128).

SECTION THREE
Adaptation and Transformation

Depopulation among Native Americans resulted not only in a diminution of numbers but also in a concomitant simplification of social structure and cultural inventory. Depopulation directly reduces what Godfrey and Monica Wilson called the "social scale" of a given ethnic group.[1] Interaction between a hundred people is inevitably far simpler than interaction between a thousand or ten thousand inhabitants of a single human settlement. A good deal of social science research[2] has noted that a growing population generates increasingly complex social organization. It must be recognized that population declines resulted in simplification of aboriginal Native American social organization. There tend to be time lags in both processes due to inertia and human conservatism. Surviving members of a governing elite required to maintain orderly social relations in a dense population strive to preserve their power and prerequisites. As the authoritarian behavior of the surviving elite members becomes progressively more dysfunctional, however, the diminished number of individuals upon whom the exactions of the elite weigh tend to shirk their traditional obligations. The complex system required to deal with a large, dense population collapses or is significantly simplified.

Part of the historical discontinuity of northern Mesoamerica was of this nature, as Woodrow Borah has stressed. In Colonial New Spain, much of the pre-Conquest political structure disappeared within a single generation. The descendants of former rulers, if recognized at all, became caciques, "an honorific group" without much remaining power. Tiers of native nobility collapsed into a single rank of "principals," who paid tribute like commoners. Even the peasants, who had been free tribute payers in a variety of ways, or serfs, all became simply peasants.[3] Mexicanists absorbed in the details of Mexican history tend to interpret this process in specific terms of a historic continuum.

Thus Borah himself attributed the cause to Spanish decrees that terminated native noble exemption from paying tribute and diminished the prerequisites of caciques to depopulation. After the decline during the 1545–1548 pandemic, the Spanish groups living upon Native American food and fiber production fought each other to minimize their losses during the necessary readjustment of tribute collection. The king and encomenderos and Native American serfs emerged from the struggle relatively well off. The native nobility and Spanish ecclesiastics lost ground. To sustain tribute payments, the Spaniards distributed land to serfs who had previously labored for Native American nobles, converting them into tribute payers.[4] Thus, Colonial administrators simplified Native American traditional social structure by collapsing both the upper and lower strata into the middle levels. Even though Spanish Colonial actions were the sufficient conditions for change, large-scale depopulation had been the necessary condition that motivated those Colonial policies.

The Latin Americanist aware that precisely the same process occurred in the Peruvian viceroyalty[5] and other areas is likely to attribute it to Spanish colonialism. Imperial administrators experienced massive losses in numbers of conquered subjects throughout the empire. Taking a broader comparative perspective, one may pose the question of whether even European colonialism was necessary or whether catastrophic depopulation itself would have produced much the same result. The French record of the final days of the Natchez in the lower Mississippi River Valley portrays the ultimate collapse of absolutist royal authority in what had been a far more populous polity. The French colonials militarily ended Natchez ethnic independence, but for three decades French traders and officials visited and dealt with autonomous Natchez not subject to Colonial rule.

Natchez population diminished rapidly to such small numbers that every family unit apparently could perform for itself all tasks save military defense more efficiently without royal supervision than with it. Migration serves as an index of early eighteenth-century Natchez social and demographic reality. In 1721, Pierre de Charlevoix visited the Natchez great or capital village. Yet he reported that it was composed of just a few dwellings. Because the Sun, or ruler, still tried to enforce his traditional right to take all his subjects' possessions, the latter had emigrated. To "get as far from him as they can," they had formed "many villages of this nation" at a distance from the chief's settlement.[6] Depopulation had reduced Natchez numbers so greatly that the effort required to maintain order in populous towns and to keep the peace between settlements in a small state two centuries earlier had become counterproductive for most of the small surviving population. Consequently, the authority of the Sun seems to have been fast disappearing in spite of continued observance of traditional forms. French traders and emissaries merely hastened the demise of traditional majority socioeconomic dependence upon royal control over resources. The

French troops ultimately defeated Natchez warriors who were already demoralized and were very probably no longer effectively commanded on the battlefield.

CULTURE-TRANSFORMING TECHNOLOGICAL CHANGES

European domination of colonized areas of the Americas resulted in rather prompt technological changes that left enduring marks on historical buildings and settlements. Except for mine camps, Spaniards plañned and then built their towns on a standard plan prescribed by the crown and derived from Roman antecedents.[7] The European understanding of how to build a true arch, along with the wheel used not only for wagons and carts but also in cogs and pulleys and mahcines for metal working, radically changed the style of architecture and the appearance of pre-Columbian public buildings.[8] On the other hand, even in areas of Colonial domination where native peoples survived, European technology often failed to spread to the sphere of domestic architecture. There the simplification of social structure that accompanied depopulation was often reflected in material objects that evidence altering and simplified conventional understandings. The dramatically transformed nature of Pueblo housing well illustrates this simplification process. Only at culturally very conservative Taos is the early sixteenth-century multistory (and easily defended) Pueblo "apartment house" preserved. Residents of other surviving Pueblos have spread out. Families have built one- or two-story homes for themselves. As interpueblo competition for circumscribed natural resources diminished with the decline in population, the need to construct compact, multistory Pueblos entered only by climbing ladders disappeared. In the specific Pueblo situation, Spaniards furnished a cultural model for simple family housing with ground-level doors and windows that may have hastened the changes in pueblo houses. When the United States annexed the Pueblo region, however, most of the surviving Pueblos still consisted of dwellings with a few small windows and small doorways. Many still maintained defensive structures entered only by ladders. Raiding by Southern Athapascans who spread across the region as Pueblo population declined had kept defensive Pueblo structures functional. When the United States pacified the southern Athapascans, still-diminishing Pueblo peoples fairly quickly moved into simpler family dwelling units. A parallel simplification of many artifacts occurred. Consequently, an archaeologist can expect to find a one-to-one correspondence between only a small fraction of early sixteenth-century and twentieth-century Pueblo tools, utensils, and housing.

DESPECIALIZATION OF ECONOMIC STRUCTURE

Spaniards brought to the New World as part of the cultural dimension of the Columbian Exchange domesticated animals. As a result they had wool for textiles, meat and nonhuman energy, small grains, many vegetables and fruits, the animal-drawn plow, crafts such as metal-smithing, leatherworking with tannin, loom weaving, button making, shoemaking, papermaking, and writing with an alphabet.[9] These additions to the total technology and economy of Colonial New Spain magnified the historical discontinuity between aboriginal and Colonial times. To the extent that Native Americans learned to work metals, weave on looms, and so on, the Colonial economy became more complex than the pre-Conquest system.

Old World additions to the pre-Columbian economic and technological base masked, on the other hand, despecialization of the Native American economic structure. As Spaniards killed members of the Native American elite, or as natives perished from Old World diseases, and the conquerors imposed European values, what the native elite regarded as luxury goods soon disappeared. Elaborate feather-worked garments and complex warriors' costumes found no market in Colonial New Spain.[10]

Abrupt shifts in the nature of the commodities valued, from jade and turquoise to gold and silver, for example, resulted from a substitution of a European for a Native American elite. Other changes in the economic structure resulted from sheer depopulation, but the Colonial power structure masked the influence of depopulation as a cause of despecialization. The same situation obtained among the Pueblo peoples after Spanish colonization in 1598. Yet at least one illustration of the long-range influence of depopulation in despecializing pre-Conquest economic structure may be discerned. Virtually every Pueblo male became a gardener as settlement contracted during Colonial times. Some early sixteenth-century Pueblos were located at such high elevations that their residents could not have relied on gardening. They must have specialized in hunting, gathering wild plants products, and the salt trade, perhaps even carrying commodities from one Pueblo to another.

In aboriginally less densely populated and less economically specialized North America, those who survived the demographic catastrophe rapidly substituted European goods for aboriginal weapons, tools, and utensils. Native Americans could obtain in trade for one commodity— furs—manufactured goods that replaced a wide variety of aboriginal specialized products. Hunting and trapping wild animals and processing their hides to trade to Europeans required a far narrower range of skills than had collecting materials and fashioning them into a broad spectrum of weapons, tools, and utensils for which European manufactured goods now substituted.

The massive depopulation that Native Americans suffered probably disproportionately thinned the ranks of skilled specialists. The more esoteric a specialty was, the more likely were its practitioners to perish during an epidemic episode. In that way, depopulation augmented Native American demand for manufactured goods. The concurrent depopulation and increasing dependence upon European commodities is well illustrated by the artifacts recovered from historic Seneca settlements. Wray and Schoff based much of their original dating of periods of village occupation on the relative quantity and type of European trade goods recovered from Seneca village sites and cemeteries. The sites dated between 1564 – 1570 and the 1574 and 1585 epidemics in table 30 yielded only a "trifling amount of trade material." A few iron axes and large iron knives were buried with bodies of the dead, and tubular brass beads and ornaments "were commonly worn."[11]

"True wampum" appeared for the first time at the sites dated in table 29 between the 1596 measles epidemic and the 1613 – 1619 bubonic plague epidemic.[12] This situation implies that the craft of fashioning wampum with metal tools began early in the seventeenth century, shortly before European colonization started. What archaeologists considered materials of Native American artisanry composed three-fourths of the goods Senecas owned.

Between the bubonic plague pandemic that ended in 1619 and the wave of contagion that began in 1633, the Senecas produced only somewhat more than half their goods. They acquired muskets and for the first time could afford to place kettles in graves.[13] Between the 1654 and 1669 epidemics, the Senecas produced only about one-fourth of their goods. They apparently no longer bothered to make their own ceramic vessels, relying on metal containers and importing a few clay ones. They seldom used stone tools or projectile points, but wampum was common. Glass beads were abundant; iron objects were commonplace.[14]

The trend in technological change is clear in this record. Senecas, and Iroquois in general, abandoned their traditional Native American crafts and acquired manufactured goods. Later, they learned Old World crafts and arts and occupations. The tools that a Mohawk or Onondaga steelworker uses in the twentieth century offer no information whatsoever about prehistoric Iroquois tools and utensils. The paper and brushes that artist and chief Oren Lyons uses likewise bear no relationship to pre-Columbian Iroquois artistry. The only artifact the author has ever seen in an Iroquois household that bore a one-to-one relationship to a prehistoric counterpart is a wooden mortar and pestle set for pounding maize kernels. That utensil is so widely used in Native North America as to have no diagnostic value to an archaeologist, and its use is well known.

WAR FOR CONQUEST AND FOR OTHER REASONS

Depopulation with concomitant diminished intergroup competition for natural resources at least allows—and probably generates—psychological changes. This phenomenon is perhaps nowhere more apparent than in recent Native American and ethnographers' attribution of motives for warfare. A.L. Kroeber, for example, asserted that the Mojave, Quechan, and Cocopah peoples "waged war gratuitously, for glory," even though he was aware that the Mojave seized Panya territory in 1827.[15] Recent claims by Native Americans in this Rancherían culture area that their ancestors never waged wars of territory conquest cannot be trusted. In recent years, Walapais participating in the "cowboy culture," with its sentimental attitudes toward horses, cannot conceive that their forebears consumed horsemeat. Yet historical evidence makes plain that mid-nineteenth-century Pai relished horseflesh.[16] Both recent cultural self-perceptions result from greatly altered circumstances—true cultural discontinuities. In the case of motivation for warfare, depopulation greatly changed Native American needs for land and resources. A reduced number of people exploited either less land or the same area less intensively.

This shift in the basis of warfare has been recognized in the archaeological remains and documents of the Native Americans of the Southeast. When de Soto's marauders explored that culture area in 1539–1543, the populous Native American ministates were fighting one another for territory.[17] The archaeological evidence in the Southeast does not include town fortifications before or after the period of peak population.[18] Wars of conquest appear to have originated as a consequence of dense population and to have ceased with depopulation.

A very striking change in psychology occurred among the Puebloan peoples. The recent remnant populations have come to view themselves and to portray themselves quite successfully to outsiders as essentially and inherently pacifist. The clear selection of easily defended natural sites on which to build fifteenth- and early sixteenth-century pueblos left physical evidence of inter-Pueblo hostilities during the period of peak population. The sixteenth-century Spanish chroniclers' descriptions of Pecos, Hawikuh, and other Pueblos clearly described large defensive settlements erected long before the first European reached the culture area. The Pueblos were populous ministates militarily competing with one another for a circumscribed environmental base.[19] Traces of Pueblo militarism generated during the late prehistoric period of population growth lingered for some time. Colonial Spaniards successfully recruited Pueblo warriors to help them during the reconquest and on numerous occasions thereafter.[20] The Pueblos convincingly demonstrated their lingering militancy and fighting ability during the 1680 Pueblo Revolt, when they temporarily laid aside their heritage of inter-Pueblo competition.[21] The Hopis and refugees from New Mexico Pueblos residing among them showed their bellicosity by destroying Awatovi in 1700 and by successfully avoiding Spanish reconquest.[22]

Again, the colonial influence after 1696 cannot be ignored. It became eminently expedient for Pueblo peoples after 1700 to proclaim their pacifism, except toward Apache raiders, and to ally themselves with the Euroamerican dominant group. At the same time, the decline in population must be recognized as having left every Pueblo with more natural resources at hand than its reduced population required. A major motive for warfare simply disappeared as Pueblo people perished.

NOTES

1. Wilson and Wilson, *Analysis*, 1945.
2. Dobyns, "Estimating," 1966, pp. 39–96.
3. Borah, "Discontinuity and Continuity," 1979, p. 10.
4. Borah, "America," 1964, pp. 175–76.
5. Dobyns and Doughty, *Peru*, 1976, p. 78, etc.
6. Swanton, *Indian Tribes*, 1911, p. 206. Charlevoix, *Journal*, 1761 (1966), vol. 2, p. 255.
7. Borah, "European Cultural Influence," 1972, pp. 35–54.
8. Borah, "Discontinuity and Continuity," 1979, p. 9.
9. Ibid., 9.
10. Ibid., 9–10.
11. Wray and Schoff, "Preliminary Report," 1953, pp. 54–55.
12. Ibid., 55–56.
13. Ibid., 56–57.

14. Ibid., 58−59.

15. Kroeber, "Nature of the Land-holding Group," 1955, p. 310.

16. Dobyns et al., "Thematic Changes," 1957.

17. Robertson, trans., *True Relation*, 1933, vol. II, pp. 153, 194; Varner and Varner, trans., *Florida*, 1962, pp. 434−44, 465−66, 487−88, 540, 544−45.

18. Larson, "Functional Considerations," 1972, p. 391.

19. Carneiro, "Theory," 1970, pp. 734−37.

20. O.L. Jones, *Pueblo Warriors*, 1966.

21. Hackett, *Revolt*, 1942.

22. Euler and Dobyns, *Hopi People*, 1971.

SECTION FOUR
Methodological Implications of Cultural Discontinuity

The second section of this essay showed that most of the epidemic chronology established for Florida also applies to an "epidemic region" of Atlantic Coast peoples north into New England. The analysis illustrated as well how dating decisive demographic events among native peoples can help archaeologists to date the abandonment and beginning of settlements. It also demonstrated how dated archaeological remains can help epidemiologists define the geographic spread of specific diseases at specific times. It is worthwhile, therefore, to explore additional implications of the techniques employed in this analysis for archaeological research on Native Americans.

First of all, epidemics of Old World pathogens spread to Native American populations in a known or knowable order. Decisive demographic events happened at documented or documentable intervals. The North American epidemic chronology is thus a tool that archaeologists can use for dating settlement abandonments and beginnings during historic and protohistoric times. This epidemic chronology is relatively absolute. That is, decisive episodes are dated in terms of specific years or very short spans of years.

SPECIFYING CAUSATION

This analysis referred to Seneca archaeological research by Charles F. Wray to illustrate how the epidemic chronology can refine the dating of settlement abandonments and beginnings dated approximately by other techniques. The earlier demonstration of how close Wray seems to have come to reconstructing the actual chronology of Seneca migrations will, I trust, allow further reference to his procedures not to appear unduly critical. Wray had no relatively full North American decisive demographic event chronology at hand on which to draw in dating Seneca migrations. His limited reference to epidemic disease in his reconstruction of the sequence of Seneca sites suggests the limitations of general knowledge that have handicapped archaeological research. Wray listed "European Epidemics" as an important event between 1550 and 1575. His list illustrates the point that resorting to epidemic disease-caused mortality as a merely general explanation does not provide the precise dates that an archaeologist needs for relating actions such as departure from one village and construction of another to each other in absolute calendrical time. For the epidemic chronology to be useful to the archaeologist, he or she must relate *specific* epidemic episodes to *particular* actions reflected in ruins and artifacts. Human response to epidemic mortality makes the demographic event decisive.

DEFINING LETHALNESS OF EPIDEMIC EPISODES

In one instance, Wray mentioned a specific epidemic episode, a "respiratory epidemic" in 1662. As table 29 shows, that specific epidemic appears not to have influenced Seneca settlement. The point is that some diseases cause greater mortality, and therefore greater behavioral consequences, than others. Evidently the respiratory ailment that spread in 1662 was not mortal enough to cause any Seneca settlement abandonments. On the other hand, the Seneca abandonment/building chronology shown in table 29 suggests that nine different decisive depopulation episodes did result in the abandonment of one or more settlements, followed by the construction of new villages a short distance away. While table 29 does not provide a complete list of major epidemics, it identifies those that occurred in 1519–1524, 1564–1570, 1613–1619, and 1633–1639 as decisive demographic events of the first magnitude in terms of their influence on Native American settlement and population. Apparently the episodes of 1585–1586, 1596, 1654, and 1669–1670 were at least regionally important and severe. Thus while table 29 is not presented as a comprehensive continental epidemic chronology, it does identify first- and second-order decisive demographic events among many Native Americans. The dates of these events are known. Archaeologists investigating ruins in areas not discussed here but between areas mentioned can anticipate encountering traces of their passing.

HISTORICAL DISCONTINUITIES AND INFERENCES FROM ETHNOLOGY

One of the scientifically successful methods of research in archaeology is the "direct historical approach." That is, the archaeologist begins with the known. In North America, that known is a surviving Native American ethnic group. The investigator excavates presently occupied settlements and then ones known formerly to have been inhabited by members of the group.[1] Where any significant depth of trash is excavated, the archaeologist can trace the housing styles and artifact preferences of the group back through time. This method at its most effective starts with ethnographic studies of the living population, its crafts, arts, settlement pattern and so forth.[2] It relies heavily upon ethnographic studies to identify the functions of various artifacts, especially those that become diagnostic of ethnic group identity in earlier sites. It follows clues in written documents as to the location of historic sites. Eventually, with sufficient skill and some luck, the archaeologist excavates prehistoric remains that can be identified as those belonging to the same ethnic group on the basis of similarities in settlement patterns, housing, and artifacts, without recourse to documentary clues. Indeed, such is the goal.

Early historic depopulation, and especially the apparent 95 percent decline in population between 1519 and 1617, created a major biological and cultural discontinuity. That discontinuity constitutes a major barrier to successful pursuit of the direct historical approach in archaeological investigation in North America. The scale of Native American depopulation indicated in this volume has serious implications for inference from ethnographic observation to pre-Columbian behaviors. This is a very complex matter that will not be fully explored here, but some basic points may be made.

Where no members of an ethnic group survived long enough to be studied by ethnographers, absolutely no inferences at all can be drawn from ethnographic studies. Such is the situation with the Timucuan-speaking peoples. Archaeologists trying to study their history and prehistory must reason from such brief and culturally biased accounts as explorers, missionaries, or Colonial administrators may have written and survived. Section 3 of essay 5 gives an assessment of canoe transportation of foodstuffs and people engaged in economic pursuits such as fishing or traveling quickly to and from hunting meadows as a major factor in Timucan sedentarism. That analysis suggests the importance of a major artifact and all of the many human behaviors centered on it, which range from selecting a tree to fell, to fashioning a dugout and charring and scraping it into shape, to the motor habits and skills required for propelling and navigating the vessel. Yet the pre-Columbian Native American canoe has been studied almost not at all by anthropologists.

Direct archaeological analysis of pre-Columbian canoes has been limited by the terrestrial nature of most excavation. Underwater archaeology has become practicable in recent decades, to be sure. Even in the New World, however, underwater archaeologists have focused their activities upon the wrecks of European ships. Treasure hunting in European cultural terms—recovering precious metals and other highly valued "antique" cargo items—is the main component of underwater archaeology. Very little research has been directed toward the pre-Columbian canoe, and the small size of such vessels and their open cargo space make recovery of instructive cargoes quite unlikely.

The prehistorian must depend primarily upon other forms of evidence in the absence of analyzable pre-Columbian canoes and their cargoes. The cultural discontinuities that most Native American peoples have suffered militate very decidedly against accurate inference from ethnographic studies to prehistoric patterns of canoe utilization. An anecdote will illustrate why. During the early 1970s, the author acted as scientific editor of forty volumes of ethnohistory of as many surviving Native American groups in the United States. A silver medallion struck with designs depicting seals of tribal governments and historically significant scenes accompanied each volume. The reservation government of each Native American group approved medallic art prior to minting and the manuscript prior to printing.[3] When the chief executive of the Chickasaw Nation saw the proposed canoe-making scene for one side of the Chickasaw medallion, he wanted to know what canoes had to do with Chickasaws. Canoes simply have not been very functional for Chickasaws in Oklahoma since the United States relocated them there.

Adjusting to the demands of a mid-continental environment, the Chickasaws over a long period of time dropped from their oral tradition recollections of the importance of canoes to their ancestors in the moister Southeastern culture area environment. Yet historical documents make clear that the Chickasaw dominated a long stretch of the Mississippi River during the eighteenth century. At different times, Chickasaw war canoes interdicted French and U.S. passage along the river. The Tennessee River was for many decades a Chickasaw stream. Moreover, the Chickasaw ranged far upstream along the Ohio River to fight western Iroquois Confederacy groups, just as the latter floated downstream to attack Chickasaws.[4] Clearly, then, accurate inferences about eighteenth-century Chickasaw canoe culture, or about earlier protohistoric Chickasaw canoe utilization, simply cannot be drawn from ethnographic research among surviving Chickasaws. Investigators must seek clues in historic documents in an effort to comprehend the fundamental importance of canoes to prehistoric and protohistoric Chickasaws.

Inasmuch as other aboriginal inhabitants of the Southeast were, like the Chickasaw, almost all forced to migrate from the area to the Indian Territory, the same ethnohistorical methods must be employed to try to understand the importance of canoes to peoples throughout the culture area. Spanish exploration chronicles contain frequent references to canoes. De Soto's marauders antagonized the peoples of peninsular Florida and had to bridge streams to cross some of them and to struggle through swamps. After wintering in Apalachee, these Spaniards may have learned how better to placate Native American chiefs and to find vessels. Approaching Cofitachique, Spanish scouts found "a landing for canoes" and shouted to the townspeople across the river by which the settlement was built. Six spokesmen crossed the river in a "large canoe" rowed by "servants" to confer with the strangers.[5] The female Townchief crossed from town to expedition in an ornamented canoe covered by a canopy, towed by a tug canoe.[6] Her people built "great rafts" to supplement their numerous canoes in order to ferry de Soto's forces across the river.[7]

Crossing the Appalachian Mountains, de Soto's marauders were not in country favorable to canoe usage. Once they entered the Mississippi River main drainage, though, they were seldom far from a populous river valley town using numerous canoes for transportation. At Ychiaha, on an island in presumably the Tennessee River, the inhabitants crossed the Spaniards in many canoes and "boats" that they prepared for that function.[8] Leaving Coza en route to Tascaluza, the Spaniards again crossed the Talise River on rafts and canoes.[9] When they reached the capital town called Tascaluza, located on a peninsula formed by the same river, they spent nearly a whole day ferrying across the stream.[10]

After losing scores of men in the battle of Mauvila, the Spaniards traveled to the Chiefdom called Chicaza. At its border town where they entered Chicaza territory, the Spaniards built their own pirogues to cross the deep river, possibly the Black Warrior, that a native army defended.[11] Upon reaching the Mississippi River, the Spaniards again made their own barges to ferry across. Native Americans in "finely wrought" canoes assembled to oppose their passage.[12] So impressive were the war canoes that the Gentleman of Elvas compared them with "a beautiful fleet of galleys."[13]

The capital towns of the riverine chiefdoms that the Spaniards visited typically were palisaded and protected by moats. Some were situated on islands. The ruling elite traveled quickly from one settlement to another by canoe.[14]

When the survivors of de Soto's grandiose plans finally decided to abandon the enterprise, they built small boats on which to return down the Mississippi River and to sail across the Gulf of Mexico. Squadrons of Native American war canoes harried them nearly all the way downstream from the point where they embarked on their voyage to the islands in the delta.[15] The "command ships" of Native American chiefs were immense: twenty-five oarsmen per side propelled them, and they carried twenty-five to thirty warriors in addition.[16] Garcilaso de la Vega, perhaps motivated by his half-Native-American heritage, interviewed survivors carefully enough to find out that the Native American paddlers sang a variety of tunes to set the rhythm for their strokes. Moreover, each leader rode a canoe painted with his color.

The Mississippi River chiefdom commodores exercised effective control over their canoe fleets in battle. Whether in their chants, or by shouting, or with visual signals, the leaders ordered their war canoes to execute maneuvers. They could travel in a single armada or could divide into three task forces, which could paddle back and forth across the river in turns so as to afford their archers the opportunity to fire volleys of arrows at enemy vessels, just as European ships of the line would on occasion sail across the path of an opposing fleet in order to deliver broadsides from their guns.[17] The Native American commodores could break contact with a hostile naval force, maintaining a tightly organized fleet, and could then quickly propel their canoes to attack a lagging enemy vessel straggling from its fleet;[18] they could also close and ram.[19] Scant as these documented details are, they are much more information than ethnographic interviews can recover from living survivors of any riverine ethnic group that engaged de Soto's forces in 1543. Some of the Native American groups on the river in 1543 have long since become extinct and cannot be studied ethnographically in any event. Historic depopulation throws an impenetrable barrier in the way of drawing accurate archaeological inferences from ethnographic studies.

Where culturally conservative peoples, such as Pueblos, survive, it is sometimes possible to identify an otherwise unidentifiable artifact by seeing a contemporary example in use. Most elegantly, an archaeologist tests his inference about a set of artifacts recovered by excavation by demonstrating a correlation between artifact and behavior that is "common" in "ethnographic reality."[20] Such is the best of all possible research worlds. Still, one-to-one correspondence between contemporary and early historic or prehistoric patterns is inevitably rare in the depopulated New World. At least two reasons for the infrequency of one-to-one correspondence between an ethnographically observed behavior and a prehistoric one have been made fairly clear in the foregoing analyses. One of the main features of the historic discontinuity in Native American cultures has been a catastrophic reduction in social scale.

At the same time, native groups altered many other cultural traits by substituting weapons, tools, and utensils of European manufacture for aboriginal ones while learning to grow several Old World domesticated plants, to ride horses from the Old World, and to care for pigs, chickens, and other animals domesticated in the Old World.

CONCLUSIONS

The numerous scholarly implications of this analysis cannot all be spelled out here. At a minimum, this study forcefully confirms William McNeill's call for historians to reinterpret human events in terms of disease. It extends that call to Indianologists, both ethnohistorians and archaeologists. This volume demonstrates that a great deal more research needs to be carried out on historic epidemiology in Native North America. The foregoing analysis shows that evidence not only in written documents but also from protohistoric Native American settlements can contribute to understanding the true scale of Native American depopulation caused by intrusive Old World pathogens. On the other hand, my analysis has indicated how little credence can be accorded to late nineteenth-century Native American statements about ancestral culture. Such statements may more or less accurately describe nineteenth-century changing cultures. Certainly those statements cannot accurately report populous, class-structured polities of the early sixteenth century prior to depopulation. Historians and anthropologists need to reformulate concepts of pre-Columbian North American societies. Accurately describing extinct pre-Columbian societies calls for a sophisticated level of combined ethnographic and archaeological analysis seldom achieved. It might be said that ethnographers and archaeologists both sorely need greater skill as ethnohistorians.

Perhaps this volume justifies optimism about the contributions archaeologists may make to understanding the scale of historic Native American depopulation and its cultural consequences. Perhaps not. On the one hand, I have indicated how documentary evidence of historic epidemics provides an absolute chronology for interpreting settlement abandonment and building, migration, and other events recorded in remains that archaeologists excavate. On the other hand, my exercise in ethnohistory has identified very substantial obstacles to successful pursuit of a direct historical approach in archaeological research on many Native American peoples. The ethnohistorical approach clearly shows that historical archaeology of Native Americans is—and because of depopulation and its sequelae must be—the study of rapid cultural change and abrupt cultural discontinuities. This fact poses a very great challenge to archaeologists, who have for the most part thought in terms of (and searched for) static cultures and continuities in cultural traditions.

My long discourse has suggested why European and Euroamerican policymakers expected Native Americans finally to disappear during the twentieth century. One method for estimating early sixteenth-century Native American population indicates that it surpassed 18 million individuals in North America. A long inquiry into food resources of Florida suggests that the estimate for that area included in the continental total is conservative. So does the estimation of early sixteenth-century Florida numbers based on epidemic mortality. By the late nineteenth-century only about one-quarter to one-third million Native Americans survived. Many of them were genetically mixed with Africans and Europeans. To employ a very simple numerical device to emphasize the amount of depopulation that appears to have occurred, one Native American lived early in the twentieth century where about seventy-two had existed four centuries earlier. Nineteenth-century policy makers can hardly be blamed, therefore, for thinking that Native Americans would become extinct.

Yet the error itself indicates a very real difficulty inherent in bringing even so quantitative a social science as demography to bear on predicting future events. A trend that exists for four centuries can change, for that is precisely what happened in the case of the Native American population. Having declined precipitously for a century, and then merely rapidly and later more slowly, Native Americans began to increase during the twentieth century. It took them some 400 years to adjust to pathogens that evolved in the Old World. Yet they did ultimately adjust. Now that Native Americans possess more or less the same immunities as other ethnic groups, they can be expected to continue to increase like other peoples in response to environmental factors other than contagious diseases—until the next decisive demographic event makes that prediction inaccurate.

NOTES

1. Steward published a seminal discussion, "Direct Historical Approach to Archaeology," in 1942. Earlier, Heizer wrote "Direct-Historical Approach in California Archaeology," 1941, pp. 98–122.

2. Guthe, *Pueblo Pottery Making*, 1925, exemplifies an ethnographic study undertaken to illuminate questions about excavated artifacts.

3. Dobyns, "Native American Publication," 1974, pp. 304–306.

4. Baird, *Chickasaw People*, 1974; Malone, *Chickasaw Nation*, 1922, pp. 251, 271–76.

5. Varner and Varner, trans., *Florida*, 1962, pp. 297–98. The Gentleman of Elvas remembered the event as four canoes crossing the stream, in one of which rode a sister of the female Townchief (Robertson, trans., *True Relation*, 1933, vol. II, p. 91).

6. Varner and Varner, trans., *Florida*, 1962, p. 299. The Gentleman of Elvas mentioned that the Townchief sat on two stacked cushions on a mat covering the canoe bottom (Robertson, trans., *True Relation*, 1933, vol. II, p. 91).

7. Varner and Varner, trans., *Florida*, 1962, p. 303. The Gentleman of Elvas remembered canoes carrying de Soto and his men across the river (Robertson, trans., *True Relation*, 1933, vol. II, pp. 92–93).

8. Varner and Varner, trans., *Florida*, 1962, p. 336.

9. Ibid., 349.

10. Ibid., 351.

11. Ibid., 393, 395. Robertson, trans., *True Relation*, 1933, vol. II, p. 140.

12. Varner and Varner, trans., *Florida*, 1962, pp. 428–29.

13. Robertson, trans., *True Relation*, 1933, vol. II, p. 161.

14. Varner and Varner, trans., *Florida*, 1962, p. 437.

15. Ibid., 578, 589; Robertson, trans., *True Relation*, 1933, vol. II, p. 275.

16. Varner and Varner, trans., *Florida*, 1962, p. 575. The Gentleman of Elvas reported that some war canoes carried 60 or 70 Native Americans (Robertson, trans., *True Relation*, 1933, vol. II, p. 276).

17. Varner and Varner, trans., *Florida*, 1962, p. 577.

18. Ibid., 582.

19. Ibid., 586.

20. R.H. Thompson, "Subjective Element," 1956, p. 329.

BIBLIOGRAPHY

Aberle, Sophie B., J.H. Watkins, and E.H. Pitney. "The Vital History of San Juan Pueblo." *Human Biology* 12 (1940):141–87.

Adicks, Richard, ed. *Le Conte's Report on East Florida*. Gainesville: Univ. Presses of Florida, 1978.

Agar, Lothian A. "The Fishes of Lake Okeechobee, Florida." *Quar. Jour. of the Fla. Acad. of Sciences* 34 (1971):53–62.

———. "Commercial Fishery on Lake Okeechobee, Florida." *Quar. Jour. of the Fla. Acad. of Sciences* 35 (1972):217–24.

Alegre, Francisco Javier. *Historia de la provincia de la Compañia de Jesús de Nueva España*. Tomos I–III. Ed. Ernest J. Burrus and Félix Zubillaga. Rome: Institutum Historicum, S.J., 1956–59.

Alexander, Taylor R. "Observations on the Ecology of the Low Hammocks of Southern Florida." *Quar. Jour. of the Fla. Acad. of Sciences* 18 (1955):21–27.

Alexander, Taylor R., and John D. Dickson III. "Vegetational Changes in the National Key Deer Refuge—II." *Quar. Jour. of the Fla. Acad. of Sciences* 35 (1972):85–96.

Andagoya, Pascual de. *Narrative of the Proceedings of Pedrarias Davila in the Provinces of Tierra Firme or Castilla de Oro and of the Discovery of the South Sea and the Coasts of Peru and Nicaragua*. Trans. Clements R. Markham. London: Hakluyt Society, 1865.

Anderson, Arthur J.O., and Charles E. Dibble, trans. *Florentine Codex: General History of the Things of New Spain*. Book 12. *The Conquest of Mexico*. By Fray Bernardino de Sahagun. Monograph 14, pt. 13. Santa Fe: School of American Research, 1955.

Anderson, W.A.D., ed. *Pathology*. St. Louis: C.V. Mosby, 1953.

Andreas, Alfred T. *History of Chicago*. Chicago: A.T. Andreas, 1884.

Anghiera, Pietro Martire d'. *De Orbe Novo: The Eight Decades of Peter Martyr D'Anghera*. Trans. Francis Augustus MacNutt. New York: Putnam's, 1912, 2 vol.

———. *The Decades of the Newe World or West India*. Trans. Richard Eden. 1555. Reprint ed. New York: Readex Microprint, 1966.

Aplin, J.A. "Pismo Clams of San Quintín, Lower California." *Calif. Fish and Game* 33 (1947):31–33.

Aranguíz y Cotes. Oficio. 1 de noviembre de 1659, San Agustín. Archivo General de Indias, Aud. de Santo Domingo, Est. 58, Caj. 2, Leg. 2. Stetson Collection, P.K. Yonge Library, Univ. of Florida, Gainesville.

Arata, Andrew A. "Effects of Burning on Vegetation and Rodent Populations in a Longleaf Pine Turkey Oak Association in North Central Florida." *Quar. Jour. of the Fla. Acad. of Sciences* 22 (1959):94–104.

Arnade, Charles W. "Cattle Raising in Spanish Florida, 1513–1763." *Agricultural History* 35 (1961):116–24.

Arnold, Lillian E. "Check List of Native and Naturalized Trees in Florida." *Proceedings of the Fla. Acad. of Sciences* 2 (1938):32–66.

Aronson, J.D. "The History of Disease among the Natives of Alaska." *College of Physicians of Philadelphia, Transactions & Studies.* 4th ser. vol. 8:4 (1940):27–40.

Arricivita, Juan Domingo. *Crónica seráfica y apostólica del Colegio de Propaganda Fide de la Santa Cruz de Querétaro en la Nueva España.* Mexico: Felipe de Zúñiga y Ontiveros, 1792.

Aschmann, Homer. *The Central Desert of Baja California: Demography and Ecology.* Ibero-Americana 42. Berkeley: Univ. of California Press, 1959.

Ashburn, Percy M. *The Ranks of Death.* Ed. Frank D. Ashburn. New York: Coward McCann, 1947.

Austin, Daniel F. "Vegetation of Southeastern Florida—I. Pine Jog." *Fla. Scientist* 39 (1976):230–35.

Bailey, Liberty Hyde, ed. *The Standard Cyclopedia of Horticulture.* New York: Macmillan, 1947.

Baird, W. David. *The Choctaw People.* Phoenix: Indian Tribal Series, 1973.

———. *The Chickasaw People.* Phoenix: Indian Tribal Series, 1974.

———. *The Quapaw People.* Phoenix: Indian Tribal Series, 1975.

Baldwin, S. Prentiss, and S. Charles Kendeigh. "Variations in the Weight of Birds." *Auk* 55 (1938):416–67.

Bancroft, H.H. *Native Races of the Pacific States. Vol. I. Wild Tribes. Vol. II. Civilized Nations.* New York: Appleton, 1875.

———. *History of Mexico.* Vol. III. *1600–1803.* San Francisco: Bancroft, 1883.

———. *History of Mexico.* Vol. II. *1521–1600.* San Francisco: History, 1886.

Bandelier, Fanny, trans. *The Journey of Alvar Núñez Cabeza de Vaca and His Companions from Florida to the Pacific, 1528–1536.* 1904. Reprint ed. New York: Allerton, 1922.

Barbour, Philip L., ed. *The Jamestown Voyages under the First Charter, 1606–1609.* 2 vols. Cambridge: Cambridge Univ. Press, Hakluyt Society, 1969.

Barrientos, Bartolomé. *Vida y Hechos de Pero Menéndez de Avilés, Cavallero de la Hordem de Sanctiago, Adelantado de la Florida: Do Largamente se Tratan las Conquistas y Poblaciones de la Provincia de la Florida, y Como Fueron Libradas de los Luteranos que dellas se avian apoderado.* Mexico: J. Aguilar Vera, 1902.

Bartlett, John R. *Personal Narrative of Explorations and Incidents in Texas, New Mexico, California, Sonora, and Chihuahua, Connected with the United States and Mexican Boundary Commission, During the Years 1850, '51, '52, and '53.* 2 vols. New York: Appleton, 1854.

Baumhoff, Martin A. *Ecological Determinants of Aboriginal California Popula-tions*. Berkeley: Univ. of California Press, Pub. in Amer. Archaeol. and Ethnol., 49 (1963).

Baxter, James P. *A Memoir of Jacques Cartier, sieur de Limoilou, his voyages to the St. Lawrence* . . . New York: Dodd, Mead, 1906.

Beals, Ralph L. "Acculturation." In *Social Anthropology*, vol. VI, ed. Manning Nash. In*Handbook of Middle American Indians*, ed. Robert Waucope. Austin: Univ. of Texas Press, 1967.

Bean, Lowell John. *Mukat's People: The Cahuilla Indians of Southern California*. Berkeley: Univ. of California Press, 1972.

Bean, Lowell John, and Katherine Siva Saubel. *Temalpakh: Cahuilla In-dian Knowledge and Usage of Plants*. Banning, Calif.: Malki Museum Press, 1972.

Benavides, Antonio de. A S. M. dando cuenta de haber hecho la visita a los indios. San Agustín. 1 de setiembre de 1727. Archivo General de Indias, Aud. de Santo Domingo, 58-1-31. P. K. Yonge Library, Univ. of Florida, Gaines-ville.

Bishop, Charles A. *The Northern Ojibwa and the Fur Trade: An Historical and Ecological Study*. Toronto: Holt, Rinehart and Winston of Canada, 1974.

Blasingham, Emily J. "The Depopulation of the Illinois Indians." *Ethnohistory* 3 (1956): part 1, 193 – 224; part 2, 361 – 412.

Bolton, Herbert E., ed. *Spanish Exploration in the Southwest, 1542—1706*. New York: Scribner's, 1908.

———. "The Mission as a Frontier Institution in the Spanish-American Col-onies." *Amer. Hist. Rev.* 23 (1917): 42 – 61.

Borah, Woodrow. "Population Decline and the Social and Institutional Changes of New Spain in the Middle Decades of the Sixteenth Century." *Akten des 34 Internationalen Amerikanisten-kongresses* (1962), 172 – 78.

———. "America as Model: The Demographic Impact of European Expansion upon the Non-European World." *Actas y memorias, XXXV Congreso Interna-cional de Americanistas, Mexico, 1962,* 3 (1964): 379 – 87.

———. "The Historical Demography of Latin America: Sources, Techniques, Controversies, Yields." In *Population and Economics*. Winnipeg: Univ. of Manitoba Press, 1970.

———. "European cultural influence in the formation of the first plan for urban centers that has lasted to our time." *Actas y Memorias del XXXIX Congreso Internacional de Americanistas, Lima, 1970,* 2 (1972): 35 – 54.

———. "Discontinuity and Continuity in Mexican History." *Pacific Hist. Rev.* 48 (1979): 1 – 25.

Borah, Woodrow, and S.F. Cook. "Conquest and Population: A Demographic Approach to Mexican History." *Amer. Phil. Soc., Proceedings* 113 (1969): 177 – 83.

Bourne, Edward Gaylord, ed. *Narratives of the Career of Hernando de Soto in the Conquest of Florida*. New York: A.S. Barnes, 1904.

Bowles, Richard. "Area Bluefish Display Their Ferocious Nature." *Gainesville Sun*, October 3, 1980.

Boyd, Mark F. "The Occurrence of the American Bison in Alabama and Florida." *Science* 84 (1936):203.

———, trans. "The Expedition of Marcos Delgado from Apalache to the Upper Creek Country in 1686." *Fla. Hist. Quar.* 16 (1937):3 – 32.

———. "Enumeration of Florida Spanish Missions in 1675." *Fla. Hist. Quar.* 27 (1948):181 – 88.

———. "Diego Peña's Expedition to Apalache and Apalachicolo in 1716." *Fla. Hist. Quar.* 28 (1949):1 – 27.

Boyd, Mark F., Hale G. Smith, and John W. Griffin. *Here They Once Stood: The Tragic End of the Apalachee Missions*. Gainesville: Univ. of Florida Press, 1951.

Brain, Jeffrey P. "The Natchez 'Paradox.' " *Ethnology* 10 (1971):215 – 22.

Brandegee, Townshend S. "A Collection of Plants from Baja California, 1889." *Proceedings of the Calif. Acad. of Sciences*, 2d ser., 2 (1890):117 – 216.

———. "Flora of the Cape Region of Baja California." *Proceedings of the Calif. Acad. of Sciences*, 2d ser., 3 (1893):108 – 82.

Brau, Salvador. *La colonización de Puerto Rico*. San Juan: Heraldo Español, 1907.

Brinton, Daniel G. *Notes on the Floridian Peninsula: Its Literary History, Indian Tribes, and Antiquities*. 1859. Reprint ed. Paladin, 1969.

Brown, David E., Neil B. Carmody, Charles H. Lowe, and Raymond M. Turner. "A Second Locality for Native California Fan Palms (*Washingtonia filifera*) in Arizona." *Jour. of the Ariz. Acad. of Science* 11 (1976):37 – 41.

Browne, J. Ross. *A Tour through Arizona: "Adventures in the Apache Country."* 1869. Reprint ed. Tucson: Arizona Silhouettes, 1950.

Brush, Stephen B. *Mountain Field and Family: The Economy and Human Ecology of an Andean Valley*. Philadelphia: Univ. of Pennsylvania Press, 1977.

Bullen, Ripley P. "Tocobaga Indians and the Safety Harbor Culture." In *Tacachale*, ed. J.T. Milanich and S. Proctor. Gainesville: Univ. Presses of Florida, 1978.

Bunzel, Ruth. *Chichicastenango: A Guatemalan Village*. Locust Valley, N.Y.: Augustin, American Ethnological Society, 1952.

Burrus, Ernest J., ed. *Kino and Manje, Explorers of Sonora and Arizona: Their Vision of the Future: A Study of Their Expeditions and Plans*. Rome: Jesuit Historical Institute, 1971.

Bushnell, Amy. "The Menéndez Cattle Barony at La Chua and the Determinants of Economic Expansion in Seventeenth-Century Florida." *Fla. Hist. Quar.* 56 (1978):407 – 31.

Cadzow, Donald A. *Archaeological Studies of the Susquehannock Indians of Pennsylvania*. Harrisburg: Pennsylvania Historical and Museum Commission, Pub. Vol. 3, No. 2, 1936.

Campbell, T.J. *Pioneer Laymen of North America*. 2 vols. New York: America Press, 1915.

Campbell, T.N. "Choctaw Subsistence: Ethnographic Notes from the Incecum Manuscript." *Fla. Anthropologist* 12 (1959):9 – 24.

Campos, Agustín de. Libro de Bautismos del Partido de San Ygnacio de Xaburic. No. 1. Pinart Collection, Bancroft Library, Univ. of California, Berkeley.

Carneiro, Robert L. "A Theory of the Origin of the State." *Science* 169 (1970):733 – 38.

Caro Baroja, Julio. "Honour and Shame: A Historical Account of Several Conflicts." In *Honour and Shame: The Values of Mediterranean Society*, ed. J.G. Peristiany. Chicago: Univ. of Chicago Press, 1966.

Carter, Annette M. "The Genus *Cercidium* (Leguminosae Caesalpinioidae) in the Sonoran Desert of Mexico and the United States." *Proceedings of the Calif. Acad. of Sciences*, 4th ser., 40 (1974):17 – 57.

Cash, Joseph H., and Gerald W. Wolff. *The Three Affiliated Tribes (Mandan, Arikara and Hidatsa)*. Phoenix: Indian Tribal Series, 1974.

Casteel, Richard W. "Two Statis Maximum Population-Density Models for Hunter-Gatherers: A First Approximation." *World Archaeology* 4 (1972):19 – 40.

Catlin, George. *The Manners, Customs and Condition of the North American Indians*. 1841. Reprint ed. Philadelphia: Leary, Stuart, 1913, 2 vol.; New York: Dover, 1973.

Ceci, Lynn. "Fish Fertilizer: A Native American Practice?" *Science* 188 (1975):26 – 30.

Chamberlain, Robert S. *The Conquest and Colonization of Honduras, 1502—1550*. Pub. 598. Washington, D.C.: Carnegie Institution, 1953.

Chapman, Charles E. *A History of Spain*. New York: Macmillan, 1918.

Charlevoix, Pierre de. *Journal of a Voyage to North-America*. 1761. Reprint ed. New York: Readex Microprint, 1966.

Chatelain, Verne E. *The Defenses of Spanish Florida, 1565 to 1763*. Pub. 511. Washington: Carnegie Institution, 1941.

———. "Spanish Contributions in Florida to American Culture." *Fla. Hist. Quar.* 19 (1941):213 – 44.

Clavijero, Francisco J. *Desertazioni sulla terra, sugli animali, e sugli abitator del Messico*. Cesena, Italy: Biasini, 1781.

———. *Historia antigua de Mexico*. Mexico: Delfin, 1944.

———. *Historia de la antigua o Baja California*. Mexico: Porrúa, 1970.

Cobo, Bernabé. *Fundación de Lima*. Madrid: Atlas, 1956.

Cohen, Mark N. *The Food Crisis in Prehistory: Overpopulation and the Origins of Agriculture*. New Haven: Yale Univ. Press, 1977.

Commissioner for Indian Affairs. *Annual Report . . . for 1849*. Washington, D.C.: Gideon, 1850.

———. *Annual Report . . . for 1898*. House Doc. 5, Part I, 56th Cong., 1st Sess., 1899.

Connor, Jeanette Thurber, trans. *Pedro Menéndez de Avilés: Memorial by Gonzalo de Solis de Merás*. 1923. Reprint ed. Gainesville: Univ. of Florida Press, 1964.

———, trans. *Colonial Records of Spanish Florida*. Vol. 1. *1570—1577*. Deland: Florida State Historical Society, 1925.

Cook, Noble David. *Demographic Collapse: Indian Peru, 1520 – 1620*. Cambridge: Cambridge University Press, 1981.

Cook, Sherburne Friend. *The Extent and Significance of Disease among the In-*

dians of Baja California, 1697—1773. Ibero-Americana 12. Berkeley: Univ. of California Press, 1937.

———. "The Smallpox Epidemic of 1797 in Mexico." *Bull. of the Hist. of Medicine* 7 (1939):937 – 69.

———. *The Epidemic of 1830—1833 in California and Oregon*. Pub. in Amer. Archaeol. and Ethnol., 43. Berkeley: Univ. of California Press, 1955.

———. *The Aboriginal Population of the North Coast of California*. Anthropol. Records 16. Berkeley: Univ. of California Press, 1956.

Cook, Sherburne Friend, and Woodrow W. Borah. *The Indian Population of Central Mexico, 1531—1610*. Ibero-Americana 44. Berkeley: Univ. of California Press, 1960.

———. *Essays in Population History: Mexico and the Caribbean*. 3 vols. Berkeley: Univ. of California Press, 1971, 1974, 1979.

Cook, Sherburne Friend, and Leslie B. Simpson. *The Population of Central Mexico in the Sixteenth Century*. Ibero-Americana 31. Berkeley: Univ. of California Press, 1948.

Corbett, Julian S., ed. "The discourse and description of the voyage of Sir Francis Drake and Mr. Captain Frobiser set forward the 14th day of September, 1585." *Papers Relating to the Navy During the Spanish War 1585—1587*. London: Navy Records Society, 1898.

Corbett, Thomas G. "Population Structure in Hispanic St. Augustine, 1629 – 1763." *Fla. Hist. Quar.* 54 (1976):263 – 84.

Cotton, John. *God's Promise to His Plantations. Old South Leaflets*, 53. Boston: Directors of the Old South Work, 1896.

Covington, James W. "La Floride: 1565." *Fla. Hist. Quar.* 41 (1963):274 – 81.

———. "Relations between the Eastern Timucuan Indians and the French and Spanish, 1564 – 1567." In *Four Centuries of Southern Indians*, ed. Charles M. Hudson. Athens: Univ. of Georgia Press, 1975.

Cox, Jeff. "Companion Planting—For Harmony and Production." *Organic Gardening* 26 (1979):56, 58 – 60, 62, 64.

Coxe, Daniel. *A Description of the English Province of Carolana, By the Spaniards call'd Florida, and by the French La Louisiana*. 1722. Reprint ed. Gainesville: Univ. Presses of Florida, 1976.

Creighton, Charles. *A History of Epidemics in Britain*. Vol. I. *From* A.D. *664 to the Extinction of Plague*. Vol. II. *From the Extinction of Plague to the Present Time*. Cambridge: Cambridge Univ. Press, 1891, 1894.

Crosby, Alfred W., Jr. *The Columbian Exchange: Biological and Cultural Consequences of 1492*. Westport: Greenwood, 1972.

———. "Virgin Soil Epidemics as a Factor in the Aboriginal Depopulation in America." *William and Mary Quar.*, 3d ser., 33 (1976):289 – 99.

———. *Epidemic and Peace, 1918*. Westport: Greenwood, 1976.

Cutler, Hugh C. "Appendix D: Two Kinds of Gourds from Key Marco." In *The Material Culture of Key Marco, Florida*, by Marion Spjut Gilliland. Gainesville: Univ. Presses of Florida, 1975.

Cypert, Eugene. "The Effects of Fires in the Okefenokee Swamp in 1954 and 1955." *Amer. Midland Naturalist* 66 (1961):485 – 503.

Dacy, George H. "His Succulency, the Florida Oyster." *The Hollywood Magazine* 1 (1925):30 – 32.

Davenport, Harbert, trans. "The Expedition of Pánfilo de Narváez." *Southwestern Hist. Quar.* 27 (1924):217 – 41.

Deagan, Kathleen A. "Cultures in Transition: Fusion and Assimilation among the Eastern Timucua." In *Tacachale*, ed. J.T. Milanich and S. Proctor. Gainesville: Univ. Presses of Florida, 1978.

De Boyrie Moya, Emile, Marguerita K. Krestensen, and John M. Goggin. "Zamia Starch in Santo Domingo." *Fla. Anthropologist* 10 (1957):17 – 40.

de Bry, Theodore. *Brevis narratio eorum quae in Florida Americae* . . . Frankfurt: n.p., 1591.

de Laguna, Frederica. *Under Mount Saint Elias: The History and Culture of the Yakutat Tlingit*. Contrib. to Anthropol., 7. Washington, D.C.: Smithsonian Institution, 1972.

Delury, George E., ed. *The World Almanac & Book of Facts*. New York: Newspaper Enterprise, 1979.

Denevan, William M. *The Aboriginal Cultural Geography of the Llanos de Mojos of Bolivia*. Ibero-Americana 48. Berkeley: Univ. of California Press, 1966.

Denig, Edwin T. *Five Indian Tribes of the Upper Missouri*. Ed. John C. Ewers. Norman: Univ. of Oklahoma Press, 1961.

de Soto, Hernando. "Letter to the Municipal Authorities of St. Jago de Cuba." In *Letter of Hernando de Soto, and Memoir of Hernando de Escalante Fontaneda*, trans. Buckingham Smith. Washington: Privately printed, 1854. In *Historical Collections of Louisiana*, . . . , ed. by B.F. French. 2d ed. Philadelphia: Daniels & Smith, 1850, pp. 91 – 93.

Díaz del Castillo, Bernal. *The Discovery and Conquest of Mexico, 1517—1521*. Trans. A.P. Maudslay. 1908. Reprint ed. Farrar, Straus and Cudahy, 1956.

Dobyns, Henry F. "Indian Extinction in the Middle Santa Cruz River Valley, Arizona." *N. M. Hist. Rev.* (1963):163 – 81.

———. "An Outline of Andean Epidemic History to 1720." *Bull. of the Hist. of Medicine* 37 (1963):493 – 515.

———. "Estimating Aboriginal American Population: An Appraisal of Techniques with a New Hemispheric Estimate." *Current Anthropology* 7 (1966):395 – 416; "Reply," 440 – 44.

———. *Hualapai Indians. Vol. I. Prehistoric Indian Occupation Within the Eastern Area of the Yuman Complex: A Study in Applied Archaeology*. 3 vols. New York: Garland, 1974.

———. "Native American Publication of Cultural History." *Current Anthropology* 15 (1974):304 – 306.

———. "Altitude Sorting of Ethnic Groups in the Southwest." *Plateau* 47 (1974):42 – 48.

———. *Native American Historic Demography: A Critical Bibliography*. Bloomington: Indiana Univ. Press, Newberry Library Center for the History of the American Indian, 1976.

———. "Brief Perspective on a Scholarly Transformation: Widowing the 'Virgin' Land." *Ethnohistory* 23 (1976):95 – 104.

————. "Breves comentarios acerca de cierta ceguera cultural evidente en las investigaciones sobre horticultura indígena americana." In *Sonora: Antropología del desierto*, coord. Beatríz Braniff C. and Richard S. Felger. Colección Científica, 27. Mexico City: Instituto Nacional de Antropología e Historia, 1976.

————. "The Study of Spanish Colonial Frontier Institutions." In *Spanish Colonial Frontier Research*, ed. H.F. Dobyns. Albuquerque: Center for Anthropological Studies, 1980.

————. *From Fire to Flood: Historic Human Destruction of Sonoran Desert Riverine Oases*. Anthropol. Pap. 20. Socorro: Ballena, 1981.

Dobyns, Henry F., and Paul L. Doughty. *Peru: A Cultural History*. New York: Oxford Univ. Press, 1976.

Dobyns, Henry F., Paul H. Ezell, Alden W. Jones, and Greta S. Ezell. "Thematic Changes in Yuman Warfare." In *Cultural Stability and Cultural Change*. Proceedings of the 1957 Annual Spring Meeting. Seattle: American Ethnological Society, 1957.

Drake, Samuel A. *The Old Indian Chronicle*. Boston: Drake, 1867.

Duffy, John. "Smallpox and the Indians of the American Colonies." *Bull. of the Hist. of Medicine* 25 (1951):324–41.

————. *Epidemics in Colonial America*. Baton Rouge: Louisiana State Univ. Press 1953.

Dumond, Don E. "The Archaeology of Alaska and the Peopling of America." *Science* 209 (1980):984–91.

Eggan, Fred. "Social Anthropology and the Method of Controlled Comparison." *Amer. Anthropologist* 56 (1954):743–63.

Enciclopedia universal ilustrada Europeo-Americana. S.V. "Amaranto." Barcelona: José Espasa, n.d.

Ehrmann, W.W. "The Timucua Indians of Sixteenth Century Florida." *Fla. Hist. Quar.* 18 (1940):168–91.

Eisner, Thomas, and Stephen Nowicki. "Red Cochineal Dye (Carminic Acid): Its Role in Nature." *Science* 208 (1980):1039–42.

Elsasser, A.B. "Indians of Lower California." *Pacific Discovery* 30 (1977):7–13.

Erasmus, Charles J. *Man Takes Control: Cultural Development and American Aid*. Minneapolis: Univ. of Minnesota Press, 1963.

————. "Monument Building: Some Field Experiments." *Southwestern Jour. of Anthropology* 21 (1965):277–301.

Escalante Fontaneda, D. de. "Memoria." In *Colección de documentos inéditos relativos al descubrimiento, conquiesta y organización de las antiguas posesiones españoles de América y Oceania, sacados de los archivos del reino y muy especialmente del de Indias*, ed. Joaquín Pacheco y Francisco de Cárdenas. Madrid: Imp. Quirós, 1864–84, Tomo V, pp. 532–48. Buckingham Smith, Trans. *Letter of Hernando de Soto, and Memoir of Hernando de Escalante Fontaneda*. Washington, 1854, pp. 11–28. *Memoir of D. o d'Escalante Fontaneda, Respecting Florida, Written in Spain, About the Year 1575*, ed. David O. True. Miami: Univ. of Miami Press, Hist. Assoc. of Southern Florida, 1944; Coral Gables: Glade House, 1945. In *New American World*. Ed. David B. Quinn. New York:

Arno Press & Hector Bye, 1979, Vol. V. In *Historical Collections of Louisiana and Florida* . . . New York: Albert Mason, 1875.

E[scalante] y Arvizu, Manuel. Proclamation. Arizpe, Son. 2 de noviembre de 1833. Bancroft Library, Univ. of California, Berkeley.

Euler, Robert C., and Henry F. Dobyns. *The Hopi People*. Phoenix: Indian Tribal Series, 1971.

Ewel, Katherine Carter, and William J. Mitsch. "The Effects of Fire on Species Composition of Cypress Dome Ecosystems." *Fla. Scientist* 41 (1978):25 – 31.

Ewers, John C. "Symposium on the Concept of Ethnohistory—Comment." *Ethnohistory* 8 (1961):262 – 70.

———. "The Influence of Epidemics on the Indian Population and Cultures of Texas." *Plains Anthropologist* 18 (1973):104 – 15.

Fairbanks, George R. *The History and Antiquities of the City of St. Augustine, Florida, founded* A.D. *1565 comprising some of the most interesting portions of the early history of Florida*. 1858. Reprint ed. Gainesville: Univ. Presses of Florida, 1975.

Feest, Christian F. "North Carolina Algonquians." In *Northeast*, Volume 15. Ed. B.G. Trigger. In *Handbook of North American Indians*, Ed. W.C. Sturtevant. Washington, D.C.: Smithsonian Institution, 1978.

Fernandez de Oviedo, Gonzalo. *Historia general y natural de las Indias*. Vol. IV. Madrid: Atlas, 1959.

Fleming, Glen, Pierre Genelle, and Robert W. Long. *Wild Flowers of Florida*. Miami: Banyan, 1976.

Folan, William J., L.A. Fletcher, and E.R. Kintz. "Fruit, Fiber, Bark, and Resin: Social Organization of a Maya Urban Center." *Science* 204 (1979):697 – 701.

Fonda, John H. "Early Wisconsin." *Wisconsin Historical Collections*. Wisconsin 5. Madison: State Historical Society of Wicsonsin, 1868, 1907.

Forbes, James Grant. *Sketches, Historical and Topographical of the Floridas: More Particularly of East Florida*. 1821. Reprint ed. Gainesville: Univ. of Florida Press, 1964.

Franz, Richard, and Lea M. Franz. "Distribution, Habitat Preference and Status of Populations of the Black Creek Crayfish *Procumburus (Ortamannicus) Pictus* (Decapodai Cambaridae)." *Fla. Scientist* 42 (1979):13 – 17.

French, B.F., comp. *Historical Collections of Louisiana, Embracing Translations of Many Rare and Valuable Documents Relating to the Natural, Civil and Political History of that State*. Pt. 2. 2d ed. Philadelphia: Daniels and Smith, 1850.

———, comp. *Historical Collections of Louisiana and Florida, Including Translations of Original Manuscripts Relating to their Discovery and Settlement, with numerous historical and biographical notes*. N.S. New York: J. Sabin, 1869.

———, comp. *Historical Collections of Louisiana and Florida, Including Translations of Original Manuscripts Relating to their Discovery and Settlement, with Numerous Biographical Notes*. 2d ser. New York: Albert Mason, 1875.

Futer, Arthur A. "The Strickler Site." in *Susquehannock Miscellany*, ed. John Witthoft and W. Fred Kinsey. Harrisburg: Pennsylvania Historical and Museum Commission, 1959.

Gannon, Michael V. *The Cross in the Sand: The Early Catholic Church in Florida, 1513—1870.* Gainesville: Univ. of Florida Press, 1965.

García, Genaro. *El Clero de México durante la Dominación Española.* Mexico: Vda. de Ch. Bouret, 1907.

Geiger, Maynard. *The Franciscan Conquest of Florida (1573—1618).* Washington, D.C.: Catholic Univ. of America, 1937.

————. *Biographical Dictionary of the Franciscans in Spanish Florida and Cuba (1528—1841).* Patterson: St. Anthony Guild, 1940.

Gentry, Howard S. *Rio Mayo Plants.* Pub. 527. Washington, D.C.: Carnegie Institution, 1942.

Gerhard, Peter. *A Guide to the Historical Geography of New Spain.* Cambridge: Cambridge Univ. Press, 1972.

Gibson, Charles. *The Aztecs under Spanish Rule: A History of the Indians of the Valley of Mexico, 1519—1810.* Stanford: Stanford Univ. Press, 1964.

Gilbert, Carter R., ed. *Rare and Endangered Biota of Florida.* Volume Four. *Fishes.* Gainesville: Univ. Presses of Florida, State of Florida Game and Fresh Water Fish Commission, 1978.

Gilliland, Marion Spjut. *The Material Culture of Key Marco, Florida.* Gainesville: Univ. Presses of Florida, 1975.

Gipson, Lawrence H., ed. "The Moravian Indian Mission on White River . . ." *Indiana Historical Bur., Hist. Coll.* 23 (1938):3–674.

Giraud, Marcel. *A History of French Louisiana.* Vol. I. *The Reign of Louis XIV, 1698–1715,* trans. Joseph C. Lambert. Baton Rouge: Louisiana State Univ. Press, 1974.

Glisan, R. *Journal of Army Life.* San Francisco: Bancroft, 1874.

Goggin, John M. "The Tekesta Indians of Southern Florida." *Fla. Hist. Quar.* 18 (1940):274–84.

————. "Cultural Occupation at Goodland Point, Florida." *Fla. Anthropologist* 2 (1949):65–91.

————. "Fort Pupo: A Spanish Frontier Outpost." *Fla. Hist. Quar.* 30 (1951):139–92.

————. *Space and Time Perspective in Northern St. Johns Archeology, Florida.* Pub. in Anthropol., 47. New Haven: Yale Univ. Press, 1952.

————. "An Introductory Outline of Timucuan Archaeology." *Southeastern Archaeological Conf. Newsletter* 3 (1953):4–17.

Goggin, John M., and William C. Sturtevant. "The Calusa: A Stratified, Nonagricultural Society (with Notes on Sibling Marriage)." In *Explorations in Cultural Anthropology,* ed. Ward H. Goodenough. New York: McGraw-Hill, 1964.

Gold, Robert L. "The Settlement of the Pensacola Indians in New Spain, 1763–1770." *Hisp. Amer. Hist. Rev.* 45 (1965):567–76.

————. *Borderland Empires in Transition: The Triple-Nation Transfer of Florida.* Carbondale: Southern Illinois Univ. Press, 1969.

Goodwin, Thomas M. "Waterfowl Management Practices Employed in Florida and Their Effectiveness on Native and Migratory Waterfowl Populations." *Fla. Scientist* 42 (1979):123–29.

Greenland, D.J. "Bringing the Green Revolution to the Shifting Cultivator." *Science* 190 (1975):841 – 44.

Guerra y Sánchez, Ramiro. *Historia de la Nación Cubana*. Havana: Historia de la Nación Cubana, 1952.

Guillory, Vincent. "Species Assemblages of Fish in Lake Conway." *Fla. Scientist* 42 (1979):158 – 62.

Guthe, Carl E. *Pueblo Pottery Making: A Study at the Village of San Ildefonso*. New Haven: Yale Univ. Press, Phillips Academy, 1925.

Haag, William G. "A Prehistory of Mississippi." *Jour. of Miss. Hist.* 17 (1955):81 – 109.

Hackett, Charles W., ed. *Historical Documents Relating to New Mexico, Nueva Vizcaya, and Approaches Thereto, to 1773, Collected by Adolph F.A. Bandelier and Fanny R. Bandelier*. 3 vols. Washington, D.C.: Carnegie Institution, 1923 – 37.

————. *Revolt of the Pueblo Indians of New Mexico and Otermin's Attempted Reconquest, 1680 – 1682*. Trans. Charmion Clair Shelby. 2 vols. Albuquerque: Univ. of New Mexico Press, 1942.

Hakluyt, Richard. *The Discovery and Conquest of Terra Florida by Don Fernando de Soto and Six Hundred Spaniards His Followers Written by a Gentleman of Elvas, Employed in all the Action and translated out of Portuguese by Richard Hakluyt*. 1609. Reprint ed. New York: Franklin, n.d.

————. *The Principal Navigations, Voyages, Traffiques, & Discoveries of the English Nation*. Vol. IX. Glasgow: James MacLehose, 1904.

Hall, Clayton C., ed. *Narratives of Early Maryland, 1633 – 1684*. New York: Scribner's, 1910.

Hall, Sharlot M. "The Story of a Pima Record Rod." *Out West* 26:5 (May 1907):413 – 23.

Hallenbeck, Cleve. *Alvar Núñez Cabeza de Vaca: The Journey and Route of the First European to Cross the Continent of North America, 1534 – 1546*. Glendale: Clark, 1940.

Harlow, Richard F. "Fall and Winter Foods of Florida White-tailed Deer." *Quar. Jour. of the Fla. Acad. of Sciences* 24 (1961):19 – 38.

Harris, Jack S. "The White Knife Shoshoni of Nevada." In *Acculturation in Seven American Indian Tribes*, ed. Ralph Linton. New York: Appleton-Century, 1940.

Hawley, Amos H. *Human Ecology: A Theory of Community Structure*. New York: Ronald, 1950.

Hedrick, Basil C., and Carroll L. Riley, eds. and trans. *The Journey of the Vaca Party*. Museum Research Records, 2. Carbondale: Southern Illinois Univ., 1974.

Heisey, Henry W., and J. Paul Witmer. "Of Historic Susquehannock Cemeteries." *Penna. Archaeologist* 32 (1962):99 – 130.

Heizer, Robert F. "The Direct-Historical Approach in California Archaeology." *Amer. Antiquity* 7 (1941):98 – 122.

Helm, June. "female infanticide, European diseases, and population levels among the Mackenzie Dene." *Amer. Ethnologist* 7 (1980):259 – 85.

Henderson, Randall. "Guadalupe Canyon in Lower California." *Desert Magazine* 9 (1946):4–8.

———. "La Mora Canyon in Baja California." *Desert Magazine* 13 (1950):4–8.

———. "We Camped with the Pai-Pais." *Desert Magazine* 14 (1951):8–11.

Herald, Earl S., and Roy R. Strickland. "An Annotated List of the Fishes of Homosassa Springs, Florida." *Quar. Jour. of the Fla. Acad. of Sciences* 11 (1949):99–109.

Hernandez Xolocotzi, Efraim. *Maize Granaries in Mexico*. Leaflet 13. Cambridge, Mass.: Harvard Univ. Botanical Museum, 1949.

Herrera y Tordesillas, Antonio de. *Historia general de los hechos de los Castellanos en las islas, y tierra-firme en el Mar Oceano*. Asunción: n.p., 1945.

Hirth, David H., and Wayne R. Marion. "Bird Communities of a South Florida Flatwoods." *Fla. Scientist* 42 (1979):142–51.

Hoebel, E. Adamson. *The Law of Primitive Man: A Study in Comparative Legal Dynamics*. Cambridge, Mass.: Harvard Univ. Press, 1954.

Holmes, Maurice G. *New Spain to the Californias by Sea, 1519–1668*. Glendale: Clark, 1963.

Horsman, Reginald. "Recent Trends and New Directions in Native American History." In *The American West: New Perspectives, New Dimensions*, ed. J.O. Steffen. Norman: Univ. of Oklahoma Press, 1979.

Hosmer, J.K., ed. *Winthrop's Journal "History of New England," 1630–1649*. New York: Scribner's, 1908.

Howard, James H. *The Ponca Tribe*. Bull. 195. Washington, D.C.: Bureau of American Ethnology, 1965.

Hubbard, William. *A Narrative of the Troubles with the Indians in New England from the First Planting Thereof in the Year 1607 to this Present Year 1677, But Chiefly of the Late Troubles in the Last Years 1675, and 1676, to which is added a Discourse about the Warre with the Pequods in the Year 1637*. London: Thomas Parkhurst; Boston: John Foster, 1677.

Hubbs, Carl L., and E. Ross Allen. "Fishes of Silver Springs, Florida." *Proceedings of the Fla. Acad. of Sciences* 6 (1943):110–30.

Hudson, Charles. *The Southeastern Indians*. Knoxville: Univ. of Tennessee Press, 1976.

Hulton, Paul ed. *The Work of Jacques Le Moyne de Morgues, a Huguenot Artist in France, Florida, and England*. London: British Museum, 1977.

———. "Images of the New World: Jacques Le Moyne de Morgues and John White." In *The Westward Enterprise*, ed. K.R. Andrews, N.P. Canny, and P.E.H. Hair. Detroit: Wayne State Univ. Press, 1979.

Hyde, George E. *Pawnee Indians*. Denver: Univ. of Denver Press, 1951.

Jacobs, Wilbur R. *Dispossessing the American Indian: Indians and Whites on the Colonial Frontier*. New York: Scribner's, 1972.

———. "The Tip of an Iceberg: Pre-Columbian Indian Demography and Some Implications for Revisionism." *William and Mary Quarterly*, 3d ser., 31 (1974):123–32.

Jameson, J. Franklin, ed. *Narratives of New Netherland, 1609–1664*. New York: Scribner's, 1909.

Jenkins, Kathleen. *Montreal: Island City of the St. Lawrence*. Garden City: Doubleday, 1966.

Jenks, Albert E. "The Wild Rice Gatherers of the Upper Lakes: A Study in American Primitive Economics." In *Nineteenth Annual Report of the Bureau of American Ethnology, 1897–98*. Pt. 2. Washington, D.C.: USGPO, 1900.

Jennings, Francis. *The Invasion of America: Indians, Colonialism, and the Cant of Conquest*. Chapel Hill: Univ. of North Carolina Press, Institute of Early American History and Culture, 1975.

Jones, B. Calvin. "Spanish Mission Sites Located and Test Excavated." *Archives & History News* 3 (1972):1–2.

Jones, Oakah L. *Pueblo Warriors and Spanish Conquest*. Norman: Univ. of Oklahoma Press, 1966.

Karns, Harry J., and Associates, trans. *Unknown Arizona and Sonora, 1693–1721: Luz de Tierra Incognita by Captain Juan Mateo Manje*. Tucson: Arizona Silhouettes, 1954.

Kearney, Thomas H., and Robert H. Peebles. *Flowering Plants and Ferns of Arizona*. Misc. Pub. 423. Washington, D.C.: U.S. Dept. of Agriculture, 1942.

Kerrigan, Anthony, trans. *Barcia's Chronological History of the Continent of Florida*. Gainesville: Univ. of Florida Press, 1951.

———, trans. *Pedro Menéndez de Avilés, Founder of Florida, Written by Bartolomé Barrientos*. Gainesville: Univ. of Florida Press, 1965.

Kessell, John L. *Kiva, Cross, and Crown: The Pecos Indians and New Mexico, 1540–1840*. Washington, D.C.: National Park Service, 1979.

Kilby, John D., and David K. Caldwell. "A List of Fishes from the Southern Tip of the Florida Peninsula." *Quar. Jour. of the Fla. Acad. of Sciences* 18 (1955):195–206.

Kimball, Solon T., and Marion Pearsall. "Event Analysis as an Approach to Community Study." *Social Forces* 34 (1955):58–63.

Kingsbury, Susan Myra, ed. *The Records of the Virginia Company of London*. Vol. III. Washington, D.C.: USGPO, 1933.

Kluckhohn, Clyde, and Dorothea C. Leighton. *The Navaho*. Cambridge, Mass.: Harvard Univ. Press, 1948.

Krech, Shepard, III. "disease, starvation, and Northern Athapaskan social organization." *Amer. Ethnologist* 5 (1978):710–32.

Kroeber, Alfred L. *Cultural and Natural Areas of Native North America*. Pub. in Amer. Archaeol. and Ethnol., 38. Berkeley: Univ. of California Press, 1939.

———. "Nature of the Land-Holding Group." *Ethnohistory* 3 (1955):303–14.

———. *Mohave Indians: Report on Aboriginal Territory and Occupancy of the Mohave Tribe*. New York: Garland, 1974.

Kurz, Herman, and Robert K. Godfrey. *Trees of Northern Florida*. Gainesville: Univ. of Florida Press, 1962.

Kushlan, James A., and Thomas E. Lodge. "Ecological and Distributional Notes on the Freshwater Fish of Southern Florida." *Fla. Scientist* 37 (1974):110–28.

Laessle, Albert M. "A Study of Quail Food Habits in Peninsular Florida." *Quar. Jour. of the Fla. Acad. of Sciences* 7 (1944):155–71.

Larson, Lewis H., Jr. "Functional Considerations of Warfare in the Southeast during the Mississippi Period." *American Antiquity* 37:3 (July 1972):383–92.

———. *Aboriginal Subsistence Technology on the Southeastern Coastal Plain during the Late Prehistoric Period*. Gainesville: Univ. Presses of Florida, 1980.

Las Casas, Bartolomé de. *The Devastation of the Indies: A Brief Account* . . . trans. Herma Briffault. New York: Seabury, 1974.

Lastres, Juan B. *Historia de la Medicina Peruana*. Vol. III. *La Medicina in la República*. Lima: Universidad Nacional Mayor de San Marcos, 1951.

Laudonnière, René. *Three Voyages*. Trans. Charles E. Bennett. Gainesville: Univ. Presses of Florida, 1975.

Lawson, Publius V. *History, Winnebago County, Wisconsin*. Chicago: Cooper, 1908.

Layne, James N., and Bette S. Johns. "Present Status of the Beaver in Florida." *Quar. Jour. of the Fla. Acad. of Sciences* 28 (1965):212–30.

Le Baron, William. *The History of Will County, Illinois*. Chicago: By the author, 1878.

Lefèvre, Edouard. *La grande encyclopédie*. S. V. "Amarante." Paris: Lamirault, n.d.

Leikind, Morris E. "Colonial Epidemic Diseases." *Ciba Symposia* 1 (1940):372–78.

León, Alonso de. *Historia de Nuevo León con noticias sobre Coahuila, Tejas, Nuevo México*. Mexico: Documentos inéditos ó Muy Raros para la Historia de México publicados por Genero García, 1909. Tomo 25.

Leonard, Irving A., trans. *Spanish Approach to Pensacola, 1689–1698*. Vol. IX. Albuquerque: Quivira Society, 1939.

Le Page du Pratz, M. *Histoire de la Louisiana contenant la decouverte de ce vaste pays; sa description geographique; un voyage dans les terres, l'histoire naturelle, les moeurs, coutumes & religion des naturels, avec leurs origines; deux voyages dans le nord du nouveau Mexique, dont un jusqu'a la mer du Sud* . . . Paris: De Bure, 1758. *The History of Louisiana, or of the Western Parts of Virginia and Carolina; containing a description of the countries that lie on both sides of the river Mississippi; with an account of the settlements, inhabitants, soil, climate and products*. Ed. Joseph G. Tregle, Jr. 1774. Reprint ed. Baton Rouge: Louisiana State Univ. Press, Louisiana American Revolution Bicentennial Commission, 1975.

Lewis, Clifford M. "The Calusa." In *Tacachale*, ed. J.T. Milanich and S. Proctor. Gainesville: Univ. Presses of Florida, 1978.

Lewis, Clifford M., and Albert J. Loomie. *The Spanish Jesuit Mission in Virginia, 1570–1572*. Chapel Hill: Virginia Historical Society, 1953.

Lewis, Henry T. *Patterns of Indian Burning in California: Ecology and Ethnohistory*. Anthropol. Pap. 1. Ramona: Ballena, 1973.

Limp, W. Frederick, and Van A. Reidhead. "An Economic Evaluation of the Potential of Fish Utilization in Riverine Environments." *Amer. Antiquity* 44 (1979):70–78.

Lindsay, George E. "Sea of Cortez Expedition of the California Academy of Sciences June 20–July 4, 1964." *Proceedings of the Calif. Acad. of Sciences*, 4th ser., 30 (1964):211–42.

Lischka, Joseph J., and Payson D. Sheets. "Comment." *Current Anthropology* 21 (1980):740.

Lockhart, James. *The Men of Cajamarca: A Social and Biographical Study of the First Conquerors of Peru*. Austin: Univ. of Texas Press, 1972.

Long, Robert W. "The Vegetation of Southern Florida." *Fla. Scientist* 37 (1974):33–45.

López de Santa Anna, Antonio. *Mi historia militar y política, 1810–1874: Memorias inéditas*. Mexico: Vda. de Ch. Bouret, 1905.

López de Velasco, Juan. *Geografía y descripción Universal de las Indias recopilada por el Cosmógrafo-Cronista Juan Lopez de Velasco desde el año de 1571 al de 1574*. Madrid: Fortanet, 1894.

Lorant, Stefan, ed. *The New World: The First Pictures of America*. New York: Duell, Sloan and Pearce, 1946.

Lowery, Woodbury. *The Spanish Settlements within the Present Limits of the United States, 1513–1561*. 2 vols. 1905. Reprint ed. New York: Russell and Russell, 1959.

Lumholtz, Carl S. *Unknown Mexico*. New York: Scribner's, 1902, 2 vol.

———. *New Trails in Mexico*. New York: Scribner's, 1912.

McBryde, F. Webster. "Influenza in America during the Sixteenth Century (Guatemala: 1523, 1559–1562, 1576)." *Bull. of the Hist. of Medicine* 8 (1940):296–302.

MacCauley, Clay. "The Seminole Indians of Florida." In *Fifth Annual Report of the Bureau of Ethnology, 1883–84*. Washington, D.C.: USGPO, 1887.

McDiarmid, Roy W., ed. *Rare and Endangered Biota of Florida*. Vol. Three. *Amphibians and Reptiles*. Gainesville: Univ. Presses of Fla., State of Florida Game and Fresh Water Fish Commission, 1978.

McGee, W.J. "The Siouan Indians." In *Fifteenth Annual Report of the Bureau of American Ethnology, 1893–94*. Washington, D.C.: USGPO, 1897.

MacLeod, William C. *The American Indian Frontier*. New York: Knopf, 1928.

McNeill, William H. *Plagues and Peoples*. Garden City: Doubleday/Anchor, 1976.

Mahon, John K. *History of the Second Seminole War*. Gainesville: Univ. of Florida Press, 1967.

Mallery, Garrick. "A Calendar of the Dakota Nation." *Bull. U.S. Geol. and Geogr. Survey of the Territories* 3 (1877):1–25.

Malone, James H. *The Chickasaw Nation: A Short Sketch of a Noble People*. Louisville: Morton, 1922.

Malthus, Thomas. "A Summary View of the Principle of Population." In *Three Essays on Population*. New York: Mentor, 1960.

Markham, Clements R., ed. *The Hawkins's Voyages during the Reigns of Henry VIII, Queen Elizabeth, and James I*. No. 57. London: Hakluyt Society, 1878.

Martin, Calvin. "Wildlife Diseases as a Factor in the Depopulation of the North American Indian." *Western Hist. Quar.* 7 (1976):47–62.

Masering, Catherine H. "Carrying Capacities and Low Population Growth." *Jour. of Anthropological Research* 33 (1977):474–92.

May, Jacques M. *The Ecology of Human Disease*. New York: MD, 1958.

Meeker, Darcy. "Florida-Based Woodstork Nears Endangered Status." *Gaines-ville Sun,* October 21, 1980.

Mellor, John W., Thomas F. Weaver, Uma J. Lele, and Sheldon R. Simon. *Developing Rural India.* Ithaca: Cornell Univ. Press, 1968.

Mendieta, Gerónimo de. *Historia eclesiástica indiana.* Mexico: Salvador Chavez Hayhoe, 1945.

Michigan Pioneer and Historical Society. *Hist. Coll.,* vol. XX. Lansing: By the author, 1892.

Milanich, Jerald T. "Excavations at the Richardson Site, Alachua County, Florida: An Early 17th Century Potano Indian Village (with Notes on Potano Culture Change)." *Bureau of Hist. Sites and Properties Bull.* 2. Tallahassee: Florida Dept. of State, Div. of Archives, History and Records Management, 1972.

————. "The Western Timucua: Patterns of Acculturation and Change." In *Tacachale,* ed. J.T. Milanich and S. Proctor. Gainesville: Univ. Presses of Florida, 1978.

Milanich, Jerald T., and Charles H. Fairbanks. *Florida Archaeology.* New York: Academic, 1980.

Milanich, Jerald T., and Samuel Proctor, eds. *Tacachale: Essays on the Indians of Florida and Southeastern Georgia during the Historic Period.* Gainesville: Univ. Presses of Florida, 1978.

Milanich, Jerald T., and William C. Sturtevant, eds. *Francisco Pareja's 1613 Confes-sionario: A Documentary Source for Timucuan Ethnography.* Trans. Emilio F. Moran. Tallahassee: Florida Dept. of State, Div. of Archives, History, and Records Management, 1972.

Milner, G.R. "Epidemic Disease in the Post-Contact Southeast: A Reappraisal." *Mid-Continent Jour. of Archaeology* 5 (1980):39–56.

Mohave County Miner (Kingman, Arizona Territory). 1887.

Moody, Harold L. "Adult Fish Populations by Haul Seine in Seven Florida Lakes." *Quar. Jour. of the Fla. Acad. of Sciences* 17 (1954):147–67.

————. "Exploited Fish Populations of the St. Johns River, Florida." *Quar. Jour. of the Fla. Acad. of Sciences* 24 (1961):1–18.

Mooney, James. "The Ghost Dance Religion and the Sioux Outbreak of 1890." In *Fourteenth Annual Report of the Bureau of American Ethnology, 1892–93.* Pt. 2. Washington, D.C.: USGPO, 1896.

————. "Calendar History of the Kiowa Indians." In *Seventeenth Annual Report of the Bureau of American Ethnology, 1895/96.* Washington, D.C.: USGPO, 1898.

————. *The Aboriginal Population of America North of Mexico.* Misc. Coll., vol. LXXX. Washington, D.C.: Smithsonian Institution, 1928.

Moore, Joseph C. "The Range of the Florida Manatee." *Quar. Jour. of the Fla. Acad. of Sciences* 14 (1951):1–19.

Moreno Ponce de León, Fray Pedro. Memorial. 7 de setiembre de 1651. Archivo General de Indias, 54-5-20. P. K. Yonge Library, Univ. of Florida, Gainesville.

Morey, Nancy C., and Robert V. Morey. "Foragers and Farmers: Differential Consequences of Spanish Contact." *Ethnohistory* 20 (1973):229–46.

Morris, Allen, comp. *The Florida Handbook, 1973 – 1974.* Tallahassee: Peninsular, 1973.

Mosher, A.T. *Getting Agriculture Moving: Essentials for Development and Modernization.* New York: Praeger, Agricultural Development Council, 1966.

Mozingo, Hugh Nelson. "A Vegetative Key to the Native and Commonly Cultivated Palms in Florida." *Quar. Jour. of the Fla. Acad. of Sciences* 17 (1954):46 – 54.

Murdock, George P. "World Ethnographic Sample." *Amer. Anthropologist* 59 (1957):664 – 87.

Murdock, George P., and Caterina Provost. "Measurement of Cultural Complexity." *Ethnology* 12 (1973):379 – 92.

Murphy, Christopher, and Charles Hudson. "On the Problem of Intensive Agriculture in the Aboriginal Southeastern United States." *Working Papers in Sociology and Anthropology.* Athens: Univ. of Ga. 2 (1968):24 – 34.

Murrill, William A. "Florida Hickories." *Quar. Jour. of the Fla. Acad. of Sciences* 9 (1946):115 – 22.

Nasatir, A.P., ed. and trans. "An Account of Spanish Louisiana, 1785." *Mo. Hist. Rev.* 24 (1930):521 – 36.

National Society of Colonial Dames of America. *Turn Left at the Plaza: A History and Tour Guide of St. Augustine and Coastal Northeast Florida.* St. Augustine: Society and Bicentennial Commission of Florida, 1976.

Neill, Wilfred T. "An Indian and Spanish Site on Tampa Bay, Florida." *Fla. Anthropologist* 21 (1968):106 – 16.

Nevile, Ella J., Sara G. Martin, and Deborah B. Martin. *Historic Green Bay: 1634 – 1840.* Green Bay: By the authors, 1893.

Newcomb, William W., Jr. *The Culture and Acculturation of the Delaware Indians.* Museum Pap. 10. Ann Arbor: Univ. of Michigan, Museum of Anthropology, 1956.

Norris, Robert A., and David W. Johnston. "Weight and Weight Variations in Summer Birds from Georgia and South Carolina." *Wilson Bull.* 70 (1958):114 – 29.

O'Callaghan, E.B., ed. *Documents Relative to the Colonial History of the State of New York.* Vol. IX. Albany: Weed, Parsons, 1855.

O'Connor, Thomas F. "Narratives of a Missionary Journey to New Mexico in 1867." *Mid-America*, n.s. 8 (1937):63 – 67.

O'Daniel, V.F. *Dominicans in Early Florida.* Monograph ser. 12. New York: U.S. Catholic Historical Society, 1930.

Onadera, Takasaki, A.B. Jenson, Ji-Won Yoon, and A.L. Notkins. "Virus-Induced Diabetes Mellitus: Reo-virus Infection of Pancreatic Cells in Mice." *Science* 201 (1978):529 – 31.

Opler, Morris E. "Themes as Dynamic Forces in Culture." *Amer. Jour. of Sociology* 51 (1945):198 – 206.

Orians, Gordon H., and Nolan E. Pearson. "On the Theory of Central Place Foraging." In *Analysis of Ecological Systems*, ed. D.J. Horn, G.R. Stairs, and R.D. Mitchell. Columbus: Ohio State Univ. Press, 1979.

Osborn, Allan. "Comment." *Current Anthropology* 21 (1980):740.

Pacheco, Joaquín, and Francisco de Cárdenas, eds. *Collección de documentos inéditos relativos al descubrimiento, conquista y colonización de las posesiones españolas en América y Oceania*. Vol. I. Madrid: Quirós, 1864.

Pareja, Francisco, Lorenzo Martínez, Pedro Ruíz, Alonso Desquera, Juan de la Cruz, Francisco Moreno de Jesús, and Bartolomé Romero. Oficio. 17 de Enero de 1617. Archivo General de Indias, Simancas, Eclesiástico, Aud. de Santo Domingo, 54-5-20. P. K. Yonge Library, Univ. of Florida, Gainesville.

Parsons, James J., and William M. Denevan. "Pre-Columbian Ridged Fields." *Scientific American* 217 (1967):92–100.

Payne, E.H., L. Gonzales Mugaburu, and E.M. Schleicher. "An Intestinal Parasite Survey in the High Cordilleras of Peru." *Amer. Jour. of Tropical Medicine and Hygiene* 5 (1956):696–98.

Pearson, Fred L. "Spanish-Indian Relations in Florida, 1602–1675: Some Aspects of Selected Visitas." *Fla. Hist. Quar.* 52 (1974):261–73.

Perceval, John. *The Journal of the Earl of Egmont*. Ed. Robert G. McPherson. Athens: Univ. of Georgia Press, 1962.

Petersen, William. *Population*. New York: Macmillan, 1961.

Polo T., José. "Apuntes sobre las epidemias en el Perú." *Revista Histórica* (Lima) 5 (1913):50–109.

Porras Barrenechea, Raúl. *Cartas del Perú (1524–1543): Colección de documentos inéditos para la historia del Perú*. Vol. III. Lima: Bibliófilos Peruanos, 1959.

Porter, Robert P., supt. *Compendium of the Elventh Census: 1890. Part I—Population*. Washington, D.C.: Dept. of the Interior, Census Office, 1892.

Portlock, Nathaniel. *A Voyage Round the World . . .* London: Stockdale and Boulding, 1789.

Powell, Philip W. *Soldiers, Indians, and Silver: The Northward Advance of New Spain, 1550–1600*. Berkeley: Univ. of California Press, 1952.

Praus, Alexis. *The Sioux, 1798–1922: A Dakota Winter Count*. Bull. 44. Bloomfield Hills: Cranbrook Institute of Science, 1962.

Priestley, Herbert I., trans. and ed. *The Luna Papers*. Deland: Florida State Historical Society, 1928.

Prine, Nathaniel. *A History of Long Island, from its First Settlement by Europeans, to the Year 1845, with special reference to its ecclesiastical concerns*. New York: Carter, 1845.

Pritchard, Peter C. H. "Florida Palms." *Fla. Naturalist* 51 (1978):12–25.

Quebbeman, Frances E. *Medicine in Territorial Arizona*. Phoenix: Arizona Historical Foundation, 1966.

Quinn, David B., ed. *The Roanoke Voyages, 1584–1590*. 2 vols. London: Hakluyt Society, 1955.

———, ed. *New American World*. Vol. I. *America from Concept to Discovery. Early Exploration of North America*. Vol. V. *The Extension of Settlement in Florida, Virginia, and the Spanish Southwest*. New York: Arno Press, Hector Bye, 1979.

Rau, Charles, trans. "An Account of the Aboriginal Inhabitants of the California Peninsula as Given by Jacob Baegert, a German Jesuit Missionary, . . ." *Annual Report of the Board of Regents of the Smithsonian Institution for the Year 1863. Ann. Report . . . 1864*. Washington, D.C.: USGPO, 1872.

Rebel, Thomas P. *Sea Turtles and the Turtle Industry of the West Indies, Florida and the Gulf of Mexico*. Rev. ed. Coral Gables: Univ. of Miami Press, 1974.

Redfield, Robert, Ralph Linton, and Melville J. Herskovits. "A Memorandum for the Study of Acculturation." *Amer. Anthropologist* 38 (1935):149 – 52.

Redfield, Robert, and Alfonso Villa Rojas. *Chan Kom: A Maya Village*. 1934. Reprint ed. Chicago: Univ. of Chicago Press, 1962.

Reid, George K. "The Fishes of Orange Lake, Florida." *Quar. Jour. of the Fla. Acad. of Sciences* 12 (1950):173 – 83.

Ribaut, Jean. *The Whole & True Discouerye of Terra Florida*. London: Rouland Hall for Thomas Hackett, 1563. (Deland: Fla. St. Hist. Soc. Pub. No. 7, 1927, Notes by H. P. Biggar; Biography by Jeannette Thurber Connor. Gainesville: Univ. of Fla. Press, 1964). Facsimile.

Rich, E.E., ed. *The Letters of John McLoughlin from Fort Vancouver*. Toronto: Champlain Society, 1941.

Richards, Cara E. *The Oneida People*. Phoenix: Indian Tribal Series, 1974.

Roberts, William. *An Account of the First Discovery and Natural History of Florida*. 1763. Reprint ed. Gainesville: Univ. Presses of Florida, 1976.

Robertson, James A., trans. *True Relation of the Hardships Suffered by Governor Fernando de Soto & Certain Portuguese Gentlemen During the Discovery of the Province of Florida. Now Newly Set forth by a Gentleman of Elvas*. Deland: Florida State Historical Society, 1932, Vol. I Facsimile; 1933, Vol. II Translation.

Rogers, Woodes. *A Cruising Voyage Around the World, first to the South Seas, thence to the East Indies and Homeward by the Cape of Good Hope*. 1712. Reprint ed. New York: Dover, 1970.

Romans, Bernard. *A Concise Natural History of East and West Florida, containing an account of the natural produce of all the southern part of British America in the three kingdoms of nature, particularly the animal and vegetable . . .* 1775. Reprint ed. Gainesville: Univ. of Florida Press, 1962.

Rostlund, Erhard. "The Geographic Range of the Historic Bison in the Southeast." *Annals of the Assoc. of Amer. Geographers* 50 (1960):395 – 407.

Rousell, Romain. *Les pèlerinages à travers les siècles*. Paris: Payot, 1954.

Rowland, Dunbar, and A.G. Sanders, eds. *Mississippi Provincial Archives, 1704 – 1743: French Dominion*. Vols. II and III. Jackson: Press of the Mississippi Dept. of Archives and History, 1929, 1932.

Ruidíaz y Caravia, Eugenio, ed. *La Florida: Su conquista y colonización por Pedro Menéndez de Avilés*. 2 vols. Madrid: J.A. García, 1893 – 94.

Ruíz de Salazar, Benito. Oficio. San Agustín, 14 de julio de 1650. Archivo General de Indias, Aud. de Santo Domingo, 54-5-10. P. K. Yonge Library, Univ. of Florida.

Russell, Frank. "The Pima Indians." In *Twenty-sixth Annual Report of the Bureau of American Ethnology, 1904 – 05*. Washington, D.C.: USGPO, 1908.

Safford, William E. "A Forgotten Cereal of Ancient America." *Nineteenth International Congress of Americanists, Proceedings*. Washington: By the Congress, 1917.

Sahagun, Bernardino de. *Historia de las cosas de Nueva España*. Mexico: Alfa, 1955.

————. *1547–1577: A History of Ancient Mexico*. Trans. Fanny R. Bandelier. Nashville: Fisk Univ. Press, 1932.

Sales, Luís. *Observations on California, 1772–1790*. Trans. Charles N. Rudkin. Los Angeles: Glen Dawson, 1956.

Saloman, Carl H., and Steven P. Naughton. "Fishes of the Littoral Zone, Pinellas County, Florida." *Fla. Scientist* 42 (1979):85–93.

Sauer, Carl O. *Aboriginal Population of Northwestern Mexico*. Ibero-Americana 10. Berkeley: Univ. of California Press, 1935.

————. "Cultivated Plants of South and Central America." In *Handbook of South American Indians*, vol. VI, *Physical Anthropology, Linguistics, and Cultural Geography of South American Indians*. Bull. 143. Washington: Bureau of American Ethnology, 1949.

————. *The Early Spanish Main*. Berkeley: Univ. of California Press, 1966.

————. *Sixteenth Century North America*. Berkeley: Univ. of California Press, 1971.

Sauer, Jonathan D. "The Grain Amaranths: A Survey of Their History and Classification." *Annals of the Mo. Botanical Garden* 37 (1950):561–632.

————. "The Grain Amaranths and Their Relatives: A Revised Taxonomic and Geographic Survey." *Annals of the Mo. Botanical Garden* 54 (1967):103–37.

Schell, Rolfe F. *De Soto Didn't Land at Tampa*. Ft. Myers Beach: Island, 1966.

Schemnitz, Sanford D. "Populations of Bear, Panther, Alligator, and Deer in the Florida Everglades." *Fla. Scientist* 37 (1974):157–67.

Schendel, Gordon, José Alvarez Amezquita, and Miguel E. Bustamante. *Medicine in Mexico: From Aztec Herbs to Betatrons*. Austin: Univ. of Texas Press, 1969.

Schlesier, Karl H. "Epidemics and Indian Middlemen: Rethinking the Wars of the Iroquois, 1609–1653." *Ethnohistory* 23 (1976):129–45.

Schoolcraft, Henry F. *Information Respecting the History, Condition and Prospects of the Indian Tribes of the United States, collected and prepared under the Bureau of Indian Affairs*. 6 vols. Philadelphia: Lippincott, 1853–60.

Sears, Elsie, and William Sears. "Preliminary Report on Prehistoric Corn Pollen from Fort Center, Florida." *Southeastern Archaeological Conf. Bull.* 19 (1976):53–56.

Secoy, Frank R. *Changing Military Patterns on the Great Plains*. Monograph 21. Locust Valley, N.Y.: Augustin, American Ethnological Society, 1953.

Segal, Charles M., and David C. Stineback. *Puritans, Indians, and Manifest Destiny*. New York: Putnam's, 1977.

Shea, John Gilmary, ed. *Early Voyages Up and Down the Mississippi, by Cavelier, St. Cosme, Le Suer, Gravier, and Guignas*. Albany: Munsell, 1861.

Sheehan, Bernard. *Savagism and Civility: Indians and Englishmen in Colonial Virginia*. Cambridge: Cambridge Univ. Press, 1980.

Shelvocke, George. *A Voyage Round the World by Way of the Great South Sea, perform'd in the Years 1719, 20, 21, 22 in the Speedwell of London, of 24 Guns and 100 Men, . . .* London: Senex, 1726.

Sheridan, Thomas E., and Thomas H. Naylor, eds. and trans. *Rarámuri: A Tarahumara Chronicle, 1607–1791*. Flagstaff: Northland, 1979.

Sherman, H.B. "List of the Recent Wild Land Mammals of Florida." *Proceedings of the Fla. Acad. of Sciences* 1 (1936):102−28.

———. "The Occurrence of Bison in Florida." *Quar. Jour. of the Fla. Acad. of Sciences* 17 (1954) 228−32.

Shipek, Florence C. *A Strategy for Change: The Luiseño of Southern California.* Ph.D. Diss. Univ. of Hawaii, Honolulu, 1977.

Sibley, John. "Historical Sketches of the Several Indian Tribes in Louisiana, South of the Arkansas River, and between the Mississippi and river Grande." *Amer. State Papers. Class II. Indian Affairs. Doc. Legislative and Exec. of the Congr. of the U.S., from the First Sess. of the First to the Third Sess. of the Thirteenth.* Vol. IV. Washington: Gales and Seaton, 1832.

Siguenza y Góngara, Carlos de. *Documentos inéditos de . . . , La Real Universidad de México y . . . el reconocimiento de la Bahía de Santa María de Galve.* Comp. Irving A. Leonard. Mexico: Juan de Eguiara y Eguren, 1963.

Silverio Sainza, Nicasio. *Cuba y la casa de Austria.* Miami: Universal, 1972.

Sims, Harold W., Jr. "Large Quahog Clams from Boca Ciega Bay." *Quar. Jour. of the Fla. Acad. of Sciences* 27 (1964):348.

Singer, Steve, John P. Holdren, Paul R. Ehrlich, Anne H. Ehrlich, John Harte, John M. Street, Gary A. Fuller, and Bruce Currey. "Bad News: Is It True?" *Science* 210 (1980):1296−1303.

Sleight, Frederick. "Kunti, A Food Staple of Florida Indians." *Fla. Anthropologist* 6 (1953):46−52.

Smith, Buckingham, trans. *Letter of Hernando de Soto, and Memoir of Hernando de Escalante Fontaneda.* Washington, D.C.: Privately printed, 1854.

———, comp. *Colección de Varios Documentos para la Historia de la Florida y Tierras Adyacentes.* London: Trubner, 1857.

———, trans. *Narratives of De Soto in the Conquest of Florida, as told by a Gentleman of Elvas . . .* Gainesville: Palmetto, 1968.

Smith, Hale G. "The Ethnological and Archaeological Significance of Zamia." *Amer. Anthropologist* 53 (1951):238−44.

Smith, John. *The Generall Historie of Virginia, New England, and the Summer Isles with the names of the Adventurers, Planters, and Governours from their first beginning An: 1584 to this present 1624 . . . 1624.* Reprint ed. New York: Readex Microprint, 1966.

Solís de Merás, Gonzalo. "Memorial, 1567." In *La Florida . . .* , ed. Eugenio Ruidíaz y Caravia. 2 vols. Madrid: J. A. García, 1893−94.

Sparke, John, Jr. "The Voyage made by the worshipful M. Iohn Haukins, Esquire, now Knight, Captain of the Iesus of Lubeck, one of her Majesties shippes, and Generall of the Solomon, and her two barkes going in his companie to the coast of Guinea, and the Indies of Noua Spania . . ." In *The Hawkins's Voyages during the Reigns of Henry VIII, Queen Elizabeth, and James I,* ed. C. R. Markham. No. 57. London: Hakluyt Society, 1878.

Speck, Frank G. *Naskapi.* Norman: Univ. of Oklahoma Press, 1935.

Spellman, Charles W. "The Agriculture of the Early North Florida Indians." *Fla. Anthropologist* 1 (1948):37−48.

Spier, Leslie. *Yuman Tribes of the Gila River*. Chicago: Univ. of Chicago Press, 1933.

Spores, Ronald. *The Mixtec Kings and Their People*. Norman: Univ. of Oklahoma Press, 1967.

Stearn, E. Wagner, and Allen E. Stearn. *The Effect of Smallpox on the Destiny of the Amerindian*. Boston: Bruce Humphries, 1945.

Steck, Francis Borgia. *Motolinia's History of the Indians of New Spain*. Washington: Academy of American Franciscan Historians, 1951.

Steward, Julian H. "The Direct Historical Approach to Archaeology." *Amer. Antiquity* 7 (1942):337 – 44.

———. "Theory and Application in a Social Science." *Ethnohistory* 2 (1955):292 – 302.

Stewart, Omer C. "Fire as the First Great Force Employed by Man." In *Man's Role in Changing the Face of the Earth*, ed. William L. Thomas, Jr. Chicago: Univ. of Chicago Press, 1956.

Stewart, Paul A. "A Preliminary List of Bird Weights." *Auk* 54 (1937):324 – 32.

Sturtevant, William C. "Historic Carolina Algonkian Cultivation of Chenopodium or Amaranthus." *Proceedings, 21st Southeastern Archaeol. Conf.* (1965), pp. 64 – 65.

———. "The Ethnological Evaluation of the Le Moyne-De Bry Illustrations." In *The Work of Jacques Le Moyne de Morgues . . .* , ed. Paul Hulton. London: British Museum, 1977.

———. "The Last of the South Florida Aborigines." In *Tacachale*, ed. J.T. Milanich and S. Proctor. Gainesville: Univ. Presses of Fla. 1978.

Swanton, John R. *Indian Tribes of the Lower Mississippi Valley and Adjacent Coast of the Gulf of Mexico*. Bull. 43. Washington, D.C.: Bureau of American Ethnology, 1911.

———. *Early History of the Creek Indians and Their Neighbors*. Bull. 73. Washington, D.C.: Bureau of American Ethnology, 1922.

———. "Notes on the Occurrence of Bison near the Gulf of Mexico." *Jour. of Mammology* 19 (1938):379 – 80.

———. "Occurrence of Bison in Florida." *Jour. of Mammology* 22 (1941):322.

———. *Indians of the Southeastern United States*. Bull. 137. Washington, D.C.: Bureau of American Ethnology, 1946.

Tanner, Helen Hornbeck. "The Glaize in 1792: A Composite Indian Community." *Ethnohistory* 25 (1978):15 – 40.

Tebeau, Charlton W. *A History of Florida*. Coral Gables: Univ. of Miami Press, 1971.

Telford, Sam R., Jr. "A Herpetological Survey in the Vicinity of Lake Shipp, Polk County, Florida." *Quar. Jour. of the Fla. Acad. of Sciences* 15 (1952):175 – 85.

TePaske, John J. "The Fugitive Slave: Intercolonial Rivalry and Spanish Slave Policy, 1687 – 1764." In *Eighteenth-Century Florida and Its Borderlands*, ed. Samuel Proctor. Gainesville: Univ. Presses of Florida, 1975.

Thomas, Mike. "Gopher Tortoise." *Fla. Naturalist* 51 (1978):2 – 3.

Thomas, Peter A. "Contrastive Subsistence Strategies and Land Use as Factors for Understanding Indian-White Relations in New England." *Ethnohistory* 23 (1976):1–18.

Thompson, H. Paul. "Estimating Aboriginal American Population: A Technique Using Anthropological and Biological Data." *Current Anthropology* 7 (1966):417–24.

Thompson, Raymond H. "The Subjective Element in Archaeological Inference." *Southwestern Jour. of Anthropology* 12 (1956):327–32.

Thwaites, Reuben G., ed. *The Jesuit Relations and Allied Documents*. Cleveland: Burrows, 1896–1901.

———, ed. *The French Regime in Wisconsin*. I. *1634–1727*. II. *1727–1748*. Vols. XVI and XVII. Madison: State Historical Society of Wisconsin, 1902, 1906.

Tomplinson, Patrick K. "Mortality, Growth, and Yield per Recruit for Pismo Clams." *Calif. Fish and Game* 54 (1968):100–107.

Toner, Joseph M. *Contributions to the Annals of Medical Progress and Medical Education in the United States Before and During the War of Independence*. New York: USGPO, 1874.

Tooker, Elizabeth. *An Ethnography of the Huron Indians, 1615–1649*. Bull. 190. Washington, D.C.: Bureau of American Ethnology, 1964.

Treitlein, Theodore E., trans. *Sonora, A Description of the Province, by Ignaz Pfefferkorn*. Albuquerque: Univ. of New Mexico Press, 1949.

Trigger, Bruce G. *The Hurons: Farmers of the North*. New York: Holt, Rinehart and Winston, 1969.

True, David O. "Some Early Maps Relating to Florida." *Imago Mundi* 11 (1954):73–83.

———, ed. *Memoir of D.o d'Escalante Fontaneda, Respecting Florida, Written in Spain, about the year 1575*. Miami: Univ. of Miami Press and Hist. Assoc. of S. Fla., 1944; Coral Gables: Glade House, 1945.

Turner, Frederick J. *The Frontier in American History*. New York: Holt, 1920.

Underhill, Ruth M. *Social Organization of the Papago Indians*. New York: Columbia Univ. Press, 1939.

Vaillant, George C. *Aztecs of Mexico*. Garden City: Doubleday, Doran, 1941.

Varner, John G., and Jeannette J. Varner, trans. *The Florida of the Inca*. Austin: Univ. of Texas Press, 1962.

Veblen, Thomas T. "Native Population Decline in Totonicapán, Guatemala." *Annals of the Assoc. of Amer. Geographers* 67 (1977): 484–99.

Vedia, Enrique de, ed. *Historiadores primitivos de Indias*. 2 vols. Madrid: Hernando, 1858.

Venegas, Miguel. *A Natural and Civil History of California*. 1759. Reprint ed. New York: Readex Microprint, 1966.

Vogl, Richard J. "Effects of Fire on the Plants and Animals of a Florida Wetland." *Amer. Midland Naturalist* 89 (1973):334–47.

Vogl, Richard J., and Alan M. Beck. "Response of White-Tailed Deer to a Wisconsin Wildfire." *Amer. Midland Naturalist* 84 (1970):270–73.

Walker, Suzanne. "lake apopka." *Fla. Naturalist* 51 (1978):13–15.

Ward, Gerald M., Thomas M. Sutherland, and Jean M. Sutherland. "Animals as an Energy Source in Third World Agriculture." *Science* 208 (1980):570–74.

Warner, Ted J. "Felix Martínez and the Santa Fe Presidio, 1693 – 1730." *N.M. Hist. Rev.* 45 (1970):269 – 310.

Watkins, John V., and Herbert S. Wolfe. *Your Florida Garden.* 5th ed. Gainesville: Univ. Presses of Florida, 1968.

Watt, Bernice K., and Annabel L. Merrill, with others. *Composition of Foods— Raw, Processed, Prepared.* Handbook no. 8. Washington, D.C.: U.S. Dept. of Agriculture, 1950.

Wedel, Waldo R. "Archeological Materials from the Vicinity of Mobridge, South Dakota." *Anthropological Papers, Nos. 43 – 48.* Bull. 157. Washington, D.C.: Bureau of American Ethnology, 1955.

Wenhold, Lucy, trans. *A 17th Century Letter of Gabriel Díaz Vara Calderón, Bishop of Cuba, Describing the Indians and Indian Missions of Florida.* Misc. Coll., vol. 95, no. 16. Washington, D.C.: Smithsonian Institution, 1936.

Wheeler-Vogelin, Erminie. "The Northern Paiute of Central Oregon: A Chapter in Treaty-Making." *Ethnohistory* 3 (1956):1 – 10.

―――. "Anthropological Report on the Ottawa, Chippewa, and Potawatomi Indians." *Indians of Illinois and Northwestern Indiana.* New York: Garland, 1974.

White, Marian E. "Neutral and Wenroe." In *Northeast*, volume 15. ed. B.G. Trigger. In *Handbook of North American Indians*, W.C. Sturtevant. Washington, D.C.: Smithsonian Institution, 1978.

Whitney, Ellen M., comp. and ed. *The Black Hawk War, 1831 –1832. Vol. II. Letters and Papers. Part 2. June 14, 1832*–October 14, 1834. Hist. Coll., vol. 37. Springfield: Illinois State Historical Society, 1937.

Wiggins, Ira L. *Flora of Baja California.* Stanford: Stanford Univ. Press, 1980.

Williams, B. O. "Survey of the State Military Road from Saginaw to Mackinaw" and "Shiawassee County." In *Pioneer Coll. Report of the Pioneer Soc. of the St. of Mich.* Vol. II. Detroit: Graham's, 1880.

Williams, Herbert H. "The Epidemic of the Indians of New England, 1616 – 1620, with Remarks on Native American Infections." *Johns Hopkins Hosp. Bull.* 20 (1909):340 – 49.

Williams, Roger. "To John Winthrop." In *Coll. Mass. Hist. Soc.* 4th ser., vol. 6. Boston: By the Society, 1863.

Williamson, William D. *The History of the State of Maine: From its First Discovery* A. D. *1602, to the Separation,* A. D. *1820, Inclusive.* Hallowell, Me.: Glazier, Masters, 1832.

Wilson, Godfrey and Monica. *The Analysis of Social Change.* Cambridge: Cambridge Univ. Press, 1945.

Wing, Elizabeth S. "Animal Remains from a Midden at Fort Walton Beach." *Quar. Jour. of the Fla. Acad. of Sciences* 30 (1967):57 – 58.

Winship, George P., trans. "The Coronado Expedition, 1540 – 1542." In *Fourteenth Annual Report of the Bureau of American Ethnology, 1892—93.* Washington, D.C.: USGPO, 1896.

Wishart, David J. "The Dispossession of the Pawnee." *Annals of the Assoc. of Amer. Geographers* 69 (1979):382 – 401.

Wissler, Clark. *Population Changes among the Northern Plains Indians*. Pub. in Anthropol. I. New Haven: Yale Univ., 1936.

Wray, Charles F. *Manual for Seneca Iroquois Archaeology*. Honeoye Falls: Cultures Primitive, 1973.

Wray, Charles F., and Harry L. Schoff. "A Preliminary Report on the Seneca Sequence in Western New York, 1550–1687." *Penna. Archaeologist* 23 (1953):53–63.

Wright, Irene. *The Early History of Cuba, 1492–1585*. New York: Macmillan, 1916.

Yesner, David R. "Maritime Hunter-Gatherers: Ecology and Prehistory." *Current Anthropology* 21 (1980):727–35, 743–50.

Zinsser, Hans. *Rats, Lice, and History*. New York: Blue Ribbon, 1934.

Zubillaga, Félix. *Monumenta antiquae Floridae (1566–1572)*. Vol. 69. Rome: Monumenta Historica Societatis Iesu, 1946.

INDEX